Networks, Markets, AND THE Pacific Rim

STUDIES IN STRATEGY

Edited by W. MARK FRUIN

New York   Oxford

Oxford University Press

1998

Oxford University Press

Oxford   New York
Athens   Auckland   Bangkok   Bogotá   Buenos Aires   Calcutta
Cape Town   Chennai   Dar es Salaam   Delhi   Florence   Hong Kong   Istanbul
Karachi   Kuala Lumpur   Madrid   Melbourne   Mexico City   Mumbai
Nairobi   Paris   São Paulo   Singapore   Taipei   Tokyo   Toronto   Warsaw

and associated companies in
Berlin   Ibadan

Copyright © 1998 by Oxford University Press, Inc.

Published by Oxford University Press, Inc.
198 Madison Avenue, New York, New York 10016

Oxford is a registered trademark of Oxford University Press

Library of Congress Cataloging-in-Publication Data
Networks, markets, and the Pacific rim: Studies in strategy /
   edited by W. Mark Fruin.
      p.   cm.—(Japanese business and economics series)
   Includes bibliographical references and index.
   ISBN 0-19-511720-4
      1. Business networks—Japan.   2. Business networks—East Asia—
Case studies.   I. Fruin, W. Mark, 1943–   .   II. Series.
   HD69.S8N477   1998
   338.6—dc21   98-5447

9 8 7 6 5 4 3 2 1

Printed in the United States of America
on acid-free paper

Preface

From the late Summer of 1997 through the Summer of 1998, the business press was filled with story after front-page story of the demise of Asian capitalism. By these accounts, Asian capitalism or "crony capitalism" was and is riddled with reckless investment, excessive borrowing, corrupt and nepotistic officials, and a discouraging lack of market discipline. The interfirm networks that interlace the economies of Japan, South Korea, Thailand, Indonesia, and greater China, were tarred and feathered along with the rest of what was once called "the East Asian miracle."

How quickly public opinion changes! Until quite recently, there was widespread agreement that the East Asian miracle was characterized by high savings, high investment, farsighted government policies, and market-friendly, high performing economies. I suspect that this interpretation will once again find favor, especially for Japan, Singapore, South Korea, Taiwan, and Thailand. After all, 20 to 40 years of solid, real economic growth is no fluke or flash in the pan, and no one argues that the road of social economic development is smoothly paved.

This book also argues that it is no fluke that a majority of well-known interfirm network organizations, such as Japan's *keiretsu,* Korea's *chaebol,* and Hong Kong and Taiwan's Chinese family business networks, are found in Asia. Indeed network forms of organization are part of the reason why Japan, South Korea, Taiwan, and other high-performing Asian economies have done so well in the past. The power of these networks, their pervasiveness, and rapid rates of economic and technical change are interconnected.

In this volume we try to consider in fairly systematic ways the immense range of social, economic, legal, and technical conditions that coexist alongside an amazing variety of network organizations in Asia. In doing so, a richer and more textured analysis of Asian capitalism should result. But integrating the literatures on organizational sociology, high-performing Asian economies, and network organizations in the Asia Pacific Region is a tall order.

To the extent that this book succeeds in doing so, I thank Howard Aldrich, Wayne Baker, Mary Yoko Brannen, Bruce Kogut, Mark Mizruchi, Mayer Zald, and the contributors to the volume. Finally, I want to thank the Asia Pacific Research

Center of Stanford University, especially Daniel Okimoto and Thomas Rohlen, and the Institute of Asian Research, University of British Columbia, for their help and support in sponsoring the Vancouver Network Conference in 1993, the genesis of this project.

Ann Arbor, Michigan   *M. F.*
Spring 1998

Contents

Contributors

Howard Aldrich is Kenan Professor of Sociology at the University of North Carolina, Chapel Hill.

Theodore Bestor is Department Head and Professor of Anthropology at Cornell University in Ithaca, New York.

Jeffrey Broadbent is Professor of Political Science at the University of Minnesota in Minneapolis.

Jeff Dyer is Professor of Management, Wharton School, University of Pennsylvania.

Mark Fruin is Visiting Professor of Corporate Strategy and Technology Management at San Jose State University and at Keio University in Tokyo.

Michael Gerlach is Professor of Business Policy at the Haas School of Business, University of California, Berkeley.

Gary Hamilton is Professor of Sociology at the University of Washington in Seattle.

You-tien Hsing is Professor of Geography at the University of British Columbia in Vancouver.

Yoshito Ishio is Professor at the Institute of Socio-Economic Policy Studies, University of Tsukuba, Japan.

Toshihiro Kanai is Professor of Management at the School of Business Administration, Kobe University.

James Lincoln is Professor of Management and Director of the Institute of Industrial Relations, Haas School of Business, University of California, Berkeley.

Hiroyuki Odagiri is Professor, Faculty of Economics, Hitotsubashi University.

Tomoaki Sakano is Professor of Sociology at Waseda University in Tokyo.

AnnaLee Saxenian is Professor of Planning at the College of Environmental Design, University of California, Berkeley.

Paul Sheard is Senior Economist at Baring Asset Management in Tokyo, Japan.

Midori Yamagishi is Professor of Sociology at Osaka International University.

Toshio Yamagishi is Professor of Behavioral Science at Hokkaido University.

Networks, Markets, AND THE Pacific Rim

1

Analyzing Pacific Rim Networks and Markets

An Introduction

W. MARK FRUIN

Networks, Markets, and the Pacific Rim

Although the world is large and human behavior diverse, there are just a few basic ways of getting things done organizationally. The three most common models and ideal types of organization are hierarchies (as bureaucracies and firms are often called), markets, and networks. Because the attention paid to hierarchies and markets has far outweighed that given to networks, in this book we underscore the importance of network organizations in and around the Pacific Rim.

Why the Pacific Rim? For two reasons. First, among the countries and territories of the Pacific Rim, including Canada, China, Japan, South Korea, Taiwan, and the United States, real economic growth during the most recent half-century has been spectacular. Indeed, it may well be the most spectacular, anywhere and anytime, in recorded history. Rapid economic growth and social technical change favor the formation of network organizations.

Second, network organizations are uncommonly abundant and influential among rapidly growing Pacific Rim economies. Why? When markets are unpredictable, gains and returns unsure, high-velocity change forces businesses to adjust quickly and often. Who will benefit, and for how long? The world is moving too fast and with too much uncertainty for the idealized organizations of microeconomic theory—independent, atomized firms—to adjust, adapt, keep up, and prosper. Network organizations are much better suited to circumstances of tumultuous economic, social and technical change.

But networks do not exist in isolation. They exist in the midst of markets and they coexist with hierarchies. That is, without markets and hierarchies, it would be difficult to talk about networks—and vice versa, although the vast literatures on markets and hierarchies give the impression that they are more preeminent and primordial. In fact, networks, markets, and hierarchies are all mixed up together, and we can talk about them separately only in an ideal world.

In the mixed-up world of real organizations, we choose to concentrate on the role and importance of networks. And because the world is messy and fuzzy, network organizations mean different things to different people. Broadly stated, a network is a set of ongoing relationships within a defined population; the population can be people or other relational nodes (Baker, 1992). So, almost anything can be a network. Networks are found among taxi drivers in New York City, fishers of salmon in Alaska and British Columbia, and Stanford University graduates in Tokyo.

Also, networking is in the air. Large firms are seemingly more networked (interrelated) than ever before. Vertically integrated and broadly diversified firms, the idealized firms of the past, are downsizing, rightsizing, and entering into more and more relation-based joint ventures and strategic alliances. They are networked and networking as never before.

But in spite of its timeliness, we do not adopt the broadest possible meaning of the network concept. Our definition focuses on networks as network *organizations* (with the emphasis on organizations), instead of just looking for patterned relations among defined populations. This narrows the field considerably, because there are a limited number of ways to identify, classify, and analyze *networks as organizations*. For example, the sociologist Charles Perrow says that every organization must accomplish four tasks: secure inputs in the form of capital; secure acceptance in the form of legitimization; marshal skills; and coordinate members and relations with other organizations, clients, or consumers (Perrow, 1969).

Perrow's list suggests the key elements to look for in viewing networks as organizations. Networks should have some resources, legitimacy, skills, and means of coordination, yet it would be surprising if they had all of these in quite the same ways and amounts as markets and hierarchies do. So, following Perrow's lead, we believe that every workable definition of network organization should have two parts: broad statements as to form, process, and purpose, and a sympathetic yet systematic relationship to markets and hierarchies. Our working definition, incorporating these elements, is as follows:

> Network organizations are composed of sets of independent actors who cooperate frequently for mutual advantage and create a community of practice.

"Sets" in this case means recurring patterns of relations among defined populations. The notion of sets, as used here, includes such concepts as "organizational set" (Evan, 1966) as well as "interorganizational field" (DiMaggio and Powell, 1983).[1] That is, sets imply ongoing, patterned relations among consenting actors who are not necessarily tied together legally or bureaucratically. So, on the one hand, think of the highly structured relations that occur among suppliers in the Japanese auto industry—consider, for example, Toyota Motor's highly efficient and complex sourcing arrangements with suppliers—and, on the other, ponder the much less structured but no less ongoing and mutually beneficial transactions that join, say, recycling centers, junk dealers, and industrial furnace operators.

While the two networks differ in many and varied ways, they both represent organizational sets or interorganizational fields, depending on your choice of language and nuance. Perhaps the notion of "tightly coupled" and "loosely coupled" helps in this respect (Granovetter, 1985). Toyota's suppliers of parts, components, and subassemblies respond to strict physical, economic, and temporal constraints exacted and enforced by Toyota. Toyota's network is tightly coupled, to say the least.

But in loosely coupled networks, fairly frequent communication and cooperation are still the norm—frequent enough, in fact, to render negligible the issue of
coordination. So, recycling centers, junk dealers, and industrial furnace operators
are likely to have highly patterned ways of keeping each other informed as to what
sorts and amounts of material they have on hand and what they are looking for.
That brings in the "mutual advantage" part of our definition. Mutual advantage is
defined by the respective goals and objectives of those involved, some of which
may have monetary value and some of which may not (Ring and Van de Ven, 1992).

Independent actors include individuals as well as institutions such as firms,
nonprofit organizations, and government agencies. Given all this, now we come to
the all-important question of cooperation. Network organizations may appear
when markets are imperfect but not always so. It is only occasionally so because
networks also appear in the interest of social and political exchange—not just economic exchange. "Social exchange," says Peter Blau, refers to the voluntary actions
of individuals, actions that "are motivated by returns they are expected to bring"
(Blau, 1964; Levine and White, 1961).

"Expected to bring" is not the same as certain to bring, and therein lies the rub
insofar as discriminating between network organizations and markets.[2] Typically,
but not always, networks emerge when market transactions are viable or when
"enough" people are willing to buy, sell, make, and trade. "Enough" has traditionally been a somewhat variable number for economists, anywhere from the many
buyers and sellers of ideal markets to the small-numbers bargaining of imperfect
markets. Imperfect, in this sense, means that buyers and sellers are too few, supply and demand unpredictable. But, in addition to enough people, network organizations come into play when a "set" of actors (institutionalized or not) is willing to buy or sell in ways that are less market based and more relation based.

Neoclassical economic analysis assumes that a well-defined and generally
known production function exists for each and every activity (Farrell, 1957). So, in
pure market-based transactions, goods and services have a more or less agreed-
upon value, whereas in network-based exchanges, they may not. For example, regularly volunteering at a local community center may increase a volunteer's social
capital and political influence, especially within a small circle of friends, acquaintances, and other volunteers, but the volunteerism is not likely to increase
personal income, at least not directly. So, while the monetary benefits of network-
based relations may be uncertain, they have value, and that value may be economic, social, or political, as well as many combinations thereof.

In short, network organizations often emerge where there could be markets but,
instead of markets, actors decide to trade and transact for reasons other than mutually agreed-upon value. This does not mean that value is unimportant, only that
clear-cut value or pricing is an insufficient condition for network-based transactions. Ambiguity or insufficiency of value (price signals) may stem from any number of factors, including that supply and demand are unreliable, as in imperfect
markets, or that traders are not comfortable because trades are infrequent and information imperfect. In network organizations, the arms-length trading relations
and pricing mechanisms of pure markets are eschewed in favor of something more
personal (relational) if less precise (Ouchi, 1980).

There are many terms for describing relation-based buying and selling—bargaining, dealing, horsetrading, and, most often, cooperating. So, any definition of

network organization must be partial at best because so many different kinds of "cooperation" are possible and because networks are mixed up with markets and hierarchies, which are themselves varied and dynamic economic organizations. Economists may still refer to exchanges and cooperation in these circumstances as "imperfect markets." We beg to differ, and in concert with Blau (1964), Homans (1958), and others, we view exchange broadly; that is, not narrowly from just a monetary or market point of view.

In our view cooperation is a basic psychological, social, political, and economic impulse. The very essence of network organization is cooperation when the value of cooperation, as in most exchanges and many transactions, is not easily calculable. But there is real value, nevertheless. Under these circumstances, a set of actors may prefer to trade cooperatively, that is, without costs and prices being determinative. Cooperation of this sort, we believe, occurs often in a wide variety of conditions.

Richard Nielsen (1988), in one typology, lists the four kinds of cooperation as exchange, pooling, complementary specialization, and experiment/contingency. The most straightforward of these, exchange, happens when, say, I give you a pound of butter in exchange for a load of firewood. When this happens, there is no doubt that something of value has been exchanged; the question is whether or not both parties are satisfied with the exchange. Good measures of satisfaction might be whether similar exchanges occur again and whether they occur on the same terms as before.

In the case of pooling, physical resources may be bought or hauled in concert, thereby reducing the cost per unit measure. Yet savings are not the same for everyone because savings are in proportion to the amount purchased or the distance hauled. Pooling may also take the form of pooled assets, as in the refining-output and freight-hauling petroleum and railroad cartels of nineteenth-century America. Holding shares in common were the means of controlling prices, output, and competition. In pooling, as in exchange, market value may be uncertain, although market-based rates and prices may be estimated with accuracy.

The more often exchanges and pooling occur among the same set of actors, the more likely they will happen again and again, and be characterized by some sort of serial equity or parity. That is, the value of what is given and taken tends to balance in the long run, even though it may be difficult to put a precise value on every single transaction or series of transactions. Quite often, cooperation involves bundled goods with lumpy social, political, and economic value (Ring and Van de Ven, 1994). Continuing cooperation signals that some sort of equitable exchange is happening, but not that an equal exchange is happening.

Thus, fair exchange may be more important than equal exchange in pursuing a strategy of cooperation, because fair is relative to the needs of each and every party, whereas equal assumes that the parties' needs are more or less the same. In other words, there may be a fine line between markets where price determination is the basis for buying and selling, and networks where some sort of serial equity or parity constitutes a basis for trading. Yet that fine line denotes rather important differences with respect to organizational form, function, and process.

Adaptation is at the heart of those differences. In market-based transactions, prices mediate buying and selling whereas in network-based transactions, something else happens. We called it "frequent cooperation" in our earlier definition.

Frequent cooperation means that certain levels of reliable exchange are realized within a relational set. Through exchange, parties not only build up trust in one another, they also adapt in the interest of further exchange, thereby deepening their investment in and commitment to ongoing cooperation. (Forsgren, Hagg, Hakansson, Johanson, Mattsson, 1995)

Some scholars argue that reciprocity is more characteristic of network-based cooperation than serial equity (Powell, 1990). We do not split hairs on the nature of network-based value, equity, or reciprocity. Simply put, we believe that network organizations are a formal realization of the value of cooperation and an informal recognition that markets price cooperation imperfectly. But, while cooperation's market value may be unclear, something of value is certainly being exchanged, pooled, given, or taken. Set-based cooperation happens—not because of or in spite of, but in the midst of markets and hierarchies (Stinchcombe, 1990; Eccles and Crane, 1988; Galaskiewicz et al., 1985).

Interorganizational and Intraorganizational Networks

There are actually two different kinds of network organizations: *inter*organizational and *intra*organizational. So far, most of what we have said applies directly to the interorganizational (or external) sort and less directly to the intraorganizational (or internal) variety. "External" and "internal" in this case refer to whether or not the ties that bind networks together are found without or within hierarchies.

Most of the essays in this book and most of the inquiry in the Asia Pacific Region have been directed towards the external, interorganizational variety. Presumably this is because external networks, such as Toyota's supplier network or the domestic and overseas networks of Chinese entrepreneurs, are so conspicuous and well developed (Skinner, 1964–65; Boisot and Child, 1988, 1996); secondarily, they challenge long-held assumptions about the nature of hierarchical organizations. Western traditions of research on network organizations have concentrated on internal or intraorganizational networks for the most part (Eccles and Crane, 1987; Baker, 1992; Ibarra, 1992; Noria and Eccles, 1992).

In intraorganizational networks, there are no organizational boundaries, except for suborganizational ones (separating those who cooperate). Such networks are often described by statements like "Who are your friends at work," and "With whom do you socialize after hours?" Obviously, without firm boundaries in the way, the frequency of communication and information exchange is likely to increase and, hence, the value of cooperation is likely to be more implicit. Intraorganizational networks may first and foremost be seeking and generating information, recognizing that the real value of information may be found more in reducing general levels of uncertainty or opportunism than in narrowing the value of this or that exchange.

Also, start-up and ongoing costs associated with intraorganizational networks are likely to be far lower than those for interorganizational networks. That is, transacting across organizational boundaries in interorganizational networks is characterized by threshold cost effects; unless the transactions achieve minimal levels of frequency, density, and duration, start-up and ongoing costs are likely to be high relative to the value realized. So, we argue that value does not need to be explicit, but there does need to be value in network-based cooperation. And if economic value is unclear, then other sorts of value—informational, political, and social— had better be obvious. In short, given that transaction costs are higher for interorganizational networks, intraorganizational networks are more numerous and less costly to start up, maintain, and shut down.

In either sort of network, cooperation is valuable and frequent enough to delimit a "set" of recognizable actors whose interactions are neither market-like nor strictly bureaucratic. By bureaucratic, we mean organizational interactions that are governed by rules, regulations, and SOPs (standard operating procedures) that were established with stable, routine tasks in mind and with a clearly defined hierarchy of authority.[3] Wages are paid to those who enforce regulations and uphold hierarchical standards. By doing so, they cooperate with one another but their cooperation is not necessarily voluntary and not always mutually advantageous.

Note that our definition of network organization stipulates neither the strength of the ties binding actors—the ties may vary from strong to weak—nor what constitutes an independent actor—they may be individuals or almost any form of institutionalized actor. So networks may be composed of individuals within the same organization as well as individuals and institutions cooperating across organizational boundaries. The notion of set assumes that the actors interact with some frequency—enough to be comfortable with and accepting of each other. Finally the ties that bind actors together may be motivated by anything that induces people to cooperate: money, power, risk reduction, influence, and access to resources.

In short, people are neither compelled nor paid to cooperate in network organizations. They cooperate for reasons other than obvious economic, legal, and administrative reasons for doing so. These observations lead us, like others, to define network organizations in terms of the nature and quality of the relations that bind actors together, assuming that the basic structural and procedural requisites of network organization are fulfilled, that is, sets of independent actors who cooperate frequently for mutual advantage. Network relations may be informal and personal, like relations among office friends, and they may be formal and impersonal, such as the relations joining large city mayors who lobby for government funds and entitlements.

Whether informal and personal or formal and impersonal, the quality of relations among sets of otherwise independent and cooperating actors defines the nature of network organizations. Relations are structured in ways that are neither market-like nor hierarchy-like. Yet relations persist, evolve, and are coordinated in ways that suggest some ordering principles are at work. The health-care networks of physicians who band together to share information on pricing and procedures without actually sharing financial risk or merging office practices are a contemporary example of this principle (Pear, 1996).

Although the costs of entering such a network (or any network) may vary widely, depending on the nature and quality of the ties binding actors together, the costs of exiting are uniformly high because exit is almost always accompanied by a loss of information, connections, and reputation (personal or institutional). While exit from markets and hierarchies may also generate losses, network-based relationships are especially hard to reconstitute once ties are broken and exit has occurred. Probably this relates to the ambiguity of value in network organizations. Trust becomes correspondingly more critical.

So, for example, physicians who have joined with others to compete with insurance companies and health maintenance organizations would suffer a loss of reputation and, more materially, referrals if they no longer cooperated fully and frequently with their erstwhile colleagues. And if the physicians in question were from several different health-care organizations, as is likely, entry and exit costs would be even higher. Crossing organizational boundaries raises transaction costs and information costs, as already argued.

Since a good number of our daily interactions are of this sort—recurring, coordinated, valuable, and based on trust or, at least, careful husbanding of relations among sets of known partners—we believe that network organizations are unusually common, varied, and vital. That belief highlights the challenge of this book: to define, clarify, and interpret network organizations—mostly of the interorganizational sort—in and around the Pacific Rim, a region where they are unusually pervasive and productive. But before we look in detail at why this may be the case, we turn toward an elaboration of network organizational types as they appear in different market circumstances around the Pacific Rim.

At Least Four Types of Networks

The collection of essays amply shows that there are many variations in the degree to which network forms of organization are formalized, managed, and integrated in different market (capitalist) systems. Based on these essays, we argue for at least four types of networks (figure 1-1):

1. networks that are naturally occurring and evolving;
2. networks that seemingly replace or diminish market transactions (a market failures perspective);
3. networks that substitute for or diminish the role of hierarchies (a bureaucratic failures perspective);
4. socially constructed networks that enhance markets without replacing or diminishing hierarchy's role and function.

Naturally Occurring Network Organizations

Network forms of organization are natural forms of social and economic exchange, as basic as markets and hierarchies are. At least, as Howard Aldrich and his colleagues argue, entrepreneurs all around the world typically rely on networking and network organizations to gather capital, co-workers, and connections. Indeed, a marshaling of network-based resources often comes well before business licenses are sought and premises are secured.

While kinsmen are the most likely recruits in emerging network organizations, as Aldrich and Sakano show (chapter 2), friends and neighbors are also candidates for likely inclusion in network-based start-ups. In fact, until recently in Japan and even now in South Korea, kinship and locality-based credit associations (*tanomoshiko* and *gei*) are popular ways of raising capital and securing the all-important

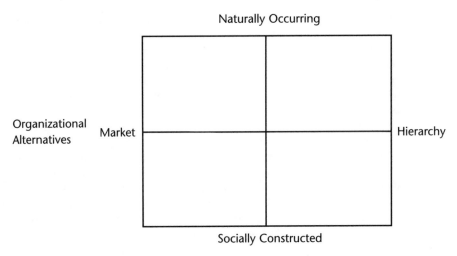

Figure 1-1 The Varieties of Network Organization

connections that lubricate entrepreneurial ventures. Indeed Japan and South Korea are not exceptional in this regard. Aldrich's work documents the importance of kinsman and locals in network organizations worldwide. In short, kinsmen-based networks are a more or less universal form of business organization.

Toshihiro Kanai's chapter (chapter 3) on new venture associations expands the point that network organizations are basic and widely found. Kanai's essay details the evolution of two different sorts of networks in Greater Boston—clubs and circles. Both of these types of networks promote entrepreneurship and new business formation, yet they vary in how they function, are structured, and recruit new members. Not surprisingly, clubs and circles likewise differ with respect to the kinds of information circulated and exchanged within groups.

Clubs are much more circumscribed with respect to membership and goals; members are elected, dues are paid, and attendance is more or less mandatory. The club format described by Kanai provides insider, almost proprietary, information concerning what works and what doesn't within a select group of high-tech entrepreneurs, most of whom have connections to the Massachusetts Institute of Technology. Circles, by contrast, are much more loosely defined; they bring together a constantly changing group of young business professionals from greater Boston. Attendance varies according to the topics and speakers on hand. Members are not elected and there are no dues.

In spite of these differences, both clubs and circles represent sets of independent actors who interact frequently for mutual benefit. This is our definition of network organization. In other words, Aldrich's kinsmen entrepreneurs and Kanai's clubs and circles describe network organizations that function and operate in ways that are neither market- nor hierarchy-like.

Yet, the human relations that underlie Aldrich's entrepreneurs and describe the activities of Kanai's clubs and circles are not the same. There is variation in the degree to which family members provide start-up funds and other non-monetary resources, and clubs are far more restrictive than circles with respect to information sharing and membership. In other words, there is significant variation within cultures as to how networks are set up, organized, and managed, and such within-culture variation turns on any number of social, economic, and political factors of the kind described by Aldrich and Kanai.

Naturally Evolving (If Not Naturally Occurring) Networks

Variation in network principles and properties is likely to increase in cross-national and cross-cultural circumstances. This is another way of saying that networks, like all organizations, evolve in response to and as part of the institutional environment. Since "institutional environment" is another way of describing what are thought to be national norms and rules of the road, country conditions powerfully affect network organizations. The same may be said of market and hierarchical organizations: country conditions affect their origins, histories, and mode of operations.

The chapters by Broadbent and Yamagishi are especially telling in this respect. Jeffrey Broadbent and Yoshito Ishio (chapter 4) suggest that Japan's state is a network organization. By this, the authors are not making the rather conventional argument that the state is composed of a number (read "network") of interrelated, special interests. Instead the authors deem the reverse: networks of existing special interests make up the state. The network is the state, not the reverse.

In this, Broadbent and Ishio echo cyber-prophets of the late twentieth century, like Scott McNealy, CEO of Sun Microsystems, who assert that the network is the computer. In other words, the Internet embodies the capabilities and connections on which computing depends. In much the same way, Broadbent and Ishio use the concept of network organization to make sense of the state's power and authority in Japan. In both instances, there are special, country-specific circumstances behind McNealy's and Broadbent and Ishio's assertions. The United States has more computers, computer users, Internet connections, and servers than any other country in the world. Surely, if there is a place where the network is the computer, it is the United States.

Neither is Broadbent and Ishio's assertion so farfetched. Until 1945, the power of the state in Japan was based on what could be called the divine right of kinship, meaning that all Japanese were related through the Imperial Family which was the nation-state's founding family. In this way, kinship was the basis of the Imperial Family and emperor's rule and, by extension, that of the government as well. So, in fact, a network of kinsmen did describe the power and authority of the state.

While the country conditions described by Broadbent, Ishio, and McNealy are not exactly naturally occurring, they are naturally evolving. In other words, the roles of the Internet in the United States or of the Imperial Family in Japan evolved in response to naturally occurring conditions that were part of the U.S.'s and Japan's institutional environment. In both cases, network organizations evolved in the context of regional and country conditions that prompted local actors to make choices affecting how they behaved, interacted with others, and organized themselves. Electronic networks and genealogy-based networks of power were the result. The emergence, evolution, and maturation of network organizations in the context of regional, national, and international circumstances help explain a great

deal about when and why such organizations take on the economic, social, and political functions that they do.

Finally, Toshio and Midori Yamagishi's chapter on trust (chapter 5) is an especially good example of how country conditions affect network organizations.
Breaking apart the accepted notion that Japan is a trusting society compared to the
United States, Yamagishi and Yamagishi argue counterintuitively that, with respect
to the commercial transactions of everyday life, Americans are more trusting, albeit
their trust is "thin" or an everyday, garden variety. By contrast, "thick" or strong
trust developed in Japan as a response to that country's uncertain past, especially
the upheavals of the mid-nineteenth century when civil war and Western intrigue
forced Japan open.

In Japan, trust exists in the context of strong, particularistic ties and generally
high levels of uncertainty. So, while markets are not especially renowned for high
levels of trust, market-mediated trust or general trust is greater in the United States
than in Japan, according to Yamagishi and Yamagishi. Actually, their chapter further distinguishes between kinship-based and information-based particularistic
trust. This distinction helps us discriminate between, say, Chinese kinship-based
business networks and Japanese trading company-based networks. In the former,
kinship and fictive kinship are all important in delineating the ties of cooperation,
whereas the frequency, intensity, and quality of information exchange seems to be
the adhesive in many Japanese business networks.

If this characterization rings true, then the more information-based networks of
modern Japan may be of fairly recent origin. In the past, Japan's networks of kinsmen,
clansmen, and loyal employees were famous for their sense of duty, faithfulness,
and reliability. This type of particularistic trust makes sense if market-mediated or
general levels of trust are low and if sources of information are few and far between. The *Forty-Seven Ronin* (masterless warriors), a drama where forty-seven
warriors avenge their master's death and then dutifully take their own lives is a famous if extreme illustration of the strong, particularistic ties that used to bind people together in historical Japan.

Market-Replacing Network Organizations

You-tien Hsing (chapter 6) likewise emphasizes the role of particularistic ties, but
in very different country and market circumstances. She demonstrates rather convincingly that the actions of Taiwanese trading companies in the fashion shoe
industry substitute for, rather than supplement, the market. Since what's hot in
fashion shoes changes four to six times a year—an especially turbulent market situation—trading houses must gather, collate, and analyze supply and demand data
all along the value chain of this fast-changing industry. They decide on a range of
choices with respect to price, quality, and delivery, and ultimately they determine
the availability of style choices and greatly influence retail margins and markups.

Trading firms provide and perform these intermediating functions on the basis
of particularistic ties uniting the many Taiwanese entrepreneurs who specialize in
this industry. These entrepreneurs and their trading firms lubricate and motivate
the fashion shoe industry's value chain. Without their intermediation or networking, the nature of the industry would be very different and it would be difficult for
others to perform the same tasks. Industry access, market information, and net-

work membership are strictly limited to insiders, a small circle of Taiwanese who know, buy, sell, and trade with each other. Most notably, there is no open bidding process among them to decide prices or terms of supply, quality, and delivery.

Trading companies (communities) function like markets in these many ways. Thus, in the absence of markets performing clearing and pricing functions, trading firms substitute for and replace markets that would otherwise be missing. But it is important to note that they do more than simply mimic or amplify markets. They also arbitrate property rights and assume numerous persona—investor, entrepreneur, innovator, bureaucrat, politician—when and where necessary. Clearly, networks of Taiwanese entrepreneurs and their trading companies are performing different functions and roles than those found among Aldrich's entrepreneurs and Kanai's clubs and circles. Networks do not simply substitute for firms when and where they may not be doing well.

Hiroyuki Odagiri's discussion on the role of networks in signalling the value of university education (chapter 7) is another example of market failure or substitution. In most rapidly developing economies, well-established labor markets for university graduates are lacking, and hence there is a general problem with respect to the pricing of the value of higher education. Odagiri believes that the prevalence and importance of old-boy networks is directly related to this problem.

Odagiri's assertions appear to be historically accurate, that is, they make sense in light of what is known about the market for university graduates in late nineteenth- and early twentieth-century Japan. But they are much less true for contemporary Japan, although they may still ring true for today's rapidly growing Asian economies, including South Korea, Taiwan, and Thailand. In these economies, the value of a university education is moot when a middle school or, at best, a high school education is the norm.

Odagiri argues that the value of a Tokyo University (Todai) education was found more in the connections that a Todai graduate enjoyed rather than in the quality of the education that he or she received. A Tokyo University diploma signaled value when the real value of higher education was uncertain. Thus, the preeminence of Tokyo University, Seoul National University, Taiwan National University, or Thailand Institute of Technology graduates in government and industry circles may be less a matter of their intelligence than it was or is a feature of the undeveloped market for higher education graduates. Old-boy networks played an important role in recruiting university graduates to government and industry service.

Theodore Bestor's essay (chapter 8) offers another example of how network organizations may substitute for markets. The story of the Tsukiji fish market is less a story of market failure, however, than one of market regulation and intervention via government licensing of brokers and mongers. Such government-sponsored business associations, like Tsukiji, have a long history in Japan. From the early eighteenth century, producers and distributors of traditional products, like foodstuffs, soy sauce, and lacquerware, were licensed, their numbers and functions regulated. The government licensed them because it did not have the means or ambition to control markets directly, such as via sales or value-added taxes. Those licensed, in turn, organized themselves into production and distribution cartels or market-replacing organizations that parceled out work on the basis of noncompetitive bidding. Prices, volumes, sales territories, brand marketing, and commercial disputes were all decided within networks of cooperating merchants and agents, much like the petroleum and railroad cartels of nineteenth-century America (Yamamura, 1973; Fruin, 1983).

Network organizations are effective in controlling supply and prices, as Bestor illustrates for Tsukiji, the largest fish market in the world. They are effective as well in maintaining the variety and quality of production, the livelihood of producers, and the availability of supply in many other industries. Most of the cartel-like arrangements have fallen by the wayside in twentieth-century Japan, as sources of supply and substitute products have become more widely available. But this has not happened for the wholesaling of fish and fish products as well as most fresh fruits and vegetables. In these product markets, traditional licensing and organizing practices continue because the rationing of supply, quality assurance, and time-to-market considerations are important for the health and well-being of Japan's 125 million, densely packed citizens. The Tsukiji fish market's network-like organization, backed by the government, regulates supply, quality, and market prices.

Hierarchy-Replacing Network Organizations

While Tsukiji's market-replacing network does not seem to upset many people, hierarchy-replacing networks are much more controversial. The public outcry in the West concerning Japan and South Korea's limited importation of manufactured goods and the bad loans and bankruptcies that ballooned in the late 1990s often point to *keiretsu* and *chaebol* as the culprits. That is, according to critics, the preferential ties and longstanding trading relationships that exist between companies in the same business group prevent outsider companies from openly buying and selling with insider companies (Lawrence, 1991). In this view, business groupings quasi-integrate production and distribution functions among member firms of the same group, and hence, pricing between firms is more akin to internal transfer pricing than market pricing. Insider relations substitute for or subvert the monitoring and managing functions normally associated with hierarchical control.

As a result, determining the difference between the value of an outcome and the likelihood that it will occur is problematic (Bernstein, 1996). In other words, frequent and recurring transactions among a set of known traders act as a substitute for hierarchy or the integration of transactions within organizations. Network organizations may accomplish what large, integrated firms otherwise do, but they seem to do so without excessive bureaucracy, rigidity, and internal rivalries that often afflict large, complex organizations. Hence, network organizations may arise out of bureaucratic failure or, better put, as alternatives to vertical and horizontal integration within single, unified organizations.

Instead of internalizing hierarchy, the 3 Cs of communication, coordination, and control are realized within the context of frequent and recurring transactions between partner-firms. Also, ownership ties, interlocking boards, and other formalized means of linking firms may buttress and ensure the quality of interfirm connections, on a case by case basis. My own essay (chapter 12), for example, analyzes the close trading relationships between a Toshiba factory and its several hundred parts and component suppliers. Yet, in this instance, Toshiba holds no shares in any of its suppliers, nor does it send them board members or administrative advisers.

In the same vein, Gary Hamilton (chapter 9) argues that the vertically integrated production cartels of South Korea greatly reduce the risks and costs of hierarchical or quasihierarchical integration. Because of the generally high levels of market uncertainty—not to mention the risks and costs—associated with establishing integrated steel, shipbuilding, chemical, and petrochemical complexes in South Korea during the 1960s and 1970s, the South Korean government stepped in to ensure that private firms had enough resources to fund, plan, coordinate, and manage such mammoth integrated production processes and complexes.

Without government credits and guarantees allowing and promoting quasi-integration, it is unlikely that South Korean companies would have had the resources and wherewithal to compete on a global scale. And, since the passage and acceptance of GATT and WTO protocols, competing globally is the only sensible strategy in industries so characterized by increasing returns to scale. Once the government steps in, credit can be more easily secured, good managers more easily recruited, and information more easily shared among an ascribed set of actors—government bureaucrats as well as bankers, insurance agents, traders, and industrialists of the same business group—with the result that information-processing costs are lowered and market obstacles circumscribed (Boisot and Child, 1988). However, higher levels of risk may occur as a result of these hierarchy-replacing practices.

Amakudari, the well-known system whereby Japanese government bureaucrats retire to lucrative and influential positions in the private sector, is a variation on this theme. As Paul Sheard (chapter 10) shows, *amakudari* and other executive transfers from banks to manufacturing firms within capital-*keiretsu* business groups are ways to monitor and reinforce interorganizational relations when hierarchical integration is unfeasible and contractual regulation inadequate (Hoshi, 1994). But it is important to recognize that network organizations, such as Japan's *keiretsu* and South Korea's *chaebol*, do not always arise in response to bureaucratic failure. There are many examples of networks that act to supplement rather than supplant hierarchies around the Pacific Rim. So, network organizations can arise when markets and hierarchies fail, as we have seen, and they can reinforce rather than simply replace markets and hierarchies, as we will now see.

Market-Enhancing Network Organizations

In Japan and South Korea, networks like *keiretsu* and *chaebol* are far more prescribed and standardized forms of organization than the more personal and informal networks of North America, or even the more ascribed and *quanxi*-based (personal-tie) networks of Taiwan and Greater China. Many *keiretsu* and *chaebol* boast long histories and in these cases, *keiretsu* and *chaebol* have evolved alongside and in tandem with industrial markets and hierarchies in Japan and South Korea.

The Mitsui and Sumitomo *keiretsu*, for example, two of the oldest business groups in Japan, began well before the American War of Independence. Their histories are critical for understanding how and why networks may become something more than a response to market and bureaucratic failure. Networks may reinforce market and firm relations, and they are most likely to do so as a consequence of long processes of adapting, adjusting, and evolving in relation to markets and firms. The longer *keiretsu* have existed, matured, and evolved, the more likely they will be market- and hierarchy-enhancing. Given enough time, markets, hierarchies, and networks will accomodate and adjust to one another.

Take the giant Mitsubishi group of several hundred companies as an example.

When the group started under Iwasaki Yataro in 1872, its assets were a few ships and a couple of warehouses. It was impossible for one part of the business not to be affected by the others. But by the 1880s, Mitsubishi was involved in coal mining, marine insurance, banking, ship repairs, shipbuilding, as well as its original shipping and warehousing businesses. Now, what happened in one part of the business was less likely to be affected by the others although there were obvious synergies between, say, shipping, ship repairs, and shipbuilding.

As the Mitsubishi empire grew, its various lines of business became more independent, so much so that a dozen or so legally independent companies were separated from the Mitsubishi Holding Company in 1917–18. Seven decades later, in 1990, the Chairman of the Mitsubishi Trading Company claimed that internal buying and selling within Mitsubishi group firms—now, several hundred strong—amounted to only 16–18 percent of total sales for the group (*Nihon Keizai Shimbun*, February 24, 1990). In the same way, Gerlach and Lincoln argue (chapter 14) that *keiretsu* may evolve into something more than a simple hierarchy-replacing mechanism.

In short, networks operate within and necessarily adapt to the institutional environment or the legal, political, social, and economic circumstances of daily life. The longer the process of adapting, the more likely networks will successfully cope with and become more intertwined with existing market and bureaucratic relations. Coevolution results. Networks become better adapted to the environment and, correspondingly, the environment better tolerates network organizations. This is a view of network organizations as complex adaptive systems; they affect, respond to, and are part of the environment (Hall, 1994; Holland 1996; Kauffman, 1993, 1995).

Such reasoning helps us understand why a *positive specialization of interorganizational assets* might have occurred in late nineteenth-century Japan, induced by two circumstances of late development (late relative to the timing of industrialization in leading Western economies). First, every imaginable kind of resource required for industrialization was in scarce supply. Second, a technology transfer-inspired emphasis on industrial specialization by function and product line forced firms into coalitions and combinations with other enterprises. In other words, firms did not have the resources and capabilities to internalize all the needed activities in ever larger enterprise structures. Instead, they joined with others in strategies of cooperation: exchange; pooling; and complementary specialization, wherein one firm specialized in this or that function, product line, or market with full knowledge that other firms were becoming more specialized in something complementary to their own activities.

Given several generations of cooperation and complementary specialization, highly formalized, elaborated, and prescribed forms of network organization have become fully integrated into the political, social, and economic fabric of contemporary Japan, South Korea, and Taiwan. Support for and understanding of network organizations are both implicit as well as explicit. Property rights are assignable, and innovation and entrepreneurship are accommodated within the form. Jeff Dyer's and Mark Fruin's chapters on supplier networks are good examples of these market-conforming and hierarchy-reinforcing qualities. For Dyer (chapter 11), supplier networks in the motor vehicle industry are learning partnerships with assemblers; for Fruin (chapter 12), good supplier relations demand that assemblers set up governance mechanisms and guidelines to supplement bilateral market relations in the rapidly changing electronics industry (Hagedoorn, 1993).

Choices that mimic the marketplace are thereby available to assemblers and suppliers alike. In this sense, Nissan and Toyota's satellite organizational system could be juxtaposed with General Motor or Ford's multidivisional model, suggesting that there are indeed many roads to Rome. The point is not to argue either for or against the functional equivalency of network organizations and multidivisional firms, but to demonstrate instead that networks do more than simply substitute for hierarchies (Womack, et al., 1991; Ring and Van de Ven, 1994).

However, in either Toyota or Toshiba's cases, one would be hard pressed to prove that their supplier networks were so market enhancing at the outset. In both instances, supplier networks were established to provide parts, goods, and services that were otherwise unavailable. Toshiba and Toyota recruited, trained, and paid suppliers to provide the parts, components, and services that they needed. In short, Toshiba and Toyota created supplier networks where previously there were none (Fruin, 1992; Nishiguchi, 1993; Fruin and Nishiguchi, 1993). Clearly Toshiba and Toyota's supplier networks began as substitutes for hierarchy, even if they did not stay that way for long. Suppliers and assemblers learned to work together by sharing information, correcting defects, shortening time-to-market, and rewarding close and enduring collaboration. Organizational and interorganizational learning emerged. Networks evolved.

The electronic networks of AnnaLee Saxenian's Route 128 and Silicon Valley (chapter 13) likewise enhance markets. Yet the flow of good ideas and people in these high-tech zones is only tangentially related to how markets work. Instead, old school connections, social and club contacts, and workplace ties grease the informal networks of Sun, Intel, Silicon Graphics, Adobe Systems, and Hewlett-Packard. Such firms are in some senses temporary recombinations of people who are bounded geographically and relationally by the interpersonal networks of Silicon Valley. Such networks reinforce rather than replace existing markets for talented employees who are the ones most likely to ride network connections to bigger and better things.

In neither Silicon Valley nor Taiwan are the rules of network organization highly formalized and prescribed, even though network membership is more narrowly ascribed in Taiwan and more obviously achieved in Silicon Valley. In both places, networks stand aside from the marketplace, supplementing market functions in Silicon Valley yet supplanting them in Taiwan. In Japan and South Korea, however, as Gerlach/Lincoln and Hamilton indicate, network organizations have become or they are becoming more market-conforming and hierarchy-enhancing.

In short, there are many sorts of networks and they coexist with many kinds of markets and hierarchies. The intersection of these might be plotted on a two-by-two matrix, juxtaposing market and hierarchy on one axis (a Williamsonian continuum) with naturally occurring and socially constructed relational sets on the other (a Granovetter-like continuum) (see figure 1-1). But this tells us little about why and when such cooperation counts. Indeed so many different combinations are possible that their coexistence and overlapping nature encourage an explanation and our attention.

Embeddedness of Networks

The four different sorts of network organization described here are not incompatible with one another. Networks may exist within networks and in tandem with markets and hierarchies. Logically speaking, embedded networks—the ones on the inside or overlapped by others—are likely to be more formal, prescribed, and tighter than those encompassing them.

An example from physical chemistry can be taken as an illustration. It is much more difficult to embed plastic in steel than vice versa. The specific gravity of plastic, ounce for ounce, is not able to stand up to that of steel. So, the heavier, denser stuff is on the inside. In much the same way, the highly sequenced, heavily managed networks of auto and electronic parts suppliers, described by Dyer and Fruin, are embedded in or, in some cases, co-exist within the loosely coupled executive exchange networks analyzed by Sheard.[4]

Sheard's executive exchange networks are bounded by numerous and broad industry associations that link managers in this or that sector with leaders from this or that peak association, such as the Keidanren or Nikkeiren, two general-interest organizations of major firms and employers in Japan. Networks may be bounded by other networks that are bounded, in turn, by other networks. So, the network of networks is the state, in Broadbent and Ishio's language.

Not surprisingly, therefore, the structure and function of Toyota's network of auto parts suppliers is rather different from, say, that of the Japan Management Association's, which is dedicated to advancing general management education. In short, many sorts of network organizations are possible and assuming functional equivalency across network organizations and functions would be a mistake. Toyota's suppliers are tightly coupled, tightly scheduled, and are likely to be good at diffusing precise, mechanical engineering information quickly and well.

Members of the Japan Management Association, some of whom are undoubtedly suppliers to Toyota, interact rather differently. The information they exchange is less frequent, less precise, and has considerably less time-value because they are not continually cooperating in the interest of supplying Toyota. Likewise, the rather ascribed and rule-bound fishmongers of Tsukiji are encapsulated by Japan's rapidly expanding supermarket chains which offer multiple, competing channels for distributing fish and marine foodstuffs. In sum, one form of network organization may be embedded within, coexist alongside, and run in tandem with other economic organizations, including networks.

The nesting of networks within other networks is precisely what makes Saxenian's Silicon Valley so much more entrepreneurial and open-ended than Route 128's self-contained networks of vertically integrated firms. Networks of Taiwanese, Hong Kong, Indian, and native-born American entrepreneurs are embedded within larger webs of interpersonal ties based on high-tech function, employment history, social clubs, and school connections. Silicon Valley networks are relational and regional in character, yet they coexist with and within the market and hierarchical structures of the Bay Area and Northern California. Such networks are certainly market-enhancing—the pressures of market competition are intense—yet in some ways they supplant hierarchies, reinforce them in others, and they are certainly "naturally occurring."

On a chronological scale, the relations that characterize network organizations

seem enduring, almost transcendental, on one end of the scale, and rather temporary, almost transitory, on the other. So, for example, some of the companies, relations, and connections that comprise the Sumitomo and Mitsui business groups
have endured for three hundred years. And if they have already survived that long,
they are likely to last a good while longer. Yet, at the same time, individual elements of these business networks, like the old Sumitomo copper pits on Shikoku
Island or Mitsui's Miike coal mines, have disappeared. So, individual elements
may come and go but networks persevere. And even as networks persevere, they
change, adjust, and adapt as befitting any dynamic (if embedded) organization.

It is this deeply embedded quality that makes nonsensical simple-minded notions of fundamentally changing or reforming network forms of economic organization. During the Allied Occupation of Japan, for example, the Supreme Command
of the Allied Powers (SCAP) wanted to dismantle Japan's giant business combinations or *zaibatsu*. *Zaibatsu*-busting was the order of the day. Indeed, numerous trading and holding company-firms were dismantled, merged and dismembered, but
within a few years of the Occupation's end, what had been broken up often recom-
bined. The recombinations were not exact copies of what had existed previously but
that would be unexpected. Since networks coexist with other forms of economic organization, as they evolve, so too network organizations evolve.

A lively debate centers around the degree to which government agencies and
bureaucrats were responsible for putting the combinations back together again.
Chalmers Johnson has been a leading advocate of the view that government—the
Ministry of International Trade and Industry (MITI) in particular—was a prime
mover in reassembling prewar *zaibatsu* as postwar *keiretsu* business groups, and
in promoting their critical role in Japan's remarkable postwar economic recovery
(Johnson, 1982).

Johnson's hypothesis has been widely debated in recent years; indeed several
contributors to this volume may be counted among critics of Johnson's "strong state
view" (Fruin, 1992; Odagiri, 1992). But in all fairness no one doubts the importance of government in establishing stable macroeconomic and fiscal conditions
and in promoting good schools, good health, and a good transportation and communications infrastructure. Beyond this, however, the effectiveness and effects of
state intervention are hotly contested.

On this question, like most others, we take the middle ground. Clearly, Japan's
government wanted a strong business sector as a springboard for postwar recovery.
And clearly the government did not enforce the Occupation's antitrust laws and
zaibatsu-busting policies as they were intended to be enforced. Instead, government cascaded one after another favor, subsidy, and benefit to various business
groups, especially during the hardscrabble years of the 1950s. But saying so and
even showing how this happened fall far short of claiming, much less proving, that
the reemergence of postwar enterprise groups was due to government intervention.

No doubt companies took advantage of everything they could, but the hoary
heads of the Mitsui and Mitsubishi *keiretsu*, for example, were and are unlikely to
take seriously the advice of bureaucrats on how to run their commercial and industrial empires. At the same time market-substituting and, to a lesser extent, hierarchy-
substituting network organizations typically appear in an institutional and regulatory context that unfolds under government auspices. At a minimum, therefore,
government bureaucrats have to look the other way if networks deal in ways that

are inconsistent with regulation. So, the reemergence of postwar business groups occurred with at least a modicum of government concurrence, if not connivance.

Accordingly, we should not expect too much from current efforts to limit the influence of *amakudari*, the ex-bureaucrats who parachute from government into lucrative and influential private sector jobs, or to dismantle their networks of favors and connections (WuDunn, 1996). *Amakudari* or something equivalent exist in every advanced industrial society although the details of how ex-bureaucrats gain power, wealth, and influence after they leave government service vary from place to place. Every once in a while, for example, legislation is introduced in the United States to limit so-called "double dippers." These are ex-government types, usually former military or foreign service officers, who retire and then work for the same civilian contractors they formerly oversaw. Double-dippers and *amakudari* are essentially the same kind of phenomenon.

So, not only are there many different kinds of network organizations but they coexist and interpenetrate one another, spatially and temporally. That diversity and complexity represent the challenge of analyzing, interpreting, and comparing networks and markets as fundamental ways of organizing human activity. In effect, there are not just four types of networks, but many. At a minimum the naturally occurring and market-conforming variety have to be considered alongside the market-supplementing and hierarchy-replacing sort. Also, the personal networks of entrepreneurs and small business owners, as described by Aldrich and Sakano, Kanai, and Yamagishi and Yamagishi, need to be compared with the more managed and institutionalized networks of parts suppliers and corporate board members, as detailed by Dyer, Fruin, and Sheard, and the trader/broker networks of fish mongers, shoe traders, and university alumni, as discussed by Bestor, Hsing, and Odagiri.

Networks, markets, and hierarchies are embedded in an institutional environment of national construction. As they adjust to and influence that environment, they adjust to each other. So, given enough time, even market-replacing networks, like Hamilton's government-backed *chaebol*, are likely to become more market friendly. This, more than anything else, explains why Gerlach and Lincoln can argue that contemporary *keiretsu* groups are both hierarchy- and market-enhancing (Granovetter, 1985).

The differential role of firms and governments in creating and advancing network organizations in Japan, South Korea, Taiwan, and the United States needs to be considered alongside systematic differences in their social, economic, and political attributes. For this, Gerlach and Lincoln (chapter 14) give us one way to look broadly at network relations, within and across cultures. Another way is to recognize that Pacific Rim countries, where network organizations are so pervasive and powerful, have shared a number of remarkable developmental similarities during the last fifty years. In concert, these help us identify the institutional rules and social–economic conditions that seen conducive to network formation across nations.

High-performing Asian Economies and Network Organization

The last half-century of come-from-behind, rapid economic growth suggests what some of these isomorphic conditions might be. When the World Bank surveyed thirteen of these runaway economies, including Japan, in the early 1990s, they were classified as High Performing Asian Economies (HPAEs) and lumped together under a banner reading "the East Asian Miracle" (World Bank, 1992). In general, the HPAEs share a gestalt of historical and institutional features that helps explain the prevalence of network forms of organization around the Pacific Rim. Among the most obvious of these are:

1. All the HPAEs experienced mid-century warfare and some of them suffered widespread destruction of physical resources and communal infrastructure. Since World War II and subsequent conflicts in Korea and Southeast Asia, all the HPAEs have shared a deep-seated nationalistic fervor to rebuild their countries, national identities, and institutions. On the North American side of the Pacific Rim, Pacific war experiences led to a rapid buildup of West-Coast–based economic resources and a pronounced shift of psychological and political attitudes with respect to the place of the West Coast in national and international, medium- to high-tech industrial development. Recovery, rebuilding, and expansion are common themes around the Pacific Rim.

2. Irrespective of geographical position on the Pacific Rim, the role of government in regional and national reconstruction has been manifest, with the state being an active agent of regulation, development, industry and policy promotion. The state's leadership role in national reconstruction has been most obvious in China, Japan, Singapore, South Korea, and Taiwan, but the visible hand of the state has been likewise obvious in promoting America and Canada's aerospace, aircraft, computer, electronics, metallurgy and new materials, optics, telecommunications, and shipping industries.

In other words, timing is an issue. There are periods when the state is more involved in economic promotion and industrial development; the last half of the twentieth century is one of those periods. Regional conflicts and persistent state intervention in industry, institutional, and regulatory development have heavily punctuated the spectacular economic growth of the last half-century. So, with respect to state and market relations, the post–World War II period has witnessed many key forking points for firm, industry, and national development within and between the nations of the Pacific Rim.

3. Given an interventionist state and rapid economic advance, law and the legal system may have been downplayed or minimized in the process of national reconstruction, particularly in the HPAEs. That is, in more or less stable circumstances, the legal system acts to regulate and maintain the status quo. But when maintaining the status quo is not so desirable or necessary, laws and the legal system carry less weight. The importance of contractual and commercial law and the enforcement of all manner of regulatory and administrative codes may be especially diminished in circumstances of rapid social, economic, political, and technical change. Following World War II and the Korean and Vietnam wars, normative sanctions were often in flux, sparsely followed and enforced. In effect, when the rules of the game are relaxed, new players of the game and new ways of playing the game are likely to appear.

4. Given widespread agreement and active intervention in favor of national reconstruction, cooperative strategies as a means of getting ahead become viable and possible. Government can cooperate with industry; industry can cooperate with labor; and firms can cooperate with one another, especially when there is a na-

tional mandate to do so, quickly and repeatedly. In such circumstances, cooperation may become a central strategy of national recovery while, at the same time, it may serve as an effective strategy deterring international competition. That is, pulling together at home is a way of both getting ahead and keeping outsiders at bay.

5. If cooperation becomes a widespread strategy of national economic recovery, it is possible to cope more easily with uncertainty. As a result, markets may not be so treacherous, and organizational constraints, such as capacity bottlenecks and capability deficiencies, may be ameliorated. Network-based cooperation becomes a major means of competition when firms can reliably and frequently turn to other firms for help and resources. In short, the institutional environment may become more conducive to all manner of cooperation, and cooperation is more likely to be prized and institutionalized in period of national emergency.

All these circumstances favor the formation of network organizations because cooperation among like-minded parties enables work to be done more easily and perhaps more economically than would otherwise be the case. But it is necessary to say a word here about motivation and incentives. Altruism does not necessarily motivate network-based cooperation; mutual advantage does. However, mutual advantage may take on a patriotic hue that could easily be mistaken for altruism when there is widespread support for national recovery and reconstruction.

Cooperating in the interest of national reconstruction would certainly characterize the motivations of many state-sanctioned and supported network organizations around the Pacific Rim. So, following our basic definition of network organization—sets of independent actors who cooperate for mutual advantage—such advantages can have social and political value because realizing maximum economic value may not be the point. Cooperation has value, in many forms and faces.

The social and institutional features that characterize the HPAEs and North America's West Coast are obviously not static. States may become less interventionist, rates of economic growth may slow, supraorganizational, patriotic feelings may wane, and cooperation may give way to competition. Nevertheless, once organizational practices and routines have become widely institutionalized, that is, accepted and acceptable, they are slow and hard to change. Thus, even though bureaucratic acts of *gyosei shido* or "administrative guidance" are now less frequent than previously in Japan and, by contrast, antimonopoly "formal hearings" or *shinpan* happen more often, secular changes of this sort are slow to unravel and reverse long-standing patterns of cooperation. Hence, while government policies toward networks may change, networks themselves are likely to persevere, adapt, and evolve in light of (and in spite of) government policy.

Old habits die hard, even when long-standing patterns of institutionalized cooperation between government and business may seem to impede competition (in Japan, for example). Highly evolved organizational routines and institutional patterns persist and change very slowly, even in the midst of turbulent times (DiMaggio and Powell, 1983; Gerseck, 1991). Thus, long-standing, institutionalized cooperation within industries, among firms, and between government and business is likely to continue, even in the face of substantial pressures for change.

In the tumult of economic, political, social, and technical change unfolding around the Pacific Rim, an increased reliance on network forms of organization seems likely. Some writers have gone so far as to claim that Pacific Rim organizations are, themselves, postmodern, in the sense that they challenge the prototypical Fordist organizational design that has dominated Western production for so long. Clegg (1990, p. 181), for example, pointed out the ways in which the flexible, niche-oriented, de-dedicated, multiskilled, and networked organizations to be found in Japan [described by Fruin (1995, 1997) as "knowledge works" or learning factories] depart radically from the bureaucratic ideal outlined by Weber. Without going quite so far, the rich evidence of this volume with respect to the nature and variety of networks gives us the opportunity to consider network organizations in new ways—new insofar as the academic work on network organizations has focused almost exclusively on networks in the context of Western society and economic organization.

Given the prevalence and persistence of cooperation among the HPAEs, it is not surprising that we can characterize them as network/networked/networking economies. Network forms of interaction, organization, cooperation, and learning are widespread. This finding points directly to another benefit of studying the Pacific Rim. If environmental circumstances and enterprise form and function are so different there as compared with Western Europe and North America, it may be possible to build a new or improved theory of network organization.

Why Pacific Rim Strategies?

For any number of reasons, some of which have been detailed here, network organizations appear to be the favored form of enterprise organization in the vast and varied Pacific Rim Region. This probably has something to do with the nature of regional opportunities, the pace of economic growth and social technical change, and the large numbers of overseas Chinese, the Japanese model of development; most likely it is related to the structure and process of network organizations. It may also have a lot to do with history, a common past linking many ethnic, cultural, and national communities with respect to a commercial and industrial development imperative. And so it obviously has to do with the fact that contemporary business interactions, structures, and strategies are related to past practices.

Japan is a perfect case in point. For more than twenty years (1953–73), no other country grew so fast for so long as Japan did. Even beyond the two decades when real annual rates of growth averaged 9 percent, Japan has continued to perform better than the average of the OECD's advanced industrial economies. Japan networks. Perhaps Japan is the quintessential networking nation. We believe that the rapid growth of Japan's economy and the prevalence of network forms of organization are interrelated because Japan's economic success has a decided organizational foundation and flavor.

From its mammoth trading companies (*sogo shosha*) that account for roughly half of all imports and exports, to its vertical *keiretsu* and horizontal bank and trading company-centered business groups (*bizunesu gurupu* or *kigyo shudan*), Japan's businesses are networked in many different ways and for many different reasons. Likewise, for South Korea and Taiwan, network organizations may well lie behind or, at least, be closely connected with their rapid economic growth, as well as the differential success of Silicon Valley as compared with Route 128. And, as Bestor shows for the Tsukiji fish market, market-replacing networks are found whenever governments regulate markets directly or indirectly. Most often, this happens for reasons of safety, security, and price stability.

Other Pacific Rim economies are experiencing what Japan has experienced previously. From 1978, the beginnings of the current economic reforms in China, to 1993, China's economy expanded at an average rate of 9 percent (Lardy, 1994). From the early 1970s, other Pacific Rim countries, like South Korea, Taiwan, Hong Kong, and Singapore have significantly outperformed the average of all developing economies in impassioned charges up the slopes of economic development.

In such regions of rapid social and economic change and discontinuous technical advance, network organizations are prevalent and notably important. We believe that there are a number of good reasons for this, four of which are outlined here. First, as argued earlier, transactions in network-based organizations do not require precise agreements as to value and price. In the short run, fair exchange rather than equitable exchange is the norm, if not the rule. Nevertheless, over the long term, a sequential equity rule may seek to even out the benefits of cooperation (Oye, 1986).

So, when supply and demand conditions are uncertain, as when total economic output doubles every four or five years—the historical case for Japan and the contemporary case for China—it is both risk-adverse and market-share expanding for firms to continue trading even though precise information as to markets, prices, and supplies may be unavailable. Risk-adverse because, as suggested earlier, there are always opportunity and reputation costs when exiting networks. Hence, if at all possible, it is safer to stay involved (networked) and to keep on trading in spite of instability and uncertainty (Abegglen and Stalk, 1985).

Once a network is exited, rejoining is always problematic because network membership assumes an ongoing relationship with a set of known trading partners. Exiters break that assumption and acquire a bad reputation. The situation is market-share expanding because in an economy that is growing rapidly, company revenues generally increase even when relative market shares remain stable. A stable share of an expanding pie is preferable to a declining share or no share at all. And if existing shares depend on maintaining good relations with established partners, then everything possible should be done to maintain good relations (Sheard, 1994).

Second, if fair transactions are repeated among a set of like-minded actors, transactional velocity will likely speed up. As velocity increases, information flows between buyers and sellers will increase as well, leading to more quickly replenished stocks of information and, therefore, to better knowledge of what buyers and sellers want. Companies are able to deal faster, more assuredly, and with less concern for legal guarantees and safeguards. In such instances, the right products with the right features at the right prices are more likely to be delivered.

Just-in-Time (JIT) strategies of supply, production, and distribution, for example, depend in crucial ways on rapid and accurate information exchange among suppliers and assemblers. The more often such cooperation occurs, the more likely it will occur again and again. The chapters by Dyer and Fruin provide graphic evidence of how network organizations may lead to increases in transactional velocity and, accordingly, to improvements in the volume and quality of information exchange, knowledge formation, and transfer among network members. Increasing transactional velocity in times of rapid economic and technical change proves broadly and mutually advantageous (Fruin, 1995).

Growing opportunities for cooperation, in short, cover a multitude of transactional shortcomings that might otherwise cause temporizing, holdup, and contractual disagreement in more stable market conditions. Rapid cost increases may be spread among many small trades in high velocity transactions, for example, rather than allow them to jeopardize less frequent, if larger, deals. In situations of rapid economic growth, "keeping up with the Joneses" is more important than trying to outperform the Joneses because maintaining relative market share beings absolute gains in sales and revenues (for everyone involved).

Third, when economies are growing quickly, companies face a double bind: They need to match internal resources and capabilities with external demand. In effect, they need to add capacity and complexity in tandem with macroeconomic growth. This is much more easily said than done. If an economy is growing at 9–10 percent annually, for example, production capacity has to be doubled every six or seven years. If a firm has, say, twenty factories, this would mean that three new factories would have to be opened and brought on stream every year, just to keep up with demand. Or, alternatively, three existing factories would have to be completely redone every year.

Finding the money to invest in three new plants per year is the first and, some would say, the easiest step in keeping up. Hiring workers, training them, transferring technologies, getting production up to reliable and competitive levels, securing the productivity and quality of the production process, effectively linking production with marketing and sales, hiring managers, training them, having them understand what they should do with whom and by when—these are some of the less obvious tasks to be mastered before new factories can be brought on stream. And in our example, such tasks would have to be mastered every year at three different locations.

But there is another way. Instead of trying to keep pace on the basis of internal resources and capabilities, much of what is needed could be outsourced. Buy rather than make. Although outsourcing comes with its own resource requirements—especially in terms of the management resources needed to monitor and manage supplier relations effectively (as Dyer, Fruin, and Sheard argue in their chapters)—outsourcing is a way to keep up with the Joneses without having to do everything the Joneses do. Indeed, unless the Joneses are extraordinarily good managers, outsourcing even a portion of new capacity and capability requirements will soon bring appreciable competitive advantages by allowing firms to focus on doing fewer internal things better. Firms can keep up with rapid growth and not lose focus or dilute capabilities (Kogut, Shan, and Walker, 1992).

Clearly, it is much less costly and more reliable to ask existing suppliers to increase output than to lay on new capacity. And if, in the course of asking suppliers to increase output, it is not entirely clear how increasing output will affect pricing, fair exchange can take precedence over equitable exchange in network organizations for as long as buyers and sellers continue trading. Due to such reputation and repetition effects, "let the buyer beware" does not appear to be as central a concern in network organizations as in hierarchies (Williamson, 1985).

Fourth, the longer cooperation endures and prospers, the more likely it will evolve. When network members can reliably buy and sell cospecialized inputs and outputs, complementary specialization represents and embodies a highly evolved form of cooperation. But, given the higher risks of opportunism associated with cospecialization, firms are likely to adopt complementary specialization strategies only when growth opportunities outstrip their abilities to supply, thereby inducing firms to initiate a search and selection of partners who can help them overcome capacity and development constraints (Clark and Fujimoto, 1991; Eisenhardt and Tabrizi, 1995).

Such an evolution underscores an pivotal point about network forms of organization: they do not begin with highly interdependent and complementary forms of cooperation. They evolve, as long as fair and mutually beneficial relations are the norm (Boisot and Child, 1996; Dore, 1983; Fruin and Nishiguchi, 1993; Salk and Brannen, 1998). Not only are a firm's own resources and capabilities evolving but so are those of the set(s) of actors with which it routinely cooperates. So, when cooperating firms search for new things to do and new ways of doing them, they have a more expanded range of routines, practices, and policies at their disposal than atomized firms do.

Rapid economic growth, a speeding-up of transactional velocity, a constant need to match enterprise resources and capabilities with environmental change, and, therefore, the emergence of complementary specialization as a viable competition strategy mean two things for organizations. On the one hand, these circumstances require a specialization of tasks to match internal resources with market opportunities; on the other hand, they require a search for ways to overcome the limits of specialization. While there may be several ways to accomplish both of these tasks, creating networks of cooperating firms is one that has proven to be both prevalent and successful around the Pacific Rim.

In all likelihood, Pacific Rim networks are so common and effective because they allow, indeed encourage, cooperation in the interest of competition. This is simply another way of saying that networks exist in the midst of markets and firms (hierarchies), but that markets and hierarchies function differently from network organizations. Compared with them, networks create different sets of incentives, engender different kinds of costs, dispense different sorts of rewards, and culminate in different patterns of coordination, control, and commitment.

Markets function best when there are many buyers and sellers and the value of market-mediated exchanges are clearcut. Prices are paramount in day-to-day transactions. Hierarchies function best when the task environment is stable and organizations are closely aligned with environmental needs. Rules, regulations, and procedures define appropriate behavior in light of environmental stability. Thus, it is easy to see when markets and hierarchies might be preferred forms of organization, but it is also easy to see when they might not. Depending on circumstances, network organizations may substitute for and replace markets and hierarchies or, alternatively, work in the midst of and alongside them. The range, versatility, and adaptability of network organizations are among their most outstanding and desirable traits.

Just as a markets and hierarchies framework makes good sense in the economic history of Western Europe and North America, so too a networks, markets, and hierarchies framework will likely make the best sense in the economic history and organizational future of the Pacific Rim Region. The thickly detailed, rich descriptions of network organizations contained in this volume may be seen as one of the necessary steps to creating such a framework, one that recognizes and emphasizes the diversity and likely heterogeneity of network organization forms and behaviors. Also, this book's emphasis on interactions—on exploring how networks, markets and hierarchies interact, evolve, and complement one another—compared with much of the existing economic and organizational literature, is exceptional (see Burt, 1992, for another exception).

The network organizations found in these chapters allow us to compare and contrast network forms in Japan, South Korea, Taiwan, and the United States according to a number of organizational and relational features, such as degrees of formalization, rule definition, and market conformance or the nature, quality, and frequency of network interactions. All this promotes a perspective on network organizations that is inclusive and useful and, as a result, we appreciate more the diversity and complexity of human experience.

Once network organizational forms are catalogued and analyzed in systematic and comprehensive ways, it may be possible to model them, assuming that some simple laws and regularities capture the richness of varietal offerings. A Pacific Rim perspective allows us to do just that: to delimit the diversity of network organizational forms and to advance more patterned analyses of network phenomena in one of the most rapidly growing and, hence, theoretically challenging regions of the world. This is good, because networks are fundamental and essential forms of political, social, and economic organization, in the past, the present, and the future.

Notes

1. The idea of "set" in studies of network organizations is a fairly old one, going back perhaps to an article first published in 1966 (Evan, 1966).

2. Some parts of this definition follow closely a model of interorganizational relations developed by Levine and White (1961) for the health-care industry.

3. A good place to start on the voluminous literature dealing with bureaucracy is Bendix (1977).

4. Mark Granovetter's seminar article, "Economic Action and Social Structure: The Problem of Embeddedness," is responsible for much of the current interest in the notion of embeddedness.

References

Abegglen, James C., and George Stalk, Jr. *Kaisha: The Japanese Corporation.* New York: Basic Books, 1985.

Baker, Wayne E. "The Network Organization in Theory and Practice." In Nitin Nohria and Robert G. Eccles, eds., *Networks and Organizations: Structure, Form, and Action.* Cambridge, Mass.: Harvard Business School Press, 1992.

Barkun, M. *Law without Sanctions: Order in Primitive Societies and the World Community.* New Haven, Conn.: Yale University Press, 1968.

Bendix, Reinhard. "Bureaucracy." *International Encyclopedia of the Social Sciences*. New York: Free Press, 1977.

Bernstein, Peter L. *Against the Gods—The Remarkable Story of Risk*. New York: John Wiley & Sons, 1996.

Blau, Peter. *Exchange and Power in Social Life*. New York: Wiley, 1964.

Boisot, Max and John Child. "The Iron Law of Fiefs: Bureaucratic Failure and the Problem of Governance in the Chinese Economic Reform." *Administrative Science Quarterly*, 33 (1988): 507–27.

Boisot, Max and John Child. "From Fiefs to Clans and Network Capitalism: Explaining China's Emerging Economic Order" *Administrative Science Quarterly*, 41–4 (Dec., 1996): 600–28.

Burt, Ronald S. "Innovation as a structural interest: Rethinking the impact of network position on innovation adoption" *Social Networks* 2 (1980): 327–55.

Burt, Ronald S. *Structural Holes*. Cambridge, Mass.: Harvard University Press, 1992.

Clark, Kim, and Takahiro Fujimoto. *Product Development Effectiveness*. Cambridge, Mass.: Harvard Business School Press, 1991.

Clegg, S. *Modern Organizations: Organization Studies in the Postmodern World*. London: Sage Publications, 1990.

DiMaggio, Paul J., and Walter W. Powell. "The Iron Cage Revisited: Institutional Isomorphism and Collective Rationality in Organizational Fields." *American Sociological Review*, 48 (April 1983): 147–60.

Dore, Ronald. "Goodwill and the Spirit of Market Capitalism." *British Journal of Sociology*, 34–4 (1983): 459–82.

Dore, Ronald. *Flexible Rigidities*. Stanford, Calif.: Stanford University Press, 1986.

Eccles, Robert G., and Dwight B. Crane. "Managing Through Networks in Investment Banking." *California Management Review*, 30 (1987): 176–95.

Eccles, Robert G., and Dwight B. Crane. *Doing Deals: Investment Banks at Work*, Cambridge, Mass.: Harvard Business School Press, 1988.

Eisenhardt, Kathleen M., and Behnam N. Tabrizi. "Accelerating Adaptive Processes: Product Innovation in the Global Computer Industry." *Administrative Science Quarterly*, 40–1 (March 1995): 84–110.

Evan, William M. "The Organization-Set: Toward a Theory of Interorganizational Relations." In J. D. Thompson, ed., *Approaches to Organizational Design*. Pittsburgh: University of Pittsburgh Press, 1966, pp. 175–91.

Farrell, M. J. "The Measurement of Productive Efficiency," *Journal of the Royal Statistical Society*, 120, Pt. 3 (1957): 253–82.

Forsgren, M., I. Hagg, Hakansson, J. Johanson, and L. Mattsson. *Firms in Networks—A New Perspective on Competitive Power*, Stockholm: Center for Business and Policy Studies, Uppsala University, 1995.

Fruin, W. Mark. *Kikkoman—Company, Clan and Community*. Cambridge, Mass.: Harvard University Press, 1983.

Fruin, W. Mark. *The Japanese Enterprise System*. New York: Oxford University Press, 1992.

Fruin, W. Mark. "Managed Competition and Supplier Network Organization in the Japanese Electronics Industry." Paper presented at the Vancouver Network Conference, Whistler, B.C., September 1993.

Fruin, W. Mark. "Competing the Old-Fashioned Way: Localizing and Integrating Knowledge Resources in Fast-to-Market Competition." In J. Liker, J. Ettlie, and

J. Campbell, eds., *Engineered in Japan*. New York: Oxford University Press, 1995.

Fruin, W. Mark. *Knowledge Works: Managing Intellectual Capital at Toshiba*. New York: Oxford University Press, 1997.

Fruin, W. Mark, and Toshihiro Nishiguchi. "Supplying the Toyota Production System." In Bruce Kogut, ed., *Country Competitiveness*, New York: Oxford University Press, 1993.

Galaskiewicz, Joseph, Stanley Wasserman, B. Rauschenbach, W. Bielefeld, and P. Mullaney. "The Influence of Corporate Power, Social Status, and Market Position on Corporate Interlocks in a Regional Network," *Social Forces*, 64 (1985): 403–31.

Geertz, C. *Local Knowledge: Further Essays in Interpretive Anthropology*. New York: Basic Books, 1983.

Gerseck, C.J.G. "Revolutionary Change Theories: a Multilevel Exploration of the Punctuated Equilibrium Paradigm." *Academy of Management Review*, 16–1 (1991): 10–36.

Granovetter, Mark. "Economic Action and Social Structure: The Problem of Embeddedness." *American Journal of Sociology*, 91 (1985): 481–510.

Hagedoorn, J. "Understanding the Rationale of Strategic Technology Partnering: Interorganizational Modes of Cooperation and Sectoral Differences." *Strategic Management Review* 14 (1993): 371–85.

Hall, Peter. *Innovation, Economics and Evolution*, Hertfordshire and New York: Harvester Wheatsheaf, Simon and Schuster, 1994.

Holland, John H. *Hidden Order*. Menlo Park: Addison Wesley, 1996.

Homans, George C. "Social Behavior as Exchange." *American Journal of Sociology*, 63 (1958): 597–606.

Hoshi, Takeo. "The Economic Role of Corporate Grouping and the Main Bank System." In M. Aoki and R. Dore, eds., *The Japanese Firm: Sources of Competitive Strength*, New York: Oxford University Press, 1994.

Ibarra, Herminia. "Network Centrality, Power, and Innovation Involvement: Determinants of Technical and Administrative Roles." *Academy of Management Journal*, 36–3 (1992): 277–303.

Johnson, Chalmers. *MITI and the Japanese Miracle*. Stanford, Calif.: Stanford University Press, 1982.

Kauffman, Stuart A. *The Origins of Order: Self-Organization and Selection in Evolution*. New York: Oxford University Press, 1993.

Kauffman, Stuart A. *At Home in the Universe*. New York: Oxford University Press, 1995.

Kogut, Bruce, Weijian Shan, and Gordon Walker. "The Make-or-Cooperate Decisions in the Context of an Industry Network." In Nitkin Nohria and Robert G. Eccles, eds., *Networks and Organizations: Structure, Form, and Action*. Cambridge, Mass.: 348–365. Harvard Business School Press, 1992.

Krackhardt, D., and J. R. Hanson. "Informal Networks: The Company behind the Charts." *Harvard Business Review*, (July/August) (1993): 104–11.

Lardy, Nicholas. *China in the World Economy*. Washington, D.C.: Institute for International Economics, 1994, p. 3.

Lawrence, R. Z. "Efficient or Exclusionist? The Import Behavior of Japanese Corporate Groups." *Brookings Papers on Economic Activity* (1991): 311–30.

Levine, Sol and Paul E. White. "Exchange as a Conceptual Framework for the Study of Interorganizational Relationships." In Amitai Etzioni, ed., *A Sociological Reader on Complex Organizations*. New York: Holt, Rinehart, and Winston (1961), pp. 117–32.

Lyotard, J. F. *The Post-Modern Condition: A Report on Knowledge*. Minneapolis: University of Minnesota Press, 1984.

Nielsen, Richard. "Cooperative Strategy." *Strategic Management Journal* 9 (1988): 475–92.

Nihon Keizai Shimbun, "Tomadou Gyokai," February 24, 1990, p. 3.

Nishiguchi, Toshihiro. *Strategic Industrial Sourcing*, New York: Oxford University Press, 1993.

Noria, Nitkin, and Robert G. Eccles, eds., *Networks and Organizations: Structure, Form, and Action*. Cambridge, Mass.: Harvard Business School Press, 1992.

Odagiri, Hiroyuki. *Competition through Growth, Growth through Competition*. Oxford: Oxford University Press, 1992.

Ouchi, William G. "Markets, Bureaucracies, and Clans." *Administrative Science Quarterly*, 25 (March) (1980): 129–41.

Pear, Robert. "Doctors May Get Leeway to Rival Large Companies," *New York Times*, April 8, 1996, pp. 1, A10.

Perrow, Charles. "The Analysis of Goals in Complex Organizations." In Amitai Etzioni, ed., *Readings on Modern Organizations*, Englewood Cliffs, N.J.: Prentice-Hall, (1969), pp. 65–79.

Pfeffer, J. "Barriers to the Advance of Organizational Science: Paradigm Development as a Dependent Variable." *Academy of Management Review*, 18 (1993): 599–620.

Powell, Walter W. "Neither Market nor Hierarchy: Network Forms of Organization." *Research in Organizational Behavior*, vol. 12. Greenwich, Conn.: JAI Press, 1990, pp. 295–336.

Rice, Ronald E., and Carolyn Aydin. "Attitudes Toward New Organizational Technology: Network Proximity as a Mechanism for Social Information Processing." *Administrative Science Quarterly*, 36 (1991): 219–44.

Richardson, G. B. "The Organization of Industry." *Economic Journal*, 82 (1972): 883–96.

Ring, Peter S., and Andrew H. Van de Ven. "Developmental Processes of Cooperative Interorganizational Relationships." *Academy of Management Review*, 19 (1994): 90–118.

Rosenau, P. M. *Post-Modernism and the Social Sciences: Insights, Inroads, and Intrusions*. Princeton, N.J.: Princeton University Press, 1992.

Salk, Jane E. and Mary Yoko Brannen, "Formal Position, Individual Attributes, and Network Centrality as Determinants of Influence in a Successful Japanese-German Joint Venture," *Academy of Management Journal*, forthcoming 1998.

Sheard, Paul. "Interlocking Shareholdings and Corporate Governance." In M. Aoki and R. Dore, eds., *The Japanese Firm*. New York: Oxford University Press, 1994.

Skinner, G. William, "Marketing and Social Structure in Rural China. Parts I, II, and III. *Journal of Asian Studies*, 24, 3–43 (1964–65): 195–228, 363–99.

Stinchcombe, Arthur L. *Information and Organizations*. Berkeley: University of California Press, 1990.

Williamson, Oliver. *The Economic Institutions of Capitalism*, New York: Free Press, 1985.

Womack, James, Daniel Roos, and Daniel Jones, *The Machine That Changed the World*. New York: Rawson Associates, 1991.

WuDunn, Sheryl. "Japan's Vaunted Bureaucrats, the Real Power Behind the Throne, Are Under Siege," *New York Times*, May 5, 1996, p. 6.

Yamamura, Kozo. "The Development of *Za* in Medieval Japan." *Business History Review* 47 (Winter 1973): 438–65.

2

Unbroken Ties

Comparing Personal Business Networks Cross-Nationally

HOWARD E. ALDRICH

TOMOAKI SAKANO

Japanese business has attracted a great deal of attention from social scientists, but almost all of it has been directed toward big firms, *keiretsu*, and cooperative alliances. Little attention has been paid to small firms, even though they are critical to the Japanese economy. In Japan, a much higher proportion of firms is in the under-100 and under-20 employee size categories than in the United States or most Western European nations. Using a very generous definition of "small," Takaoka (1989) argued that 99.4 percent of all Japanese businesses are small, employing about 60 percent of the workforce. He defined "small" for each of three sectors: (a) manufacturing: an incorporated company whose capital is no more than 100 million yen or with fewer than 300 employees, or a sole proprietorship with fewer than 300 employees; (b) wholesale: an incorporated company whose capital is no more than 30 million yen, or a sole proprietorship with fewer than 100 employees; and (c) retail and service: an incorporated company whose capital is less than 10 million yen, or a sole proprietorship with fewer than fifty employees (Takaoka, 1989), Miwa (1993) also noted that the proportion of establishments in the private sector (not including agriculture and fisheries) that are small has remained very stable over the past thirty or forty years.

The picture of the Japanese economy painted in most accounts is one in which personal obligations are extremely important and very slow to change. Marketing and distribution channels, manufacturer–supplier relations, and other business relationships are portrayed as a maze of overlapping ties and obligations. Yamagishi and Yamagishi (1993, p. 12) posited that "extensive networks of stable relations play a more prominent role in the Japanese society in general, and in the Japanese business in particular, than in the American society." Because many firms involved in these relations are small, we could infer that strong ties of reciprocal dependence are the bedrock upon which the nature of the Japanese economy rests. (For an ethnographic account of a Tokyo neighborhood, Miyamoto-chò, that is structured around "homes, inexpensive apartments, small factories, and shops operated as family businesses, see Bestor, 1989, p. 7.)

We now take it as axiomatic that economic action is embedded in networks of

32

social relationships (Granovetter, 1985. However, we also take it as axiomatic that entrepreneurial action is fraught with paradoxes and contradictions (Kanai, 1993). How might the networks of Japanese business owners be constructed? Should we expect the personal networks of Japanese business owners to look like those in other capitalist nations? Or do business owners in Japan construct different kinds of networks, given their goals and circumstances?

In comparing business networks across countries, we have found it helpful to consider two models of how networks are formed, based on Granovetter's (1985) work: (1) an embeddedness model—positing that networks are products of long-standing affiliations and relationships, and (2) an instrumental model—positing that networks are pragmatic, instrumental tools of fleeting duration.

Model 1 rests on the assumption that the social relationships of owners resemble those of other people, with a core of close personal relations built on ties of reciprocal interdependence and a periphery of weaker ties assembled on a more haphazard basis. At the center of owners' networks are the people they have known for many years: friends, family, schoolmates, business associates, and former co-workers. Ownership is a risky business, and strong ties of intimate friendship can provide the social support needed to weather crises and hardships.

Model 2 rests on the assumption that the social relationships of owners are quite different from those of everyone else, with a core of weak ties assembled on a pragmatic basis and a few close personal relations built on ties of reciprocal interdependence. Because owners have a strong interest in making the best deals possible, they pick members of their inner circle on an instrumental basis. Accordingly, because strong ties of intimate friendship may cloud an owner's vision and prevent the clear thinking needed to make robust business decisions, owners may sever ties to the people they have known for many years: friends, family, schoolmates, business associates, and former co-workers.

Which of the two models of business owners' networks would we expect to find in Japan? Do cultural norms of respect for hierarchy and duty mean that Model 1—strong-tie, long duration networks—is the modal pattern? Indeed, are there any grounds to expect that Model 2 even remotely fits Japanese conditions, given Model 2's portrayal of business relations as driven by instrumental rather than affective considerations? In Japan, with its reliance on complex webs of interdependent relations, networks might well be very different from societies with more arms-length business ties.

Research Design

To investigate this question, we studied the personal networks of small- and medium-sized firms in five countries: Japan, the United States, Italy, Northern Ireland, and Sweden.

The Questionnaire and Sampling

Investigators in the five countries used a standardized questionnaire, with some modifications, to collect information on the characteristics of current and potential entrepreneurs and their personal networks. In most countries, questionnaires were mailed to people selected from the records of groups, agencies, or educational institutions concerned with entrepreneurial education and development. In a few cases, questionnaires were filled out by persons attending entrepreneurship classes. Questions focused on networking activities and the characteristics of the five people who were the closest members of the respondent's network.

The Japanese survey was carried out in 1989, sampling respondents in the Tokyo metropolitan area (Kanagawa, Chiba, and Saitama prefectures) from a list of businesses with 300 million yen or less in capital. The sample was stratified using three criteria: (a) male or female owner, (b) industry (manufacturer versus all other industries), and (c) capital (more than 500,000 yen or not), producing a 2 × 2 × 2 design of eight cells. We randomly sampled 125 addresses from each cell and mailed 1,000 questionnaires, of which 147 returned usable replies by February 1990. (This response rate is typical for Japanese mailed surveys.)

The U.S. sample was conducted in the Research Triangle area of North Carolina in 1986 and provided data on 266 respondents. The Italian study was carried out in 1988 and 1989 in Milan and sampled 109 participants in the Gemini Project of the SDA Bocconi Business School. The Northern Ireland sampling list was drawn up from information supplied by directors of small firm advice and assistance centers. From the list, 1,150 firms were randomly selected in 1988, and questionnaires were returned by 274 respondents. In 1987, the Swedish study sampled 898 persons from five different sampling lists and obtained 383 completed questionnaires. For our analysis, we included only the persons in these national samples who were currently operating a business. Characteristics of the sample in each nation are shown in table 2-1.

Our Japanese sample contained a slightly higher proportion of owners over 55 years old than the other samples, and it also contained the highest proportion of women. Due to the way the sample was drawn, about 38 percent of the sample were women, making it comparable to the Italian sample, which was also deliberately stratified to include more women. The percent of married owners was about the same in Japan as in the sample average. In all nations, about eight or ten were married, with the exception of Italy, where the sample consisted mainly of young, urban Italians who tend to marry at an older age.

About 54 percent of Japanese owners had self-employed fathers, indicating a high degree of occupational inheritance, a social process common for this stratum in all industrialized nations. (In all nations, a high percent of owners had self-employed fathers when they were growing up.) A smaller proportion of the Japanese owners also had self-employed mothers. Female owners were more likely to have had self-employed mothers than male owners. In Japan, 10 percent of the men but 24 percent of the women had self-employed mothers; in the United States, 7 percent of the men and 17 percent of the women had self-employed mothers. In both nations, self-employed mothers apparently served as role models for their daughters and may have been a motivating factor in their daughters seeking self-employment.

In Japan, almost none of the owners were in the start-up phase of their business careers; only 4 percent had businesses less than 2 years old. Across the national samples, Sweden included the highest percent of new firms. In both Japan and Ireland, about 68 percent of the businesses are five years old or older, but we found enough businesses in the intermediate years—2–5 years old—to spot any life cycle effects on personal networking.

Table 2-1. Sample Characteristics.

Characteristic	All Nations	Japan	United States	Italy	Ireland	Sweden
Age: *(percent)*						
17–34 Years	30	10	20	71	36	32
35–44 Years	34	29	41	19	35	36
45–54 Years	25	39	25	2	23	22
55 + Years	11	22	13	8	6	9
Total	100	100	99	100	100	99
N	(786)	(142)	(142)	(52)	(244)	(206)
Average Age	41.2	47.8	43.0	34.6	39.2	39.8
Sex: *(percent)*						
Women	24	38	15	36	23	18
N	(776)	(142)	(142)	(52)	(240)	(200)
Marital Status: *(percent)*						
Married	79	77	85	49	78	86
N	(774)	(141)	(140)	(49)	(239)	(205)
Family: *(percent)*						
Father Self-Employed	46	54	43	66	(NA)	39
N	(526)	(138)	(139)	(47)		(202)
Mother Self-Employed	13	14	8	23	(NA)	13
N	(467)	(138)	(142)	(44)		(143)
Business Age:						
0–1.9 Years	24	4	13	31	13	56
2–4.9 Years	32	27	38	42	19	44
5+ Years	44	68	49	27	68	0
Total	100	99	100	100	100	100
N	(786)	(142)	(142)	(52)	(244)	(206)
Business Size:						
0–4 Employers	56	21	44	46	75	71
5–9 Employers	12	18	18	12	10	6
10–19 Employers	10	21	13	17	5	3
20–49 Employers	11	18	14	8	7	9
50 + Employers	11	22	11	17	3	11
Total	100	100	100	100	100	100
N	(786)	(142)	(142)	(52)	(244)	(206)

The Japanese sample included fewer small firms and more large firms, proportionately, than the other samples. Whereas between 44 and 75 percent of the businesses in the other nations had fewer than five employees, only 21 percent of the Japanese firms were that small. The proportion of firms with more than 50 employees was twice as high in Japan as in the other nations (22 percent vs. 11 percent). These differences reflect the sources of our sampling lists; the bank that supplied our list in Japan clearly has an interest in dealing with well-capitalized firms.

Differences in sample composition, particularly business age and number of employees, suggest that we should exercise caution in interpreting any raw differences we discover. However, with multivariate analysis, we can control for such compositional differences and examine the *net* effect of national differences.

The Relations Database

The centerpiece of the questionnaire we used in all nations was an item that directed business owners to "Please indicate up to five (5) people with whom you feel especially willing or able to discuss your ideas for a new business or your ideas about running your current business." Respondents listed the names or initials of up to five people and then provided information on their personal characteristics (for example, age, sex, and their relationship to the respondent—friend, family member, business associate). We also asked how they met the network person and if a third person was involved (as a broker). Additional questions about network members were also added by investigators in each nation; in this chapter, however, we only used those developed especially for the Japanese sample.

Using this format, we potentially had information on five personal network members for each owner in our samples. However, not every respondent answered all questions, and some named fewer than five people. In our analysis, the unit of analysis was the owner-network member pair, with the number of pairs on which information is available varying from 235 in Italy to 799 in Sweden. The number of pairs available for analysis varied because of missing data on certain variables.

Characteristics of Network Members

Are persons recruited to be members of an owner's personal network, or do they simply slide imperceptibly from one form of association (such as "friend") to another? The embeddedness model suggests that owners will turn for business advice to the people with whom they have relatively long-standing relations and with whom they have developed trust. In this sense, personal network members are not recruited to the network but simply are already available because of prior associations. The instrumental model suggests that owners might well segregate their relationships into business and nonbusiness, with a special group of people reserved as business advisors. Such people would be chosen for their expertise, rather than social similarity to the owner.

An ideal test of such ideas would involve following panels of owners from the time before they became owners up to the point where they began making difficult business decisions. We would see whether their personal networks were marked by strong continuities or sharp discontinuities, as economic exigencies pressed in upon the new owners. Also, ideally, we should study all the members of an owner's network to discover whether owners confine their business-oriented interactions to one sector or spread them around to all members. Neither design was economically feasible for us. Thus, we limited ourselves to examining the characteristics of persons currently in owners' personal networks and drew inferences about which of the two models was more strongly supported by such indirect evidence.

Using an open-ended question, we asked respondents what kinds of relationships they had with the people they identified as those to whom they would turn

Table 2-2. Characteristics of Persons in Owners' Personal Networks.

Characteristic	All Nations	Japan	United States	Italy	Ireland	Sweden
Percent of Members Who Are:*						
Family	17	13	14	24	13	23
Friends	38	45	50	28	32	32
Business Ties	58	60	65	54	55	54
Other	8	4	6	2	0	22
N	3005	571	615	235	785	799
Percent Who Are Women	16	13	15	18	16	19
(S.D.)	(37)	(34)	(36)	(39)	(37)	(39)
N	2886	581	588	232	697	788
Average Age of Network Members	44.0	49.8	43.4	40.4	42.3	42.5
(S.D.)	(11.1)	(10.9)	(10.6)	(12.6)	(9.6)	(10.5)
N	2531	517	576	227	436	775

*Multiple responses were possible, so percentages do not add to 100.

for business advice. Responses were coded into four categories: family ties, friends, business ties (such as customers, suppliers, employees, former employers), and other. Allowance was made for multiple responses, but most people gave only one response. However, multiple responses varied by nation. The percentages in the first panel of table 2-2 do not add to 100 because of multiple responses.

Most persons in the owners' personal networks were identified as having some sort of business tie to the owner. Remarkably, the percent of members with a business tie varied only slightly across the five nations: from 54 to 65 percent. Friends made up the second largest category of network identifications, from a low of 28 percent in Italy to a high of 50 percent in the United States. Japan was closest to the United States in this regard, with 45 percent of network members identified as "friends." Family members were the third largest category, with Japan, the United States, and Ireland almost identical—13 or 14 percent. Clearly, we have solid evidence that some basic structural properties of small- and medium-sized firm owners' strong-tie networks are highly similar across capitalist nations, as well as evidence that Japan does not stand out as an exceptional case.

Owners in Japan, the United States, and Sweden were reasonably conscientious about completely filling out our questionnaire, and many owners listed more than one relationship with network members. In these three nations, very few members were identified as *both* a family member *and* a business associate: 3 percent in the United States and 4 percent each in Japan and Sweden. The combination of "friend" and "business associate" was more common: 28 percent in the United States, 19 percent in Japan, and 15 percent in Sweden. The importance of multiplex ties involving "friendship" and "business" was more evident when we computed the proportion of that subset of ties defined as "business" that were also defined as "friends." In the United States, 44 percent of business ties also involved a friend; in Japan, it was 31 percent; and in Sweden, it was 28 percent. Regardless of outsiders' perceptions, strong business ties in Japan are no more encrusted with friendship bonds than are strong ties in other nations.

Women were not major figures in the personal networks of owners in any nation, as shown in the second panel of table 2-2. About one in seven network members was a woman, with a low of 13 percent in Japan and a high of 19 percent in Sweden. Women owners had more women in their networks (about 40 percent of their network members were women), compared to men (every other man had one woman in his network, on average). As we argued previously (Aldrich, et al., 1989), the low percentage of women in owners' networks undoubtedly reflects the existing distribution of economic resources and power in these nations, as well as their occupational distributions. Women are not found at the head of major corporations, nor are they key players in the financial services sector, where they might be able to forge strong ties with small- and medium-sized business firms.

Women made up 35 percent of the family ties among all owners, but only 11 percent of all business ties. Of the ties that were both family and business, women constituted 29 percent, but of those that were both friendship and business ties, women constituted only 11 percent. In these respects, owners' personal networks appear to mirror the social structures of the surrounding societies, thus lending strong support to the embeddedness model.

In traditional societies, anthropologists tell us, the aged are revered as sages and looked to for advice. In modern societies, their role is no longer so clear-cut. To whom have our respondents turned for business advice? As shown in the last panel of table 2-2, the average age of network members resembled very closely the average of the owners in each sample. The average age of all owners was 41.2 years, and the average for all network members was 44 years. Japanese owners were the oldest in our sample: the average owner was 47.8, and the average network member was 49.8. (We think this is mainly a reflection of our sampling criteria, rather than a picture of true differences between Japan and other nations.)

In each nation, the network members were slightly older, on average, than the owners. However, the gap is far too small to support the proposition that owners are turning to older and wiser people. Moreover, a regression of network member's age on owner's age showed that, whereas there is an association between the ages of owners and members (R^2 was .11), owners are not simply choosing people similar in age to themselves or slightly older. Instead, many other factors are clearly at work, and we suspect "age" is dominated by other, more important characteristics in establishing strong ties, such as the kind of relationship between owners and members.

For only the Japanese owners, we regressed the network member's age on the owner's age. R^2 was only .06, and an examination of the scatter plot of member's age against owner's age revealed many younger owners linked to members many years older than they, and vice versa. About 40 percent were tied to people less than 5 years older or younger, whereas about 32 percent were tied to people more than 10 years older or younger. The plot revealed a slight tendency for network members to be older than the owner, with about 10 percent of the network members 20 or more years older than the owner. Nonetheless, the overall picture is of owners in Japan being connected to network members across the entire age range, thus supporting the embeddedness model: most owners turn to their age-peers for strong ties, rather than those very much older or younger than themselves.

Brokered Relationships

Owners who rely solely on people they meet face to face probably have a greater chance of meeting others very much like themselves than those using third parties to meet others. Meeting "friends of friends" is more likely to expand the diversity of an owner's network than only meeting people at one's place of work or worship. This possibility is blunted, of course, to the extent that one's friends also choose people like themselves. The instrumental model of networking suggests that pragmatic owners ought to use brokers to meet others whenever they can, whereas the embeddedness model suggests that third-party induced ties are more matters of chance than planning.

We asked owners if they had met their network members at their initiative or through a third party. If they indicated a third party was involved, we asked if that person was one of the five people they already listed in the questionnaire. If the broker was not already listed, we asked what the owner's relation was with the broker. Our results are shown in the first two panels of table 2-3.

Slightly less than one in three (31 percent) of the owners' personal network members were met via a broker. Cross-national variation was substantial, from a low of 23 percent in Sweden to a high of 48 percent in Italy. Japanese owners most closely resembled the Italians, with 44 percent of the ties stemming from third-party contacts. Italy and Japan were the nations with the proportionately largest small business sectors in our studies and arguably are also the most traditional in their social structures. Without the benefit of the Italian comparison sample, we might have been tempted to conclude that Japanese owners were very broker-oriented because of something distinctively Japanese. However, because we have other nations in the sample, we know that brokers are also an important feature of business networks elsewhere. We suspect that Japan and Italy stand out because "broker" is a well-defined social role in each country and because our samples in those two countries are from heavily urbanized areas (Tokyo and Milan), where brokers are enlisted to help owners cope with urban complexity and diversity.

Japan and Italy were also similar in the proportion of brokers who were members of the owner's personal network—20 percent in Japan and 23 percent in Italy. Overall, about one quarter of the brokers for whom we have some information were members of the owners' personal networks. Missing data limit our ability to say much about the brokers who were *not* members of owners' networks, but we do have information on 283 of them. About 9 percent were identified as family, 47 percent as business ties, 39 percent as friends, and 5 percent as "other." Figures for Japan only were very similar: 10 percent were family, 43 percent friends, 45 percent business ties, and 10 percent "other." This distribution was similar to that for the network members themselves.

Are the people met through third-party contacts different in any important respects from network members met directly by owners? To answer this question, we turned to logistic regression analysis. We created a dummy variable, taking the value "1" if a network member was met via a broker and "0" otherwise. We then regressed this variable on characteristics of the owners and the members who were met via a broker. We carried out an analysis for the entire dataset and then one separately for just Japanese owners. Results are shown in table 2-4.

In building our regression model, we were guided by the hypothesis that bro-

Table 2-3. Nature of the Relationships Between Owners and Members of Their Personal Networks.

Relationship	All Nations	Japan	United States	Italy	Ireland	Sweden
Met Through a Broker *(percent)*	31	44	29	48	29	23
(S.D.)	(46)	(50)	(45)	(50)	(45)	(42)
N	2929	537	614	214	774	790
Broker is a Network Member *(percent)*	24	20	31	23	18	35
Average Number of Years Known	10.9	13.9	10.6	11.9	8.1	11.6
(S.D.)	(10.6)	(11.1)	(10.6)	(11.3)	(8.5)	(11.3)
N	3013	573	621	221	812	790
Average Number of Meetings Per Week	3.1	(NA)[a]	2.5	3.8	2.8	3.7
(S.D.)	(4.08)		(4.5)	(5.0)	(3.4)	(4.0)
N	2430		603	210	812	805

[a]Japan has been excluded because of possible differences in the interpretation of this question.

kered ties would connect owners to people whom they would otherwise be unlikely to reach. Barriers to reaching potentially useful network members include age, sex, and being outside the family circle. We were also guided by the hypothesis that brokered ties would be less important to owners who had been in business a long time, had large social networks, and spent a lot of time developing and maintaining contacts. In our analysis, we also controlled for the order in which members were mentioned in the questionnaire, in case there were any unmeasured characteristics of first-named persons that we didn't capture with our variables. We found no effect of order, and so it is not displayed in the results shown in table 2-4.

Could older owners have any advantages in networking over younger owners? From the perspective of our instrumental model of networking, older owners have had more opportunities to go beyond their traditional associates. If nothing else, they have certainly had the opportunity to be exposed to many more people than younger owners. Pragmatic owners might, therefore, have kept an implicit inventory of possible brokers and used them to link with desired network members. For our Japanese sample, these expectations were not confirmed. Our analysis revealed that neither the owner's nor the member's age was important in influencing whether the relationship was brokered. Findings for the total sample were similar.

The instrumental model, following this logic, can also be used to generate expectations about the effect of business experience on brokered ties. Just as growing older means more exposure to networking opportunities for rational owners, additional years in business means more chances at forming ties to people who can act as gateways to distant others. However, this expectation also was not confirmed: years in business had no effect on whether a relationship was brokered, either in Japan or the full sample. Thus, brokers are used by owners of all ages to link

Table 2-4.   Use of Brokers: Logistic Regression of Whether a Broker Mediated the Relations Between Ego and Alter (Order Controlled but not Shown).

| | Dependent Variable (1 = Yes, Broker) | | | |
| | All Nations | | Japan Only | |
Variable	Effect on the Log-Odds	Effect on the Odds	Effect on the Log-Odds	Effect on the Odds
Intercept	−0.60	0.55	1.21	3.34
Age of Alter	−0.01	0.99	0.02	1.02
Age of Alter^2/1000	0.06[a]	1.00[a]	−0.21	1.00
Age of Ego	0.02	1.02	−0.08	0.92
Age of Ego^2/1000	0.25	1.00	0.70	1.00
Years in Business	0.00	1.00	0.01	0.99
Man Ego/Woman Alter	−0.12	0.89	0.49	1.63
Woman Ego/Man Alter	0.68[b]	1.98[b]	0.62[a]	1.85[a]
Woman Ego/Woman Alter	−0.38	0.68	−1.25[a]	0.29[a]
Ego Married	0.07	1.07	−0.26	0.77
Alter: Family	−1.12[b]	0.33[b]	−0.90[a]	0.41[a]
Alter: Friend	−0.09	0.92	0.15	1.17
Alter: Business	−0.02	1.08	0.06	1.06
Size of Network	0.01	1.00	0.00	1.00
Hours Developing Contacts	0.00	1.00	0.01	1.00
Hours Maintaining Contacts	0.00	1.00	−0.02	0.92
Country:				
Italy	0.73[b]	2.07[b]	(NA)	(NA)
Ireland	−0.13	0.88	(NA)	(NA)
Japan	0.45[b]	1.56[b]	(NA)	(NA)
Sweden	−0.40[b]	0.67[b]	(NA)	(NA)
Chi-Square	164.40[b]		39.26[b]	
df	23.00		19.00	
N	2033.00		402.00	

[a]Significant at .05.

[b]Significant at .01.

them with strong ties of all ages, apparently because other characteristics take priority over age.

Brokers play a more important role for female owners than for men, according to our results. In Japan, as well as in the full sample, female owners were twice as likely to have met a male network member through a broker as men were to meet another man through a broker. Otherwise, in the analysis for all nations, man-to-woman and woman-to-woman ties were no more likely to be brokered than man-to-man ties.

One difference between the analysis for Japan and the full analysis is that woman-to-woman ties in Japan were only about one third as likely to be brokered as man-to-man ties (the odds ratio was .29, significant at the .05 level). There is a hint of this effect in table 2-4 in the full analysis for all nations (the odds ratio for woman-to-woman ties was .68), but the coefficient was not statistically significant. Do the Japanese female owners in our sample have some avenue for meeting other female owners that is not available to men? And why are women using brokers to reach male network members but not women? Clearly, in Japan, the pattern of social relations in which female owners are embedded differs in some important ways from that of men. However, the pattern in Japan of women using brokers to reach men was quite similar to that in the other four countries, indicating that gender barriers are a cross-national phenomenon that is *not* specifically Japanese.

We included a dummy variable for an owner's marital status on the hunch that spouses might provide a link to persons outside of an owner's family and business circle. However, in neither Japan nor the full sample was the coefficient significant. At least for an owner's closest five business advisors, spouses played no linking-pin role.

We expected that ties to family members in an owner's personal network would *not* be brokered, and that expectation was confirmed. Ties to family members in an owner's network were one-third as likely to be brokered as ties to outsiders. (Odds ratios were very similar in the full sample and in the Japanese sample: .33 and .41, respectively, giving us added confidence in our results.) By contrast, we suspected that third parties might play some role in linking owners to business associates and maybe also a few friends. However, ties neither to friends nor business associates were significantly more likely to be brokered than other ties. This result is the same for the full sample and for Japan.

Three indicators of how much owners had invested in developing, maintaining, and expanding their networks were simply not associated with whether a tie was brokered. We asked owners "Over the past six months, with how many people would you estimate you have discussed aspects of starting a business or running your own business?" The average number of persons spoken with varied from a low of five in Japan to a high of twelve in the United States. (This variable is labeled "size of network" in the tables.)

In Japan, we asked owners an additional question: "How many of the people you talked with were women?" Men and women spoke with about the same number of people, on average: 4.5 for men versus 5.8 for women. However, two-thirds of the men had not spoken to *any* women, whereas about two-fifths of the female owners had spoken to at least one other woman. Twenty of the eighty-two Japanese men who answered the question had spoken with one woman, five with two women, one with three women, and one with four women. By contrast, twenty of the fifty-four Japanese female owners had spoken with one woman, five with two women, one with three women, two with nine women, one with ten women, and one with thirteen women. Few male or female owners in Japan had turned to women for their strong ties in business—as is also shown by the composition of their personal strong-tie networks in table 2-2—but most Japanese women owners had been in touch with at least one woman. This result strengthens our earlier finding, regarding the *absence* of third parties standing between Japanese female owners and female members of their personal business networks.

Owners reported spending between four to six hours per week in developing and maintaining their networks in all nations but Italy (Aldrich et al., 1989). On both measures, Japanese owners were at the low end of the range (3.6 hours developing and 4.3 hours maintaining networks). Regardless of hours invested in networking activity, the odds of having a brokered relationship to a personal network member did *not* change. This result challenges the instrumental model of networking, as it implies that owners who invest considerable time in meeting people are no less likely to have a brokered tie to a personal network member than are other owners. (About a third of all ties to personal network members were established via a third party.)

Net of the characteristics of owners and their network members, we still find national differences, as shown in the last rows of Table 2-4. All national effects are expressed as differences from the United States, which is the omitted country. Each nation was entered as a dummy variable for each relationship. Ireland was not significantly different from the United States in the odds that a relationship will be brokered, whereas in Italy and Japan, odds were one and one-half to two times greater than a relation will be brokered than in the United States. In Sweden, by contrast, the odds of a brokered relation were only two-thirds as great as in the United States. By definition, these significant coefficients represent either our failure to include other owners' and members' characteristics that are generic to all nations *or* the operation of some national cultural factors that transcend individual characteristics.

In Japan, greater dependence on brokers for extending one's network may reflect their relatively circumscribed networking system, in which relationships are sustained over long periods by loyalty and general trust (Yamagishi and Yamagishi, 1993), whereas the United States has a more open, market-like system. In the Japanese system, owners' attitudes toward unknown people are indifferent, and it is difficult for owners to extend their networks by themselves. But, with the help of a broker, owners can trust others even without firsthand knowledge of the others' trustworthiness. As Bestor (1989) pointed out, "broker" is a culturally marked category in Japan, and brokers play a socially recognized role in linking people.

The greater presence of brokers in relationships between female owners and male network members is another reflection of barriers to outsiders in networks in Japan. The role of brokers in women's networks is to overcome gender barriers, not only in Japan but also in the other nations we studied. By contrast, women owners have much less need of brokers for meeting other women.

On balance, we found little support for the instrumental model of owners' personal networking in our analysis of brokered relationships, either in Japan or the other four nations. There were no returns to age or business experience, and investments in networking activity also seemed to have little payoff for owners. We found some evidence of gender barriers, because the importance of brokers differed substantially between the sexes. Brokers were less likely to join women to women and more likely to join women to men than they were to join men to men, or men to women. We interpreted this result as support for the embeddedness model.

Duration of Relationships with Network Members

The embeddedness model of business-oriented personal networks, as we have portrayed it, posits strong-tie, long-duration relationships between owners and members of their networks. The instrumental model, by contrast, posits weak-tie, short-duration relationships. Thus, an analysis of the duration of ties and the factors influencing duration can help us understand the empirical implications of the two models.

The evidence favored the embeddedness model, rather than the instrumental model. On average, owners knew the people in their networks about 10.9 years, as shown in table 2-3. In Japan, the average was almost 14 years, 2 years longer than in Italy and Sweden, more than three years longer than in the United States, and almost 6 years longer than in Ireland. Some of these differences, however, reflect the differing age, sex, and relationships composition of the national samples. Therefore, we turned to multivariate analysis to see whether national differences persisted after controls were introduced, and thus whether the embeddedness model was still supported.

In Table 2-5, we report the unstandardized coefficients from a regression of the number of years an owner has known a network member on a set of twenty variables. The explanatory power of the model is quite good for all nations and for Japan alone, with R^2s of .46 and .42, respectively.

Based on the embeddedness model, we would expect an owner's age to be strongly associated with the duration of his or her ties to network members. If owners form strong ties with associates that they are reluctant to break, even when business conditions change, then owners' personal network ties ought to age with them. If, however, owners are more instrumental in their associations, then they should disregard the years they have invested in a tie and break it when conditions change. Because we have only cross-sectional data, any inferences are weaker than if we could follow owners over time, watching their ties form and dissolve.

In Japan, the association between owners' ages and the duration of a relationship was very strong: the regression coefficient of .92 indicates that, as Japanese owners age, their ties age at about the same rate. Our results showed that, on average, each year of an owner's age adds a little more than one-third of a year (.37, to be exact) to his or her length of association with a network member. The relationship appears linear, as a test for nonlinearity—adding a squared age term—is nonsignificant. Age of the network member, however, makes no difference to the duration of a relationship. This result complements our earlier finding that the correlation between owners' ages and those of their network members is quite low. Just as in the full sample, there was *no* association between how long an owner has been in business and the duration of an owner's ties. Put alongside our earlier finding that years in business did *not* affect whether a relationship has been created via a third party, this result again suggests the importance of nonbusiness context for an owner's business ties. Owners are carrying ties with them as they age, rather than cutting and pruning their networks.

Cross-sex relationships are of shorter duration than same-sex relationships. In the full sample, male owners knew female members of their networks an average of about two and one-half years less than they knew the male members. Female owners knew male members of their networks an average of about two years less than they knew the female members of their networks.

The pattern of results for Japan was similar, but none of the coefficients was statistically significant. In Japan, we found that female owners were much less likely to have their ties to other women mediated by a broker than were men. Women-to-women ties seem particularly strong in Japan, perhaps as a reaction to women's exclusion from the personal business networks of men.

Table 2-5. Multiple Regression of Years Alter Known to Ego on Relationship
Characteristics (Unstandardized Coefficients: Order Controlled but not Shown).

Variable	Dependent Variable	
	All Nations	Japan Only
Intercept	−9.60[b]	−23.38[a]
Age of Alter	0.03	0.21
Age of Alter^2/10	0.02	0.00
Age of Ego	0.37[b]	0.92[b]
Age of Ego^2/10	−0.02	−0.01
Years in Business	0.02	0.06
Man Ego/Woman Alter	−2.45[b]	−0.52
Woman Ego/Man Alter	−1.28[b]	−0.99
Woman Ego/Woman Alter	0.79	2.28
Ego Married	−0.22	0.11
Alter: Family	16.34[b]	14.68[b]
Alter: Friend	3.03[b]	1.32
Alter: Business Tie	0.22	−1.21
Brokered Tie	−3.46[b]	−4.72[b]
Size of Network	0.04[a]	−0.03
Hours Developing Contacts	−0.06	0.07
Hours Maintaining Contacts	0.01	0.01
Country:		
Italy	3.45[b]	(NA)
Ireland	−0.04	(NA)
Japan	1.66[b]	(NA)
Sweden	1.11[a]	(NA)
R^2 (Adjusted)	.46[b]	.42[b]
N	2001	399

Dependent Variable = Years Alter Known to Ego.

[a]Significant at .05.

[b]Significant at .01.

We expected family-based ties would be of longer duration than others, and our
expectations were confirmed. Compared to a baseline of "miscellaneous" ties (non-
friendship, nonbusiness), family ties averaged more than 15 years longer in Japan
and almost 16 years longer in the total sample. Friendship ties were much less
durable, lasting about three years longer in the total sample and a statistically insignificant amount longer in Japan.

More important for our models, business-based ties were of no greater duration
than miscellaneous ties in either the full sample or in Japan taken by itself. Indeed,
before introducing controls for age and sex, business ties were of the second short-
est duration of the four we emphasized: Mean durations were 8.4 years for miscellaneous ties, 8.5 for business ties, 10.7 for friendship ties, and 24.4 for family
ties. Clearly, 8.5 years is still a relatively long duration, and thus this result provides little support for the instrumental model of owner networking. Even in their
business-based connections, owners are maintaining ties over fairly long periods,
thus supporting the embeddedness model.

Brokered relationships are of shorter duration than others, by a substantial margin. When a broker was involved as a go-between in a tie, it was about 3.5 years shorter than a non-brokered tie in the full sample and 4.7 years shorter in the Japanese sample. Perhaps such relationships are more likely to be established when there is no "natural" basis for a relationship (e.g., owners and members did not meet at an association meeting or through normal business dealings), and thus they have been formed more recently than other relationships. (Because our study was cross-sectional, our measure of duration was formally equivalent to a measure of how recently the ties have been formed.)

As in our analysis of brokered ties, we included three indicators of how much owners had invested in developing, maintaining, and expanding their networks. And, as in our earlier analysis, instrumental investments in networking were simply *not* significantly associated with a tie's duration. The number of people talked to in the preceding six months had a small positive association with duration (the coefficient was .04), but this effect would be important only for someone at the upper bound of our results for network size. For example, someone who had talked with twenty-five people had relations that averaged about 1 year more than someone who had only talked with one person, and less than 5 percent of our respondents had twenty or more members in their networks.

Net of the characteristics of owners and their network members, we still found national differences, as shown in the last rows of table 2-5. All national effects were expressed as differences from the United States, which is the omitted country. Each nation was entered as a dummy variable for each relationship. As in our analysis of brokered relations, Ireland was not significantly different from the United States in the duration of relationships. In the other three nations, ties have lasted between 1 and almost 3.5 years longer than in the United States. We tested the significance of the differences between country coefficients and found that Japan and Sweden did not differ significantly. All the other differences were significant.

As with our analysis of brokered relationships, we found little support for the instrumental model of owners' personal networking in our analysis of the duration of business-oriented relationships, either in Japan or in the full sample. There were no returns to years of business experience, and investments in networking activity also seemed to have little payoff for owners. As owners age, the duration of their ties increases, which we take as evidence for the embeddedness model. Cross-sex ties are of shorter duration than same-sex ties, suggesting the existence of gender barriers.

Even business ties are of relatively long duration, but family ties are, understandably, the most durable. Only by comparison to family- and friendship-based ties do business ties look remotely instrumental. We believe our findings, on balance, support the embeddedness model.

Relationships in Japan

We asked owners how frequently they met the five people they listed as those to whom they turned for business advice, and the results are shown in the last row of table 2-3. Except for Japan, the frequency of meeting network members was remarkably consistent across nations—the average was 3.1 meetings per week (ex-

Table 2-6. Japanese Owners Only: Relations with Network Members.

	Family Only	Family and Business	Friend Only	Friend and Business	Business Only
Expertise *(percent)*					
Member Is Specialist	21	17	38	30	50
Member Is Generalist	79	83	62	70	50
Total	100	100	100	100	100
(N)	(48)	(18)	(145)	(104)	(208)
Where Meet? *(percent)*					
Outside Office	67	36	61	37	22
In Office	26	55	34	48	67
Both	7	9	5	15	10
Total	100	100	100	100	99
(N)	(54)	(22)	(152)	(106)	(212)
Continue to Meet? *(percent)*					
No	0	6	5	7	20
Yes	100	94	95	93	80
Total	100	100	100	100	100
(N)	(48)	(18)	(145)	(102)	(205)

cluding Japan), varying from a low of 2.5 in the United States to a high of 3.8 in Italy. Japan stood out sharply on this issue, for Japanese owners told us they only saw their network members 3.5 times *per month* (standard deviation of 5.4), which is one-fourth the average of the other four countries. It is possible that our Japanese respondents narrowly interpreted the question as asking only about times when specific business questions were discussed, rather than all contacts. If so, then the figure may be misleading. However if it is accurate, it suggests a different pattern of networking in Japan than in the other nations we studied.

We turned to some other questions that were only asked in the Japanese questionnaire to see if we could shed any light on this anomaly. Owners were asked, "Is the person a general expert who consults on a great many issues with you, or a specialist who only consults on finance, or marketing, or production, etc.?" About 62 percent of the 555 owners answering this question said the member was a general expert. There was no difference in the times per month these two types of members are met.

To determine whether Japanese owners' contacts with their network members differed by relationship type, we constructed table 2-6. Members were classified by type of relationship and may appear only once in the table. The "other" category was omitted, because it was too mixed to allow easy interpretation. About 77 percent of the owners listed only one type of relationship to a member, a simple tie, with the remainder listing two types of relations, or multiplex ties. As a percent of all 571 members on whom we have information, the breakdown of simple ties was as follows: friend only, 26 percent; business only, 37 percent; family only, 9 percent; and other, 4 percent. The breakdown of multiplex ties—for the remaining 131 that listed more than one type of tie—was as follows: 106 (or 18 percent) labeled a member both a friend and a business tie, and 22 (or 14 percent) labeled a member both a family member and a business tie. Only one owner listed someone as a family member and a friend, and the other two members were other combinations.

As shown in the first section of the table, members with a family tie to the owner were more likely to be seen as generalists than other members, whereas members without a family tie were more likely to be seen as specialists. Members whose ties to the owner are solely via business were the most likely to be labeled specialists, suggesting that their interactions with the owner are more limited than other network members. Family members, known for much longer periods than nonfamily, consulted with owners on a wide variety of issues. Most network members, however, were seen as generalists rather than specialists, suggesting that owners keep only a *few* specialists in their inner circle. Specialists might be the people who are sought on a more instrumental basis.

We asked, "Where do you usually meet the person?" About 42 percent met the person outside the office, 48 percent met in their office, and 9 percent met in both. As shown in the second section of table 2-6, persons who are tied solely via family and friendship relations were more likely to be seen outside the office than others, with about two-thirds of owners saying they meet family and friends at least some of the time outside of their offices. By contrast, for persons named as solely business ties, two-thirds were met only in their offices.

Finally, we asked, "Will you continue meeting after your business transactions are completed?" About 90 percent answered "yes" to this question. As expected, all members with a purely family relationship to the owner were seen as people the owner would continue to meet. Even members listed as business ties were seen as persons with whom the owners would continue their relationships, although one-fifth were evidently expendable.

Thus, combining the information in table 2-6 with that in table 2-5 presents a picture of Japanese owners as possessing a core of family members in their networks who function as generalists, who are seen mostly outside the owner's place of business, and with whom owners expect to maintain relations into the foreseeable future. About one-quarter of family ties are also business ties. Most network members are exclusively labeled as friends (26 percent) or business ties (37 percent), with another sizable group having multiplex business–friendship ties (19 percent). Business ties are the most specialized, are met mostly in offices, and have been known fewer years than family members.

Friends fall somewhere in between, with more specialists than among family members but fewer than among pure business ties. They are met both in offices and outside and have been known a few years longer, on average, than business ties.

Summary and Conclusions

We began our analysis of business owners' strong-tie networks with the presupposition that economic action is embedded in networks of social relationships (Granovetter, 1985), but that embeddedness is a variable. Some kinds of action might be deeply embedded and slow to change, whereas others might be more shallowly embedded and thus subject to the more transitory pressures of frequently changing circumstances. Entrepreneurial economic action is of particular interest, given a fiercely globally competitive economic environment and strong admonitions to entrepreneurs to choose business relations wisely. Indeed, networking among business owners might even be taken as a mantra of the 1990s, with articles on networking routinely appearing in the business and popular press (Aldrich and Dubini, 1989; Dubini and Aldrich, 1991).

Our study design not only allowed us to examine which of two models—an embeddedness or an instrumental model—seemed to describe better the behavior of small- and medium-sized businesses in Japan, but also to test their cross-national validity. Data on business owners' personal networks were collected in five countries, using the same questionnaire, and thus we could look for cross-national variation in owners' networks. In particular, we were interested in which of the two models of business owners' networks fit the Japanese case better.

Summary of Findings

Are the strong-tie networks of small- and medium-sized firms in Japan substantially different from those in other parts of the world? As in all the other nations we studied, Japanese owners' closest personal networks are made up of a mix of family, friends, and business ties, with family ties the least significant in terms of proportion. As in other nations, family ties are the longest lived. The personal networks of business owners in all five nations are composed of four major groupings: a small minority of family members, almost none of whom are also in a business relation with the owner; a large group of business associates who are defined by the owner in strictly businesslike terms; a smaller group of business associates who are also considered "friends" by the owners; and a fourth group who are strictly defined as "friends," without an apparent business tie also being present.

Very few women are in Japanese owners' networks, just as in other nations. Female owners quite often have the help of a third party in establishing ties to a man, just as in other nations. Women are sparse in the personal strong-tie networks of all owners, probably because women's place in the existing distribution of economic resources and power in these nations is very similar. Women do not occupy the key jobs to which entrepreneurs need connections.

Japanese owners do not simply choose people similar in age to themselves, nor do the owners in the other nations we studied. Instead, many factors affect who becomes embedded in owners' networks, and "age" is not as important as other characteristics, such as the kind of relationship between owners and members.

In their use of brokers and in the duration of their ties, Japanese owners look more like Italian owners than anyone else. A large proportion of the owners' personal network members were met via a broker, with about one-fifth of the brokers being members of the owners' personal networks. The distribution of brokers by type of relation to the owners is very similar to that for the network members themselves, suggesting, at the very least, that the third parties were part of the social relationships in which owners were already embedded.

In multivariate analyses of brokered relationships in Japan and the other four nations, we found little support for the instrumental model of owners' personal networking. There are no returns to age or business experience, and investments in networking activity also seem to have little payoff for owners. We found some evidence of gender barriers, as the importance of brokers differs substantially between the sexes. Brokers are less likely to join women to women and more likely to join women to men than they are to join men to men, or men to women.

On average, owners have known the people in their networks for a long time. In a multivariate analysis of relationship duration, we found little support for the instrumental model of owners' personal networking. There are no returns to years of business experience, and investments in networking activity also seem to have little payoff for owners. As owners age, the duration of their ties increases, and we found some evidence of gender barriers, as cross-sex ties are of shorter duration than same-sex ties. Family ties are, understandably, extremely durable, and even business ties are of relatively long duration.

The Two Models Revisited

To understand the structures of Japanese owners' personal business networks, we proposed two models for how the networks of business owners are constructed: (1) an embeddedness model—networks as products of long-standing affiliations and relationships, or (2) an instrumental model—networks as pragmatic, instrumental tolls of fleeting duration. The first model builds on the hypothesis that the social relationships of owners resemble those of everyone else, with a core of close and interdependent personal relationships and a periphery of weaker ties. In many respects, the first model resembles the "club mode" identified by Kanai (1993), who pointed out that the Executive Dialog Group of the Smaller Business Association of New England (SBANE) had low turnover, a lengthy time commitment, and high internal cohesion. The second model builds on the hypothesis that the social relationships of owners are quite different from those of everyone else, with a core of instrumentally based weak ties and a few close personal relations built on ties of reciprocity. In many respects, the second model resembles the "circle mode," as described in Kanai's (1993) paper and chapter, which has high turnover, short time commitment, and lower internal cohesion than the "club mode."

Our results show that the embeddedness model fits Japan and the other four nations we studied very well. At the center of owners' networks are the people they have known for many years: friends, family, schoolmates, business associates, and former co-workers. Ownership is fraught with uncertainty, and strong ties of intimate friendship provide the social support needed to weather crises and hardship. Relationships of long duration are cemented by loyalty and trust and stand as a bulwark against an owner's being exploited by people out only for short-term gain. At least among the five people closest to the owners we studied, personal networks are fairly resistant to change. Many business owners are the sons or daughters of parents who were also business owners, and lessons learned about the importance of maintaining and protecting strong ties are undoubtedly passed on between the generations.

The instrumental model, which posits that owners pick members of their inner circle on a pragmatic basis, also sheds some light on business owners' networks. Many owners' strong ties were met via third parties, only a minority of whom were other inner circle members. Also, a sizable fraction of the inner circle is described as only business ties, rather than family or friends. However, even these ties have been known a long time. In Japan, even the strictly business ties, who are met mainly in owners' offices, are persons whom owners said they will continue to meet, even after their transactions are concluded.

We suspect a reconciliation of these two models will build on the idea that almost all relationships in a business context are inherently ambivalent (Yamagishi and Yamagishi, 1993). Owners seek other people they can trust, but firsthand knowledge of trustworthiness is hard to obtain. We believe some of our findings provide evidence that Japanese networks are a more closely tied, relatively circumscribed system than networks in other nations. Once a relationship is established, consultation and information-seeking go around within the circumscribed network. However, if owners limit themselves to only well-known others, with whom they have gained enough experience to grant trust, their business world will be very narrowly circumscribed. Therefore, owners must form associations with people they do not know very well. Accordingly, many relationships will be entered into with a great deal of uncertainty as to the outcome, and many owners will, ultimately, be disappointed.

Caveats

As several people noted at our conference, we must be cautious in generalizing from our results because of the way we collected our data. We asked owners to tell us about their five closest business relationships, rather than all their relationships. Thus, our analysis reflects the nature of owners' strong ties, rather than their weak ties. By choosing strong ties, we increased our chances of finding support for the embeddedness model, rather than the instrumental model. Future researchers could investigate owners' weak ties, examining whether cross-national similarities still obtain in relationships that are potentially more instrumental.

Note

This chapter was originally prepared as a paper for presentation at the Vancouver Network Conference, Whistler, British Columbia, September 10–12, 1993; the conference was organized by the Institute of Asian Research, the University of British Columbia. Thanks to Elisa Bienenstock, Pat Ray Reese, Bill Woodward, Ben Rosen, Paola Dubini, Bengt Johannison, and Sue Birley for help with the various national studies. Deborah Tilley designed the tables and shaped the manuscript into its final form.

References

Aldrich, H.E., & Dubini, P. "Le Reti e i Processi di Sviluppo Delle Imprese." *Economia e Politica Industriale*, 64 (1989): 363–75.

Aldrich, H.E., P.R. Reese, and P. Dubini. Women on the Verge of a Breakthrough?: Networking Among Entrepreneurs in the United States and Italy. *Journal of Entrepreneurship and Regional Development*, 1–4 (1989): 339–56.

Bestor, T.C. *Neighborhood Tokyo*. Stanford, Calif.: Stanford University Press, 1989.

Dubini, P., and H.E. Aldrich. Personal and Extended Networks are Central to the Entrepreneurial Process. *Journal of Business Venturing*, 6 (1991): 305–13.

Granovetter, M. Economic Action and Social Structure: The Problem of Embeddedness. *American Journal of Sociology*, 91 (1985): 481–510.
Kanai, T. *Seven Entrepreneurial Paradoxes and the Taxonomy of Networking: The
   Cases of the MIT Enterprise Forum, Smaller Business Association of New Eng-
   land, and the Yokohama Venture Business Club*. Paper presented at the Van-
   couver Network Conference, Whistler, B.C., September 1983.
Miwa, Y. *Organizations, Networks and Network Organizations in Japan*. Paper pre-
   sented at the Vancouver Network Conference, Whistler, B.C., September 1993.
Takaoka, Y. *Small Business in Japan Today*. Paper presented at the University of
   Southern California Invited Symposium on Entrepreneurship, Los Angeles,
   California, 1989.
Yamagishi, T., and M. Yamagishi. *Trust and Commitment as Alternative Responses
   to Social Uncertainty*. Paper presented at the Vancouver Network Conference,
   Whistler, B.C., September 1993.

3

Entrepreneurial Networking Organizations

Cases, Taxonomy, and Paradoxes

TOSHIHIRO KANAI

Entrepreneurship is nurtured by networking, and, clearly, entrepreneurial networking is not an abstract activity. With help from their friends and acquaintances, entrepreneurs make things happen. There are specific places to make things happen, such as the Greater Boston area and Silicon Valley, where there are various kinds of networking opportunities for entrepreneurs and those who want to be entrepreneurs. In other words, networking can be facilitated by more or less formalized organizational arrangements for meeting others and encouraging entrepreneurship.

In this chapter, I first present a comparative case description of two networking organizations for entrepreneurs in the Greater Boston area. One organization is the Massachusetts Institute of Technology (MIT) Enterprise Forum, and another is the Executive Dialog Group of the Smaller Business Association of New England (SBANE). These two cases were chosen because of their theoretical contrast, although the descriptor is purely empirical. Second, based on a comparison of these cases, I construct the theoretical taxonomy of entrepreneurial networking organizations. The two contrasting types are the "circles type," drawn from the MIT Enterprise Forum, and the "clubs type," drawn from the SBANE's Dialog Program. Third, the ways these ideal types interact with each other are discussed. The organization of this chapter is rather unconventional, in that two cases are first described and then the relevant literature is reviewed when I discuss theoretical taxonomy and paradox.

Entrepreneurial Networking Organizations

The Greater Boston area as an entrepreneurial community is replete with many networking organizations. Two entrepreneurial networking organizations have been selected to show the contrast between different types of organizations.

A Brief Note on Method

At the beginning of this study, efforts were made to locate organizations by "snow-balling"—whenever I interviewed those who attended a networking organization, I asked them to name other networking organizations. If it is easy for an alien like myself (I came from Japan and was not an entrepreneur) to locate more than twenty networking organizations, it must be even easier for those who live in the area and are entrepreneurs to locate such organizations.

Among these organizations, two were selected because of their distinctive contrasts, and this should be helpful in constructing a theoretical taxonomy of networking organizations based on native views and theories (Glaser and Strauss, 1967). Originally, the case description was intended to provide ethnographic accounts based on interviews with participants, observations of meetings, archival records, and field- and mail-administered questionnaires. However, because these accounts were fully reported elsewhere (Kanai, 1989), in this chapter only vignettes of cases are presented.

Contrasting the Forum and the Dialog

The two selected sites were the MIT Enterprise Forum and SBANE. Short histories of these two organizations are summarized in table 3-1.

The MIT Enterprise Forum began small as a "private counseling" session for start ups. It emphasized high-tech start-ups and growing, technology-based companies. SBANE was an association created to increase the political clout of small business. In the beginning, the Forum was the small, cozy meeting where friends and acquaintances met, whereas SBANE from its inception was a large gathering. At the time when the Forum was born, risk capital was short, so it was a "misery loves company" kind of meeting.

Today, the situation is reversed. The Forum has grown into a large, open arena. SBANE has spawned the Dialog, where a small group of people express their ideas in a snug, warm atmosphere. Table 3-2 shows the specific foci of the current study, the Forum's monthly case-presentation meeting and the SBANE's Dialog.

There are about 2,000 people on the Forum's mailing list. Out of these 2,000 (plus those not on the list who happen to hear about the session), normally about 200 participants come to a meeting. A person can attend on a selective basis. Members of the Executive Committee and other "addicts" attend regularly. There seems to be almost no entry threshold.

In contrast, the Dialog has a deliberately designed threshold for entry. Being interested is insufficient reason to be allowed to attend Dialog sessions. First and foremost, one must be an SBANE member to sign up for the program. Second, one must pay substantial membership dues, which eliminates noncommitted members. This reflects the responsibilities required for running a business. Someone who is planning to become an entrepreneur cannot be a member of the Dialog. The third factor that screens members is the required time commitment. One is expected to attend all sessions throughout the Dialog year. Unlike the Forum, one cannot be selective by attending only certain Dialog sessions.

Whereas the monthly Forum has been a core activity of the MIT Enterprise Forum from its inception in 1978, the Dialog was a latecomer inside the SBANE,

Table 3-1. Contrasts Between MIT/EF and SBANE.

MIT/EF	SBANE
• Established in 1978.	• Established in 1938.
• The voluntary association geared to high tech businesses.	• The oldest political association for small businesses.
• Began as an informal clinic to discuss cases in a small group of people known to each other, when the time was tough for entrepreneurs because of the lack of risk capital.	• Organized as a vehicle to convey collective voices of small business owners, when Franklin D. Roosevelt sought a new wing of his political constituency—started with a critical mass where members were not known to each other.
• Currently over 2,000 people subscribe to the Forum Reporter.	• Currently over 2,000 small business owners are its members.
• No dues or qualifications for membership —there is no concept of membership.	• Dues are determined by the size of the company ($185 to $1,200) and member-ship is limited only to those who are substantially responsible for running the business (CEO, Chairman, president, and owner).
• Institutionally supported by the MIT Alumni Association.	• Incorporated as an independent, not-for-profit organization; associated with a national association, SBU, for legislative objectives.
• Financially supported by twenty-two outside organizations (including SBANE).	• Financially operated by membership dues and other fees for functions.
• The focal activity of this study is monthly case presentation meeting (simply called the Forum or a "large" Forum).	• The focal activity of this study is the Executive Dialog Program (simply called the Dialog).
• National Director is a major informant.	• Director of Educational Services is a major informant.
• The meeting is announced through a formal media, the Forum Reporter.	• The notice of the next session is a personal letter, followed by a phone call by the host to each member as a reminder.
• Competitors of presenters can come; the presenter might not know who is in the meeting.	• Competitors, customers, and suppliers are not permitted to be in the same group.
• What you hear at the meeting is regarded as being in the public domain.	• What you hear at the session should not be disseminated. There is an explicit norm for confidentiality.
• In the past, focus has been upon high tech companies.	• The business areas run the whole gamut.
• Currently trying to have service companies as presenters.	• Concerned about keeping the balance between manufacturing and service. Natural tendency is toward more service people.
• Experts are on the panel. They are regarded as resources.	• Consultants and other experts are a potential threat to the idea of a peer group. Some, not all of the members, regard them as resources.

Table 3-2. Factual Contrasts Between the Forum and the Dialog.

The Forum	The Dialog
• Began at the inception of the MIT/EF.	• Began thirty years after the inception of SBANE.
• Initiated by the founders of the Forum, following the format of the New York Venture Clinic.	• Invented and founded by a member in collaboration with SBANE headquarters.
• The core of all of the Forum activities.	• The program of highest reputation (according to 1985 survey).
• Fluid membership and the lack of boundary of insiders. • Everyone can attend the session (The Forum officially does not have a concept of membership for participants). • MIT/EF has no membership fee and attendance at case presentation is also free except for a presenter who pays a nominal cover charge ($200).	• Limited membership and a clear definition of its population from which members are drawn. Only the SBANE members are allowed to sign up for the Dialog program. • SBANE members who are in the Dialog still must pay a fee for the Dialog ($75).
• On average, about two hundred participants attend the session.	• In total, about 150 signed up for the Dialog in 1986–87.
• They meet together at an MIT classroom.	• They are in ten separate groups. Each group meets at the host's company (on-site meeting).
• Participants are not expected to attend all of the monthly presentations throughout the Forum year. In other words, selective attendance does not cause any problem. One attends a session only when interested in a presenting company and panelists.	• Once one signs up for the program and is assigned to a specific group, one is required to attend all the sessions, in principle. Only when something very urgent happens, nonattendance is acceptable. In other words, a continued attendance is a valued norm.
• Participants are not necessarily known to each other.	• Members typically become close associates as time goes by because the same members meet throughout the year.

even though SBANE was founded in 1970. The Dialog group was a brainchild of an SBANE member who wanted to have a group of "peers" with whom to discuss business problems. Albeit relatively a recent addition to SBANE's activities, the Dialog received high praise, according to a 1985 survey conducted by an outside marketing research firm. The Dialog has become a core activity in the SBANE's educational branch.

SBANE's limited entry threshold and enrollment are believed to be necessary to ensure that the group be composed of committed "peers." In contrast, the Executive Committee of the Forum allows casual onlookers to contribute to discussions; the Dialog committee makes efforts to avoid somebody who cannot be a true "peer."

These organizations are also different in meeting formats, as summarized in the vignettes in table 3-2. The monthly Forum is more formal and sophisticated. Any speaker, before presenting his or her ideas in front of 200 people from the entre-preneurial community, must be prepared. Spontaneity is discouraged. The meeting can be threatening for a young, vulnerable company representative because of the pressure of a large group and its unknown nature. Often, experts in a specific area can be quite tough, and a presenter has no way to know who will be in the audi-ence. Anybody, competitors included, can come to the meeting. Low threshold to entry, or open membership, enables a free and diverse exchange of ideas and re-sources, but this element may be threatening for presenters.

The Dialog session is much more formal. First, it is an on-site meeting, with some food and beverage, including some liquor. Members must travel where the host is. The host may face some pressure, especially when he or she expresses some of his or her problems or weaknesses. Second, because of the limited mem-bership in combination with the rules for allocating members into groups, the host, ideally, should not be threatened by the configuration of the group. The member-ship rules try to ensure that members will not include competitors and customers (and suppliers). Third, rules of the Dialog operations make it explicit that what is discussed in the Dialog should be kept confidential. Fourth, the size of each Dia-log group has been limited to no more than fifteen (ideally ten to twelve). The size of the meeting is kept small enough to allow an informal atmosphere. As the pro-gram has grown, SBANE has increased the number of groups, instead of increasing the size of each group. Unlike the Forum, all Dialog members (in different groups) do not meet together except for a kick-off dinner.

The Forum's monthly sessions are held in an MIT classroom, ten times a year at the same place. There are two sessions per night at the Forum. The *Forum Reporter* provides an notice of the coming sessions. In contrast, there are nine to ten ses-sions throughout the Dialog year, and the site is rotated among the members' busi-ness locations. Each Dialog member hosts the session that takes place at his or her business. The group may meet during the summer or more than once a month so that every one in the group can host. Because the same members meet throughout the year, as time goes by, members become close associates or "business" friends. A personal touch is another hallmark of the Dialog; the host is expected to make a personal call (not through his or her secretary) as a reminder of the session. The primary means of notification of the next session is a personal letter from the host that describes his or her (often private) problems.

At the Forum, few presenters are willing to address weaknesses of the firm (or self). Instead, they point out the strengths of their company. The exception is of course the area where financial resources are sought. For instance, if the entrepre-neur is trying to raise money, the presenter must emphasize the strength of his or her product to impress the audience, who usually includes people from the finan-cial community. In contrast, at the Dialog, the host is expected to be "honest" about his or her problems and weaknesses or, at least, to share information. The sharing of weaknesses is the cornerstone upon which peer discussion rests in Dialog. Some Dialog insiders who also know the Forum presume that the differences may not be so much in honesty as disclosure. Both the Dialog hosts and the Forum presenters are selective in varying degrees.

In the Forum, experts are regarded as valuable additions if they represent re-sources available in the community. The Forum is the place where these resources, which otherwise would remain dormant and invisible, are uncovered and discussed. Most supporting organizations of the Forum, by virtue of this visibility, support the Forum's activities because of their exposure. On the other hand, experts in the Dialog, especially consultants, are not authentic peers and thus are problematic in the group.

In terms of demographics, Dialog members are older and more seasoned (as measured by age and years spent in small business) than Forum participants. Dialog members have been in the Boston area longer than Forum members, and Dialog members seem, therefore, to be more socially embedded in the community than are Forum participants. The majority of people in both groups have experience in big businesses, although the percentage is higher for Forum participants. According to interviews with members, there is a trend toward an increasing number of female participants in both groups. There are, however, more female entrepreneurs in the Dialog than in the Forum. One out of four Dialog members is a female entrepreneur. In an ethnographic description of the Dialog in Kanai (1989), I relied on many quotations from female entrepreneurs. As one member noted, "We female entrepreneurs must be more 'vocal' than male counterparts."

Finally, in terms of educational backgrounds, Forum participants, on average, are better educated. The median and mode category for the Forum respondents is Masters degree level (the next category in terms of frequency, surprisingly, is a doctoral degree). Typical Dialog members, by contrast, are college graduates with a bachelor's degree. Company profile differences show that Dialog members represent companies that are more established and larger in the number of employees and revenues. Dialog members are more likely to have taken over a family business or acquired a business started by somebody else. Because of the open membership that allows those who are aspiring to be entrepreneurs to be present, there are company employees and students in the Forum. They seem to have a mindset very different from those who take over a family business, for example. One Dialog member refers to the fact that he used to learn a lot from an association called the Sons of Bosses. There are more people from traditional professions (like certified public accountants and lawyers—"white-collar services") in the Forum, and many are engaged in R&D activities. In the Dialog, manufacturing represents the largest portion of companies, although even in the Dialog, services in a broader sense are a dominant force. Services are equally distributed between white-collar and blue-collar service businesses.

The Taxonomy of Entrepreneurial Networking Organizations

Two contrasting types of networking organizations are presented as ideal types in a Weberian sense, or genotypes in a Lewinian sense. As such, *circle* and *club* are conceptual terms. However, the taxonomy is constructed through detailed qualitative accounts of two organizations to make it grounded (Glaser and Strauss, 1967). The basic taxonomy is based on four basic attributes or dimensions: basis of ties, benefits to members, entry requirements, and basis of operation. The taxonomy is summarized in table 3-3.

Table 3-3. Ideal Types of Networking Organizations: Comparisons of Circle and Club.

Attributes (Dimensions)	Categories (Types) of Networking Organizations	
	Circle (e.g., the Forum)	Club (e.g., the Dialog)
• Basis of ties and connections	• Weak ties • Variant value • Preference over diversity and discontinuity • Loose coupling • Appealing to the need to fly	• Strong ties • Value homophyly • Preference over common grounds and continuity • Tight coupling • Appealing to the need to be rooted
• Benefits	• Instrumental tool • Access to broader information and resources • Exchange at lower context	• Expressive-consummatory value • A deeper dialogue that may attribute a new meaning even to information already in hand • Confirmation at high context
• Entry	• Open membership or the lack of membership qualification	• Closed or limited membership qualifications are stipulated
• Basis of operation and procedures	• High turnover • Low time commitment • Nonregular, sporadic attendance • Indirect interactions utilized, and chain effects as a part of anticipated result • Lower internal cohesion and permeable to outside which may be conducive to macro integration • Grow as a whole group and potentially larger in maximum size	• Low turnover • Longer time commitment • Regular, and continued attendance • Direct face-to-face interactions valued, and chain effects, if happens, are a byproduct • Higher internal cohesion; but may entail macro fragmentation • Grow and divide to reduce the size of each group

Basis of Ties and Connections

The dimensions of entry and basis of operation and procedures provide design parameters. They are under the control, in varying degrees, of founding or central members of a networking organization. Moreover, the basis of ties and connections describes the very mechanism by which people gather.

People gather to exploit the strength of weak ties (see Granovetter, 1973). They believe that being weakly tied to various, diverse constituencies is an efficient way to get access to unexpected information or untapped resources. If they stick together too closely, meeting the same members over and over again, (which happened at the failing New York Venture Clinic, a predecessor of the Forum), then members believe that the meetings are boring and lack fresh perspectives. If the heart of the entrepreneurial process is to generate "new" combinations, weak ties seem suitable. The weaker the tie, the more novel the information and resources derived from the tie. Circles are based on weak ties. They look fragile, but they are strong in bringing new elements into networks.

Clubs, in contrast, rely on strong ties to create situations in which people can develop trust. People become friends. People gather in clubs because they find others who are wrestling with similar problems. Members believe that getting together has value. Therefore, participants do not attend circles to make friends; they want to meet people they have not known before.

Two rival hypotheses deal with the relationship between similarity of values and the formation of ties. One proposes that integration across diverse people occurs because they have different values (within certain limits). This is called the variant value hypothesis (Turk, 1963). Turk presumed a complex organizational setting where people from different occupational communities need to cooperate to achieve an organizational objective. For instance, in a hospital, nurses and doctors must cooperate, because of differences in their background, abilities, and values. The Forum has a loose but unique integrity, perhaps because participants represent variances in values. Forum members believe that entrepreneurs not only want to see their fellow entrepreneurs but also to be integrated with people in the financial community, for instance. Among them, venture capitalists have values that presumably are different from loan officers at a bank. Still, both of them are needed to help CEOs of small businesses. Companies at different stages and plans seek different sources of money. Typically, venture capitalists (VCs), especially the seed capital providers, are less risk averse than other sources of money, like banks.

On the other hand, a network may be formed because its members seek community. A propensity to seek others who have values similar to oneself is called *value homophyly* (see Laumann et al., 1974). In clubs, people gather out of value homophyly to seek strong ties and to feel "I am one of them." The hallmark of the Dialog is its character as a "peer" group. The metaphor of "group therapy" implies that the group has a problem-solving ("therapeutic") power because its members share a feeling of commonality. Clubs are meeting places to see old friends who are linked strongly.

A careful examination of these rival hypotheses—the variant value hypothesis and the value homophyly hypothesis—reveals the differences in research sites between Turk (1963) and Laumann et al. (1974). Turk studied a hospital as a community in which different professionals (such as doctors versus nurses) form ties because of differences. They need to be integrated because cooperation between different occupations, rather than between people in the same occupation, is more strongly required. In this sense, the hospital can be construed as an "occupational ecology" in which different pieces fit into a jigsaw puzzle (see Long, 1958). The Forum is one such example of an "occupational ecology" in which people with different values, skills, and resources from different occupations who are concerned about entrepreneurship play their own games. Different constituencies fulfill different objectives through the Forum.

Laumann et al. (1974), by contrast, studied community influence structures.

People who are influential in the community have their identity as political peers (even if their business and professional domains are different), and politicians belong to *one* occupational category. The social network Laumann et al. studied is closer to an "occupational community" (see Van Maanen and Barley, 1984). If small business owners, regardless of differences in business areas, are regarded as a single occupational category, the Dialog (like the community elites network) is closer to an emerging "occupational community."

In terms of motives to attend a network, the native views are closer to Maki's (1977) dual categorization of needs. (He developed this idea through a critique of a series of studies by Carlos Castaneda.) In Maki's understanding, people are driven by both the need to "fly" and the need to "be rooted." Apparently, Forum participants, especially those people who are dreaming and aspiring to be entrepreneurs, attend the Forum because the place appeals to the need to fly. They see others fly, and they may find the connections that might enable the need to fly. The Dialog, in contrast, appears to be attractive to those who have already flown but need to find the place to fold their wings for a while, which eventually may have a positive effect by allowing them to fly further.

In an ideal sense, circles are more strongly associated with a need to fly, and clubs are based on people's need to be rooted or to be embedded. The Forum is almost a showplace for entertaining the general audience and showing off presenters' businesses. The Dialog is a place for commiseration and group therapy. With regard to this contrast, a typical comment on motives by Forum participants is that "I need these kinds of people to start up my business," but Dialog members a need a place "just to talk."

Benefits

If an entrepreneur would like to experiment (or play) with an innovative idea, a loosely coupled association that brings contacts with the outside world is beneficial for access to a broad range of information and resources. For this purpose, a networking organization is an instrument. As one Forum member put it, the Forum is the place to utilize otherwise untapped resources by making them visible.

If entrepreneurs, after launching a new venture with their ideas, face problems that appear too overwhelming to be solved alone, they want to be associated with other peers just to express frustrations, worries, and weaknesses. As most Dialog members pointed out, learning that others are having the same problems is beneficial and relieving.

Ideally, circles provide instrumental benefits, whereas clubs provide expressive benefits. More specifically, circles are instrumental in gaining access to novel, unexpected information and resources from broader sources; clubs are places where one can express what one would like to share with peers. As such, the Forum is less personified, and it can inevitably serve as "another market." Exchanges of information and resources do not require circle participants to know others at a deeper level. Contextual subtlety and personal backgrounds of other networks are not important. In clubs, however, members are supportive of each other, and networking organizations begin to have a consummatory value. At the Dialog, peers work on problems presented by the host. To promote such conversations, each member must share context. With a higher context, members may develop new meanings for the seemingly familiar matters they discuss. Therefore, in clubs, generation of meaning is more salient than access to unexpected information and untapped resources.

The most frequently heard metaphors about the Forum and the Dialog are "show business" and "group therapy," respectively. The circle demands presentation of a "strong" self, whereas clubs sometimes allow (even encourage) people to unveil a "weak" self for commiserating with others.

Entry and Membership

The two remaining attributes in table 3-3 include dimensions that are controlled by founders of a network. As such, they provide clues for designing networking organizations of circles or clubs.

The Forum decided officially not to use the term "member" to refer to those who attend the Forum's monthly presentation. People simply participate without being bothered by membership qualifications. In contrast, the entry threshold is high in Dialog: SBANE membership dues, additional fees to sign up for the Dialog, and membership qualifications limited to those who run a business. The value put on continued attendance and the required time commitment also build the entry threshold higher yet. In short, entry to the Forum is free and open, and entry to the Dialog is relatively costly and selective.

As a design parameter, there are many ways to control the entry stage of networking organizations. The fee size is one dimension. Exclusivity of membership is another. Obligation, duties, and other forms of commitment are other design choices. The entry controls are easy to design. Once decided, however, they cannot be changed easily without jeopardizing the image and purpose of the organization. Both high and low entry thresholds have their own merits and demerits. Kanda and Teramoto (1986–87) studied the Japanese networking organizations for entrepreneurs known as techno-mixing groups (*igyoshukoryu*). They found a negative correlation between membership fees and the perceived information and manpower flow, as well as a positive correlation between membership fee and the serious joint efforts to develop and sell products. That correlation implies that high entry fees have a detrimental effect on free and relaxed exchange of ideas, but they have a positive effect on a group's collective efforts to develop businesses. Circles are good for exchange and weak for cohesive, collective efforts; the opposite is true for clubs.

Basis of Operation and Procedures

In terms of format and other procedural process, many contrasting features are found between the Forum and the Dialog. First, circles and clubs are characterized by high and low turnover, respectively. Although turnover is inevitable, even in clubs, selection at entry is a check against people who are insufficiently committed. Ideally, if networking organizations are chosen to be closer to the club concept, they should be based on the principle of low turnover. The turnover rate of the Dialog is estimated to be about 30 percent. This number, however, reflects the average turnover rates of different Dialog years. Within the same year, attrition is much lower.

Conversely, in the Forum, the number of people who attend is constantly changing from one session to another, depending on the cases being presented on that day. Indeed, the Forum does not urge continued attendance. Only those who are interested attend. As a design feature, circles are based on a principle of high turnover. A corollary is that high turnover means the lack of a heavy time commitment. One can leave as easily as one can enter. Thus, participation in meetings is rather sporadic. The Forum, however, was not *deliberately* founded on this principle; the format evolved.

The issue of whether high turnover is really a conscious principle of design is not necessarily supported by the Forum designers. A careful examination of the interview data reveals that it is regarded as a design element, not a principle, or so insiders believe. First, they created the Annual Workshop so that a much larger number of people could meet, assuming that the monthly session is not supposed to be attended by everyone on the mailing list (physically, it is impossible). Second, continuity of membership is more salient in the Forum's New Venture Clinic (NVC). In the process of designing the NVC, members of the Forum's Executive Committee reportedly discussed the high turnover in monthly case-presentation meetings. Turnover rates, at least retrospectively, are believed to be a design parameter. It should be noted, however, that the Forum insiders unanimously emphasize the evolutionary (versus designed) nature of their activities. Therefore, a native understanding of "designability" is very subtle. Other groups in the area, such as the 128 Venture Group, are more explicitly designed and operated on a principle of high turnover (Kahn, 1985). As the founder of 128 VG noted, "If a person ceases to attend a session, this means that he or she has got what is wanted. High turnover, therefore, indicates the success of our meetings."

Another contrast is high and low use of a "chain effect" in circles and clubs, respectively (Maguire, 1983). The use of a chain effect in circles is deliberate and intended, whereas its use in clubs is more haphazard, more a byproduct of a social gathering. The chain effect, for instance, enables Person A to reach Person D, because Person A knows Person B and Person B knows Person C who knows Person D.

To access information and resources, Forum insiders believe that the chain effect is important. In Forum sessions, participants may not meet a targeted person but will find that person through an introduction from someone in the meetings. Apparently, indirect interaction after the session often provides more valuable information and resources than direct contacts in and immediately following meetings. In an ideal sense, circles are just instruments or vehicles for getting things done later. A reliance on chain effects and indirect interactions are congruent with the instrumental benefits of circles.

On the other hand, the chain effect is not central to clubs. Dialog members believe that one needs to see other members face to face, because the group has a consummatory value for them. Moreover, a full, subtle grasp of a host's problems demands direct interaction. In reality, a chain effect does occur in the Dialog in the form of referrals and introductions through other members of the group. This benefit, however, is believed to be secondary in Dialog sessions. The ground rules explicitly prohibit the use of a Dialog session for soliciting business. However, the chain effect is more strongly expected by white-collar service members of the Dialog. One Dialog member, who is a consultant, noted that "the Dialog is a marketing tool for me." The emphasis on direct, face-to-face contacts in clubs is congruent with the dominance of expressive benefits.

The size of social gatherings is another design parameter. It is related to selectivity at the entry level, but it is an independent dimension. The Dialog started as a small pilot group and has grown. However, the operating principle for coping with growth in the Dialog is "grow and divide." Ideally, clubs stay small. (If they become large, other features are devalued.) Circles, on the other hand, rely on indirect as well as direct interactions. Potentially, they can be large, and the Forum is much larger than the Dialog.

Clubs, therefore, are more suitable for creating internal cohesion at the risk of shutting out wider contacts. A major complaint about the Dialog is that members do not learn what is happening in different Dialog subgroups. Circles, by contrast, create ties with various constituencies that, at first glance, appear to be outside. These other constituencies can be partially included at the risk of circles becoming somewhat chaotic, without cohesion. The boundaries of circles are more fluid than those of clubs. In Granovetter's (1973) terms, clubs generate "micro integration" at the cost of "macro fragmentation"; circles help achieve "macro integration" and lose internal cohesion.

Two Types of Interaction

Circle and club attributes do interact. Perhaps networking organizations that work effectively incorporate both elements in a complementary way. But seeking both from the very beginning causes an insurmountable challenge, because, viewed from a developmental perspective, their coexistence and interaction are very subtle. Clubs evolve into circles, and circles spawn clubs. A careful reexamination of the Forum and the Dialog interviews revealed that both elements coexist subtly.

The Formative Period of the Two Groups

In the early days, the Forum was more like a club. The founding members unanimously pointed out that it was born because they "felt miserable" with the "harsh environment for small businesses." Risk capital was low, and the Route 128 high-technology start-ups were suffering. Participants met in a small group to discuss their plight and console each other. It was, however, the founders' deliberate efforts to introduce circle elements in order to avoid the mistakes of the New York Venture Clinic, namely, the mistake of the "same old faces." Among their deliberate choices was "open membership" beyond the MIT community. Thus, the Forum evolved toward a circle.

By contrast, the very origin of SBANE, a matrix for the Dialog, was established as a legislative "instrument." It was a political circle to mobilize the voices of small businesses. For this purpose, even at the very beginning, SBANE had to reach a critical mass. It was a circle with a political purpose. Dialog groups under the auspices of the SBANE, in a metaphoric sense, are isolated, protected islands in a sea of circles.

The NVC for the Forum and the NEBC
for the Dialog

A pure type of anything can be vulnerable. Ideal circles lack internal solidarity, whereas ideal clubs lack access to wider resources. The very nature of the Forum's monthly session, such as open membership and low threshold, is a potential threat to the "young" companies that the Forum originally wanted to help. Competitors can come, and comments can be too brutal to be accepted by fledgling companies that have to be "incubated." Because of the Forum's brutality, the Executive Committee formed the New Venture Clinic (NVC)—also called the incubator—as a club for fledgling companies. In the NVC, the number of members is limited, and they meet to help young companies in a protected atmosphere. The NVC was added to the MIT Enterprise Forum activities to support and encourage fledgling ventures. As all founders alluded, the NVC is reminiscent of the old Forum (e.g., it is a gathering close to clubs).

On the other hand, one of the most common complaints about the "well-protected" Dialog is that members cannot learn from the mistakes of others. Each Dialog Group is an "isolated island." That isolation enables sincere expressions of problems inside the island, but risks not knowing anything about the surrounding ocean and other Dialog groups. (The "island" metaphor is native, not necessarily shared by all Dialog insiders.) SBANE has established the New England Business Conference (NEBC). The SBANE staff does not formally claim that the NEBC is a countermeasure to cope with the closed nature of the Dialog. However, some Dialog members expect the NEBC to be an opportunity to be exposed to the overall SBANE population and other participants beyond the cozy but small world of each Dialog group. In 1987, the NEBC had fifty-two sections and installed an exhibition called "The Marketplace." The Marketplace is an "instrument" for small business owners to get access to procurement managers in major corporations in New England. The NEBC serves as a circle for Dialog members in the club.

The Executive Committee of the Forum and
the Dissolution Rule of the Dialog

Circles as an ideal type are a very loosely connected group. They will dissolve, unless they have a dedicated core of members. They are thin, fragile, and weak. These attributes imply the weaknesses of circles.

The Forum has been working well, reportedly because of the efforts of the Executive Committee of the Forum. The committee embraces most founding members. They are the hub of the Forum's activities. The committee members believe that without their efforts, a loosely organized network like the Forum would be easily unsettled. The Executive Committee was construed as a club by one of the general participants of the Forum, when he complained "Make it [the Executive Committee] less clubby" (according to a survey conducted by the Forum, an internal document). He coined "clubby" in a negative sense. However, without this "clubby" element inside circles, operations could not be easily maintained. The committee is the only centripetal force uniting all other loosely defined Forum activities.

Circles need club elements to give continuity to its activities. In a similar vein, the club needs the circle's elements to neutralize the limits associated with clubs. The NEBC is one such example. In considering what makes the Dialog attractive, the dissolution rule should not be underestimated, as most Dialog insiders suggest. Some members resent this uncompromising rule. However, because of this rule, Dialog members not only have close ties with some SBANE members but also have access to a different set of people from the more diverse SBANE population.

Another hybrid element in the Dialog is the appearance of consultants. Consultants are received with mixed feelings by the entrepreneurial peers in the Dialog. They may negate the "peer feeling" inherent in clubs if they use the Dialog as a marketing "instrument." However, their addition can deepen the discussion and may enable the Dialog to utilize professional networks and associations (but at the risk of jeopardizing the spirit of a "self-help" peer group). Therefore, it comes as no surprise to find some Dialog interviewees who welcomed the inclusion of consultants, CPAs, and lawyers. As a result, the Dialog is not a pure club. Its closed nature is attenuated, and weak ties and chain effects occur.

Interaction of the Circle and the Club in a Community

On a macro level, an entrepreneurially active community like the Greater Boston area has various kinds of networks for entrepreneurs. Naturally, they include both circles and clubs. Both types may interact, like the Forum and the Dialog. For instance, the program chair of the 1987 NEBC was a member of the Executive Committee of the Forum. The National Director of the Forum sometimes calls the Educational Director of SBANE to ask for informal cooperation, and vice versa. SBANE has been a supporter of the Forum. The Forum similarly has been a supporter of SBANE and the Dialog's educational activities. The interaction became more explicit and visible in the 1987 NEBC.

Interactions are not limited to core members of the two organizations. Interactions can be found among general members and participants. Overlapping membership in both types enables members to reap the benefits of both groups. The exact number of overlapping cases is not clear, but it is not large. (I matched the mailing list of the *Forum Reporter* and the membership list of the 1986–87 Dialog.) Few people were on both lists. There are two reasons for this small number: I checked only the past nine years of Dialog applications, and the names on the mailing list of the *Forum Reporter* are changing. I only looked at the list of current members who have paid their dues most recently. Because those who are not on the list can come to the Forum, the degree of overlapping membership can be easily underestimated.

Overlapping membership is not so pervasive between the Forum and the Dialog as it is between the Forum and SBANE. According to my field-administered survey, 18 percent of the Forum participants in a specific session were also members of SBANE (though less than 10 percent of SBANE members signed up for the

1986–87 Dialog). (In a mail survey, the result of the equivalent question would be 15.1 percent of Forum respondents.)

There are, at least, four notable cases of overlapping. One person in both groups is a manufacturing entrepreneur, an experienced businessman who acquired a company started by three MIT graduates. He has attended the Forum for a long time and has twice been a member of a Dialog group. Another case of overlapping involves a high-tech businessperson who is new to both the Forum and the Dialog. He is becoming active in both groups. The third case involves an older businessman, an old-timer in the Dialog, who once was invited to the Forum as a guest speaker. The last case involves one of the Forum's Executive Committee members who used to be active in the Dialog and then quit. An interaction of circle and club elements is found inside networking organizations. In addition, in an "interorganizationally" rich area like the Greater Boston area, an organization closer to circles and another closer to clubs can interact on a community level. They coexist.

Empirical Foundations of Seven Entrepreneurial Paradoxes

In concluding this chapter, seven entrepreneurial paradoxes are proposed and examined with reference to the two organizations described previously. These paradoxes are conceptually constructed through an extensive literature review. They are epitomized in the empirical realities of the two networking organizations.

A Basic Entrepreneurial Paradox

One becomes an entrepreneur, because one wants to be on one's own. Self-reliance and autonomy are keys to entrepreneurial success. After starting one's company, one has to understand deeply how one relies on others for information, resources, and other forms of support. Kets de Vries (1977) revealed that entrepreneurs create a work environment of high dependency on others while professing a high need for independence and a low need for support. They face a psychological dilemma of hoping for independence and, at the same time, finding themselves dependent upon others for critical resources. This is the basic entrepreneurial paradox.

The founders of the MIT Enterprise Forum started this networking organization when risk capital had dried up and entrepreneurs felt helpless. Entrepreneurs started their business only to find out that they lacked critical resources, especially venture capital. On a deeper level, to cope with the basic entrepreneurial paradox of simultaneously being self-reliant and dependent on others for help, they started the Forum to help themselves as entrepreneurs. The Forum was designed as an instrumental device to help entrepreneurs, by bringing in diverse ideas, information, and resources.

The founder of the SBANE's Executive Dialog program more clearly admitted that entrepreneurs were lonely. The survey study of the SBANE reported that many members of the SBANE felt entrepreneurial solitude. There prevails a heroic image of entrepreneurs who start their business, people on their own. In reality, they gather in a peer group to attenuate this feeling of solitude. Being at the top of small businesses means that it is difficult to talk on a deeper level to someone inside the company. The Dialog, as a selective club, enables entrepreneurs to share this feeling, although the group is also useful for joint problem solving.

The Weak-Tie Paradox

Weak ties are important in locating resources and information from a broad range of sources and gaining access to them. Given the fundamental "dependence paradox," the search for critical resources necessary for new ventures should be thorough and efficient for entrepreneurs who are quite likely to be reluctant to rely on others. Remote acquaintances (weak ties) rather than close friends (strong ties) should help this search (Granovetter, 1973). Granovetter (1973, 1982), however, admitted that strong ties have the function of enhancing internal cohesiveness of the group at the risk of macro fragmentation; exclusive concern for weak ties may achieve macro integration, potentially at the risk of micro fragmentation (loss of cohesive primary groups).

Granovetter's finding, in short, is that weak ties are "better" (or "stronger") than strong ties. The strength of weak ties is a paradox that deserves attention. This paradox, however, does not deny the "strength of strong ties," a statement too obvious to notice. Obviously, strong ties have their own advantages. "Strength" is a tricky term. The question is what is meant by "better" (or "stronger") in Granovetter's paradox. It is a term relative to the dimension of benefits one expects from the use of ties. Maguire (1983) suggested an interesting proposition on this point:

> Individual networking for resources . . . depends on who is doing the networking and their purpose. In general, personal and emotional support and guidance is best provided by either long-standing, intimate friendship or kin network. Material resources and less readily available or more technical resources or services must be provided by more diverse, less intimate, second-order networks, that is, network members known wholly or primarily through another or even a series of other contacts (p. 70).

This observation can be reinterpreted that strong ties are functional for the expressive use of networks; weak ties are functional for the instrumental use of them. Granovetter's definition of the "strength" of an interpersonal tie refers to the degree of intimacy, an expressive, emotional aspect. However, the way he used "strength" when he described the strength-of-weak-tie paradox focuses on the instrumental aspect of finding a job. Granovetter not only unearthed this paradox but also suggested a subtle relationship between the expressive and instrumental use of networks.

The MIT Enterprise Forum was designed to make full use of the strength of weak ties. Its predecessor, the New York Venture Clinic, was suffering from the too-clublike nature of the group. Members began to learn that the same people gathered to exchange the same remarks. The Forum, based on this experience, was intended to be the place where people with different backgrounds met to mobilize resources. In its evolutionary process, the Forum's Executive Committee, the Forum's core group, was sometimes criticized as being too closed and clubby. Participants of the Forum wanted to make it an open place to exchange ideas with unknown people and acquaintances who were linked only through weak ties. The instrumental use of network resources was the key issue among the Forum participants.

In stark contrast, SBANE's Dialog groups are characterized by their emphasis on strong commitment to the development of strong ties among members. The expressive use of the network was the dominant concern among Dialog members. SBANE, however, introduced other networking arrangements, such as the New England Business Conference, to provide members with the opportunity for enjoying the strength of weak ties.

The Diversity–Homogeneity Dilemma

There are two opposing arguments about whether similarity or heterogeneity of members produces better relations. Again, the dilemma is centered on the question, "Better in what sense?" Each argument is most appropriately represented by the value-homophyly hypothesis or the variant-value hypothesis.

Value homophyly is defined by Laumann et al. (1974) in connection with an underlying hypothesis:

> Value homophyly, the term we shall use to refer to the variable degree of value, attitude, and belief similarity or congruence between two individuals, may promote or prevent a social relationship, depending on the type of relationship being considered. Obviously, high value homophyly is not required in a highly *instrumental* relationship as in a business transaction between a buyer and seller (p. 166).

An implicit pair hypothesis is that value homophyly is more crucial in a highly *expressive* relationship. Therefore, Laumann and his associates carefully avoided the universal argument that value homophyly is important in every kind of relationship. Unlike other major concepts in social networking analyses, value homophyly is on the side of motivational orientation rather than structural positional attributes. It is worth examining whether the actors in a structurally equivalent position are going to have similar value attitudes over time. In the current issue, it is assumed that value homophyly or value variance is an antecedent to networking behavior. Moreover, the dynamic changes of value orientation over time is beyond the scope of this study.

The variant-value hypothesis (Turk, 1963) posits that different (rather than similar) value orientations between different professions bring higher cohesion in their social relationship. The "cohesion of a structurally differentiated system rests on some tolerated variability in the values to which its various parts are oriented" (p. 37). The diversity–homogeneity dilemma, if simply stated, is that without a minimum degree of commonality (or something universal at a deeper level), it would be difficult to relate oneself to others. At the same time, without some degree of diversity, one is much less likely to get fresh and invigorating perspectives and novel (unexpected) information and resources.

This dilemma reminds us of the contrast between functions of strong ties and those of weak ties. There is a clear parallel. Granovetter (1982) treated the concept of value homophyly as an attribute of strong ties, loosely defining it as the tendency to choose friends from people who are similar to oneself. Parallelism is more than this aspect, because strong ties and value homophyly are strongly associated with *expressive* needs of members in a network. On the other hand, both weak ties and value variance are linked to the *instrumental* use of a network. We need both in networking.

The MIT Enterprise Forum represents the diversity of participants. Everyone can attend if he or she has an interest in entrepreneurship. Even onlookers who just want to know about entrepreneurship can attend. By making the Forum a monthly meeting open to everyone, it attracts people with diverse backgrounds. The common tie among participants is their interest in entrepreneurship, although the degree of interest differs from one participant to another.

SBANE's Dialog Group was intended to be a homogeneous group. Those who want to sign up for the Dialog must be a member of SBANE. Membership qualification of SBANE is very strictly limited. In principle, only CEOs or owners of small businesses can attend. As such, members are homogeneous in that they run small businesses. However, the areas of business activity are diverse, ranging from gas stations, to high-tech ventures, to restaurants. Without homogeneity, members cannot talk on a deeper level; at the same time, without diversity in business backgrounds, members cannot get fresh insights from peers.

The Redundancy–Reliability Paradox

Landau (1969) contended that redundancy enhances the reliability of communication and the adaptability of a system. He applied insights from natural automata (natural networks) to studies of social networks. His basic tenet was that a natural organism is a self-organizing system that is characterized by richly redundant networks with a considerable degree of "overlapping" and equifinality (multiple routes to the same end). This characteristic makes a natural system, despite its complexity, relatively free from errors and failures of communication among elements in the system, as compared with an artificial system.

Redundancy or multiplicity in the context of networking is multiple memberships. Why does one bother to attend various similar associations? Why is an "interorganizational leader" needed in addition to an "organizational leader" (Perrucci and Pilisuk, 1970)? The Home Brew Computer Club in Silicon Valley is a classic example of a network born out of a grass-roots movement. It was the product of an evolution rather than a careful design "from above," that is, by the state or federal government. As a natural, emergent, and evolving system, the Home Brew Computer Club might have characteristics similar to natural automata, which allowed redundancy and hence reliability and flexibility of communication among members. Moreover, what is more important in Silicon Valley is that there are so many networks in the area. The Home Brew Computer Club, albeit prominent, is not the only network. Moreover, people in Silicon Valley know that multiple networks exist (see Rogers and Larsen, 1984) One can enjoy creative redundancy by maintaining multiple memberships in more than a few similar organizations.

Multiple membership is germane to the function of weak ties. If one wants to be relaxed in an internally cohesive group, one may not be actively seeking weak ties. Weak-tie seekers (in terms of a position in the network) are more inclined to be engaged in various associations. ("Weak-" or "strong-tie seekers" do not refer to human characteristics like personality. The terms are used just for convenience. They imply a position orientation in the network.)

Overlapping, multiple memberships not only facilitate macro integration but also improve reliability of communication. Why do entrepreneurial "networkers" attend two or more associations? Multiple membership provides a circuit of credibility through which one becomes more likely to meet not only longtime friends but also relative newcomers. Redundancy has its own function. Thus, multiple memberships in similar organizations are not fruitless.

On the surface, it is paradoxical to know that redundancy has a positive effect in networking. At the same time, it may not sound like a paradox, because it is almost a cliché that repeating the same message (at the risk of losing succinctness) assures communicative reliability. It is more like a trade-off between redundancy (especially a loss in time) and reliability, rather than a paradox.

The Greater Boston area and Silicon Valley are widely known as places where various kinds of networking organizations for entrepreneurs exist. One can easily find both circles and clubs. Multiple membership in two or more networking organizations may be redundant, but through this redundancy, reliability of communication is maintained in an entrepreneurial community.

The Paradoxical Role of Professionals in Networks

How can outside professionals be involved with a natural, grass-roots network without deteriorating the essence of "self-help/mutual aid" as its most prevailing goal? The paradoxical role of professionals in a naturally occurring network has been well documented in a special issue on self-help groups in the *Journal of Applied Behavioral Science*, published in September 1976. For instance, Back and Taylor (1976) argued that "[p]rofessionals have failed in the client's view, while a lay group, a group of persons having the same deficiency, has been able to help. . . . One of the most striking characteristics of self-help adherents is *distrust of professionals* (pp. 299, 301, emphasis added)."

What appears to be a crisis, or at least something critical or unusual, for laypersons is routine for professionals. Examples are replete in modern life: suing or being sued, for clients of lawyers [see Black and Baumgartner (1980), for legal services in general]; neurosis for patients of psychiatrists [see Illich (1976), for Medicare in general]; and clients of consultants who write business plans for venture capitalists (see Parthe and Schaufeld, 1984).

Usually a self-help movement has more of an expressive origin to help people discuss their problems, worries, and anxieties. Its participants typically are weak, deprived, or stigmatized (Goffman, 1963). Confession plays an important role in mutual encouragement that "I am not the only one" in the closed, protected terrain of a self-help group (Hurvitz, 1976). Goffman's (1963) label of "huddle-together" groups is revealing. By contrast, professionals (as an ideal type—professionals do have their share of loneliness and emotional reactions) are more specifically trained to be instrumental. They may or may not show empathy with a layperson's expressive needs, but by no means do they show their personal concerns. Moreover, they look strong or even omnipotent in their specialized area. A self-help/mutual aid movement, in this respect, is an antiprofessional movement that often claims at the initial organizing stage that professionals are not omnipotent (see Blumer, 1969). Back and Taylor (1976) applied Blumer's framework to self-help movements and argued that agitation and unrest in the first stage of such movements typically are about the distrust of professional omnipotence.

Self-help groups, as a kind of resource exchange network, *ideally* should be "likes and helping likes" [e.g., women helping women, teachers helping teachers) (see Sarason and Lorentz, 1979, p. 48) or entrepreneurs helping entrepreneurs)], not professionals helping laypersons. However, most self-help groups *in reality* lend themselves to some kinds of professional help and advice (Maguire, 1983; Steinman and Traunstein, 1976).

A third point is related to this issue. A critical fact when attempting to create a "self-help" network is that professionals need access to various kinds of resources that one would not be even aware of without their help. If one plans to organize peer groups for young entrepreneurs, how does one know where they are? A layperson may not, but venture capitalists, new venture consultants/advisors, or other professionals do. For example, because one of venture capitalists' primary tasks is to screen business plans, they are in a better position to meet entrepreneurs. A layperson can do that by asking friends and snowballing the list of potential members. Asking friends may work and is perfectly fitted with the norm of "self-help." (This is why a directory of members becomes a valuable asset in self-help networks.) The method, however, might not be as far reaching and efficient as one supported by professionals, because professionals are more likely to have a database of clients.

Therefore, in reality, self-help networks do rely on professionals. For example, researchers in an empirical study of forty-eight self-help groups reported that 38 percent willingly used the services of trained professionals, and an additional 58 percent of groups used professional services, though unwillingly (Steinman and Traunstein, 1976). In other words, almost all (forty-six of forty-eight groups surveyed) relied on professional help in some way. Maguire (1983) admitted the potential danger of introducing professionals into a self-help network. He also argued that one factor that makes the modern self-help movement distinctive from a traditional natural network (like kinship ties) is a partial inclusion of professionals. Using human services that involve social workers as an example, Maguire (1983) illustrated partial inclusion:

> By definition, self-help groups are run by and for people who share a concern or problems; this excludes professionals who do not personally share the problem. However, professionals have devised a great many ways of working with self-help groups so as not to undermine their autonomy and self-reliance. . . . There are four specific instances when the need for social work intervention with self-help are most clearly indicated. The first is where the individual clearly has no personal and material *resources* or is extremely deficient. The second is where the *resources* are not readily perceived by the person or where they are dormant. The third is where the problem is sufficiently serious so that professional social work assistance in developing the *resources* becomes crucial to successfully working through the problem. Finally, social workers must encourage the self-help capabilities of a client when the nonpersonal *resources* needed are not as available to the client as they are to a professional social worker. (p., 36, emphasis added)

Kleiman et al. (1976) provided a case of collaboration between lay volunteers and professionals, but empirical evidence of the collaborative model is rather thin when compared with the cases of distrusting professionals. Maguire (1983) may be too optimistic. The paradoxical role of professionals in self-help movements remains very subtle and tenuous, even if there are some cases of collaboration. Therefore, inclusion of professionals in self-help groups is a mixed blessing. The dilemma is derived from the double-edged power of professionals and the powerlessness of laypersons as potential clients in broadening access to various resources "out there."

Two theoretical grounds account for the importance of peers in self-help movements. The first is Festinger's (1954) theory of social comparison. If one is thrown into an uncertain situation, one usually observes how others behave in a similar situation. Situational norms can be learned through vicarious rule-learning (Bandura, 1977). People are most sensitive to others whom they perceive to be similar to themselves. Those people serve as a reference group in coping with problems. Psychological modeling and observational learning are put into operation in a peer group. Unless professionals are as empathic as peers (which is doubtful), observational rule-learning through sharing experiences is facilitated more in a peer group than in a group initiated and maintained by somewhat "detached" professionals.

Second, consider the social construction of reality (Berger and Luckman, 1967) through mutually expressing (confessing) one's thoughts and ideas. Phenomenologically, not only professionals and experts are outsiders to members who share a common world, but they may also have their own cosmology and define the world separately. Insiders find peers to help define their world. Intersubjectivity is not a one-way street imposed by experts upon laypersons. We live in this world, because we define our world.

Antze (1976) examined the formal mission statements of Alcoholics Anonymous, Recovery, Inc., and Synanon and concluded that ideology is an integrating concept for self-help movements. His recommendation is quite straightforward: "The first rule for professionals working with these groups [self-help peer groups] must be a scrupulous respect for their teaching"—because "[w]henever outsiders try to support or cooperate with one of these organizations [self-help organizations], they run some risk of tampering with its ideology" (p. 344).

If professionals, consultants, and other service providers are simply "bad guys," the solution is simple: "Exclude them!" If such were the case, there would be no paradox. What makes the role of professionals in self-help groups critically paradoxical is that they do have expertise and access to various other resources. Those resources are either invisible or unreachable for laypersons. Professionals may not be deeply engaged in the inner world of a self-help group in which "confession, catharsis, mutual identification, and the removal of stigmatized feelings" characterize the psychological process of "sharing experiences or feelings with *a body of like-minded others*" (Antze, 1976, pp. 323–24, emphasis added). On the other hand, they may have their resources and broader ties to profession-based networks.

Lawyers, CPAs, consultants, and other professionals attended the MIT Enterprise Forum to solicit prospective clients. This is inevitable, because the Forum is open for everyone and its monthly meeting serves as a marketplace. This openness may have a negative effect on a peer atmosphere but circles, like the MIT Enterprise Forum, could not thrive without professionals. Although the appearance of professionals is problematic, they can serve as a positive addition to networking organizations.

Because the SBANE's Dialog highly valued a peer atmosphere, inclusion of professionals was much more problematic. Consultants, however, sneaked into the group by asserting that they were also the president or CEO of a consulting firm (even though the firm was a one-person operation). If consultants and other professionals try to find clients in a group originally invented for entrepreneurial group therapy, they are no longer peers in the eyes of other members. But some Dialog members benefited from professionals in the group who provided expert advice. As such, inclusion of nonpeer professionals is a mixed blessing for clubs.

The Formalization (Institutionalization) Paradox

Formalization is the extent to which legitimate rules and standard operating procedures are written. It is a major dimension of bureaucracy. Along with their warning about professionalism, Steinman and Traunstein (1976) warned that bureaucratization is another factor that undermines self-help movements. Sarason and Lorentz (1979), in analyzing several case studies of resource exchange networks, raised the same question: How does a network of loose, informal, resource-exchange, face-to-face relationships change (if they do) as a consequence of becoming a formal organization having a structure, defined tasks, leadership roles, and a need to pursue financial support?

The *raison d'être* of a grass-roots, self-help movement is that there are no professionals or experts for helping to solve the problems at hand. Other persons who share the same problems are the only sources for useful information. The "liability of newness" (Stinchcombe, 1965) is inherent in the embryonic stage of an emergent network. One solution to cope with this liability is the inclusion of well-established professionals. But, as the professionals' dilemma shows, even the partial inclusion of professionals in a self-help network is problematic. Another remedy that is quite likely to happen is institutionalization, thereby formalizing the project in a community or larger society (Meyer and Rowan, 1977).

As Kimberly (1979, 1980a,b) demonstrated by his case analysis based on organizational life cycle theory, institutionalization is a double-edged sword. It may eliminate inefficiencies derived from the newness and innovative nature of programs. But, in return for the stability realized through institutionalization, one may have to give up exhilarating, innovative projects. Balancing innovation and stability is a basic dilemma of organizing as an evolutionary process (Weick, 1979). A networking organization for entrepreneurs is no exception.

The emergence of a format for meetings is one element of formalization. The monthly meeting of the MIT Enterprise Forum had a very specific format. With this format, activities became stable, but the meeting lost its original informal atmosphere. In the early days, the meeting was almost like personal counseling for a case presenter. The atmosphere was cozy. Formalization is more often required for circles than for clubs, because the former attracts more diverse people with different backgrounds. Thus, some level of formalization was necessary in Forum activities. To cope with the formalization paradox, the MIT Enterprise Forum introduced the MIT New Venture Clinic, whereby invited participants could enjoy a more personal atmosphere without being bothered by the introduction of a detailed format. (Note that NVC is closer to clubs.)

As a peer group, SBANE's Dialog maintained a cozy, friendly atmosphere. But the growth of the Dialog program forced the SBANE headquarters to formalize activities for the program, like scheduling kick-off meetings, selecting group coordinators, and developing an evaluation format for Dialog sessions. The more formalized activities were introduced to preserve the friendly atmosphere of each group. Because the meeting is held at a host's house (or a conference room at his or her company) and members discuss topics while having light snacks, wine, and beer, the atmosphere is very informal. Higher levels of institutionalization did not permeate such groups, although SBANE had become considerably institutionalized because of its long history and its political activities.

The Expansion Paradox

Expansion may be a cursed course of action for self-help movements. Small clubs where members are linked by strong ties might lose some of their original momentum in the process of rapid expansion. A displacement of goals might result (Merton, 1968). Strong ties, coupled with an expressive focus, cannot be maintained as self-help networks grow rapidly and significantly beyond the level of cozy clubs.

The mixed feelings accompanying growth are well documented in the Essex network project partly based at Yale. The academic planners of the project (Sarason and Lorentz, 1979) recalled:

> To anyone seeking to develop a resource exchange network, the thorny question is, "What would the network have to look like to make each person in it more accessible to every other person in it for the purposes of resource exchange and expanding the numbers and variety of people (resources) in it?" Not "anyone" seeks to develop a resource exchange network, but rather self-selected people with a mission (and we do not use that word in any pejorative sense). (p. 170)

There seems to be a certain limit of "desirable" growth for groups in which members are known to each other based on strong ties and in which members seek expressive needs.

Summary and Conclusion

These paradoxes seem to reflect the elusive nature of entrepreneurial networking (see table 3-3). Although they seem to be diverse and less powerful in terms of parsimony (as compared to one predictor—n-Ach—paradigm of McClelland), all paradoxes repeatedly center around the same notions of strong versus weak ties, instrumental versus expressive needs of networkers, and individual versus organizational requirements.

As a circle, the MIT Enterprise Forum did not suffer from growth in the number of participants in the monthly case-presentation meeting. As explained previously, however, many old-timers missed the early days. One way to handle the expansion paradox in the case of the MIT Enterprise Forum was diversification of activities. Instead of just expanding the monthly case-presentation meeting, the Forum introduced other new activities, such as the Annual Workshop and a week-long Independent Activities Program (IAP) seminar at MIT. The Annual Workshop by its design could easily accommodate 500 participants, three times as many as the monthly case-presentation meeting, which had already reached a plateau after rapid growth.

In the early days before SBANE headquarters began to promote the Dialog program, the Dialog groups were often referred to as "SBANE's best kept secret." The Dialog started to grow after a membership survey showed that members of Dialog reported high satisfaction with the program. One important rule to cope with the expansion of the Dialog program is to increase the number of groups rather than increase the size of each group. Therefore, expansion of each group did not occur, albeit the number of members became a bit higher than ten, which SBANE headquarters thought was the ideal group size for a Dialog session. As in the case of the Annual Workshop at the MIT Enterprise Forum, if a circle is needed for SBANE activities, members could use other opportunities provided under SBANE, such as the New England Business Conference.

These comparative case studies suggest the universality of the seven paradoxes and a theoretical taxonomy of networking organizations. To move beyond suggestion to prediction, however, more thorough ethnographic accounts are needed to describe a diversity of research sites from different locations around the Pacific Rim.

References

Antze, P. "The Role of Ideologies in Peer Psychotherapy Organizations: Some Theoretical Considerations and Three Case Studies." *The Journal of Applied Behavioral Science*, 3 (1976): 323–46.

Back, K. W., and R. C. Taylor. "Self-help Groups: Tool or Symbol?" *The Journal of Applied Behavioral Science*, 12–3 (1976): 295–309.

Bandura, A. *Social Learning Theory*. Englewood Cliffs, N.J.: Prentice-Hall, 1977.

Berger, P. L., and T. Luckman. *The Social Construction of Reality: Treaties in the Sociology of Knowledge*. New York: Doubleday, 1967.

Black, D., and M. P. Baumgartner. "On Self-help in Modern Society." In D. Black, ed., *The Manners and Customs of the Police*. New York: Academic Press, 1980, pp. 193–208.

Blumer, H. *Symbolic Interactionism: Perspective and Method*. Englewood Cliffs, N.J.: Prentice-Hall, 1969.

Festinger, L. "A Theory of Social Comparison Processes." *Human Relations*, 7 (1965): 117–40.

Glaser, B. G., and A. P. Strauss. *The Discovery of Grounded Theory: Strategies for Qualitative Research*. Hawthorne, N.Y.: Aldine, 1967.

Goffman, E. *Stigma: Notes on the Management of Spoiled Identity*. New York: Simon and Schuster, 1963.

Granovetter, M. S. "The Strength of Weak Ties." *American Journal of Sociology*, 78 (1973): 1360–80.

Granovetter, M. S. "Strength of Weak Ties: A Network Theory Revisited." In P. V.

Marsden and N. Lin, eds., *Social Structure and Network Analysis.* Beverly Hills, Calif.: Sage, 1982, pp. 105–30.

Hurvitz, N. "The Origins of the Peer Self-help Psychotherapy Group Movement." *The Journal of Applied Behavioral Science,* 12–3 (1976): 283–95.

Illich, I. *Limits to Medicine—Medical Nemesis: The Expropriation of Health.* London: Calder and Boyars, 1976.

Kahn, J. P. "Networking: A Little Help from Your Friends." *Inc. Magazine,* 7–6 (June 1985): 55–64.

Kanai, T. *Entrepreneurial Networking: A Comparative Analysis of Networking Organizations and Their Participants in an Entrepreneurial Community.* Ph.D. diss. Massachusetts Institute of Technology, 1989.

Kanai, T. *Kigosha netowakingu no sekai (The World of Entrepreneurial Networking).* Tokyo: Hakuto Shobo Publisher, 1994.

Kanda, R., and Y. Teramoto. "Igyoshukoryu no shinka to management (Evolution and Management of Techno-mixing Groups)." *Keizai Kenkyu (Meiji-Gakuin University),* 76 (1986–87): 25–48, 78, 63–83, 79, 24–47 (in Japanese).

Katz, A. H. "Self-help and Mutual Aid: An Emerging Social Movement?" *Annual Review of Sociology,* 7 (1981): 129–55.

Kets de Vries, M. F. R. "The Entrepreneurial Personality: A Person at the Crossroad." *Journal of Management Studies,* 14 (1977): 34–57.

Kets de Vries, M. F. R. "The Dark Side of Entrepreneurship." *Harvard Business Review,* 63 (1985): 160–67.

Kimberly, J. R. "Issues in the Creation of Organizations: Initiation, Innovation, and Institutionalization." *Academy of Management Journal,* 22 (1979): 437–57.

Kimberly, J. R. (1980a). "The Life Cycle Analogy and the Study of Introduction." In J. R. Kimberly, et al., eds., *The Organizational Life Cycles: Issues in the Creation, Transformation, and Decline of Organizations.* San Francisco: Jossey-Bass, 1980a, pp. 1–43.

Kleiman, M. A., J. E. Mantell, and E. S. Alexander. "Collaboration and Its Discontents: The Perils of Partnership." *The Journal of Applied Behavioral Science,* 12–3 (1976): 403–10.

Landau, M. "Redundancy, Rationality, and the Problem of Duplication and Overlap." *Public Administration Review,* 29 (1969): 346–57.

Laumann, E. O., L. M. Verbrugge, and F. U. Pappi. "A Casual Modeling Approach to the Study of a Community Elite's Influence Structure." *American Sociological Review,* 39 (1974): 162–74.

Long, N. E. "The Non-contractual Relations in Business: A Preliminary Study." *American Sociological Review,* 28 (1958): 55–69.

Maguire, L. *Understanding Social Networks.* Beverly Hills, Calif.: Sage, 1983.

Maki, Y. *Kiryu no naru oto: Kokyo suru commune (The Sound of Airstreams: An Orchestrated Commune).* Tokyo: Chikuma Shobo, 1977 (in Japanese).

Merton, R. K. *Social Theory and Social Structure.* New York: Free Press, 1968.

Meyer, J. W., and B. Rowan. "Institutionalized Organizations: Formal Structure as Myth and Ceremony." *American Journal of Sociology,* 83 (1977): 340–63.

Meyer, J. W., and W. R. Scott. Eds. *Organizational Environments: Ritual and Rationality.* Beverly Hills, Calif.: Sage, 1983.

Parthe, Jr., A. C., and J. J. Schaufeld. "The MIT Enterprise Forum: A Resource for Growing Technology-based Organizations." *IEEE Transactions on Engineering Management,* 31 (1984): 204–06.

Perrucci, R., and M. Pilisuk. "Leaders and Ruling Elites: The Interorganizational

Bases of Community Power." *American Sociological Review*, 35 (1970): 1040–57.

Rogers, E. M., and J. K. Larsen. *Silicon Valley Fever: Growth of High-technology Culture*. New York: Basic Press, 1984.

Sarason, S. B., and E. Lorentz. *The Challenge of Resource Exchange Network*. San Francisco: Jossey-Bass, 1979.

Steinman, R., and E. M. Traunstein. "Redefining Deviances: The Self-help Challenge to the Human Services." *Journal of Applied Behavioral Science*, 12–3 (1976): 347–62.

Stinchcombe, A. L. "Social Structure and Organizations." In J. G. March, ed., *Handbook of Organization*, 1965, Chicago: Rand McNally, pp. 142–93.

Turk, H. "Social Cohesion through Variant Values: Evidence from Medical Role Relations." *American Sociological Review*, 28 (1963): 28–37.

Van Maanen, M., and S. M. Barley. "Occupational Communities: Culture and Control in Organization." *Research in Organizational Behavior*, 6 (1984): 287–365.

Weick, K. E. *The Social Psychology of Organizing*, 2nd ed. Reading, Mass.: Addison-Wesley, 1979.

4

The "Embedded Broker" State

Social Networks and Political Organization in Japan

JEFFREY BROADBENT
YOSHITO ISHIO

Introduction

Businesses and other organizations operate under conditions strongly influenced by politics and government—the state. In all the industrialized capitalist democratic societies, the state allocates major resources, both financial and regulatory. Its "interference" in markets and business operations, especially in the form of regulations, has long been a source of complaint among business leaders. In East Asia, the state exercises much weaker formal regulatory control over business, but it engages and "guides" business in more subtle ways. Just as relational networks act to coordinate markets in East Asia, so too do they work to coordinate political organization and control. This chapter empirically demonstrates the web of political networks that stretch between and within state and society in Japan.

Recent work has attributed much of the success of the East Asian economies to the way the state is "embedded" into society through the exchange and solidarity relationships that we call networks (Evans, 1995; Johnson, 1982). Japan, for instance, has the reputation for operating through informal negotiations (*nemawashi*) which involve exactly what we measured: the trading of information, trust, and support (Nakane, 1970). Through these networks, the thesis goes, rather than leave growth to the "chaos" of the market, the East Asian state provides business with guidance that allows coordinating collective efforts toward producing a stronger national economy. Business trusts the state to absorb business' concerns and give good collective guidance based on it.

In this sense, the term state "guidance" is actually shorthand for what should properly be described as state formulation of policies that "rationalize" the collective best interests of the business community as a whole (Skocpol, 1995). The guidance takes place, not so much through heavy-handed bureaucratic regulatory commandism nor macroeconomic fiscal manipulation, but in the form seen among businesses themselves, as reported by many of the chapters in this volume—networks of communication, trust, and resource exchanges.

State guidance includes helping "sunrise" or targeted industries to grow rapidly with protection, and helping "sunset" industries to decline gracefully with a minimum of disruption to business productivity and the workforce (Johnson, 1982). State guidance also covers policies that adjust and affect business–labor relations, such as wage levels, worker retraining, health insurance schemes, the privatization of state owned firms, and levels of consumer taxation. Rather than the content of policy, however, this chapter is concerned with the means by which that "guidance" takes place.

The state–society relationship can be studied in many ways. Most studies look at a particular sector of the state or society, such as one agency like the Japanese Ministry of International Trade and Industry (MITI). In contrast, the interorganizational network approach used here incorporates information on exchanges among all the major players in the political system concerning labor-related policies. This approach permits a systematic evaluation of the overall pattern of influence flow. These flow pathways, or interorganizational relationships, indicate the important sinews of the body politic. Taken together, they provide a systemic view of the state–society relations. Laumann and Knoke (1987) referred to this as the "organizational state" approach.

This systemic viewpoint allows us to generate some new perspectives on Japanese politics and state–society relations. In particular, it allows us to study the social structural position of the actors within the network of influence relations between state and society. Applying this viewpoint to the state, we label it the "embedded broker" model. The vaunted but "enigmatic" power of the Japanese state derives not so much from its formal authority, but from its structural location as a *broker* between organized business and organized labor, deeply embedded in social relations to both groups.

This approach takes a distinctly sociological viewpoint, emphasizing group structure and process (Knoke, 1990). In everyday usage, the term *group* refers to a number of people. But in sociology, the members of a group can be organizations as well as individuals, as long as they have some relationship among themselves. *Group structure* refers to the division of labor and power into roles and relationships. *Group process* refers to the exchanges between and among the actors that produce and maintain this structure (Homans, 1974).

The essential relationship in democratic politics is that of influence, but influence can be either conflictual or cooperative. Influence builds up into and eventuates in power, the ability to accomplish a task, from constructing a factory to collecting taxes. In human affairs, task accomplishment usually requires a collective effort among a number of actors. The exercise of influence can be seen as ways of drawing actors into coordination. Accordingly, the analysis of influence is crucial to understanding politics. Studies distinguish different sorts of sanctions that actors give out to others in order to exercise influence: coercion, legitimate authority, economic inducement, vital information, persuasion, moral conviction, and emotional identification (Broadbent, 1989; Etzioni, 1968; French and Raven, 1959).

The transmission of these sanctions creates networks of relationships (social and otherwise) among actors, which can be considered the influence "capillaries" of the body politic. They stretch among the major actors in state and society—government ministries (or departments), political parties, business and labor associations, public interest groups, and others—forming subtle but distinct and important types of social structures. The presence (or lack) and precise form of these networks may have great bearing upon the operation and outputs of state and society.

Among these, a social network-type relationship generates influence not through raw coercion, nor through pure impersonal economic considerations, but through a heavy dash of trust and persuasion built up over many exchanges. Social networks operate by transmitting vital information from trusted others that causes the recipient to change their course of action. The Ministry of Labor (Rodosho), for instance, may provide a union with valuable information, thus influencing its course of action on an issue. Or the Liberal Democratic Party (LDP) may consult with ministerial officials, thus affecting the content of a policy proposal. The network relationship does not remove, for instance, the actor's rational calculation of profit-goals, but it allows it to be expressed within a broader collective context and ideology—that of "the elites" or "the nation."

In the Japanese case, state–society social networks do not often degenerate into mere cronyism (corruption for the sake of individual actor profit) because the ministries are not entirely captured by the interest groups they are supposed to regulate (Evans, 1995). As the analysis will show, this relative "autonomy" of the state (Skocpol, 1985) depends upon its structural position within the networks of information and trust that span the entire political domain.

In this chapter we trace and measure the exchange of four types of resources or sanctions among important actors in the domain of labor politics. These four types of sanctions include: (1) the provision of vital information, (2) perception of being in a relationship of mutual aid with another organization, (3) the provision of political support, and (4) the provision of work for another organization. As actors give and receive these sanctions, they create habituated channels of exchange and solidarity that take on a certain autonomy or life of their own.

Many investigations focus on a single or a few actors. This is necessary for case study research, but may rather truncate the field of vision. Network analysis, in contrast, measures the relations among all the relevant organizational actors. This resultant information allows discussion of the state–society relationship from a comprehensive, systemic viewpoint. The network method's sensitivity to variations in the patterns and qualities of these relationships not only permits tests of existing models, it also allows the construction of a whole new class of models. This in turn opens the door to much better comparative cross-national studies. The data for this chapter were, in fact, collected as part of the first systematic cross-national study of political networks. This study compared the network patterns of labor policy-making in Japan, the United States, and Germany (Knoke et al., 1996).

State–Society Models

In characterizing the state–society, especially state–business, relationship in Japan, many scholars have supported variations of the *corporatist* model. In this model, the leaders of relevant government ministries sit down with the leaders of organized business (and to some degree labor) to decide the main aspects of public policies close to their interests (Inoguchi, 1983; Okimoto, 1989). In this model, the state acts as a partner with dominant groups in society to create an "orderly, stable, and effective" arrangement of politics (Schmitter, 1981, p. 293).

Within the corporatist family, authors disagree on the degree of participation from other sectors of society. Three main models—"corporatism-without-labor," the network state, and osmotic corporatism—present different versions of this theme. The *corporatism-without-labor* model recognizes a very strong connection between the state and business in the policy-making process, but sees little participation from labor. To cite from the model's authors, Japan "presents a curious anomaly: a high degree of corporatized interest mediation in many sectors, but virtually none in the important area of labor" (Pempel and Tsunekawa, 1979, p. 245). Okimoto's *network state* model (1989) also focuses exclusively on the state–business connection, but emphasizes that the central power of the state comes, not from its formal authority, but from its "network of [cooperative] ties to the private sector" and the "structure of LDP-[state] bureaucracy-interest group alignments" (p. 226). In this view, peak federations for the business community negotiate collective policies with the state, which their member groups then accept "without obstruction." Nakane (1970) labels this situation the "vertical society" (p. 102), as cited in Okimoto (1989, p. 226).

Others argue that the state's cooperative network relationship also extend to other sectors of society. Inoguchi (1983) called this "bureaucratic–inclusionary pluralism" (*kanryo hokatsuteki tagenshugi*). Muramatsu and Krauss (1988) pointed to a similar "flexible and responsive . . . patterned pluralism" following guidelines set by the bureaucracy (cited in Okimoto and Rohlen, 1988, p. 209).

Tsujinaka's model of *osmotic corporatism* carries the power of societal groups further, arguing that the new Rengo Federation of Labor gives labor a stronger voice in Japanese corporatist policy-making, especially compared to its predecessor, the more left-leaning Sohyo Federation. Tsujinaka (1993) argues that Rengo attains this new power by acting as its own sort of network hub—a "node for the exchange of information among innumerable enterprise unions" (p. 203). During our data collection period, both Sohyo and Rengo still coexisted, so we can test this hypothesis by comparing their roles as peak federations.

All these variations on the corporatist theme suffer from some flaws. First, they ignore the important stipulation by the theorists of corporatism that this state–society arrangement permits "the better-organized, collaborative actors to pass on the costs of their mutually self-serving agreements to the un- or underorganized" (Schmitter, 1981, p. 322). Hence, corporatistic policy-making can skew the flow of benefits toward the organized sectors. Second, they tend to portray the state as a monolithic entity. Yet all states suffer from some degree of balkanization into ministerial turfs or "subgovernments." As Campbell (1984) noted, "Subgovernments . . . constitute a set of interest-based cleavages that divide the entire decision-making system" (p. 301). A better model would include these aspects.

Methods

In our research framework, we considered organizations (not individuals) to be the major players in politics in the modern state. Organizations constitute the state and the interest groups of civil society. They include government ministries and agencies, political parties, advisory councils, business organizations, labor organizations, public interest groups, and social movements of all sorts. The Japanese organizations include all that were active and influential in labor policy between 1982 and 1988. We culled organizations from mentions in newspaper and specialized journal accounts of labor policy decisions (events) for that time; we also asked experts to add groups we had missed. This resulted in a list of the 122 most active and important organizations in the labor policy area. These organizations range from ministries (*sho*) and bureaus (*kyoku*) within the administrative state, advisory councils (*shingikai*) appointed by the state, political parties in the national legislature (Diet), and a host of organizations in civil society: business and labor sectoral organizations (*gyokai* and *kumiai*), their peak associations (such as Nikkeiren and Rengo) and public interest groups and social movements of many types.

In like fashion, we assembled a list of the most important labor-relevant policy decisions for the same time period. We found that the total array of issues dealt with in the Japanese labor-policy domain fell within the list already assembled for the U.S. and German cases, so we used that list. We then submitted the two lists to five Japanese experts in labor policy; the experts came from a wide spectrum of ideological positions. They each noted the organizations and events they felt to be most important and added more we had not listed. In this way, we constructed our final lists of actors, events, and issues. These lists became the basis of our questionnaire.

In the questionnaire, we gathered data on a number of relevant topics. In approaching each organization, we sought out the officer who was most knowledgeable about the political activities of the organization. For each type of influence relationship, the survey requested that the officer pick from the actor list those organizations with which they had an important relationship. As noted previously, these included the sending or receiving of vital information (*hitsuyo joho*) (two checklists) the presence of trust in a mutual aid relationship (*mochitsu motaretsu*) with the other organization (one checklist), the receipt of political support (*seijiteki shien*) from the other organization (one checklist), and work performed for the other organization (one checklist).

These four types of exchange relations express and characterize important ways that organizations exert informal influence over each other. Each one forms a unique network of relationships among the 122 actors, with varying degrees of overlap. Each has its own effects upon the distribution of power and influence among organizations. One important method of analysis would be to compare these networks in their relative contribution to the overall pattern of influence. However, for this chapter we take a more synthesizing route to get at the general pattern first. Rather than examine each network separately and compare their consequences, we treated them as equal in weight and combined them into a single, multistranded relational fabric. The resulting pattern exhibits the general structure of influence relationships among the 122 major political players. As such, it allows us to assess the validity of the different political models noted previously and refine them.

Strictly speaking, the data used in this chapter refer only to the domain of labor policies, not to all types of policies. Accordingly, the findings most strongly model the operation of power in the Japanese labor-policy domain per se. However, a strong argument can be made that the findings have wider relevance. First, the organizational actors found in this domain include all those generally acknowledged as most important for policy-making as a whole (such as MITI and the LDP), along with others important only in this specialized domain. Second, the events, although chosen because they affected labor, ended up including eight out of the ten most crucial Japanese policy events of the 1980s. Study of these events provided our initial lists of actors. Therefore, the data very likely represent a wider pattern of politics in Japan, though that remains a question for further research.

From the relational data, how do we know which actors are more important? In any network, some actors are very central. They act as hubs for the receipt and dispersal of important sanctions such as information, trust, support, and help. Other actors are of middling status in this regard, sending to and receiving from a limited number of partners. Some are peripheral, having few contacts with others, or are isolates, out of the loop altogether. Network analysis has techniques that determine the relative centrality of an organization in a network. As noted previously, we found that an organization's degree of network centrality in the support network, rather than in the information network, turned out to predict its influence better (see the next section) (Knoke et al., 1996).

Findings

Clusters

The large number of organizations (122) produced a complex mesh of relationships that required simplification. First, we used the method of structural equivalence to partition or sort the 122 organizations into twelve clusters (Burt, 1989). This sorting method is based on the similarity of an organization's pattern of relationship with all the other organizations. The most relationally similar organizations went into the same cluster (irrespective of whether or not they had relations with each other). For instance, if the two peak labor federations both had numerous relations to many labor union associations, but not to other types of organizations, the two would end up in the same cluster. Similarly, union associations that affiliated with those two peak organizations more than any other organization fell into the same cluster. This method separated leaders from followers, and different types of each from each other.

Table 4-1 presents the twelve clusters by number, with a descriptive name, a brief description of members, and sometimes the names of the most important members. (The appendix presents the organizational names.) Political leaders appear in the first four clusters. Followers or those not actively engaged groups appear in the others. The last cluster contains isolates not closely affiliated with the leaders. This clustering reveals a hierarchy of power, in which some organizations play the major leadership roles in the labor policy-making system. The cluster names Core, Secondary, Follower, and Isolate indicate their ranking in this hierarchy.

Cluster Hierarchy

Other measures of the average political power of clusters reinforce the claim that they form a hierarchy of power. We used two measures to assess the power of an organization: its power as perceived by others and its power as assessed by its own officer. We arrived at the perceived-influence scores by asking the respondents to check off all organizations that they thought "especially important" in the labor-policy domain. The organization's score is the total number of checkmarks received. The cluster's score is the average. We produced the self-assessed measure, on the other hand, by asking the respondent to indicate the degree that their organization, for each of thirty-four policy events, had been able to attain its political goals (see table 4-1). For each of the thirty-four policy events in which they participated, an organization's respondent scored their goal-attainment (*mokuteki tasseido*) on a scale from 0 to 5 (complete success). The organization's score is the average on the thirty-four events. The cluster score is the average for all the cluster members.

First, let us consider perceived influence. The Ministry of Labor (MOL) Core Cluster had the highest reputation for influence (a score of 82) (table 4-1, column 3). The fact that the MOL Core Cluster has only one member, the Labor Policy Bureau, meant that the cluster score was the same as the organizational score. The Business Core (69) and the Labor Core (63) achieved fairly high influence scores. These core clusters were small and active; they did not contain weaker members that would reduce their cluster average. The Productivity Core, however, despite the presence of MITI, ranked only in the middle range (32) of perceived influence. In the Secondary/Follower categories, the MOL Secondary Cluster attained the highest score (59), but the remaining clusters ranked much lower. By this measure, the MOL, Business, and Labor Cores were the real movers and shakers of the system.

Self-assessed goal-attainment scores also produce a hierarchy of power (see table 4-1, column 4). The only clusters to receive high influence scores by this measure were some government-related clusters. They averaged in the top range, above 4. This indicates they felt they achieved most or all of their objectives. Business clusters, along with some other government ministry clusters, ranked in the middle tier (the 3 range). Labor-related clusters uniformly ranked in the 2 range, indicating "very little" goal attainment.

These scores indicate that government agencies exercised the strongest levels of influence in the system. Among them, the MOL Core Cluster occupied the peak of power. Its single member, the Labor Politics Department (LPB, Roseikyoku), handled the politics of negotiating with labor unions and guiding them on attainable goals. The LPB's (MOL Core Cluster's) self-assessed goal-attainment scores exceeded its influence reputation. In other words, the MOL Core Cluster thought more highly of its power than others did. In contrast, both Business and Labor Core Clusters thought less of their power than others did. The gap between perceived influence and self-assessed influence was especially big for labor.

Why did this gap occur? One reason is frequency of participation in policy events. The more an organization participated in public policy struggles, the more its reputation for influence increased. The Labor Core participated in more policy events (20.74) than any other cluster, making it very visible. The Core's peak associations, Sohyo and Rengo, had to get involved in every policy fight of interest to labor, even if the policy was of peripheral importance. They could not delegate some tasks, as business did. By being so active, they increased their reputation for influence, even if not their actual influence. Business' smaller gap between other-

Table 4-1. Twelve Clusters in the Labor Policy Domain.

Name and Number of Members (in paren.)	Internal Density	Average Influence Reputation Score	Average Goal Attainment Score	Description
1. Productivity Core (6)	54%	32	3.47	Cross-sectoral: MITI and two related technocratic productivity-espousing quasipublic organizations, with the Democratic Socialist Party (DSP) and two unions.
2. Labor Core (4)	54%	63	2.79	The two peak union confederations (Private Sector Trade Union Confederation [Rengo] and General Council of Trade Unions [Sohyo]) cluster with the Japan Socialist Party (JSP) and a Ministry of Labor-related labor policy research institute.
3. Ministry of Labor (MOL) Core (1)	N.A. (one actor)	82	4.11	The Labor Politics Bureau of the Ministry of Labor (generally recognized as its most powerful bureau) stands alone, taking the mandated broker role.
4. Business Core (3)	71%	69	3.44	The peak business association that specializes in labor policy, Federation of Employers' Associations (Nikkeiren) clusters with the Liberal Democratic Party (LDP) and one industrial association.
5. Ministry of Health and Welfare (MHW) Secondary Cluster (5)	44%	27	3.62	All three Ministry of Health and Welfare (MHW) bureaus cluster with Ministry of Posts and a union.
6. Business-Ministry Secondary Cluster (9)	16%	32	4.03	Cross-sectoral: Remaining four peak business federations (Federation of Economic Organizations, Fedederation for Economic Development, Federation of Chambers of Commerce and Industry, National Center for Medium and Small Enterprises Organizations) with five government ministries (MOC, MOT) and agencies.
7. Advisory Council Secondary Cluster (16)	4%	27	4.16	All government advisory councils, also Ministry of Finance (MOF), mandatory insurance federations, and employment related public interest groups (ILO).

8. Ministry of Labor (MOL) Secondary Cluster (4)	21%	59	4.16	Remaining four Ministry of Labor bureaus.
9. General Business Follower Cluster (29)	7%	6	3.28	Thirty-two business industrial associations (*gyokai*).
10. Private Sector Unions Follower Cluster (26)	15%	16	2.71	Twenty-two private sector union confederations with two centrist political parties (Clean Government Party and Social Democratic Federation) and two policy-study public interest groups.
11. Public Sector Unions Follower Cluster (26)	47%	16	2.45	Five government (public) workers' union confederations (such as Japan Teachers' Union) with the Buraku Liberation League (a civil rights movement).
12. Public Interest Isolate Cluster (13)	7%	10	2.63	Medical and service workers' unions confederations cluster with the Japan Medical Association, the Pharmaceutical Industrial Association, four public interest groups in our survey (including the national governors' and mayors' associations), two mandatory insurance associations, and the Japan Communist Party.

perceived and self-assessed influence for business resulted from their greater division of labor. The Federation of Employers' Associations (Nikkeiren) handled only labor-policy events, leaving fights over other types of policies to the Keidanren or the Keizai Doyukai. But the Federation drew on the resources of the larger organizations when necessary. This practice raised the organization's own assessment of its influence.

Government ministries and agencies, on the other hand, preferred to work "behind the scenes," exerting influence in as invisible a way as possible. Nonetheless, they were very effective. These habits made their publicly perceived influence lower than their self-assessed influence.

Clusters as Groups

A cluster is not necessarily a group (with ties among its members). This is important to keep in mind. Being put into the same cluster by the sorting program does not mean cluster members related to each other or acted in concert. Organizations might have no communication with each other and still be in the same cluster. Some clusters were that way. But others had very high internal densities of relationships (see table 4-1, column 2). A high internal density indicated a cluster's strong cohesion as a group, which meant a greater likelihood of political solidarity and cooperation. A low internal density indicated just the reverse. The Business Core Cluster had the highest internal density, with 71 percent of the possible ties made among its members. Next were the Productivity Core and the Labor Core Clusters, each with 54 percent of possible ties made. Of the remaining clusters, only the Ministry of Health and Welfare Secondary and the Public Sector Union Follower Clusters had high densities, 44 and 47 percent, respectively. The rest of the clusters had very low rates of internal density, indicating they did not cohere as groups. They were "follower" clusters with members that looked upward, not sideways, for support and leadership. They sent their network ties to peak leadership clusters.

These findings indicate two sorts of clusters: those that have the potential for autonomous collective action and those that do not. Clusters with high density scores enjoy stronger ties of communication, trust, and support (political and work) among members. The figures indicate that those clusters enjoy more solidarity, common ideology, and willingness to help each other. Many scholars recognize these qualities as important preconditions for collective action (Tilly, 1978; McCarthy and Zald, 1977).

All the core clusters had high internal densities. They had the potential to become collective political actors, acting in defense of their group interests. But the follower clusters lacked important preconditions, with one exception. This lack rendered them unlikely to engage in autonomous collective action. The Public Sector Unions Follower Cluster was the exception. It had close to 50 percent internal density, indicating a higher degree of internal organization. This density gave it stronger potential for autonomous action and control over the activities of its peak associations. This may have been important in making the influence relations of Public Sector Unions Follower Clusters with the Labor Core more democratic, compared to other clusters. In other words, if any cluster is likely to contradict Nakane's prediction of state authority transmitted without resistance down the hierarchy, it is this cluster. In comparison, relations between the Business Core and its follower clusters or between the Labor Core and the Private Sector Union Follower Cluster should be more docile. The Public Sector Unions are better organized to define and defend their interests and defy elites if necessary.

Further researchers should examine the exact patterns of relationships within each cluster. This would likely yield important information about their internal power structures and their internal patterns of cliques and isolates.

The Macrosystem

The data allowed us to produce a systemic map of the entire political system of the labor-politics domain. Having defined the clusters, we analyzed the strength of the influence relationships between them. To do so, we assumed that the more the members of one cluster had connection with members of another, the stronger the influence between the clusters. Social network analysis calls this the "density" of the ties. We calculated the density of ties between all pairs possible among the twelve clusters (as well as calculating the density of ties among the members internal to each cluster) for each of the four types of exchanges (communication, trust, political support, and work support). To find the total density of influence between any two clusters, we calculated the average of the (average) densities of their relationships on each of the four exchange networks in both directions (for both the A sends to B and the B sends to A relationships). The more that members of one cluster related to members of another cluster, the higher the density of their relationship.

For instance, in a relationship between twelve-member cluster A and six-member cluster B, the total possible number of cross-cluster organization-to-organization ties would be (12 × 6 =) 72. If only six members of Cluster A and only three members of Cluster B had ties (6 × 3 = 18), the density of the cluster-to-cluster relationship would be 25 percent (18/72 = .25). Only one-quarter of the possible ties would be consummated between these two clusters, which is not a strong, influential relationship by this scale. If, however, the density turned out to be 50 or 75 percent, it would indicate a much stronger intercluster relationship.

We then used the density percentage number as an indicator of the "social distance" between each cluster on an "influence map" (figure 4-1). The closer the two clusters are on the map, the more they exchange resources and hence influence each other. This method of analysis results in a rough but valid and readily graspable visual representation of the pattern of influence relationships among all the actors comprising the total system.

We portray this system as a sociographic map of influence distances among the clusters. This map is not an impressionistic rendering; like a highway map, it is derived from the measured relationships. In figure 4-1, we superimposed a grid of concentric rings to emphasize the relative centrality of the clusters. We also drew lines to indicate the strongest vectors of influence going among the clusters (those with density scores over 50 percent between them). The pattern of the sociographic map resembles the structure of the solar system, with the most important unit at the center. In the Japanese labor-politics universe, the MOL Core Cluster occupies the central position. Close to it lies the Productivity Core, home to the Ministry of International Trade and Industry (MITI) and other organizations. Their closeness indicates that these two clusters are the central actors of the system.

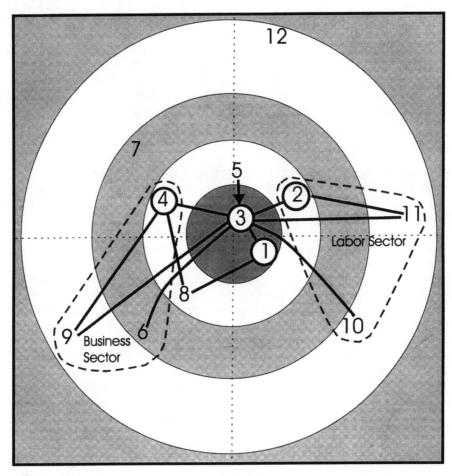

O   = Block with high exchange among members

──   = Two-way exchange relationship

➤   = One-way exchange relationship

Figure 4-1 The Japanese Power Structure. Resource Exchange Pattern in the Labor Policy Domain.
KEY: CLUSTER NAME: 1. Productivity (MITI/DSP) Core; 2. Labor Peak Association/Party Core; 3. Ministry of Labor Core; 4. Business Peak Association/Party Core; 5. Ministry of Health and Welfare Secondary Cluster; 6. Business-Ministry Secondary Cluster; 7. Advisory Council Secondary Cluster; 8. Ministry of Labor Secondary Cluster; 9. General Business Follower Cluster; 10. Private Sector Unions Follower Cluster; 11. Public Sector Unions Follower Cluster; 12. Isolate Cluster.
Stress = 0.189 (Spatial distance among twelve blocks: two-dimensional ALSCAL Analysis of interblock densities, averaged over four networks with exchanges over 50 percent noted as lines).

The second concentric ring around the center, slightly further out, holds four clusters. The Ministry of Health and Welfare (MHW) Secondary Cluster, containing all the ministry's bureaus, is the closest to the MOL Core. But the rest are only slightly further away. Appropriately, the Business Core and the Labor Core, which contain the peak associations and political parties of those two opposing sectors, stand on opposite sides of the MOL Core. The remaining bureaus of the MOL, in the MOL Secondary Cluster, stand just beyond that distance. These four clusters constitute the second tier of influence.

The third concentric ring holds two clusters: one with the remaining government ministries and peak business associations and one with all the advisory councils (a group of mainly progovernment academics and business leaders, appointed by the government to discuss and comment on newly forming policy initiatives within a narrowly focused, specialized domain, such as minimum wage). The grouping of the remaining ministries and business peak associations into one cluster, close to the MOL Secondary Cluster, indicates they have similar relations to the center. These ministries and business peaks have great potential power. But their location makes it clear that, in the labor-policy domain, they delegate that power to organizations mandated for the tasks (the MOL and the Nikkeiren). This practice indicates a strong functional division of labor in the government and business sectors.

In this third ring, the Advisory Council Cluster is located closest to Nikkeiren, indicating that those councils have stronger ties with that business peak association than with any other cluster. The MOL Core and the MHW Cluster are only a little farther away. The lack of other clusters in the area of the Advisory Council Cluster indicates its members operate in a fairly isolated fashion. This isolation is appropriate, because they are appointed to conduct an independent review of government policies. Figure 4-1 indicates, however, that they are likely to operate with a considerable probusiness slant.

The fourth concentric ring holds the three follower clusters and the single isolate cluster. This ring is a zone of isolation for organizations that enjoy little or no direct influence over the policy-decision process. Still, those organizations that have strong connections to peak associations may be able to exert a measure of indirect influence through them on policy decision-making. This influence depends upon how representative (versus authoritative) their peak associations are.

In this system of influence, the Business Follower Cluster is located on the left side of the map, nearest to the Business-Ministry Cluster. Next nearest to it is the MOL Secondary Cluster, holding the remaining MOL bureaus. This positioning indicates that even in the labor-policy domain, the business associations (*gyokai*) of the Business Follower Cluster have the Federation of Economic Organizations (Keidanren) "intermediate" their interests. Keidanren formulates their collective labor policy before Nikkeiren implements it.

This arrangement indicates a strong societal corporatism that complements and reinforces the state corporatism. For the purposes of labor policy-making, the business sector is organized hierarchically under a single peak association (Nikkeiren). It is connected to and facilitates the state corporatism of the larger system, indicated by the presence of the MOL Core at its absolute center.

In the fourth concentric ring, the two labor follower clusters, the Private Sector Union and Public Sector Union Follower Clusters, are located on the right side of figure 4-1, to the right of the Labor Core. (In this figure, "left" and "right" only de-scribe a location, not an ideological meaning). Comparing the two, the Public Sec-tor Union Follower Cluster is closest to the Labor Core, as would be expected. Its union associations (such as the Japan Teachers' Union) have a socialist, antigov-ernmental orientation. Within the Labor Core Cluster, the peak association (Sohyo) espouses a similar orientation. On the other hand, although the Private Sector Union Follower Cluster is also located close to the Labor Core, it is even closer to the Productivity Core Cluster (DSP and MITI). The Productivity Cluster, in other words, has stronger ties with the Private Sector Unions than the Labor Core does.

The same systemic pattern of relationships may be discerned through an alter-nate method called bloc-modeling. The inter- and intracluster relational densities appear in table 4-2. If we give a 1 to all values over 50 percent, and a 0 to all val-ues less than that, and then reorder the rows and columns (so that the most active, well-connected clusters go into the upper left corner), we get the simplified repre-sentation of the table in table 4-3. The cells with 1's represent the lines between clusters in figure 4-1.

These data show that occupancy of the center gives more than figurehead status. Clearly, most action centers around the MOL Core. Most communication and sup-port pass through it, and it is the central object of trust. Apart from it, only the busi-ness sector establishes its own reciprocal, independent base of power; business core and business follower clusters have strong relationships. The Labor Core sends influence strongly to one of its follower clusters, but not to the other. This partiality indicates a fragmented, weakened sector, compared to the tight organi-zation of the business sector and the overall centrality of the MOL Core.

Looking at the percentages in table 4-2 refines this impression. The most intense or densest intercluster relationship runs from the Business Core to the MOL Core (83 percent). The reciprocal relationship is almost as dense (75 percent). The only other relationship of that density runs from the Productivity Core to the MOL Core (75 percent). At a slightly lower density, the MOL Core reciprocates strongly with the Productivity Core (63 percent). The Business-Ministry Secondary Cluster (with Keidanren and a number of key ministries) and the Business Follower Cluster also have many ties with the MOL Core Cluster (67 and 63 percent, respectively). All these strong ties center on the MOL Core. The only set of strong reciprocal ties that does not center on the MOL Core runs between the Business Core and the Business Follower Clusters. Finally, the Labor Core sends strong ties to the Public Sector Union Follower Cluster (61 percent).

These results show that the MOL Core is by far the most active sender and re-ceiver of ties of all sorts. It has more than twice as many relationships with others than its nearest competitors do. But after the MOL, this symmetry of sending and receiving breaks down. The next most active sender is the Business Core, with the Productivity Core and Labor Core close behind. Other clusters do much less send-ing. But the next most active receivers are the Labor Core and the Business Core. The other clusters do much less receiving. This set of relationships reinforces the MOL Core as the pivotal role in the system.

In figure 4-1, it is surprising to find that the Private Sector Union Cluster is closer to the Productivity Core than to the Labor Core. This indicates that the Pro-ductivity Core has denser ties with private sector unions than does the Labor Core, its official representative. This may be significant for our understanding of how the

Table 4.2. Mean Density of Ties Between 12 Clusters.

Cluster	1	2	3	4	5	6	7	8	9	10	11	12
1	54	53	75	42	24	29	16	28	14	48	20	10
2	48	54	56	27	41	22	32	47	04	42	61	18
3	63	50	00	75	40	56	33	56	50	50	50	48
4	33	25	83	71	47	45	27	69	50	06	04	11
5	26	43	55	48	44	30	22	38	04	10	12	20
6	22	21	67	48	18	16	12	27	07	03	01	02
7	11	25	31	27	17	09	04	17	04	05	02	05
8	18	45	56	71	25	27	16	21	16	12	04	05
9	13	03	63	50	07	09	04	23	07	02	01	01
10	48	43	57	07	09	04	05	12	03	15	07	01
11	18	57	50	06	06	02	02	07	00	06	47	04
12	06	16	35	14	12	01	03	01	01	01	03	07

Japanese political economy works. Perhaps the Democratic Socialist Party (DSP), in the Productivity Core, is not the only cluster that has great influence over the private sector unions; and its agencies may have strong influence as well. Firmer conclusions await a more detailed analysis of the interorganizational data.

The centrality of the Productivity Core indicates its importance. It is located next to the MOL Labor Politics Bureau, which is the government agency mandated to coordinate the political process in the labor-policy domain. Its centrality, within a bailiwick formally belonging to the Ministry of Labor, indicates an interesting hypothesis on how MITI may exercise its vaunted but little understood "guidance" over all sectors and actors of the national economy (e.g., industrial targeting, structural adjustment, import control). MITI may monitor many policy domains as it does the labor domain—not as the most central actor, but as an ancillary, information-gathering, and advice-giving presence. This role would allow MITI to keep in touch with all sectors of the economy and related policies.

Table 4.3. Reordered Image Matrix of Mean Density Table (density values >50 percent=1).

Cluster	3	2	4	1	8	9	11	6	10	5	7	12
3	0	1	1	1	1	1	1	1	1	0	0	0
4	1	0	1	0	1	1	0	0	0	0	0	0
1	1	1	0	1	0	0	0	0	0	0	0	0
2	1	1	0	0	0	0	1	0	0	0	0	0
8	1	0	1	0	0	0	0	0	0	0	0	0
9	1	0	1	0	0	0	0	0	0	0	0	0
11	1	1	0	0	0	0	0	0	0	0	0	0
5	1	0	0	0	0	0	0	0	0	0	0	0
6	1	0	0	0	0	0	0	0	0	0	0	0
10	1	0	0	0	0	0	0	0	0	0	0	0
7	0	0	0	0	0	0	0	0	0	0	0	0
12	0	0	0	0	0	0	0	0	0	0	0	0

Discussion

The Nature of the State

These data tell us a great deal about the social organization of the state and society. The state encompasses the organizations of formal policy-making for the society, including the executive leadership, the administrative bureaucracy, the legislature and the judiciary. In Japan, the dominant political party or coalition in the Diet chooses the Prime Minister, who then selects the Cabinet following party negotiation. The administrative bureaucracy, consisting of ministries and agencies, is much stronger than in the United States. Some models place it at the center of policy-making power in Japan. Unlike the Supreme Court in the United States, the Japanese judiciary does not take a lead role in policy-making. Accordingly, questions of power within the state revolve around the influence relations among ministries and agencies, and between them and the ruling party (at that time, the LDP).

The relationships among ministries and agencies can be studied through these data. The MOL Core clearly occupies the center of the administrative system. Other ministries, agencies, and appointed advisory councils are situated in six clusters; some of these clusters are of mixed composition. What sort of internal centralization and coordination does their arrangement imply for the state, given that its many ministries and bureaus are so scattered?

First, let us examine the internal organization of the MOL. Excluding the Labor Politics Bureau (the MOL Core), the other MOL bureaus form a single cluster. This cluster has a fairly low internal density (21 percent) but a much higher relational density with the MOL Core (56 percent). In other words, the MOL Secondary bureaus worked in relative isolation from each other and sent their policy decisions to the Labor Politics Bureau for coordination and implementation.

Other than the MOL Core and Secondary Clusters, only the MOF stayed in anything close to a cluster composed only of governmental organizations. The Ministry of Finance (MOF), true to its reputation, stands aloof from possibly compromising connections with civil society. The MOF clustered with the advisory councils, indicating their mutual concern with an objective assessment of societal conditions.

Except for those three clusters, state agencies clustered with organizations in civil society that pursued similar interests. MITI and DSP, for instance, have similar concerns with productive and harmonious management–labor relations. The MOT and MOC are well-known for their close relations to the business world (as many kickback scandals testify).

Does this picture indicate a state fractured into a plurality of subgovernments and further pulled apart by close or collusive ties with client organizations in civil society? Or does it simply reflect a functional division of labor within the state, which remains self-disciplined and well coordinated despite that?

Both tendencies seem to exist. The fact that all the governmental clusters (except the Advisory Council Cluster, which consists of very specialized organizations) have high density ties with the MOL Core indicates functional coordination. (The Advisory Council Cluster has a lower density tie with the MOL Core because an advisory council is attached to one specific ministry. The MOL had only a few such councils.) The dispersal of a number of ministries into clusters with organizations from civil society raises the possibility that the state lacks autonomy, that the regulators have become captured by their targets.

A close examination shows that the data do not support this hypothesis, however. The main cluster in which co-membership occurs, the Business-Ministry Secondary Cluster, exhibits low internal density among its members (16 percent). This low density indicates that its members have little contact with each other, which means they are not in collusion. Those ministries do not succumb to the enticements of interest groups in civil society.

The political parties appear in clusters with their main supporters and allies, the LDP in the Business Core Cluster and the Japan Socialist Party in the Labor Core Cluster. First of all, this indicates their partisanship. The fact that those two clusters have high internal density makes it likely that those partners consciously participate in a political alliance with the co-member peak associations. To anyone familiar with Japanese politics, this finding will come as no surprise. The implication for the larger pattern of power is that the parties are very partisan. They do not act as impartial arbiters for the whole society. Rather, they are the representatives of special interests.

The overall pattern of relationships indicates that, within the labor-policy domain, the ministries of the Japanese state exhibit strong integration around the functional (task-specific) leadership of the MOL Core. The MOL Core, as the mandated broker for this policy domain, straddles and binds the class divisions between business and labor. The strength of ties among several government clusters indicates a high degree of mutual solidarity and coordination. If other domains behaved similarly, the state overall would enjoy a high degree of functional coordination.

The Organization of Civil Society

Civil society encompasses the many types of organizations, groups, and communities outside the state, as well as the unorganized populace. Civil society has its own patterns of organization that articulate with and hamper or facilitate the efforts of the state. The most obvious fissure in Japanese society revealed by our network analysis follows class lines. It neatly divides most of the politically active organizations into two main sectors, business and labor. This division is intensified by the strong corporatistic integration of each sector under its peak associations. Another, less obvious, fissure in civil society runs between the corporatistic and noncorporatistic sectors. Organizations in the corporatistic sectors participate in national politics indirectly, through their peak federations. But those not in the corporatistic sectors have much less political voice. This is all the more true for those who are not members of political organizations. This category includes the nonunionized two-thirds of the labor force (mostly women), as well as students, the unemployed and the retired.

In our data, the corporatist business sector appears in three clusters: the Business Core, the Business-Ministry Secondary Cluster, and the Business Follower Cluster. The Business Core contains the peak business association that takes the lead in labor negotiations, Nikkeiren, as well as the political party that checks the broader feasibility of measures Nikkeiren might propose, the LDP. The Business-Ministry Secondary Cluster contains other powerful peak business associations and the ministries they are closest to or have the same concerns as (such as Construction and Transport). The composition of the Business Follower Cluster illustrates the intense unanimity of the business community behind its peak leadership. It contains all but two industrial associations (*gyokai*). Each type of industry—steel, petrochemicals, autos, etc.—although composed of a number of separate firms, has an industrial association that represents its members' collective political interests and coordinates the members' response to government policies.

Overall, the power pattern of the business sector looks much like that within the state. The organization with the mandate to handle the specific type of problem takes the lead and receives lots of information and political support from the other organizations in its sector. It reciprocates by making and pushing the policies that the others support and want. This increases the net quantity of trust and loyalty within the sector. Such practices produce a highly integrated and coordinated corporatism within the business sector, imbued with a strong sense of solidarity and collective interest. This contrasts with the more fragmented quality of the U.S. business community (Vogel, 1995).

Compared to the Japanese business sector, the Japanese labor sector is more fractured and undisciplined, overseeing a weaker form of organization. Labor unions are more scattered, appearing in four clusters: the Labor Core, the Productivity Core, the Public Sector Follower Unions, and the Private Sector Follower Unions. The Labor Core contains the two peak labor federations, along with the Japan Socialist Party and the Japan Institute of Labor (an MOL-established research agency). Each labor peak orients toward a different set of unions. The Productivity Core contains two union associations and the political party that represents conservative unions (the DSP), plus MITI and the others noted previously.

The Private Sector Unions belonged mostly to the old Domei federation, which advocated cooperation with management to increase productivity. The DSP had been their representative. It dissolved to form the new Rengo federation, which its members entered.

The Public Sector Unions, in contrast, belonged mostly to the Sohyo federation, which took a more leftist stance in opposition to the ruling elite and the state. The Japan Socialist Party (JSP) had been their representative.

Within-cluster densities differ greatly. In the Labor Core, Rengo, Sohyo, and the JSP had strong ties with each other, as the cluster's high density (54 percent) indicates. The two labor follower clusters differed strikingly in their internal densities. The Public Union Cluster had fairly strong internal density (47 percent), but the Private Union Cluster had a very weak internal density (15 percent). In other words, the public sector unions exhibit a classic working class solidarity, but the private sector unions do not. This difference is not accidental. It resulted from a long and largely successful campaign by Japanese business to transform unions from being industrywide, independent organizations to firm-specific, compliant ones.

Among the four clusters in the labor sector relationships are weaker than in the business sector. The Labor Core has strong ties to the Public (Sector Union Follower) Cluster (61 percent), but only moderate ties with the Private (Sector Union Follower) Cluster (42 percent). The presence of the JSP, closer to Sohyo, in the Labor Core, may explain this. In contrast, the Private Cluster has a moderately strong relationship to the Productivity Core (48 percent), where the DSP is located. But the Public Cluster has a weak relationship to the Productivity Core (20 percent). These patterns followed the interest group/party alliances of the 1955 system and weakened the independent political potential of organized labor. Since this research, the decline of Sohyo and change in the party and electoral systems has transformed this balance of forces in uncertain ways.

Having accounted for the organized, corporatistic sectors of Japanese society (government, business, and labor), relatively few organizations remain in our group of 122. The rest of the organizations played narrowly focused or peripheral roles in labor politics. By virtue of this, they all fell into the Isolate Cluster.

The membership of the Isolate Cluster highlights the weakness of the voluntary sector in Japanese civil society. It consists of groups marginalized for different reasons: the radical left (including the Japan Communist Party), interest groups that are not part of corporatistic sectors or have little to do with labor policy (like the Medical Association), and quasigovernmental groups that tend passively to reflect government policy (like the National Mayors' and National Governors' Associations or mandatory insurance associations). No voluntary groups that serve the generalized "public interest" (like, for instance, the liberal U.S. group Public Citizen or the conservative Heritage Foundation) appear, even in the Isolate Cluster.

The Isolate Cluster had little cohesion as a cluster (7 percent) and not much contact with other clusters. It had a moderately strong connection to the MOL Core (48 percent), which tried to keep in touch with all actors. It had weak connections to the Ministry of Health and Welfare Cluster (20 percent) and to the Labor Core (18 percent). Otherwise, the Isolate Cluster had virtually no outside connections (the densities range from 11 to 1 percent).

Japanese civil society, as indicated by these data, splits into three large corporatistic sectors (business, public sector labor, and private sector labor) and a large, politically unorganized mass. The peak associations sway or make decisions for their corporatistic membership. This pattern severely reduces the potential of new, unorganized groups to mobilize and take on autonomous political activity. It has important organizational and operational implications for each sector and the entire political system.

State–Society Relations

The state has close ties with the peak federations, of course. But some state organizations, especially the MOL and Productivity Cores, also have close direct relationships with ties the ordinary member associations in the business and labor follower clusters. These direct relations are not mediated by peak associations, as corporatist theorists presume (Schmitter, 1981). The peak federations do not enjoy the role of full "interest intermediation" of being the only gatekeepers between their sector membership and the state. Some members of the follower clusters broke corporatistic discipline, sidestepped their peak associations, and established their direct relations with the MOL and Productivity Cores.

The Private Sector Unions Cluster went the furthest in this regard; it had stronger relations with the MOL Core than with its Labor Core. Some members of the Business Follower Cluster also broke corporatist solidarity and had direct ties with state clusters. Both follower clusters had low internal solidarity. This finding means their members received policy influence from both their peak federations and from the state, and had little chance to organize any contrary preferences among themselves. In a word, parallel to debates about state relative autonomy (Skocpol, 1985), they had little relative *class* autonomy. Consequently, they would be more likely to follow elite directions about policy matters. This situation makes them both likely candidates for Nakane's idea of deferential corporatism—the vertical society that accepts the state's decisions without resistance (Nakane, 1970). The Public Sector Union Follower Cluster, on the other hand, had more internal solidarity and a more dedicated connection to its own sectoral peak federation. This helped give that cluster more of an independent voice and a peak association (Sohyo) that would represent that voice, to the discomfort of the state and business interests.

The two major political parties appear to be more creatures of society than creatures of the state. They appear solidly within the core clusters of the interest groups they represent: business and labor. In the Labor Core, the two main labor peak associations work with each other and the JSP. In the Business Core, the LDP works closely with the Japan Federation of Employers' Associations (Nikkeiren). But they are in close touch with the Federation of Economic Organizations (Keidanren), the "parent" business federation that sets Nikkeiren's general goals and monitors its progress very closely. The industry-specific business associations (*gyokai*) dutifully group themselves into one deferential follower cluster.

Within the state, the government ministry appropriate to the policy domain, the MOL, played the central role in the policy-making process. Within the Labor Ministry, a single specialized bureau, the Labor Politics Bureau, formulated overall Ministerial policy and represented it to the outside. It was closely shepherded, though not controlled, by the Productivity Core, MITI. This system of shepherded mandate autonomy allowed ministries to enter into close relations with clientele while reducing the risk of being captured by them.

Within society, three main camps (business and two labor) assumed strongly corporatistic formations, but with important differences among them. The findings indicate a moderate level of internal solidarity in the business sector, but one of a very hierarchical nature that ties the sector to the state. Follower members looked to their peak federations—in the case of labor policy, Nikkeiren—for leadership. Because of a lack of connections among themselves, followers had little ability to generate an autonomous voice. The Business Core (with Nikkeiren) had a closer relationship (and one of mutual exchange of influence) with the MOL Core than any other cluster except the Productivity Core (with MITI). This indicates a very tight alliance between the Business and MOL Cores. The business followers looked not only to the Business Core, but also directly to the MOL Core for leadership. In fact, a higher proportion of them sent vital information and other resources to the MOL Core (63 percent) than to Nikkeiren (50 percent). This weakened Nikkeiren control and strengthened MOL's chances for control over all business politics in the labor domain.

The degree and style of state influence within the business sector runs completely contrary to expectations based on U.S. or European experience. The nature of *gyokai* organization explains these results. In the field, *gyokai* officials complained to the first author that they had to accept retired officials (*amakudari*) from the government ministries onto their boards of directors (*rijikai*). These officials usually took the position of managing director (*jomu riji*) of the *gyokai*, which gave them great influence over *gyokai* decisions. This situation reinforced state surveillance and control of the *gyokai*.

The findings indicate that influence between the state and the business sector is likely to flow like Nakane's idea of the vertical society would have it—downward. The organizational pattern is likely to transmit the voice of state authority, as she contends, down the line without resistance (and in fact, the business sector was the empirical referent for her generalization).

Private sector labor had a weak connection to the Labor Core. Surprisingly, they sent more resources to the MOL Core (57 percent density) and the Productivity Core (48 percent) than to the Labor Core (43 percent). They also received resources in the same order. Their loyalties were at least splintered, and perhaps lay more with the state than with their own peak federation. Coupled with the private sector unions' low internal cohesion (15 percent density), this indicates a sense of sectoral solidarity much weaker than either the business or the public unions sectors.

The public labor union follower cluster, on the other hand, showed strong internal cohesion (47 percent). It sent more resources to the Labor Core (57 percent) than to the MOL Core (50 percent) and also received resources in the same proportion. Unlike the private sector unions, it sent and received very little resources with the Productivity Core (18 and 20 percent, respectively). The strong internal solidarity of this cluster, coupled with its preference for resource exchange with its own peak federations, indicates a much more participatory and democratic relationship between peak and followers. Its preference for relations with the MOL Core over the Productivity Core further strengthened its position. As historical research has shown, the MOL has often worked to improve the situation of labor and legitimize the position of labor unions (Garon, 1987). Accordingly, the pattern of influence flow between the Public Sector Unions and their peak confounds the Nakane vertical society characterization. This is why the some state ministries and the business elite worked to destroy it.

In the state–society relationship, the mandated state agency clearly mediates between business and labor, bridging the major divide of the society. The MOL works with the peak federations of the two sectors, but also bypasses them to penetrate directly into their follower clusters. This structural broker location gives the MOL unparalleled ability to draw in demands from all sides and to interpret them with considerable autonomy according to its own agenda. The structural position also enhances MOL's ability to persuade sectoral follower-level organizations to go along with its decisions, and to build societywide acceptance of compromise policies.

No other clusters have as strong a capacity to act as influence bridges across the business–labor divide. The Productivity Core comes close. It has high density ties with the Labor Core (53 percent). But, it dips below the 50 percent mark in its ties to the Business Core (42 percent). Other government clusters have strong relations with either the Business Core or the Labor Core, but not with both. The MOL Secondary Cluster also comes close. It has the highest density of ties with the Business Core (71 percent), but it falls below 50 percent in its ties to the Labor Core (45 percent). The Ministry of Health and Welfare Secondary Cluster is below the 50 percent level in its ties to both Business and Labor Cores. So is the Business-Ministry Secondary Cluster. Neither do Business and Labor Cores have the ability to directly mediate their disputes over policy matters. They have low levels of direct relationship between themselves (27 and 25 percent, respectively). However, they and all these governmental clusters have very strong direct ties to the MOL Core. This indicates that the MOL Core has, by far, the strongest capacity to mediate between factions and integrate the system. Therefore, the MOL Core, for the labor-policy domain, creates whatever degree of reality there is to the networked, consensual image of the Japanese polity.

The relative intensity of relation between the Isolate Cluster and the MOL core strengthens our impression of the central role of the ministry in integrating the society around its policies. The MOL Core keeps in touch with all sectors of society, even those in the nether regions. To achieve this, the Ministry must earnestly pursue its role as social integrator within its policy domain.

These findings indicate a pattern of corporatism that ignores the public sector outside the three big blocs (government, business, and labor). Corporatism can be either state led, or it can exist as a form of negotiation between autonomous sectors of society and the state. The latter is, of course, more democratic, if not pluralistic. Japanese corporatism includes the highly organized business and labor sectors, but excludes the less or unorganized majority. Even the included sectors, however, with the exception of the declining Public Sector Unions, does not appear have at least the best structural locations for autonomous bargaining with the state.

Assessing the Models

The findings indicate a polity organized by both state and societal corporatism, with the state bureaucracy playing the central hub role. It has a relatively efficient division of labor within the state and within each sector, divided functionally among mandated state bureaucracies and peak federations. Strictly speaking, these results only apply to the labor-policy domain. But given the openness of our definition of labor policy and the centrality of the issues, the policies sparked the attention of most influential actors in the entire political system. Accordingly, the findings are likely to indicate patterns of more general prevalence in the Japanese political organization.

Principles of network analysis help us understand the power implications of these findings. Network researchers have found a close relationship between an actor's power or influence and its centrality in a network. Being a necessary intermediary or broker between two other actors gives a third actor great power (Marsden, 1982; Marsden, 1983; Freeman, 1979). Clearly, the MOL Core occupies the perfect social location for brokering between business and labor. Business, labor, and their political parties have virtually no independent contact with each other. To know of each other's positions and to negotiate or coordinate national policy, they need to go through a government bureaucracy—most likely the MOL Labor Policy Bureau. The peak associations of the public sector unions enjoy a similar broker role with respect to their own sector. Their roles similarly exemplify the key corporatist role of "interest intermediation." The peak federations of the business and private union sectors enjoy less exclusivity in that role, because the state agencies are in direct contact with their members.

The systemic broker role enjoyed by the MOL gives it a decided structural advantage. Its position strengthens its autonomy and helps it act as a political entrepreneur, relatively free from dependency upon or constraint from other actors (Burt, 1980). Given its location within habituated, embedded social networks, the mandated state agency achieves high autonomy because of its structural location. It enjoys power, not so much because of its monopoly over coercive domination (as Western theorists are wont to assume), but because of its exclusive brokerage centrality in societal network structure. This finding leads us to characterize the Japanese state as a mandated broker state firmly embedded in a social network, or in short, an "*embedded broker state*." To a lesser degree, the business and private sector union peaks enjoy a similar autonomy with their sectors, but their power relies in part upon the central structural role of the state.

As for asymmetrical power generated by resource dependency, clearly the control over important resources augments an organization's influence in the total system. True, the flow of such resources among elites is usually two-way. In that sense, both are dependent upon the other, suggesting an egalitarian relationship. But power equality depends upon the existence of alternative sources for the same resources. The state enjoys this. It can get information and help directly from labor and business groups rather than peak federations, if it so chooses. But the business and labor peaks, not to mention their follower groups, do not enjoy those alternative sources. In that sense, they are dependent on the state for information about the whole system.

These findings indicate the general relevance of the corporatist model. But insofar as this model leads us to expect the peak federations to fully "intermediate" between their followers and the state, they fail. The Japanese state has direct connections to the business and labor follower clusters that circumvent the peak federations. To some extent, the state itself is the main peak federation of both corporatist sectors in society.

This connection may encourage the voices of business and labor to seep "osmotically" into policy decisions, as Tsujinaka asserted in his Japan- and Rengo-specific model. But with the transfer to Rengo, this seepage depends entirely upon the paternalistic good will of the state, not on labor's independently organized strength. With privatization and other policy events in the 1980s, state paternalism weakened the voice of labor, making "corporatism without labor" more constructable at the whim of the state.

The societal network state model comes closest to our findings because it attributes the state's power to its networks of contacts with, specifically, the business sector. Inoguchi's expansion of this network model to include state–labor relations also fits the findings. Both versions assume that follower organizations accept state policies passed down to them by their peak federations.

But our data show this is not always the case. The Japanese state sometimes bypasses the peak associations and communicates directly with the follower clusters. Also, the whole noncorporatistically unorganized sector is denied much paternalistic inclusion. Accordingly, the findings modify the societal network state model, suggesting a power structure in Japan that would more accurately be called a "mandated, embedded broker" arrangement.

One of the biggest problems with Japan's state broker political system lies in its lack of incorporation and participation for the noncorporatistically organized sector. This sector includes the majority of the population: the workers at small- and medium-sized companies and shops; the "part-time," female employees of large corporations; housewives; the elderly; consumers; students; intellectuals; and participants in social movements. If these portions of society become more and consistently politically active, as they no doubt will, demands upon the system will increase, making the state's embedded mandated broker role increasingly difficult to maintain.

However, this system has been beneficial for Japan's business climate and has supported its rapid economic growth. Centralized domains can reach authoritative decisions faster than decentralized ones (Laumann and Knoke, 1987). Until the 1990s, Japan's high degree of state and societal corporatism strongly contributed to its powerful ability (for a large society) to orchestrate its political economy to meet the changing world market. Relations between Japanese firms in the manufacturing and distributing process also depend on embedded networks, as this book makes clear. These trust relations largely replace both market and hierarchy, reducing their inefficiencies. However, they require a stable and sensitive political and labor–management context to operate well.

The mandated "embedded broker" state system described in this chapter provides this context for firms and reproduces a similar elite paternalism at that level. Further research is needed to demonstrate how the favorable structural location of the state articulates with other sources of influence in the political system. It may be that in some circumstances, for instance, the economic resources and centrality to national economic health of the business sector would make the state less politically autonomous than its structural location alone would indicate. Certainly, Japan's financial troubles of the 1990s indicate that. Under other circumstances, however, the state's formal authority may join with its structural location in informal networks to produce state-initiated and effectively implemented regulatory policy decisions (Broadbent, forthcoming).

Note

Jeffrey Broadbent gratefully acknowledges the grants that made this research possible: Japan–United States Educational Commission (JUSEC), USDOE Fulbright–Hays (Prog. 84.109, App. PO19A80047) and NSF (NSF/INT-8821714), awarded for 1988–1990.

References

Broadbent, J. "Environmental Politics in Japan: An Integrated Structural Analysis." *Sociological Forum*, 4–2(1989): 179–202.

Broadbent, J. *Environmental Politics in Japan.*: Networks of Power and Protest Cambridge: Cambridge University Press, 1998.

Burt, R. "Autonomy in a Social Topology." *American Journal of Sociology*, 85 (1980): 892–925.

Burt, R. *Structure Version 4.1.* New York: Center for the Social Sciences, Columbia University, 1989.

Campbell, J. "Policy Conflict and its Resolution within the Governmental System" in E. Krauss, T. Rohlen, and P. Steinhoff (eds.) *Conflict in Japan* Honolulu: University Press of Hawaii, 1984.

Etzioni, A. *The Active Society*. New York: Free Press, 1968.

Evans, P. *Embedded Autonomy: States and Industrial Transformation*. Princeton N.J.: Princeton University Press, 1995.

Freeman, L. "Centrality in Social Networks. I: Conceptual Clarification." *Social Networks*, 1 (1979): 215–39.

French, J., and B. Raven. "The Bases of Social Power." In D. Cartwright, ed., *Studies in Social Power*. Ann Arbor: University of Michigan Press, 1959.

Garon, S. *The State and Labor in Modern Japan*. Berkeley: University of California Press, 1987.

Homans, G. *Social Behavior: Its Elementary Forms*. New York: Harcourt, Brace, Jovanovich, 1974.

Inoguchi, T. *Gendai Nihon Seiji Keizai No Kozu (The Structure of Contemporary Japanese Political-Economy)*. Tokyo: Toyo Keizai Shuppansha, 1983.

Johnson, C. *MITI and the Japanese Miracle*. Stanford, Calif.: Stanford University Press, 1982.

Knoke, D. *Political Networks*. Cambridge: Cambridge University Press, 1990.

Knoke, D., F. Pappi, J. Broadbent, and Y. Tsujinaka. *Comparing Policy Networks: Labor Politics in the US, Germany, and Japan*. Cambridge: Cambridge University Press, 1996.

Laumann, E. O. and D. Knoke. *The Organizational State*. Madison: University of Wisconsin Press, 1987.

Marsden, P. "Brokerage Behavior in Restricted Exchange Networks." In P. Marsden and N. Lin, eds., *Social Structure and Network Analysis*. Beverly Hills, Calif.: Sage, 1982.

Marsden, P. "Restricted Access in Networks and Models of Power." *American Journal of Sociology*, 88–4 (1983): 686–715.

McCarthy, J. D. and M. N. Zald. "Resource Mobilization and Social Movements: A Partial Theory." *American Journal of Sociology*, 82–6 (1977): 1212–41.

Muramatsu, M. and E. Krauss. "The Japanese Political-Economy Today: The Patterned Pluralist Model." In K. Yamamura and Y. Yasuba, eds., *The Political Economy of Japan*, vol. 1, Stanford, Calif.: Stanford University Press, 1988.

Nakane, C. *Japanese Society*. Berkeley: University of California Press, 1970.

Okimoto, D. *Between MITI and the Market: Japanese Industrial Policy for High Technology*. Stanford, Calif.: Stanford University Press, 1989.

Okimoto, D. and T. Rohlen, eds. *Inside the Japanese System*. Stanford, Calif.: Stanford University Press, 1988.

Pempel, T. and K. Tsunekawa. "Corporatism without Labor? The Japanese Anomaly." In S. a. Philippe and Gerhard Lehmbruch, eds., *Trend Toward Corporatist Intermediation*. Beverly Hills, Calif.: Sage, 1979, pp. 231–70.

Schmitter, P. "Interest Intermediation and Regime Governability in Contemporary Western Europe and North America." In S. Berger, ed., *Organizing Interests in Western Europe*. Cambridge: Cambridge University Press, 1981, pp. 285–327.

Skocpol, T. (1985) "Bringing the State Back In: Strategies of Analysis in Current Research." In P. Evans, T. Skocpol, and D. Reuschmeyer, eds., *Bringing the State Back In*. New York: Cambridge University Press, 1985.

Skocpol, T. "Political Response to Capitalist Crisis: Neo-Marxist Theories of the State and the Case of the New Deal." In T. Skocpol and J. L. Campbell, eds., *American Society and Politics*. New York: McGraw-Hill, 1995, pp. 48–73.

Tsujinaka, Y. "Rengo and its Osmotic Networks" in G. Allinson and Y. Sone *Political Dynamics in Contemporary Japan* Ithaca: Cornell U. Press, 1993.

Tilly, C. *From Mobilization to Revolution*. Reading, Mass.: Addison Wesley, 1978.

Vogel, D. (1995) "Why Businessmen Distrust Their State: The Political Consciousness of American Corporate Executives." In T. Skocpol and J. L. Campbell, eds., *American Society and Politics*. New York: McGraw-Hill, 1995, pp. 247–71.

Appendix: Twelve Cluster
Organizational Membership

1. Productivity Core (6)

Labor Unions
  General Federation of Private Railway Workers Unions of Japan (Shitetsu Soren)
  International Chemical and Energy Workers Unions—Japanese Affiliates Federation (Kagaku Energii Rokyo)
Public Interest
  Social Economic Council of Citizens (Shakai Keizai Kokumin Kaigi)
  Japan Producitivity Center (Nihon Seisansei Honbu)
Ministry
  Ministry of International Trade and Industry (Tsusansho)
Political Party
  Democratic Socialist Party Policy Council (Minsha To)

2. Labor Core (4)

Unions
  Japan Private Sector Trade Union Confederation (Zenminroren, Rengo)
  General Council of Trade Unions of Japan (Sohyo)
Public Interest
  Japan Institute of Labor (Nihon Rodo Kyokai)
Political Party
  Japan Socialist Party Policy Council (Nihon Shakai To)

3. MOL Core (1)

Ministry
  Ministry of Labor Labor Politics Bureau (Rodosho Rosei Kyoku)

4. Business Core (3)

Business
  Japan Steel Industry Federation (Nihon Tekko Renmei)
  Japan Federation of Employers Association (Nikkeiren—Nihon Keieisha Dantai Renmei)
Political Party
  LDP Policy Research Council Labor Committee (Jiyu Minshu To Seichokai Rodo Bukai)

5. Ministry of Health and Welfare Secondary Cluster (5)

Union
  General Federation of National Construction Workers Unions (Zenken Soren)
Ministries
  Ministry of Health and Welfare (MHW) Social Affairs Bureau (Koseisho Shakai-kyoku)
  MHW Social Insurance Bureau (Koseisho Hoken Kyoku)

MHW Pension Bureau (Koseisho Nenkin Kyoku)
Ministry of Posts and Telecommunications (Yuseisho)

6. Business-Ministry Secondary Cluster (9)

Business
Federation of Chambers of Commerce and Industry (Nihon Shoko Kaigisho)
JFEC—Japan Federation of Economic Organizations (Keizai Dantai Rengokai, Keidanren)
JCED—Japanese Committee for Economic Development (Keizai Doyukai)
NCMSEOJ—National Center for Medium- and Small-Sized Enterprises Organizations in Japan (Zenkoku Chusho Kigyo Dantai Chuokai)
Ministries
Administrative Management and Coordination Agency (Somucho)
Cabinet Secretariat (Naikaku Kanbo)
Ministry of Construction (Kensetsusho)
Ministry of Transport (Unyusho)
Economic Planning Agency (Keizai Kikaku Cho)

7. Advisory Council Secondary Cluster (16)

Public Interest
International Labor Organization Tokyo office (ILO Tokyo Jimukyoku)
Japan Institute for Promoting Employment for the Handicapped (Nihon Shogaisha Ko yo soku shin kyoukai)
Employment Promotion Corporation (Koyo SokushinJigyodan)
Mandatory Insurance
Federation of Health Insurance Associations (Kenko Hoken Kumiai Rengokai)
Federation of Welfare Annuity Insurance Funds (Kosei Nenkin Kikin Rengokai)
Ministries
Ministry of Finance (Okurasho)
Advisory Councils
Economic Advisory Council (Keizai Shingikai)
Industrial Structure Advisory Council (Sangyo Kozo Shingikai)
Social Security System Advisory Council (Shakai Hoken Seido Shingikai)
Special Council for Promotion of Administrative Reform (Rinji Gyosei Kaikaku Suishin Shingikai)
Central Minimum Wage Advisory Council (Chuo Saitei Chingin Shingikai)
Advisory Council for Health Insurance for Aged Persons (Rojin Hoken Shingikai)
Social Insurance Advisory Council (Shakai Hoken Shingikai)
Employment Advisory Council (Koyo Shingikai)
Central Labor Standards Advisory Council (Chuo Rodo Kijun Shingikai)
Central Employment Stability Council (Chuo Shokugyo Antei Shingikai)

8. Ministry of Labor Secondary Cluster (4)

Ministries
MOL Labor Standards Bureau (Rodosho Rodo Kijun Kyoku)
MOL Human Resources Bureau (Rodosho Shokugyo Antei Kyoku)

MOL Womens Affairs Bureau (Rodosho Fujin Kyoku)
MOL Vocational Ability Development Bureau (Rodosho Shokugyo Noryoku Kai-
hatsu Kyoku)

9. General Business Follower Cluster (32)

Business
Japan Paper Processing Industry Federation (Nihon Seishi Rengokai)
Federation of Japan Pharmaceutical Industry Organizations (Nihon Seiyaku Dan-
tai Rengokai)
Maritime Business Employers Association (Gaiko Romu Kyokai)
Automobile Industry Employers Association (Jidosha Sangyo Keieisha Renmei)
Japan Federation of Taxicab Associations (Zenkoku Joyo Jidosha Rengokai)
National Construction Industry Association (Zenkoku Kensetsugyo Kyokai)
Electrical Industry Federation (Denki Jigyo Rengokai)
Japan Chemical Industry Association (Nihon Kagaku Kogyo Kyokai)
Japan Chemical Textile Industry Assoc (Nihon Kagaku Seni Kyokai)
Japan Machine Industry Association (Nihon Kikai Kogyo Rengokai)
Federation of Japan Construction Industry
Organizations (Nihon Kensetsugyo Dantai Rengokai)
Japan Mining Association (Nihon Kogyo Kyokai)
Japan Rubber Industry Association (Nihon Gomu Kogyokai)
Japan Industrial Machine Industry Association (Nihon Sangyo Kikai Kogyokai)
Japan Shipowners Association (Nihon Senshu Kyokai)
Japan Securities Business Association (Nihon Shokengyo Kyokai)
Japan Shipbuilding Industry Association (Nihon Zosen Kogyokai)
Japan Steel Industry Federation (Nihon Tekko Renmei)
Petroleum Industry Federation (Sekiyu Renmei)
Japan Electric Machine Industry Association (Nihon Denki Kogyokai)
Japan Spinning Industry (Nihon Boseki Kyokai)
Japan Private Railway Association (Nihon Minei Tetsudo Kyokai)
Japan Chain Store Association (Nihon Chenstoa Kyokai)
Japan Department Store Association (Nihon Hyakkaten Kyokai)
Japan Trade Association (Nihon Boekikai)
National Federation of Bank Associations (Zenkoku Ginko Kyokai Rengokai)
Life Insurance Company Association (Seimei Hoken Kyokai)
Indemnity Insurance Company Associations (Nihon Songai Hoken Kyokai)
Realtor Association (Fudosan Kyokai)
Japan Gas Industry Association (Nihon Gasu Kyokai)

10. Private Sector Unions Follower Cluster (26)

Unions
International Metalworkers Federation—Japan Council (IMF—JC)
Japan Federation of Iron and Steel Workers Unions (Tekko Roren)
National Metalworkers Union (Zenkoku Kinzoku)
National Federation of Metal Trade Unions (Zenkin Domei)
All Japan Federation of Electrical Machine Workers' Unions (Denki Roren)

National Federation of Shipbuilding and Heavy Machinery Workers' Unions (Zosen Juki Roren)
General Federation of Japan Automobile Workers' Unions (Jidosha Soren)
General Federation of Paper and Pulp Processing Workers' Unions (Kamipa Sorengo)
Federation of Petroleum Industry Workers Unions (Sekiyu Roren)
Federation of National Gas Workers Unions (Zenkoku Gasu)
Federation of National Electric Power Workers Unions (Denryoku Roren)
Federation of Japan Transport Workers Unions (Kotsu Roren)
Federation of Indemnity Insurance Workers Unions Conference of Construction Employees Unions (Nikkenkyo)
Federation of Japan Commerce Workers Unions (Shogyo Roren)
Japan Federation of Textile Workers Unions (Zensen Domei)
All Japan Transport Union (Zennitsu)
National Metalworkers Union (Zenkoku Kinzoku)
All Japan Federation of Food Workers Unions (Shokuhin Roren)
National Federation of Life Insurance Workers Unions (Seiho Roren)
Federation of All Japan Railway Workers Unions (Tetsudo Roren)
Telecommunication Workers Union of Japan (Zendentsu)
All Japan Seamens Union (Zen Nihon Kaiin Kumiai)
Public Interest
Peace Economy Council of Citizens (Heiwa Keizai Kokumin Kaigi)
Contemporary Policy Studies Group (Gendai Sogo Kenkyu Shudan)
Political Parties
Clean Government Party Policy Council (Komei To)
Social Democratic Federation Policy Council (Shakai Minshu Rengo Seisaku Shingikai)

11. Public Sector Unions Follower Cluster (6)

Unions
Japan Teachers Union (Nihon Kyoshokuin Kumiai)
All Japan Prefectural and Municipal Workers Unions (Zen Nihon Jichidantai Rodo Kumiai)
Conference of Government-Related Public Corporations Workers Unions (Seirokyo)
Japan Postal Workers Union (Zentei)
Federation of Japan Metropolitan Transport Workers Unions (Toshiko)
Public Interest
Buraku Liberation League (Buraku Kaiho Domei)

12. Isolate Cluster (13)

Unions
Japan Federation of National Public Servants Unions (Kokko Roren)
Conference of Mass Communication, Information and Culture Workers Unions (Nihon Masukomi Bunka Joho Roso Kaigi)
Federation of City Banks Employees Unions (Shiginren)
Japan Medical Workers Unions Federation (Nihon Iroren)

Business
  Federation of Japan Pharmaceutical Industry Organizations (Nihon Seiyaku Dantai Rengokai)
Professional
  Japan Medical Association (Nihon Ishikai)
Public Interest
  National Social Welfare Conference (Zenkoku Shakai Fukushi Kyogikai)
  National Governors Association (Zenkoku Chijikai)
  National Association of Municipal Mayors (Zenkoku Shichosoncho Kai)
  Five Member Committee for Promotion of Administrative Reform (Gyokaku Suishin Gonin Iinkai)
Mandatory Insurance
  Federation of National Health Insurance Associations (Kokumin Kenko Hoken Chuokai)
  Federation of National Civil Servants Benefit Societies (Kokkakomuin Kyozaikumiai Rengokai)
Political Party
  Japan Communist Party Policy Council (Nihon Kyosan To)

5

Trust and Commitment as Alternative Responses to Social Uncertainty

TOSHIO YAMAGISHI
MIDORI YAMAGISHI

Trust has been recognized as an important variable to characterize business operations in East Asian countries. For example, Redding and Tam (1985), Redding and Wong (1986), and Redding (1989) pointed out that the inability of Chinese entrepreneurs to develop business networks beyond family and kin networks has contributed to the dominance of small family businesses in Hong Kong. Studying more than forty large businesses in Taiwan, Kao (1989) concluded that "personal trust" is one of the key mechanisms of *guanxi*, which Hamilton (1989) called the Chinese type of capitalism in Taiwan. Furthermore, Whitley (1990) proposed that trust mechanisms between strangers is a crucial societal context that differentiates dominant forms of business organization in Japan, Korea, Taiwan, Hong Kong, and the United States.

Although trust is generally assumed to be a necessary condition for developing interpersonal and interorganizational relationships, the nature and process of trust mechanisms have been little understood. Specifically, little has been known about the effect of sociocultural differences on trust formation. The treatment of trust in comparative management studies to date has been mostly speculative—historical analysis of social phenomena or impressionistic observations of current business operations. Empirical research is thus needed to clarify the concept of trust and its role in developing network structures. In addition, processes that mediate individual and macro level social phenomenon need to be examined.

Are Americans More Trustful Than Japanese?

The research in this chapter is an attempt to clarify dimensions of trust, first by theoretically examining different types of trust and then by experimentally demonstrating the relationship between trust and uncertainty. Before presenting the findings, we briefly introduce the background to our research. For more than a decade, we have been conducting a series of small group experiments in the United States and Japan. These are experiments on cooperation in social dilemma situations.

"Social dilemma" is a term used by social psychologists to refer to the problems of public goods provision and free riding. (See Dawes, 1980, and Yamagishi, 1995a, for reviews of social dilemma literature.) Participants in these experiments typically face a decision between two actions, C (cooperation) and D (defection). The incentives, that is, the outcomes of this choice to the participants (usually a small amount of money, $30 or so), are structured such that D (defection choice) always gives a participant a better outcome (i.e., more money) than C (cooperation choice), regardless of the choices of the other participants. However, this more beneficial choice will result in a less desirable outcome if all participants take it.

For example, each participant is given one dollar and is asked to "donate" any portion of the money for the group of participants. The amount donated by the participant is doubled in value and equally allocated to the other three members. For each participant, not donating yields a better outcome, because the "bonus" generated by their own "donation" does not directly benefit themselves. However, if all four members take this more beneficial action and donate nothing, each will end up with the original one dollar. On the other hand, they can earn two dollars instead of one if all of them donate one dollar. This kind of decision-making is repeated many times during the experiment.

A large literature in social psychology concerns the factors promoting cooperative choices in such situations. Among the major findings in such experimental studies is the importance of trust. People who trust other participants and expect that others will be cooperative tend to make cooperative choices themselves. This finding corresponds to the argument in economic literature that trust provides a "cheap" solution to the market for lemons (e.g., Akerlof, 1970; Dasgupta, 1988; Frank, 1988). The importance of trust has been also demonstrated in our experimental studies conducted in the United States and Japan (Yamagishi, 1986, 1988a,b, 1992; Yamagishi and Sato, 1986). For example, the average level of trust among 852 U.S. participants was about two-thirds higher (of the within-country standard deviation) than the average level of trust among 212 Japanese participants (Yamagishi, 1988b). Several follow-up studies involving more than 2,000 respondents in each country repeatedly found a similar difference (see Yamagishi and Yamagishi, 1989).

Our research project on trust, the outline of which first appeared in Yamagishi and Yamagishi (1989), was prompted by this consistent finding related to trust in this series of experiments; the level of general trust among the U.S. participants was substantially higher than that among the Japanese participants. Furthermore, U.S. participants were generally more cooperative than their Japanese counterparts. It is possible, of course, to disregard this finding—which seems to be opposite to the "common-wisdom" belief that the Japanese are more trustful than Americans—as a result of a poor methodology and/or biased (i.e., student) samples. [Although these studies conducted by Yamagishi and his associates used students as samples, a more systematic study done by the Institute of Statistical Mathematics (Hayashi et al., 1982), using representative national samples, reported a similar cross-national difference.] Instead, we launched a research project, tentatively assuming that the finding that Americans are more trusting than Japanese is valid and meaningful, to investigate the reasons for and the implications of this difference. In this chapter, we present an outline of the theoretical arguments we have developed so far and the findings from an initial experiment. We also are conducting a cross-national questionnaire survey to test some elaborate theoretical ideas based on the line of reasoning developed in this study. (See Yamagishi and Yamagishi, 1994, for a preliminary report of this study.)

Two Widely Accepted Views of Trust

Trust, as we deal with it in this chapter, concerns only intentions of the interaction partners, not their ability. As Barber (1983) suggested, these two factors are qualitatively quite different. Even a person who does not fully trust the ability of the pilot of the plane he or she is on would not suspect that the pilot may intentionally crash the plane. Similarly, many Japanese would have high trust in the ability of the high-ranking government bureaucrats, but not trust at all in their intentions. Social uncertainty is relevant only to trust in the intention of the partners, not in the ability of the partners.

Despite the elusiveness of the concept of trust, most researchers working on problems related to trust tend to agree on two general propositions. First, trust is considered important because it facilitates social and economic exchanges, especially in situations devoid of direct, intimate, stable, and long-lasting relations. Trust provides a foundation for exchanges that are potentially mutually beneficial but often fail to take place because of the potential risks. Trust is often considered to play the role of lubricant for social and economic exchanges in such situations. This functional importance of trust entices social scientists to work on this predominantly psychological phenomenon. Second, it also seems to be widely accepted that trust is engendered in close and stable relations. Furthermore, the trust engendered in such close and stable relations is considered to develop into more general kinds of trust that play a role in situations beyond the initial close and stable relations.

These views of trust—that trust plays the role of social lubricant and trust is engendered in close and stable relations—are usually considered to be mutually compatible. Most people would not feel uneasy to accept both views simultaneously. It is often considered that trust engendered in close and stable relations is diffused to interpersonal relations in general and plays the role of lubricant in the latter settings. We challenge this common sense view of trust. More specifically, we believe that the key to understanding the counterintuitive, cross-cultural difference in the level of trust between U.S. and Japanese participants in our previous studies lies here (that is, in the incompatibility of the two aspects of trust). We consider that the two are incompatible with each other because the "demand" for trust assumed in the first view is created by the lack of close and stable relations; in other words, the demand for trust as social lubricant is created by the lack of factors generating trust. Thus, *trust is needed most in the situations in which it is least likely to emerge.* For example, the market for lemons—that is, selling low-quality used cars (Akerlof, 1970)—exists in the situation that is least likely to engender trust (that is, among strangers). Who would sell a lemon to a close friend? This example is discussed in more detail in the next section.

The seeming inconsistency between the two views of trust is derived from a confusion between two types of trust: *particularistic trust* (trust in a particular individual one knows well) engendered in close and stable relations and *general trust* (trust in human beings in general), which plays the role of lubricant outside close and stable relations. Proponents of these widely accepted views of trust assume that general trust is a watered-down version of particularistic trust. In contrast to this view, we introduce the idea that these two types of trust are qualitatively different. As Hawthorn (1988) wrote, "if friendship is the model of interpersonal trust, . . . interpersonal trust itself cannot, as it stands, be a model for enduringly cooperative and trusting relations between strangers" (p. 113). We further argue that general trust is higher among Americans than among Japanese and that particularistic trust is higher in Japan than in the United States.

Trust and Social Uncertainty

The view that trust (general trust) plays the role of social lubricant, or that trust provides a solution to the market for lemons, is based on an assumption of a high level of social uncertainty. Social uncertainty produces a strong demand for general trust. We use the phrase *social uncertainty for an actor in a social relationship* to refer to a mixed-motive incentive structure in which the actor does not have the capability of correctly detecting a partner's intentions or motivations. The *market for lemons* (Akerlof, 1970) is a good example of such a socially uncertain situation. Buyers of used cars usually cannot tell the real quality of cars displayed on used car lots. Buyers know about the possibility of getting a lemon and reflect this in their offering price. At this depressed price, the seller cannot make much profit by selling high-quality cars and is thus even more strongly motivated to sell lemons. This vicious circle would eventually drive high-quality used cars out of the market.

The market for lemons is based on two conditions; the lack of either condition will make it unproblematic. First, buyers do not have the capability to detect correctly the seller's intentions. Lemons will no longer dominate the market once buyers become capable of telling honest sellers from dishonest sellers. Second, there must be room for the seller to profit from acting dishonestly. There is not much to hide with regard to new cars, and thus there is not much incentive for a new car salesperson to act dishonestly. Detecting whether the salesperson is honest is less important when one buys a new car. Social uncertainty exists in a situation characterized by these two conditions—when someone is incapable of correctly detecting interaction partners' intentions, and when partners have incentives to act dishonestly.

The lack of trust in socially uncertain situations, as in the market for lemons, prevents all parties from obtaining the potential benefits of honest transactions. Trust can thus provide a solution to the problem of failed transactions in socially uncertain situations. [It is interesting to note the similarities of the arguments presented, without references to each other, by economists and social psychologists (e.g., Akerlof, 1970; Gambetta, 1988a; Pruitt and Kimmel, 1977).] On the other hand, this kind of trust (which we call general trust) is not needed in close and stable relations because very little uncertainty is involved in such relations. There are at least three reasons why social uncertainty is reduced in committed relations. First, people in such relations accumulate information sufficient for allowing certainty about the partner's intentions. Second, a variety of "hostages," ranging from mutual emotional attachments to relation-specific assets (Helper and Levin, 1992), will develop in committed relations, and these hostages can be mobilized to provide deterrence against unilateral defection (Shapiro et al., 1992). Finally, it is possible to induce a partner to take a certain course of action with the use of strategies such as "tit for tat" (see Axelrod, 1984). That is, people often have mutual control over each other in such close and stable relations. One important result of a reduction of social uncertainty in mutually committed relations is a decrease in the need for general trust. People can tell what kind of person the partner is; because they know, they do not need to infer. Furthermore, they have bilateral behavior control (Thibaut and Kelley, 1959), and thus, even egoists would cooperate in mutually committed relations (Axelrod, 1984). When there is little social uncertainty, partners do not infer each other's intentions to be assured of the partner's benign behavior.

Because of the lower level of social uncertainty achieved in close and stable relations, people in such relations often feel secure about the consequences of the partner's choices. They feel that they trust the partner. As described previously, we call such trust in a particular person with whom one has close and stable relations particularistic trust. Particularistic trust refers to the lack of uncertainty in a partner's choices. It is based on reliable information or on the controllability of a partner's action. Thus, the level of particularistic trust should be a function of the availability of information about a partner's intentions or the ability to impose structural constraints on a partner's choices. In short, the level of particularistic trust is a function of the nature of an interpersonal relationship devoid of social uncertainty.

We further distinguish two types of particularistic trust, *knowledge-based* particularistic trust and *relation-based* particularistic trust. Partners in close and stable relations assume that they will not be betrayed for two reasons. First, they have plenty of information about the partner. Second, they can control the action of the partner through tit for tat strategies. When such assurances come from knowledge of the partner, it is knowledge-based trust. When it comes from the controllability of the partner's action, it is relation-based trust.

In sum, there are two means by which people deal with socially uncertain situations: they either generate general trust or they remove uncertainty from the situation through developing close and stable relations (i.e., by forming mutually committed relations). Societies characterized by high levels of general trust tend to be low in levels of particularistic trust, and societies characterized by high levels of particularistic trust tend to be low in levels of general trust. Whether a society is characterized by high levels of general trust or particularistic trust depends on how densely networks of mutually committed relations are established in the society. If dense networks of mutually committed relations develop in a society, it is expected that the general level of social uncertainty is reduced and the overall level of general trust is reduced as well. In a society characterized with dense networks of mutually committed relations, the general level of particularistic trust (both knowledge-based trust and relation-based trust) is expected to be high.

The distinction between general trust and particularistic trust helps us resolve the puzzle posed by the aforementioned finding that Americans are more trustful than Japanese. The trust scale used in those studies measured levels of general trust (Yamagishi, 1986, 1988a,b; Yamagishi and Yamagishi, 1989, 1994). Trust in particular persons is believed to be higher in Japanese society. The relative lack of general trust among the Japanese moves them toward establishing networks of mutually committed relations. A fear of strangers (i.e., a low level of general trust) motivates the Japanese toward establishing mutually committed relations with persons they feel they can trust. In the experiment reported next, we empirically demonstrate that those who are low in general trust tend to form committed relations. Before presenting this experiment, however, we take a closer look at general trust.

What Is General Trust, and How Is It Generated?

If particularistic trust is a mental representation of interpersonal relations devoid of social uncertainty, general trust is not a watered-down version of particularistic trust. General trust is not based on the stability of interpersonal relations or on low levels of social uncertainty. When general trust is generated, it is independent of specific interpersonal relations. It is a belief that others will generally act in a socially responsible and altruistic manner in a variety of situations. In short, general trust is the belief in human benevolence.

Particularistic trust is easy to explain: It depends on a lack of social uncertainty based on stable and durable interpersonal relations. Facing socially uncertain situations, people seek to form mutually committed relations with particular partners. By forming mutually committed relations, they can reduce social uncertainty. They feel secure from the possibility of being cheated and exploited, and thus they "trust" their partners. In contrast, it is difficult to identify structural factors that produce general trust. Social uncertainty is a necessary condition for general trust but not a sufficient condition; social uncertainty creates a demand for general trust, but the existence of a demand by itself does not "explain" its supply. What we need is a theory explaining how individuals come to accept or generate a belief in human benevolence, especially under conditions of social uncertainty.

Often, when we try to explain systematic differences in beliefs about human nature in general, and in human benevolence in particular, we resort to cultural or psychological explanations. However, neither of these approaches is satisfactory. Cultural explanations do not explain cross-cultural differences in belief; they simply describe them. Psychologists have been trying to provide explanations for the development of particular types of belief, but none of these seems to bridge the chasm separating social uncertainty and general trust. Only two theories seem to serve as candidates for what we are seeking. One is the commitment model of emotion (Frank, 1988), and the second is the "cognitive-miser" theory of cooperation's advantage by Orbell and Dawes (1991, 1993).

Frank's Commitment Model of Emotion

Frank (1988) proposed a theory of human emotion in which emotion is a device to commit individuals to a certain course of action. It is a "strategy" of self-control in which individuals make no conscious decisions. Roughly, according to Frank's argument, the long-term interests of individuals are served by being consistently honest in socially uncertain situations (situations in which trust is needed). Certain emotions "force" people to act honestly, even when acting opportunistically might yield better short-term outcomes. Frank speculated that humans have evolved certain emotions as solutions to the "commitment problem" or the problem of social uncertainty. An implication of Frank's theory is that emotions related to honesty or trustworthiness play a more important role in socially uncertain situations than in socially certain situations. Simply put, being honest pays off in socially uncertain situations, whereas honesty is irrelevant in socially certain situations.

Two comments on Frank's commitment model of emotion need to be made here. First, the relationship between the benefit of being honest and social uncertainty is mediated by reputation. There is no need for reputation in socially certain situations, because people can make accurate predictions about the partner's choices anyway (or there is no need to make predictions). On the other hand, a good reputation may not be enough to convince people about the trustworthiness of a partner in extremely uncertain situations. Therefore, the relationship between the benefit of honesty and social uncertainty will take an inverted U-shape. Second, Frank's theory explains why people are more honest in socially uncertain situations than in certain ones, but it does not explain why they are more trustful. Although Frank himself is not explicit on this point, it is easy to derive an explanation for the genesis of trustfulness. That is, honest and trustworthy people would prefer to interact with other honest and trustworthy people, avoiding dishonest and untrustworthy people. Because of this process of mutual selection, they interact mostly with others who are honest and trustworthy. This process may underlie the empirically well-established correlation between cooperativeness and trustfulness (e.g., Dawes et al., 1977; Marwell and Ames, 1979; Messick et al., 1983; Yamagishi and Sato, 1986; Tyszka and Grzelak, 1976; Yamagishi, 1986, 1988a). According to this line of reasoning, a high level of general trust (or belief in human benevolence) in socially uncertain situations is a byproduct of a high level of honesty (which serves one's long-term interests). In short, according to Frank's theory, a sizable portion of people facing socially uncertain situations come to be honest because of the effects of reputation, and then they selectively interact mostly with other honest people.

Orbell and Dawes' "Cognitive-Miser"

Orbell and Dawes' (1991, 1993) arguments start with an assumption of the aforementioned positive relationship between cooperativeness (or honesty) and truthfulness (i.e., cooperative people tend to be trustful of others). This correlation can be explained by the mutual selection of honest people through reputation, as described previously. This correlation may also be explained by the social psychological phenomenon of false consensus. *False consensus* refers to the tendency of most people to perceive others as similar to themselves. A good example of this is an experiment by Ross et al. (1977). They asked college students to walk around the campus wearing large sandwich boards. Some agreed with this request; some did not. They were then asked to estimate the proportion of people, among other participants like themselves, who would or would not agree with this request. Those who agreed to wear the sandwich boards estimated that 62 percent of their peers would agree; those who did not agree thought that 67 percent would not. Similar "consensus" effects have been observed in more than 100 empirical studies, according to Fiske and Taylor (1991). Orbell and Dawes (1991, 1993) argued that an empirical correlation between trustworthiness (or cooperativeness) and trustfulness is based on the false consensus effect.

The existence of this correlation between cooperativeness and trustfulness, Orbell and Dawes argued, provides a safety net for cooperative–trustful people in situations involving social uncertainties, risks, and potential rewards. Given a choice between a socially uncertain but potentially beneficial situation and a situation that yields a certain but less attractive benefit, trustful people would choose the former more often than would less trustful people. This is because trusting people think that others will also be honest and cooperative so that the risk of being exploited in such situations is low. As a result, trustful people congregate in socially uncertain situations in which a majority of the participants turn out to be honest and cooperative in such situations; they enjoy high levels of benefit generated by mutual cooperation in such situations.

Orbell and Dawes (1993) demonstrated this effect in an experiment. Participants were given a choice between joining and not joining a social dilemma game. The incentive structure of the game was such that mutual cooperation yielded a better individual payoff than the payoff of staying away. High trusters in this experiment tended to join the game more often than did low trusters. As a result, those who joined were mostly trustful–cooperative ones. They cooperated in the game and earned more than did the less trustful–cooperative participants, who did not join the game. In sum, according to this theory, honest people tend to think that others are also honest and will self-select into socially uncertain situations in which the majority turn out to be honest and trustful. As a result, honest–trustful people are better off than dishonest–fearful people.

In both of these explanations, trustful people are better off than less trusting ones. According to Frank, people can distinguish trustworthy ones from less trustworthy ones through reputation and other signaling devices. According to Orbell and Dawes, mutual selection of trustworthy people does not even require reputation and other signaling devices, because trustworthy people are at the same time trustful. It should be noted, however, that either explanation implies that only when social uncertainty is relatively high and people have choices of interaction partners are people with high levels of general trust better off than those with lower levels of general trust. In other words, dense networks of mutually committed networks prevent general trust from developing.

Thus, the relationship between the level of general trust and the development of networks of mutually committed relations is bidirectional. On the one hand, a low level of general trust promotes development of mutually committed relations, as discussed previously. On the other, prevalence of networks of mutually committed relations prevents general trust from developing. Therefore, the two form a mutually reinforcing feedback loop. This feedback system will lead to one of the following "ideal typical" societies. In one type, the general level of social uncertainty is low because of extensive networks of mutually committed relations; in this society, the level of general trust is low. This is a society in which people do not need to be honest and trustworthy; the networks of mutually committed relations take care of potential problems of social uncertainty. We postulate that Japanese society is closer to this ideal type than is U.S. society. In the second type, networks of committed relations are not so extensive and, as a result, the general level of particularistic trust is low. Nevertheless, people have a high level of general trust or a strong belief in human benevolence. This is a society in which people benefit from being honest and trustful. This is also a society in which people are honest and trustworthy; otherwise, social and economic exchanges will not take place smoothly. We postulate that the U.S. society is closer to this ideal type than is Japanese society.

An Experiment

We conducted the following experiment to test some predictions derived from our model. One hundred Japanese college students, recruited from various classes at a large national university, participated in the experiment. Monetary incentives were emphasized at the time of recruitment. At the time of recruitment (at least two months before the experiment), subjects' levels of general trust were measured with the eight-item trust scale used in Yamagishi's previous studies (Yamagishi, 1986, 1988a,b). Potential participants were classified into three groups: low trusters, medium trusters, and high trusters. Fifty low trusters and fifty high trusters were scheduled for the experiment. One-half of the subjects on each level of trust (twenty-five high trusters and twenty-five low trusters) were placed in the high-incentive condition, with the rest in the low-incentive condition. The subject's level of general trust was again measured with a postexperimental questionnaire using the same eight-item scale and a newly developed fourteen-item scale. The preexperimental measure of general trust was correlated with either of the two postexperimental measures ($r = .75$ with the same eight-item scale and $r = .72$ with the newly developed fourteen-item scale; the correlation between the two postexperimental measures was .86), and few subjects' scores dramatically changed between the pre- and postexperimental measures. We thus adopted the fourteen-item postexperimental measure (with the reliability of $\alpha = .83$) instead of the preexperimental measure for use in the analysis. Subjects were reclassified as high or low trusters according to the score on the fourteen-item scale.

As in Kollock's (1994) experiment that demonstrated that uncertainty promotes commitment formation and particularistic trust, the experiment simulated transactions between several sellers and buyers. Subjects were instructed that they would be randomly assigned the role of a seller or a buyer, but all were actually assigned the role of buyer. Upon arrival at the laboratory, each subject read the initial instructions. Each subject was given 500 yen (about $4.50 at the time) in cash as an initial fund to be used for the transactions. The reward to the subject for the participation (which took a little over one hour) was whatever profit he or she would make through transactions plus the initial 500 yen.

The subject read the initial instructions, was randomly assigned the role of buyer, and was given the initial fund of 500 yen. Then he or she was given an instruction sheet specifically written for the buyer, which contained the information shown in the Appendix. In brief, each subject-buyer interacted with two potential sellers, one of whom, Seller A, took advantage of opportunities to "rob" some money from the subject, whereas another seller, C, did not take advantage of such opportunities.

The first twenty periods were used to let subjects have experiences with Sellers A and C. Seller A took advantage of the exploitation opportunities, whereas

Seller C did not. At the end of the twentieth period, Seller A was replaced by Seller F. The subject had no previous information about Seller F. The choice for the subject during the last ten periods was thus between Seller C, who was known not to have taken advantage of the exploitation opportunities, and a new seller, F, who offered a better deal. Without commitment to C, the subject should have almost exclusively dealt with F, who offered better deals. The frequency of transactions with Seller C during the last ten periods (periods 21–30) is thus defined as a measure of commitment to C in the following analysis. This variable, however, had more than one mode in each cell, so that it was dichotomized (1 = commitment formed, with six or more transactions with C; 0 = commitment not formed with five or fewer transactions with C). Another dependent variable, particularistic trust, was measured through the subject's responses to two postexperimental questionnaire items. One item asked how trustworthy C (the "nice" seller) was (1 = not trustworthy, 5 = trustworthy). The other item asked how trustworthy F (a new seller) was. The subject's level of particularistic trust in C was measured as the difference between his or her responses to these items. That is, the subject's particularistic trust in C is how strongly he or she trusted C compared to strangers (in this case, F).

The percentage of subjects who formed a commitment was much higher in the high-uncertainty condition (71 percent) than in the low-certainty condition (37 percent), χ^2 (1) = 10.62, p <.01. This result clearly shows that uncertainty leads people to commitment formation with particular partners. People more strongly prefer dealing with those with whom they can feel safe under conditions when they can be exploited. The result also shows that the level of particularistic trust in C is much higher than among those who formed a commitment with C than among those who did not form a commitment (1.56 vs. 0.15, t(78) = 5.79, p = .01. People who are committed to a particular person trust that partner much more than strangers. Finally, the level of particularistic trust was higher in the high-uncertainty condition (1.20) than in the low-uncertainty condition (0.63), t(98) = 2.7, p <.05. People trust each other more strongly when they live in a social jungle than when they live in a safe world. These results support our idea that uncertainty promotes particularistic trust by making people seek mutually committed relations. Furthermore, our theoretical predictions concerning the effect of general trust on commitment formation were also supported. Particularly, general trust interacted with uncertainty, χ^2 (1) = 2.80, p <.10. When the level of social uncertainty was high, low trusters formed a commitment more often (83 percent) than did high trusters (58 percent), χ^2 (1) = 3.69, p <.05. When the level of social uncertainty was low, however, the difference (40 percent vs. 35 percent) was not significant χ^2 (1) = 0.13, ns.

The experimental results clearly support our theoretical discussions on trust. First, high uncertainty did promote commitment formation and particularistic trust. Furthermore, under highly uncertain situations, general trust was negatively related to commitment formation. These findings clearly indicate that general trust and particularistic trust are qualitatively different.

Conclusion

We started with a puzzling empirical finding. Japanese questionnaire respondents have repeatedly shown lower degrees of trust than their U.S. counterparts. This is puzzling to those who think that close, stable, long-term relations are the cradle of trust. If we accept the conventional view that stability of interpersonal and interorganizational relations is one of the distinguishing characteristics of Japanese society, especially in comparison with the United States, it seems likely that stronger trust would be nurtured in Japan. Yet, what seems logical is inconsistent with previous survey results (Hayashi et al., 1982; Yamagishi, 1988b; Yamagishi and Yamagishi, 1989, 1994). The puzzle is solved only when a clear distinction is made between general and particularistic trust. The two are qualitatively different.

High-trusters, who have a positive view of human nature, tend to form less committed, particularistic relationships than low-trusters. Low-trusters, who have a more negative view of human nature, by contrast, form more committed and stable relationships but with a much smaller set of partners. So, general trust "frees" people from forming strongly committed relationships and facilitates exploration of more open-ended opportunities. Particularistic and general trust play totally different, even opposing, roles.

The image of a commitment-based society in which networks of "strong ties" (Granovetter, 1973) provide secure and stable relations for its members reminds us of the notion of collectivistic culture (Hofstede, 1980). Numerous studies have contrasted how insiders and outsiders are treated in such cultures (e.g., Triandis, 1994). We (Yamagishi, 1988a, 1988b, 1996; Yamagishi and Yamagishi, 1994) too have depicted Japanese society as one where mutual trust is largely confined within the boundaries of particularistic groups and relationships. Our approach, however, does not take the particularistic quality of trust as a cultural given in Japan.

Instead, we argue that Japanese consolidate committed relations as a way of minimizing opportunity costs. In difficult and turbulent times, closing one's doors to outsiders and seeking harmony and cooperation within is a wise strategy for minimizing opportunity costs. To be more precise, it is wise insofar as the transaction cost savings that are generated among insiders exceed the opportunity costs incurred by excluding outsiders. Historically, it would seem that Japan has capitalized on this strategy. However, as outside opportunities increase (and this is what seems to be happening in and around Japan), the maintenance of committed, particularistic, insider relationships, such as *keiretsu* networks, may become increasingly costly.

In sum, strong, committed, and particularistic relationships may promote a stable society (Putnam, 1993, 1995) but overly strong, committed, and particularistic relationships may prevent the development of general trust (Fukuyama, 1995). Japan has been a puzzle in this respect: a high-trust society for insiders and a low-trust society for outsiders. Today, with mounting pressures of liberalization, transparency in business relations, internationalization and globalization, there is an inevitable weakening of the particularistic ties that have been so important in the past. But it is not inevitable that high levels of general trust will appear as a result. An emergence of general trust depends not only on a weakening of particularistic relations but also on the existence of open social, political, and legal systems. The two are interdependent and given this, Japan may remain a puzzle for some time to come.

Note

Our research project on trust has been supported by the Institute of Nuclear Safety System, Kyoto Japan. We thank Professor Juji Misumi and Mr. Akira Yamada of the Institute for encouraging our research as well as providing valuable insights and comments. Additional supports for the research came from an Abe Fellowship granted to Toshio Yamagishi. Our thanks also to Professors Karen Cook, University of Washington; Mary Brinton, University of Chicago; Peter Kollock, University of California, Los Angeles; Motoki Watabe, Hokkaido University; Tatsuya Kamed, Toyo University; Taro Kamioka, Hitotsubashi University; and Ichiro Numazaki, Tohoku University, for providing invaluable comments and insights to our project on several occasions. We also thank Kumiko Mori, Nahoko Hayashi, Nobuhito Jin, and Nobuyuki Takahashi for providing useful input and conducting aspects of our project at various phases.

References

Akerlof, G. "The market for 'Lemons': Qualitative Uncertainty and the Market Mechanism. *Quarterly Journal of Economics*, 84 (1970): 488–500.

Axelrod, R. *The Evolution of Cooperation*. New York: Basic Books, 1984.

Barber, B. *The Logic and Limit of Trust*. New Brunswick, N.J.: Rutgers University Press, 1983.

Dasgupta, P. "Trust as a Commodity." In D. Gambetta, ed., *Trust: Making and Breaking Cooperative Relations*. Oxford: Blackwell, 1988.

Dawes, R. M. "Social Dilemmas." *Annual Review of Psychology*, 31 (1980): 169–93.

Dawes, R. M., J. McTavish, and H. Shaklee. "Behavior, Communication, and Assumptions about Other People's Behavior in a Commons Dilemma Situation." *Journal of Personality and Social Psychology*, 35 (1977): 1–11.

Fiske, S. T., and S. E. Taylor. *Social Cognition*, 2nd ed. New York: McGraw-Hill, 1991.

Frank, R. H. *Passions within Reason: The Strategic Role of the Emotions*. New York: Norton, 1988.

Fukuyama, F. *Trust: The Social Virtues and the Creation of Prosperity*. New York: Free Press, 1995.

Gambetta, D. "Can We Trust Trust?" In D. Gambetta, ed., *Trust: Making and Breaking Cooperative Relations*. Oxford: Blackwell, 1988a.

Gambetta, D. "Mafia: The Price of Distrust." In D. Gambetta, ed., *Trust: Making and Breaking Cooperative Relations*. Oxford: Blackwell, 1988b.

Granovetter, M. S. "The Strength of Weak Ties." *American Journal of Sociology*, 78 (1973): 1360–80.

Hamilton, G. "Patterns of Asian Capitalism: The Case of Taiwan and South Korea." Program in East Asian Culture and Development Research Working Paper Series, No. 28. Institute of Governmental Affairs, University of California, Davis, 1989.

Hawthorn, G. "Three Ironies of Trust. In D. Gambetta, ed., *Trust: Making and Breaking Cooperative Relations*. Oxford: Blackwell, 1988.

Hayashi, C., T. Suzuki, G. Suzuki, and M. Murakami. *A Study of Japanese National Character*, vol. 4. (In Japanese with an English summary.) Tokyo: Idemitsushoten, 1982.

Helper, S., and D. Levin "Long-term Supplier Relations and Product–Market Structure." *The Journal of Law, Economics and Organization*, 8 (1992): 561–81.

Hofstede, G. *Culture's Consequences*. Beverly Hills, Calif.: Sage, 1980.

Kao, C-S. "The Role of "Personal Trust" in Large Businesses in Taiwan." Paper presented at the International Conference on Business Groups and Economic Development in East Asia, 1989.

Kollock, P. "The Emergence of Exchange Structures: An Experimental Study of Uncertainty, Commitment, and Trust." *American Journal of Sociology*, 100–2 (1994), 313–45.

Luhmann, N. "Familiarity, Confidence, Trust: Problems and Alternatives." In D. Gambetta, ed., *Trust: Making and Breaking Cooperative Relations.* Oxford: Blackwell, 1988.

Marwell, G., and R. E. Ames. Experiments on the Provision of Public Goods, I: Resources, Interest, Group Size, and the Free-rider Problem. *American Journal of Sociology*, 84 (1979): 1335–60.

Messick, D. M., H. Wilke, M. Brewer, R. M. Kramer, P. E. Zemke, and L. Lui. "Individual adaptations and Structural Change as Solutions to Social Dilemmas." *Journal of Personality and Social Psychology*, 44 (1983): 294–309.

Orbell, J. M., and R. M. Dawes, "A 'Cognitive Miser' Theory of Cooperator's Advantage." *American Political Science Review*, 85 (1991): 515–28.

Orbell, J. M., and R. M. Dawes. "Social Welfare, Cooperators' Advantage, and the Option of Not Playing the Game." *American Sociological Review*, 58 (1993): 787–800.

Pruitt, D. G., and M. J. Kimmel. "Twenty Years of Experimental Gaming: Critique, Synthesis, and Suggestions for the Future." *Annual Review of Psychology*, 28 (1977): 363–92.

Putnam, R. D. "The Prosperous Community." *American Prospect* (Spring 1993): 35–42.

Putnam, R. D. *Making Democracy Work: Civic Traditions in Modern Italy.* Princeton, N.J.: Princeton University Press, 1995.

Redding, G. *The Spirit of Chinese Capitalism.* Berlin: deGruyter, 1989.

Redding, G., and S. Tam. "Networks and Molecular Organizations: An Exploratory View of Chinese Firms in Hong Kong." In K. C. Mun and T. S. Chen, eds., *Perspectives in International Business.* Hong Kong: Chinese University Press, 1985.

Redding, G., and G. Y. Y. Wong. "The Psychology of Chinese Organizational Behavior. In M. Bond, ed., *The Psychology of the Chinese People.* Oxford: Oxford University Press, 1986.

Ross, L., D. Greene, and P. House. "The 'False Consensus Effect': Distortions in the Attribution Process." In L. Berkowitz, ed., *Advanced in Experimental Social Psychology*, vol. 10. New York: Academic Press, 1977.

Shapiro, D. L., B. H. Sheppard, and L. Cheraskin. "Business on a Handshake." *Negotiation Journal*, 8 (1992): 365–77.

Thibaut, J. W., and H. H. Kelley. *The Social Psychology of Groups.* New York: Wiley, 1959.

Triandis, H. C. *Culture and Social Behavior.* New York: McGraw-Hill, 1994.

Tyszka, T., and L. J. Grzelak. "Criteria of Choice in Nonconstant Zero-Sum Games." *Journal of Conflict Resolution*, 20 (1976): 357–76.

Whitley, R. D. Eastern Asian Enterprise Structures and the Comparative Analysis of Forms of Business Organizations. *Organizational Studies*, 11 (1990): 47–74.

Yamagishi, M., and T. Yamagishi. "Trust, Commitment, and the Development of Network Structures." Paper presented at the Workshop for the Beyong Bureaucracy Research Project, Hong Kong, 1989.

Yamagishi, T. "The Provision of a Sanctioning System as a Public Good. *Journal of Personality and Social Psychology*, 51 (1986): 110–16.

Yamagishi, T. "Seriousness of Social Dilemmas and the Provision of a Sanctioning System." *Social Psychology Quarterly*, 51 (1988a): 32–42.

Yamagishi, T. "The Provision of a Sanctioning System in the United States and Japan." *Social Psychology Quarterly*, 51 (1988b): 264–70.

Yamagishi, T. "Group Size and the Provision of a Sanctioning System in a Social Dilemma." In W. B. G. Liebrand, D. M. Messick, and H. A. M. Wilka, eds., *A Social Psychological Approach to Social Dilemmas*. New York: Pergamon Press, 1992.

Yamagishi, T. "Social Dilemmas." In K. S. Cook, G. Fine, and J. House, eds., *Sociological Perspectives on Social Psychology*. Boston: Allyn and Bacon, 1995a.

Yamagishi, T. (1995b). "Have Americans Really Become Distrustful?" Paper presented at the American Sociological Association Annual Meetings, Washington D.C., August 19–23, 1995.

Yamagishi, T., and K. Sato. "Motivational Bases of the Public Goods Problem." *Journal of Personality and Social Psychology*, 50 (1986): 67–73.

Yamagishi, T., and M. Yamagishi. "Trust and Commitment in the United States and Japan." *Motivation and Emotion*, 18 (1994): 129–66.

Zucker, L. G. "Production of Trust: Institutional Sources of Economic Structure, 1840–1929." *Research in Organizational Behavior*, 8 (1986): 53–111.

Appendix: A Summary of the Experimental Instructions and the Uncertainty Manipulation

1. The buyer will be paid the amount he or she made in the transactions during the experiment plus 500 yen.
2. The transaction will be repeated many times.
3. At each transaction period, the subject deals with two sellers. A transaction is completed as the subject chooses between offers from two sellers. The subject has to choose one of two offers.
4. Each seller has multiple buyers as well. Therefore, if one of the sellers completes a deal with another buyer, the subject is forced to deal with the remaining seller.
5. Of the two sellers the subject deals with, one (Seller C) remains S's partner throughout the experiment. The other seller (Seller A) is replaced by yet another seller (Seller F) after a certain, randomly determined number of periods.
6. Each period starts with sellers setting their selling prices. Then, buyers decide from which seller they will purchase.
7. The "standard resale value" of the commodity is 140 yen. However, the quality of the commodity the subject purchases may be above or below the standard. If the quality is higher than the standard, its resale value is above 140 yen; if it is lower, its resale value is below 140 yen. The profit for the buyer is the difference between the purchasing price (which the seller determines) and the resale value. There is no way the buyer can know the quality of the commodity before actually purchasing

it. The seller has a rough idea about the quality of the commodity he or she sells, but the information provided to the seller (on a computer screen) may not be correct. The subject who purchases low quality goods is thus not sure if the seller cheated.

8. After each transaction is completed, there is a "roulette chance." A roulette spins on the subject's (as well as the seller's) screen. And, if a ball hits the "strike" (the apparent probability is one-sixth), the seller with whom the subject made a deal is given a chance to exploit. That is, the seller is given a chance to "rob" a certain amount of money from the buyer. A seller is free not to use this option. Although the subject is not informed in advance, the amount of "rip-off" increases as the period proceed; from 120 yen (periods 1 through 7) to 190 yen (8–14), 260 yen (15–21).

9. The subject is led to believe that the roulette is random. In fact, the roulette hits "strike" twice with each seller during the first twenty periods. Seller A takes advantage of the opportunities and "robs" the subject the amount specified here. Seller C, on the other hand, refrains from taking advantage of these opportunities.

Manipulation of social uncertainty was carried out in the following way. After the twentieth period, Seller A was replaced by Seller F, with whom the subject had had no previous interactions. The offering price of F was generally lower than the offering price of C, the seller who had not taken advantage of the exploitation opportunities. In the high-uncertainty condition, the "rip-off" amount was increased to 400 yen. In the low-uncertainty condition, the roulette was removed from the screen, and the subject was told that there would be no more roulette chances.

6

The Work of Networks in Taiwan's Export Fashion Shoe Industry

YOU-TIEN HSING

This chapter discusses the mechanisms of coordination used by production and marketing networks in Taiwan's fashion shoe industry. Contrary to the conventional wisdom, the competitiveness of Taiwan's export fashion shoe industry is not based simply on low production costs. Instead, competition unfolds on three fronts at the same time: securing the lowest costs and the highest quality in the least amount of time. In producing the highest possible quality shoes at the lowest possible costs, Taiwanese export fashion shoe makers have been quick in responding to market signals, punctual in making deliveries and operating with short production cycles.

These characteristics, in turn, are based on an interfirm organization of production, which I call *networks of creative imitation*. The networks of creative imitation are composed of small to medium-sized independent manufacturers, suppliers, and subcontractors who adopt intermediate-level production technologies and product design and development strategies. Effective coordination within and between production and marketing networks has been the reason why Taiwanese shoe makers can deliver fast-changing fashion shoes to the world markets at competitive quality and costs.

Based on my interviews with Taiwanese fashion shoe trading and manufacturing companies in Guangdong Province, China, and Taichung, Taiwan, between July 1991 and May 1992, I analyzed the major mechanisms that explain effective coordination with interfirm networks. In this chapter, I focus on the active role that Taiwanese trading companies have played in the networks. Taiwanese trading companies have not been constrained by their role as intermediaries; that is, they have not been passively representing overseas buyers who place orders with local manufacturers. Instead, they are actively involved in organizing, integrating, and coordinating the production and distribution of export fashion shoes from the earliest stage of order negotiation to the final stage of delivery. They oversee production processes and schedules, provide technical support, undertake quality control, and ensure punctual deliveries. In some cases, trading firms also share risks with manufacturers in fluctuating export markets. Most of all, trading companies' direct and frequent contact with international markets have made them into clearing-houses of information for innovation such as fashion trends, new production equipment, and new materials. Based on their local knowledge of industrial conditions and individual manufacturers, trading companies are crucial in helping individual manufacturers achieve economies of scope through more effective coordination of production and distribution networks.

Trading companies' close working relationships with Taiwanese shoe manufacturers on the one hand and with foreign buyers on the other have contributed to the establishment of information networks and effective coordination. Yet "inter-firm" coordination is not simply production planning and facilitative arrangements "between" individual firms in a purely technical sense. Trading companies cannot build networks by themselves. Coordination is an interactive rather than an independent operation undertaken by isolated trading companies. Trading companies are a part of the social networks that are themselves built upon the interpersonal relationships among actors in networks. Although physical and legal boundaries between firms are clearly defined, long-term interpersonal relationships among factory owners, managers, and quality inspectors of trading companies, suppliers, and subcontractors are more intertwined, and they lead to a social construction of networking and networked arrangements.

Social networks and information flows in the industry are enhanced through job hopping and high enterprise mortality and fertility. Hence, the forms of linkages among individuals change constantly. A factory owner may be an ex-employee of a trading company and may have a long-term friendship with the managers of a trading company; a quality inspector for a trading company may have been a factory owner and, therefore, is well known by many suppliers and subcontractors. Interpersonal relationships across firm boundaries constitute a basis for effective coordination between firms. In addition, mutual investment schemes and credit sales between suppliers and manufacturers are two more institutionalized mechanisms that contribute to network coordination in the industry.

This chapter is divided into two sections. The first section is devoted to the way trading companies coordinate production and marketing in Taiwan's export fashion shoe industry. The second is focused on the social base for effective coordination. I discuss job hopping and high enterprise fertility and mortality as mechanisms that facilitate the formation of interpersonal networks. I also describe the institutionalization of mutual investment and credit arrangements as ways to share risks and reinforce cooperation.

Trading Companies in Production and Marketing Networks

Trading companies are the link between Taiwan's export manufacturers and the world market. The initial impetus behind Taiwan's shoe exports in the early 1970s was provided by Mitsubishi, the leading Japanese trading firm dealing in footwear, when it decided to shift the manufacture of plastic sandals for the U.S. market from Japan to Taiwan. Thus, Taiwanese plastic shoe makers became linked to world markets through Japanese trading firms (Levy, 1991).

In 1983, there were 36,000 domestic trading companies in Taiwan (Chen, 1991).

Table 6-1. Channels of Export of Taiwanese Footwear Manufacturers (1985)

Export Channels	No. of Factories	Percentage
Direct exports by factory		
Accounted for less than 20% of total exports	131	57
Accounted for more than 20% of total exports	41	18
Accounted for more than 50% of total exports	59	26
Total number of factories	231	
Domestic trading firm as intermediary		
Accounted for less than 20% of total exports	79	11
Accounted for more than 20% of total exports	56	7
Accounted for more than 50% of total exports	611	82
Total number of factories	746	
Foreign buying office or trading firm as intermediary		
Accounted for less than 20% of total exports	182	46
Accounted for more than 20% of total exports	65	16
Accounted for more than 50% of total exports	148	38
Total number of factories	395	

Source: Taiwan Footwear Manufacturer Association and Taiwan Industry Bureau, The Ministry of Economics. Report on the Current Situation of the Shoe Industry. Taipei. 1986, pp. 90.

By 1986, the number had jumped to 65,000, about half the number of manufacturing companies in Taiwan (Liu, 1991). In the export shoe industry, as the number of export shoe manufacturers and the total volume of shoe exports increased, the number of independent shoe exporters also increased and came to dominate Taiwan's shoe exports. Sales through local trading companies are the most important marketing channel for most Taiwanese export shoe producers. According to a survey of the shoe industry in Taiwan, more than 80 percent of 844 shoe manufacturers reported that domestic trading companies handled at least 50 percent of their exports (see table 6-1). According to another survey, 72 percent of Taiwanese shoe factories sold more than half of their products through domestic trading companies; 19 percent sold more than half of their products through foreign buying offices. Only 7 percent of all surveyed companies sold directly to foreign buyers (Taiwan Shoe Manufacture Association, 1989).

   The majority of Taiwanese trading companies were small, with seven employees on average (Liu, 1991). Although there has been a lack of information on the average size of trading companies specializing in shoes, my survey shows that shoe trading companies share this general size characteristic. This is especially distinctive when comparing trading companies in Taiwan to their counterparts in South Korea (see table 6-2). As shown in table 6-2, in Taiwan, the number of export traders grew from 2,777 in 1973 to 20,597 in 1984. In that time, the average value of industrial exports per trader remained constant at $1,400,000. The number of export traders in South Korea has grown more slowly than in Taiwan, from 1,200 in 1973 to 5,300 in 1984. In that time, the average value of industrial exports per trader rose from $2,400,000 to $5,200,000. Compared to Taiwan's shoe exports, South Korean shoe exports are more concentrated in the hands of fewer exporters (Levy, 1991). One of the reasons for the concentration is that South Korea has spe-

Table 6-2. Export Trading Companies in South Korea and Taiwan, 1973–84.

	South Korea		Taiwan	
	No. of Export	Avg. Value	No. of Export	Avg. Value
1973	1,200	$2,400	2,777	$1,400
1975	1,900	2,500	4,430	1,000
1978			8,899	1,300
1980	2,300	7,000	13,320	1,300
1982	3,500	5,800	14,117	1,500
1984	5,300	5,200	20,597	1,400

Source: Levy (1991:157).

cialized in producing large-volume, brand-name athletic footwear, such as Nike and Reebok, which have a more direct route from production to marketing (Gereffi and Korzeniewicz, 1990).

In the beginning of Taiwan's shoe exportation to the United States in the 1970s, U.S. trading companies or importers bought shoes from Taiwanese manufacturers through domestic trading companies and sold them to U.S. wholesellers with an average 40 percent markup. U.S. wholesellers then distributed the shoes to domestic retailers. After a few years' experience in dealing with Taiwanese companies, the U.S. chain stores and department stores bypassed U.S. wholesellers and began to place orders directly with Taiwanese trading companies. Since the 1980s, as competition in the world market has become more demanding and U.S. and European department stores have accumulated more experience with Taiwan's manufacturing system, Western department stores have begun to trim their procurement system. Stores have set up buying offices in Taiwan to deal directly with local producers. Some large Taiwanese shoe manufacturers even have their own marketing/trading departments to deal directly with foreign buyers. Accordingly, the role of local trading companies seems to be diminishing.

However, in the women's fashion shoe segment, foreign buyers still depend on trading companies to coordinate production locally. This dependence occurs because product design changes occur much more often in the women's fashion shoe industry, and women's shoes require more complex material and component compositions and have a greater potential for quality inconsistency because of the high levels of manual work involved. United States buyers still need Taiwanese trading firms to coordinate numerous producers in the network and to undertake the tedious work of quality inspection in individual factories.

Quality Control and Punctual Delivery

From foreign buyers' point of view, major reasons to use local traders as intermediaries in purchasing are to ensure product quality and punctual delivery. This is especially true considering that the buyers are on the other side of the ocean, 6,000 miles away from production operations.

The involvement of trading companies in production may begin as early as the product development process. Generally, there is at least one shoemaker master in a trading company of eight to ten employees. The master is responsible for generating basic measurements on the basis of the sample provided by a foreign buyer. When a foreign buyer places an order with a trading company, the requirements of the order are often rather abstract, suggesting loose specifications, such as "make it tighter in the middle" or "do not make the leather surface too shiny." The trading company has to translate these requirements from English into Chinese, as well as translate the abstract description of specific requirements into technical language. They also make suggestions to manufacturers for achieving the buyer's specifications, such as "adjust the front part of the last model" or "apply a certain type of finishing or moisturizer on the leather." Manufacturers produce sample shoes for buyers to confirm shoe designs before mass production starts. To speed the process, some trading companies are given the authority to approve sample shoe designs for buyers. In product development as well, trading companies frequently share responsibilities with manufacturers in searching for and securing materials and components specified by buyers.

At the final stages of production, a trading company will send quality inspectors to partner factories to oversee the production process. Almost all of a trading company's quality inspectors have had experience in manufacturing and, as a result, they are often entrusted by foreign buyers to carry out quality inspections. Manufacturers need to obtain an inspector's signature to ship the product overseas. Therefore, if a batch is rejected, both the trading company and the manufacturer take responsibility for the loss. In formal contracts, manufacturers are typically responsible for a loss caused by a buyer's rejection of a delivery. Yet, if a delivery is rejected, trading companies will usually assist manufacturers either by finding another buyer or by negotiating with the original buyer, as a way to gain the trust of the manufacturer for longer-term collaborations.

Trading companies' quality inspectors either pay daily visits to partner factories or even live in the dormitory of the major partner's factory. (This after a majority of Taiwanese export shoe manufacturers shifted their production operations to China since the late 1980s). Quality inspectors work with production managers and technicians to ensure that each step of production—from cutting, stitching, and assembling to final packaging—is uninterrupted. Their previous experience in manufacturing provides them with sufficient technical knowledge to undertake troubleshooting on the shop floor. When there is a rush delivery, quality inspectors stay on the shop floor, even if it means staying up all night to ensure that the order is completed on time. As shoe styles become more varied and the style more complicated (i.e., more materials and component items are involved, more stitching steps, etc.), demand for quality inspection increases. In some cases, quality inspectors even have to deal with the suppliers of partner manufacturers to gain better control over the quality and delivery of materials and components.

The verb in Chinese that quality inspectors use most frequently is to *ding* the factory. It means scrutinizing with extreme care and "nailing down something with one's eyes," or "not letting one's eyes off the object." A Taiwanese quality inspector pointed out that a quality inspector's capacity to communicate, to work with local manufacturers, and to "stay in dirty factories all day long" are the reasons why foreign buyers still depend on Taiwanese traders. Since the majority of Taiwanese export shoe factories moved to China in the late 1980s, overseas buying representatives have been even less willing to go from factory to factory along the bumpy roads of rural China to inspect shoe factories, nor are they able to endure the monotony of dull evenings spent in factory dorms in the midst of rice fields. In addition, there is a linguistic barrier between local manufacturers and foreign purchasing representatives, which makes communication on the shop floor very difficult.

Quality inspectors follow daily production progress and ensure timely delivery of the order. Delivery deadlines are followed religiously in export manufacturing. A late delivery usually leads to a two-month delay in payment, and the buyer has the right to deduct a penalty totaling 5 to 10 percent of the payment. A delayed payment is a rather severe penalty for small manufacturers who have limited operating capital on hand. Trading companies usually have to share in any losses resulting from delayed delivery. Their 5 to 10 percent commission from the manufacturer is paid only after payment is received from the buyer.

Trading companies are crucial to the coordination of production and delivery schedules, because manufacturers practice just-in-time purchasing, production, and delivery. Manufacturers and their suppliers produce shoes in accordance with orders, with minimum inventories, and hence have little control over their production schedules. In the fashion industry, most orders are rush orders, and there is always a lot of anxiety over timing issues. Since production has shifted to China, there have been greater problems with the delivery and shipping of materials. To minimize losses resulting from delayed delivery, trading companies have to negotiate constantly with buyers. Trading companies push buyers to provide preliminary orders so that manufacturers can start ordering materials early. While manufacturers are waiting for the materials to arrive, buyers prepare formal, detailed orders. When the formal orders are ready, the materials are delivered right away, and final production starts immediately without having to wait another one to two weeks.

Product Design and Development

Traders and manufacturers do not have a clear-cut division of labor between marketing and production. Small factory owners play multiple roles in the factory, including management, financing, accounting, and dealing with trading companies. Therefore, shoemakers have little energy and time left over to assess what is going on outside factories and to cultivate market information. In addition, because they do not often possess the linguistic and cultural skills necessary to negotiate directly with foreign buyers, shoemakers deal with foreign customers through an intermediary: the trading company.

Manufacturers are still responsible for many complex international trading procedures, such as shipping, storage, delivery, insurance, freight handling, and customs. But trading companies' frequent contacts with foreign buyers and many different manufacturers expose them to new trends in fashion design, technology, and materials. Such exposure to timely information is particularly crucial in strengthening a firm's competitiveness in the fashion shoe industry.

Some Taiwanese trading companies have set up branch offices or affiliated firms in the United States or Europe to gather fashion information and to explore new markets. Larger trading companies may even hire designers from Europe and employ them to work with Taiwanese shoemaker masters. Although they follow the fashion trends led by Paris and Milan, like everyone else in the business, trading companies have to take the initiative in designing new styles to compete for orders. On average, only 10 to 30 percent of the styles provided by trading companies are accepted by foreign buyers, so trading companies have to develop numerous styles to capture a sufficient number of orders.

One characteristic of the "creative imitation" strategy is the low-cost reproduction of high-end products. Taiwanese fashion shoemakers seldom imitate original designs with 100 percent precision, because that would be too costly. Instead, they integrate and transform fashion concepts into their "designs." A trading company owner pointed out that the meaning of "design" in the context of the export shoe industry is "to catch the drift" of fashion trends and apply them to local production circumstances. For example, when shoes with brightly colored fabric and floral patterns were popular in Europe, Taiwanese companies designed several shoe lines with locally designed and produced colorful fabrics and patterns.

A capacity for correctly catching trends and developing new styles is critical to the competitiveness of trading companies. Naturally enough, new styles under development are commercial secrets. The sample room of a trading company is not open to competing trading companies and factories, and it is usually located far in the back of an office. Once I met the boss of a trading company when he was visiting his partner factories. The first place he visited at each factory was the sample room. He checked the kind of shoes under development as a way to be in touch with market trends and to get "inspiration."

Trading companies are also important in introducing new production techniques and materials. The introduction of the so-called "Brazilian technique" is a good example. Brazilian shoemakers have a special technique for processing leather. They apply several layers of water-based wax and a finishing called "Antico" to leather shoes, then polish the leather repeatedly until the shoes show fine grains of leather with a slight differentiation in color, giving the shoes a natural leather look. This kind of "natural and authentic-looking" shoe has been very popular in the United States and sells at a higher price. A Taiwanese export company brought several Brazilian technicians to Taiwan, who taught local manufacturers this technique. Soon many shoemakers mastered the technique and were able to produce this type of shoe at low cost.

Coordination of Interfirm Scale and Scope Economies

If economies of scope are defined as cost reductions that occur when related products run through the same institutional facilities, and economies of scale are cost savings realized through the production of large volumes of a small number of products, then theoretically there may be a trade-off between economies of scope and economies of scale (Fruin, 1992). Yet, in the case of the Taiwanese fashion shoe industry, I have observed that both scale and scope can be achieved through a hierarchy of specialization and networks of production among independent producers. It seems safe to propose that, given the small-enterprise-based structure of Taiwan's export sector, network forms of production organization in the fashion shoe industry have achieved levels of scale and economies of scope that would not be easily achieved within individual firms.

The question is not whether scope economies outweigh scale economies. Rather, it is how to achieve both economies when orders tend to be small with frequent changes in product design. This situation is close to Fruin's (1992) analysis of the Japanese enterprise system, in which economies of scope are scale economies based on plant-specific economies. In the Japanese case, the system is coordinated by effective management at different levels or organization. In Taiwan's fashion shoe industry, local trading companies coordinate interfirm networks to achieve both economies.

Trading companies have built well-entrenched networks with local manufacturers. A typical shoe trading company usually has twelve to fifteen partner manufacturers. To offset an increase in production costs associated with small production runs and limited demand for each order, trading companies coordinate and allocate orders in accordance with the specialization of individual factories (e.g., Does the factory specialize in PU or genuine leather shoes? if the latter, does the factory specialize in shoes made of pig, cow, snake, or sheep leather? pumps or flats? is the factory focused on the U.S. or European market?) to maximize interfirm economies of scale. For example, some factories specialize in the U.S. market, whereas others specialize in the Japanese or European market. Each market has its own special demands. According to the manufacturers I interviewed, U.S. women have narrower feet than European and Japanese women, and the last models used to make shoes sold in U.S. markets are narrower in the middle than those used for the shoes sold in Europe and Japan. By focusing on one specific regional market, factories prepare one type of model and therefore save on production.

Long-term relationships between trading companies and their partner factories provide traders with detailed information about partner factories. For example, trading companies usually have a clear idea about the type of last models and cutting dies that its partner manufacturers have. Traders can take into account whether a factory can work with a set of used models and cutting dies to produce a specific batch of shoes, and thus can allocate orders accordingly. If a set of used models and cutting dies can be re-used to produce a new batch, manufacturers can absorb orders as small as several hundred to one thousand pairs, and the unit price will still be competitive.

If an order requires both women's and children's shoes of the same style but of very different sizes (requiring different sets of models and cutting dies), a trading company may place the order for women's shoes in one factory and children's shoes in another. Each factory can concentrate on a segment of the order and save the cost of extra models and cutting dies. Trading companies may also sell one line of shoes to several buyers, using different colored leather or fabrics but the same set of models and cutting dies, thus realizing economies of scale through interfirm coordination.

Cost savings are not the only benefit of trading companies' coordination. Trading companies provide as information on the managerial and financial condition of manufacturing factories, especially their partner factories. Trading companies also keep track of the size and number of orders each partner factory has received from other trading companies. This helps trading companies estimate if the factories have reached the upper ceiling of their production capacity.

Trading companies require good understanding of the managerial capabilities of partner factories to assess if factories are able to deliver rush orders on time. For example, if the most competent manager of a partner factory is rumored to be planning to start his own factory, trading company management may be considering shifting orders to the new factory. Managers may also ask if the proposed factory has the necessary support from its suppliers to ensure punctual deliveries of materials, and thus punctual deliveries of final products. According to the manager of a trading company, even gossip about owner's having a mistress can be a valuable piece of information, because that may affect a company's financial situation and the credit worthiness of a factory owner. In short, timely information helps trading companies allocate orders to factories that will result in the highest quality product appearing in the least amount of time.

Risk Sharing

According to international trading rules, immediately after the order is placed, foreign buyers should deposit a Letter of Credit (L/C) in a bank for the entire payment owed to the manufacturer. The manufacturer then orders materials after receiving the L/C. Practice in the Taiwanese export shoe industry, however, has been that buyers do not deposit L/Cs until two weeks before delivery dates. Manufacturers have to order materials and start production before the L/Cs are received. If the market reaction to a style is not as good as predicted, buyers might cancel orders even after production has started. Order cancellations happen more often during market downturns. A factory owner told me that he had at least three orders canceled a year, each cancelled order worth from $100,000 to $200,000, amounting to 7 to 14 percent of annual sales. In another case, a small company went bankrupt because a single order was canceled, and the owner is now working for an export firm as a quality inspector. Increasingly rigorous competition in world markets has also made foreign buyers tougher with manufacturers on delivery times and quality. Any delay or defect can lead to a rejection of an entire order.

Generally speaking, trading companies' risks are not as high as manufacturers'. Their profits are based mainly on commissions, and hence they have little fixed investment. Even shoes rejected on the basis of quality may be saleable. When an order has been rejected, trading firms may cycle export clothes and shoes into the underground economy. It is part of urban night life in Taiwan to go shopping in streets filled with vendors selling rejected export clothes in front of department stores. There are also special discount stores that sell rejected export clothes and shoes at low prices.

In these ways, trading companies do not share fully in losses from order cancellations or rejections. Manufacturers pay a 5 percent commission fee one month after an order is delivered, no matter what happens later. However, because most orders are placed through trading companies, they help factories minimize losses, either by searching for other buyers or by negotiating with the original buyer. To minimize its own risk even more, especially when the chances of order rejections or penalties are high (e.g., rush orders), trading companies may place orders with two different factories without informing either factory that they have competitors. Then trading companies accept the output from the manufacturer who completes the order first and cancels the order with the other manufacturer, using an excuse of poor quality or late delivery as a reason for cancellation.

Social Networks and Interfirm Coordination

As mentioned previously, trading companies are at the center of Taiwan's export fashion shoe industry informational networks, which provide the basis for effective coordination in the industry. Coordination effectiveness is the result of long-term relations between individuals in the industry, and it is not limited by the boundaries of companies. Indeed, long-term relationships are not always conflict free and they do not necessarily guarantee cooperation among firms. In fact, competition between firms has always been fierce. However, social networks serve as one of the most valuable sources of background information on the individuals with whom one is dealing—be they competitors or partners.

Effective coordination and cooperation are not simply based on things as arbitrary as personality and interpersonal relationships. Other mechanisms have been built in with the intention of ensuring more consistent network functioning. The following discussion is focused on the mechanisms that have contributed to the formation and effective operation of interpersonal networks in the fashion shoe industry in Taiwan. I begin with high enterprise mortality and fertility, as well as job hopping, which lead to constant personnel flows among firms and, unintentionally, to a tight social circle of experienced entrepreneurs in the industry. Then, I turn to more institutionalized mechanisms, such as mutual investment and credit sales of merchandise, which represent mechanisms for engendering mutual trust and risk sharing between suppliers and manufacturers.

Flows of Personnel Among Firms and
Interpersonal Relationships Across Firms

High enterprise fertility and mortality result in frequent personnel flows among firms in Taiwan's export shoe industry. When a factory goes bankrupt, the owner may work for another factory as a manager or for a trading company as a quality inspector, and then experienced factory managers or quality inspectors often start independent subcontracting operations after they have accumulated sufficient social capital in industrial networks. Furthermore, weak ties between employers and employees in most small- and medium-sized firms encourage frequent job hopping.

The prevalence of family-based enterprises in Taiwan also has a destabilizing effect in the industry. One reason is that non-family members in family-based companies have a lower chance of being promoted to key positions, and so they tend to change companies frequently as a way to move up the career ladder. The popularity of diversification strategies in Taiwan has an effect. As a company diversifies into various segments of the same industry or even into different industries, employees have ample opportunities to move to different companies. For a detailed analysis see Shieh (1992), Liu (1990), and Greenhalgh (1988).

Job Hopping

In a small- to medium-sized firm, a group of senior managers compose the *bandi* of the firm. *Bandi* are the inner circle of the company and form an important support group around the boss. They share in the work of daily operations on the shop floor as well as in administrative matters. *Bandi* members have expertise in a variety of fields, such as production management, product development, manufacturing technologies, personnel management, financing, and marketing. Some may also possess strong personal connections with trading companies. Some *bandi* may be family members of the boss, but many have simply developed a patronage relationship with the boss after working for the company for a long time. Liu (1991) described the *bandi* phenomenon as the basis for a "quasi family" type of organization in Taiwanese small- and medium-sized firms. Given the important role that *bandi* members play, the boss is understandably concerned with the danger of losing them to other companies. Bonus systems and senior-level profit-sharing schemes are used to keep *bandi* on board. Not surprisingly, competent *bandi* technicians and managers are sought after by other firms. Firms will "dig the base of another's wall," by luring away the *bandi* of other companies with lucrative salaries and benefits. Competition for competent managers and technicians generates tension between firms.

Since production has shifted to China, there has been an increasing demand for experienced factory and trading company managers. "Digging at the base" has become ever more intense. In summer 1992, a quality inspector told me that when he met with his business friends after the New Year, there are always rounds of business card exchange among old friends. Because Chinese New Year marks the end and beginning of business years, most people receive their end-of-year bonus and then change their jobs after New Year. The exchange of business cards during the reunion allows everyone to keep track of who is going where in the new year.

Changing jobs is also a way to expand experience in different industrial sectors. Quality inspectors in trading companies and manager/technicians in manufacturing firms are constantly changing jobs—not only between firms of the same sort but also between trading and manufacturing firms. In fact, it is a prerequisite for trading company quality inspectors to have production experience in manufacturing. Managers with export business experience are also in demand by manufacturing firms.

Job hopping may seem damaging to individual firms. Yet a constant flow of personnel between firms results in closer interpersonal relationships in the industry as a whole. Such relationships extend beyond the boundaries of individual firms, which in turn facilitate interfirm coordination. Not all previous relationships are pleasant ones, nor will personnel relationships necessarily influence substantial business matters. As one shoe factory manager put it, "if I am dealing with someone I have known from before, I will at least have a better idea about this person's history and personality, and such information helps me to determine my negotiation attitude and business strategies." In another case, a factory owner learned the price that a partner trading company had offered his competitor. This helped him prepare his bid for a shoe order.

Job hopping also facilitates the flows of information regarding new technologies, fashion trends, and new marketing channels. In the case of the "Brazilian technique," when it was first introduced in Taiwan, it was a business secret. But it spread quickly once it was introduced at a few selected manufacturers. The process was not very complicated, and the key material, Antico, quickly became commercially available. Most of all, interpersonal relationships in the industry make it difficult to keep any secrets, and job hopping facilitates the flow of technology from one firm to another.

High Enterprise Fertility and Mortality

The high fertility and mortality of small firms also contribute to the flow of personnel among firms. Shei (1992), in a sociological study of Taiwan's subcontracting system, suggests that the ideology of "everyone can be a boss if one works hard enough" and the mentality that "it is better to be a chicken head than an ox's tail" explains the high growth and failure rates of small- and medium-sized enterprises. The Taiwanese fashion shoe industry well represents such a trend.

The entry threshold for starting a business is low. Initial capital can be as low as $500,000. Experienced managers in trading companies and manufacturing firms accumulate sufficient monetary and human capital (by organizing their own *bandi* and partners), identify promising sources of orders, and spin off and start their own companies as independent assemblers or subcontractors.

However, the industry's high fertility is accompanied by high mortality. Owners of failed factories then work for other manufacturers or trading companies as managers or quality inspectors. More than half of the Taiwanese factory managers and quality inspectors I interviewed in southern China and Taiwan used to have their own businesses. They all had stories about their experiences with trading companies, customers, material suppliers, and so on. High enterprise mortality resulted in the formation of a pool of managers/entrepreneurs with wide experience in the trade. Their areas of expertise included production management, marketing, finance, quality control, export-import regulations and procedures, machinery maintenance, and technical troubleshooting on the shop floor. A pool of experienced managers/entrepreneurs and their extensive personal contacts in the industry further facilitated an interaction between different segments of the industry.

The following case study illustrated the way interpersonal networks are developed in Taiwan's fashion shoe industry. An 800-worker shoe company, Dali, had two owners, Wang and Chen. (The names of firms and owners are fictitious.) Wang used to work for a shoe trading company as a quality inspector; he switched to a large shoe factory as a manager seven years ago. Wang's industrial experience helped him to establish good relationships with foreign buyers and other trading companies. After working for the family-based factory for seven years, however, he felt that further advancement in the factory was blocked because he is not part of the family owning the firm.

The other partner of Dali, Chen, used to work in a family-based sole factory started by his father. There had been serious tension among three brothers who ran the family firm. Chen then decided to start an independent shoe-manufacturing venture. Chen knew Wang because the family firm was a long-time supplier to the factory for which Wang used to work. Just as Chen was planning to establish a new firm, Wang was ready to make a career move. Wang's experience in shoe manufacturing and marketing would complement Chen's capital and ownership experience. A partnership between Wang and Chen was thus established. They first talked to a trading company, Wenji, to secure a sufficient number of orders, and a new firm, Dali Shoe Company, was established in 1986. They each owned half of Dali's shares.

Wenji was also a newly established company. The owner of Wenji is a Japanese who worked as a purchasing representative for a U.S. shoe trading company, Metro, in Taiwan for more than 10 years. Wenji had two other partners. One was a U.S. colleague who headed Metro's marketing department in the United States; the other was a Taiwanese woman who was experienced with Taiwanese manufacturing companies. Thus, the newly established Wenji Trading Company had marketing and information-gathering channels in the United States and manufacturing experience in Taiwan. Wenji needed a reliable manufacturing partner that was committed to Wenji and was willing to give it top delivery priority during peak season. The Dali Shoe Company was ideal in these respects. In addition, Dali, a new firm itself, was desperately in need of stable orders. As a result, 90 percent of Dali's first orders came from Wenji. After three years, Dali began to seek orders from other trading companies. By capitalizing on Wang's interpersonal connections, and by proving their capability to produce complicated shoe styles, by 1991, Dali reduced the percentage of their orders form Wenji from 90 percent to 60 percent.

Interpersonal contacts did not directly result in lucrative orders, as Wang explained to me. Instead, *interpersonal connections* helped to bring customers to the door, but only good-quality shoes help a company maintain a stable source of orders. In other words, if Wang wanted to start a business relationship with another trading company, he would invite the purchasing manager to dinner by getting an old friend who worked in the trading company to issue an invitation. After sending some follow-up gifts to the manager of the trading company, he might receive a small order from that company. This was his opportunity to impress both the trading company and its U.S. buyer with his high-quality products and punctual delivery.

Sales of Merchandise on Credit and
Mutual Investment Between Suppliers
and Manufacturers

Sales of merchandise on credit are common. Manufacturers purchase materials and parts on credit and pay for them only after they are paid for the finished products. Accordingly, suppliers share losses with manufacturers if an order is canceled or payment delayed. Suppliers are not supposed to issue the invoice to manufacturers for at least one month after the merchandise has been delivered. A manufacturer sends a pay voucher to a supplier three to four weeks after the invoice has been issued. A check that can be cashed within a week is considered as good as cash, and a manufacturer can receive a 3–5-percent discount for paying in a timely manner. Typically, suppliers have to wait at least two months for payment after materials have been delivered, and often, major negotiations are required to ensure that payments can be collected in two months.[1]

In many cases, suppliers have to wait another three months before checks can be cashed. If an order is canceled or batch rejected, suppliers have to wait as long as half a year before a check can be cashed. As competition intensifies and markets become more unpredictable, cancellations and delayed payments increase. For better or for worse, suppliers and manufacturers are inextricably linked by such risk-sharing mechanisms.

Credit sales are not normally supported by legally valid contracts. Instead, sales are based on the creditability of manufacturers and cooperation between suppliers and manufacturers. If manufacturers lose creditability with suppliers, they will not be able to get materials from suppliers on credit. Then they have to use some other manufacturer's account to obtain materials. Credit complications inevitably slow the production process.

Joint investment is another common practice for building cooperation between suppliers and manufacturers. For suppliers, investing in partner manufacturing firms ensures more stable sources and timely payments. It also opens information channels regarding a partner's financial conditions. For manufacturers, investing in suppliers helps ensure delivery priority. Joint investments by shoe manufacturers and leather tanneries are an example. Because the supply of leather is very unstable, especially during rush periods, manufacturers hold some shares in a tannery to secure a priority position in leather supply and to purchase supplies on long-term credit.

However, joint investment is less popular between trading companies and manufacturers. For trading firms, nevertheless, holding shares in a partner manufacturing firm gives them more bargaining power when negotiating with buyers. Negotiations are faster and more direct. Investment in manufacturing firms by trading companies enhances a manufacturer's trust in a trader and may secure priority deliveries.

But the disadvantages of investing in partner manufacturers usually outweigh these advantages. To increase sales and achieve economies of scale, small, specialized firms should build connections with as many customers and firms as possible, while at the same time not becoming too involved with any single company (Granovetter, 1973). The key to establishing a network is a subtle balance between intimacy and distance among firms. Inspection of partner factories by trading companies requires a certain distance and independence between the parties, and financial involvement in partner manufacturing firms will inevitably diminish the former's objectivity in performing quality inspections. A quality inspector of a trading company, for example, complained to me that one of their partner manufacturers had become rather uncooperative and reluctant to accept his suggestions on quality improvement. The quality inspector refused to sign an approval for an order that did not meet quality standards. The manufacturing firm's owner threatened to call the inspector's boss, claiming that a loss to the manufacturer would also be a loss to the trader. The conflict damaged the relationship between the two firms, affecting the ability of the two firms to interact effectively.

A trading company usually has more than ten partner manufacturers. To win the support and trust of these partners, it is important for trading firms to appear to be fair with all partner manufacturers. Being fair means that trading firms will not favor particular manufacturing firms by ordering at higher prices or larger volumes. If a trading company is a shareholder in a partner manufacturing firms, other manufacturers will inevitably suspect the trading company of bias, and their trust in the trading company will be shaken. A reputation for being unfair will weaken a trading company's capacity to mobilize and coordinate manufacturers. As a consequence, it will be more difficult to absorb rush orders, respond quickly to design changes, and deliver high-quality products on time. Maintaining connections with all kinds of factories in order to widen the range of available products is an important cornerstone of every trading company's strategy.

On the other hand, trading companies need a small number of highly reliable manufacturers. During the peak season when factories have more orders than they can handle or when rush orders are forcing reschedulings, a "balanced" relationship is needed for trading firms to secure production priority from partner factories. The strategy of most trading firms is to establish special partnerships with a limited number of core partner manufacturers in its business network.

The importance of maintaining a well-balanced relationship with all partner manufacturers also holds true the other way around; manufacturers usually have more than one partner trading company. If manufacturers own shares in a trading company, other trading companies believe the manufacturer will give top priority to its partner company's rush orders, to the detriment of other trading companies. So, other trading companies lose confidence in this manufacturer and are reluctant to send profitable orders in its direction. Mutual shareholding may make it more difficult for both sides to establish good working relationships with other companies in the network.

Conclusion

Based on this examination of Taiwan's export fashion shoe industry, there appear to be two critical factors for interfirm networks to work effectively. One is the existence of coordinating agents—in this case, trading companies. The other is strong social ties underlying the mechanics of network coordination.

The key to network coordination in Taiwan's fashion shoe industry is the effective management of information at both macro and micro levels. Keeping domestic shoemakers informed about rapidly changing fashion trends and technologies depends on trading companies' connections with international markets. This is particularly important in the case of small- and medium-sized Taiwanese shoe manufacturers because of their limited organizational capacity to collect such information. Trading companies, for their part, generally have updated local knowledge concerning the financial, managerial, and technical conditions of individual manufacturers. This helps them plan and even accelerate production processes in a highly segmented division of labor. Based on such information, trading companies can place orders with specialized manufacturers to achieve network economies of scope. This is particularly important for the fashion shoe industry, because most orders are for small volumes and a large number of styles. Because of effective network coordination, Taiwan's fashion shoe industry is able to compete in time, quality, and price in the world market.

Trading companies do not orchestrate networks like a conductor. Rather, along with other actors in the networks, they are parts of a social network of interpersonal ties. Long-term relations between individuals, rather than companies, facilitate a flow of information and coordination among producers and between producers and traders. In this chapter, I have suggested that some of the institutional bases of these networks are mutual investment schemes between suppliers and manufacturers, risk sharing embedded in a system of credit sales, and an interfirm flow of personnel through job hopping and high enterprise mortality and fertility. High turnover is destabilizing for individual firms, but for the industry as a whole, it has a positive, (though unintended) effect of building tight interpersonal connections across company boundaries.

Other culturally informed business practices that have facilitated the establishment of trust between network actors will be examined in future research. It is common, for example, to establish a "brotherhood" among suppliers, manufacturers, contractors, and subcontractors, as a way of securing mutual support. It would be useful to find out how and in what ways "brothers" enhance network operations. Compared with Japanese trading companies that are also deeply involved in production organization and risk sharing (Yoshino and Lifson, 1986; Sheard, 1989), Taiwanese trading firms seem to have similar functions but much looser institutional rules and requirements. Perhaps this is because the particularistic ties that link network members are more relation-based (including fictive relations) in Taiwan and more information-based in Japan (see Yamagishi and Yamagishi in this volume). Comparative studies of trading companies will help us better understand the governance of interfirm networks.

Note

1. Chen Jie-shuen's (1991) research on subject matter experts (SMEs) describes the culture of payment collection. A representative of the supplier firm visits the manufacturing firm many times before he can collect. He might be blocked by all kinds of excuses: company accountant is sick; the check requires the signature of the president of the firm, who happens to be in the United States with his buyer; or the company found some defects in the materials, so they cannot pay the full amount—maybe 15 percent less. After all kinds of trouble and delays, payment is made, but it is rarely the amount that was originally agreed upon.

Acknowledgments   I benefited tremendously from discussions with Mark Fruin, AnnaLee Saxenian, and Paul Sheard. I also thank the National Science Foundation in the United States and the Institute of East Asian Studies at the University of California at Berkeley for providing the research grants for the project on Taiwanese manufacturing investment in Southern China. This chapter is a part of the results of the project.

References

Chen, J. *Social and economic characteristics of the small- and medium-sized enterprises in Taiwan.* Ph.D. diss. Graduate School of Sociology, Dong-hai University, Taiwan.

Fruin, W. M. *The Japanese Enterprise System: Competitive Strategies and Cooperative structures.* Oxford: Oxford UP.

Gereffi, G., & Korzeniewicz, M. Commodity chains and footwear exports in the semiperiphery. In W. G. Martin (Ed.), *Semiperipheral states in the world economy* (pp. 45–68). New York: Greenwood.

Greenhalgh, S. Families and networks in Taiwan's economic development. In E. Winckler & S. Greenhalgh (Eds.), *Contending Approaches to the Political Economy of Taiwan* (pp. 224–45). New York: M. E. Sharpe.

Levy, B. "Transactions Costs, the Size of Firms and Industrial Policy: Lesson From a Comparative Case Study of the Footwear Industry in Korea and Taiwan." *Journal of Development Economics*, 34 (1991): 151–78.

Liu, J. "Taiwanese Small- and Medium-Sized Enterprises and International Division of Labor. Trans. L. Huiying *Taiwan Research Quarterly* (Xiamen) 1 (1991): 25–40.

Liu, J. Taiwanese Small- and Medium-Sized Enterprises and International Division of Labor. Trans. L. Huiying *Taiwan Research Quarterly* (Xiamen) 2/3 (1990): 45–54.

Liu, J. Taiwanese "Small- and Medium-Sized Enterprises and International Division of Labor. Trans. L. Huiying *Taiwan Research Quarterly* (Xiamen) 4 (1990): 83–92.

Sheard, P. The Japanese General Trading Company as an Aspect of Interfirm Risk-sharing. *Journal of the Japanese and International Economies*, 3 (1989): 308–22.

Shieh, G. S. *"Boss" Island: The Subcontracting Network and Microentrepreneurship in Taiwan's Development.* New York: Peter Lang, 1992.

Taiwan Footwear Industry Association and Taiwan Industry Bureau, The Ministry of Economics. *Report on productivity improvement of traditional industries: The footwear industry.* Taiwan Footwear Industry Association and Taiwan Industry Bureau, 1990.

Taiwan Shoe Manufacture Association. *Thirty Years of Taiwan's Shoe Industry.* Taipei: Taiwan Shoe Manufacture Association, 1989.

Yoshino, M. Y., and T. Lifson. *The Invisible Link: Japan's Sogo Shosha and the Organization of Trade.* Cambridge, Mass.: MIT Press, 1986.

7

Education as a Source of Network, Signal, or Nepotism

Managers and Engineers during Japan's Industrial Development

HIROYUKI ODAGIRI

A recurrent theme in Japan's industrial development is how its labor market evolved and operated, particularly at the level of administrators, management staff, technicians, and engineers. In the early years of Japan's modernization, say, in the mid- to late nineteenth century, only a handful of Japanese had the required knowledge and experience. Furthermore, it was often difficult for prospective employers to know where to find qualified people.

An employer's search for those with expertise and workers' search for jobs were made in a yet undeveloped and uninformed market. At the start of Japan's industrialization, as a result, the most common method of recruitment was for employers to use their former co-workers and other acquaintances, such as *samurai* (warriors and officials) from the same *han* (clan or local government under the feudal system during the Tokugawa Era, 1603–1867). As a few people became known to have particularly valuable information, many employers and prospective employees started to seek information from them. Like matchmakers (*nakodo*) in arranged marriages (*miai kekkon*), these information keepers acted as hubs of an information network. Shibusawa Eiichi, a businessman, and Fukuzawa Yukichi, an educator, are two well-known cases. (Following the Japanese convention, the surnames appear first.)

As the system of higher education became established, schools, particularly colleges and universities, started to play similar roles. For example, employers often hired their former classmates and others they came to know during school years. Schools also started to send signals; people assumed that a graduate from a certain department or a certain university must have a certain sort of knowledge and ability. Schools then started to function as a hub of informational and human networks as well as a provider of signals, in addition to their original role as educational institutions.

When people came to rely excessively on educational background as a sign of knowledge and experience, however, school or academic nepotism (*gakureki*-ism) resulted. In this chapter, I describe the historical development of the role of schools as networks of information. *Schools* indicates various higher educational institutions.

The Development of Engineering Education in the Late Nineteenth Century

Japan's effort to industrialize started after the end of Seclusionism in 1854, which, for more than two centuries, had prohibited relations with foreign countries other than China, Korea, and the Netherlands. In the Meiji Restoration of 1867, lower ranked, young *samurai* of western provinces overthrew the rule of the Tokugawa Shogunate (*bakufu*) and established a new government with Emperor Meiji as the head of the State. The tasks facing this new government were enormous. It had to draft a new constitution and create new judicial, military, educational, communication, transportation, financial, and business systems. Naturally, the need for knowledgeable and experienced people was urgent in every field and at every level. The country needed people with knowledge of the political, social, and scientific systems of the West; it also needed people with the capacity to manage.

The government hired foreigners and sent Japanese students to the United States and Europe. At the peak of 1875, the number of hired foreigners was 527, including 205 engineers and 144 teachers (Nippon Kagaku-Shi Gakkai, 1964). Some of these foreigners received exorbitant salaries; for instance, one foreigner was paid 2,000 yen when the Prime Minister (*Dajo Daijin*) himself earned only 800 yen (Yuasa, 1980). Such high salaries indicated the value the Japanese government placed on the knowledge and expertise these people were expected to bring.

To deal with daily administration, the government often relied on the officials of the former government, whether at the central *bakufu* level or at the local *han* level. For example, among the 704 personnel of the Ministry of Finance in 1870, 328 (47 percent) were former *bakufu* officials (Uemura, 1974). In view of the antagonistic relationship between the people who eventually came to lead the Meiji government and the *bakufu*, the large proportion of ex-*bakufu* officials in the new government is a testimony to its desperate need for experienced people.

The government was, of course, keenly aware of the need to cultivate people, particularly the younger generation, so that they could replace the foreign advisors and those with obsolete skills. Thus, one of the Meiji government's priorities was to establish an educational system, both at the elementary and higher levels.

Higher-level education was by no means absent during the Tokugawa era. In addition to public institutions, most of which taught purely Japanese or Chinese studies such as Confucianism, there were a few private schools teaching medical sciences using Dutch books. The best known of these schools was Tekijuku in Osaka, taught by Ogata Koan, who had learned Dutch medical science in Nagasaki. Among his students were Ohmura Masujiro, who later designed the Meiji military system (but was assassinated before the system was completed), and Fukuzawa Yukichi, who later spent a year in Europe and then introduced Western democratic thought to Japan. In 1868, Fukuzawa started a school to teach Western thought, including economics and business. He named it Keio, which later became one of Japan's first private universities.

Toward the end of its regime, the Tokugawa government made a few efforts to teach Western science. Only after the Restoration, however, were full efforts made to teach science and engineering in higher-level institutions. I will concentrate on engineering education, because Japan's success in playing technological catch up was the most important factor in its rapid industrial development.

Kobusho (the Ministry of Industries) hired a British citizen, Henry Dyer, to plan an engineering college. In 1873, Kogakuryo (Imperial College of Engineering) was established with Dyer's curriculum and with eight British staff (five professors, a modeler, and two assistants), in addition to Dyer. In the first year, the school admitted fifty-two students between fifteen to eighteen years old for a six-year course. The school offered studies in seven fields and, between 1879 and 1885, produced 211 graduates. The number of graduates by field were civil engineering, 45; mechanical engineering, 39; telegraphy, 21; architecture, 20; practical chemistry, 25; mining, 48; and metallurgy, 5. Later, shipbuilding was added, and eight students graduated. The eagerness and high quality of both the faculty and the students made the college successful. It hired more foreign (mostly British) professors and then, beginning in 1882, replaced them with its Japanese graduates. One of the first replacements was Fujioka Ichisuke, who would later become one of the founders of Toshiba (Odagiri & Goto, 1996).

Kogakuryo was renamed Kobu Daigakko in 1877 and then, in 1886, was merged with the Department of Technology at the University of Tokyo. This department was originally established by the Tokugawa government to teach science and technology with the help of Dutch, French, and German advisors and teachers. The merger resulted in the Engineering Department of Tokyo Imperial University (now the University of Tokyo), which had a three-year course instead of Kogakuryo's six-year curriculum. The college and the university produced graduates who later founded many major Japanese manufacturing companies.

The program at Kogakuryo emphasized an interaction between classroom studies and on-site training at laboratories and works within the college and Kobusho. Dyer's originality should be noted, because this balance between the academic and practical aspects of education was lacking in European schools at the time. Dyer left in 1882 to return to Glasgow, where he tried to introduce a similar engineering education program in a new technical college. Apparently, the Japanese government emphasized practical engineering education at the time when more developed countries regarded learning pure science as superior to engineering. Even in Germany, where technical education was more accepted than in England, practical engineering was taught in technical schools (*Hochschule*) but not in universities, which were the "centres 'for scholarship and knowledge'" (Locke, 1993, p. 61). This environment gave Dyer an opportunity to experiment with his ideas on engineering education and, with his Japanese experience, he persuaded his fellow Scotsmen of the importance of engineering education.

That the college was supported by the Ministry of Industries also helped Dyer's objective. The facilities at the Ministry could be used, and the students received a scholarship on the condition that they would work at the Ministry for several years after graduation. Hence, students were eager to learn practical knowledge. Merging with the Imperial University implied the loss of this connection with the Ministry, because the college came under the authority of the Mombusho (Ministry of Education). As a result, a shift occurred from practice to academia, according to Miyoshi (1979).

Tokyo Imperial University was the only national university until 1897, when Kyoto Imperial University (now Kyoto University) was established. In addition, Tokyo Shokuko Gakko was established as a practical technical school in 1881. It later became Tokyo Kogyo Gakko and then the Tokyo Institute of Technology. It offered a three-year course (plus a one-year preparatory course) in chemical engineering and mechanical engineering.

For business education, Tokyo Koto Shogyo Gakko (the predecessor to Hitotsubashi University) was established in 1885. Private colleges were also established during the nineteenth century. In addition to Keio, the predecessors of Hosei, Senshu, Meiji, Waseda, and Chuo universities were established during 1879 to 1885. All of these mainly taught law.

Managers' Educational Background before World War II

These universities—especially Keio, Tokyo, and their predecessors such as Kogakuryo—supplied a dominant share of managers to the business community in Meiji Japan. Ishikawa (1974) studied businesspeople (*Jitsugyoka*) born before 1869 and listed in a "Who's Who." Of the 246 whose educational background was known, 172 received formal education after the Meiji Restoration. Of these 172, 45 (26.2 percent) were graduated from Keio and 34 (19.8 percent) from Tokyo. Thirteen of these 34 studied law and 8, engineering. In terms of industrial distribution, the number of Tokyo graduates was disproportionately large in mining, banking, electric power and equipment, and chemicals, including pharmaceuticals, whereas the number of graduates of Keio was disproportionately large in banking, insurance, transportation, and textiles.

Morikawa (1973) studied 170 professional managers of large firms in the Meiji Era. By *professional managers*, he meant full-time directors who did not have a major share in ownership at the time they joined the firm. He found that 115 (67.6 percent) received higher education; 51 were graduated from Tokyo and its predecessors and 28 from Keio. Of those from Tokyo, 24 had studied law and 21, engineering. He also found that the proportion of those who had studied science and engineering was lower in *zaibatsu* companies (18.2 percent) than in non-*zaibatsu* companies (42.6 percent).

The significance of Tokyo graduates increased in later years. Morikawa (1975) studied 1,415 managers who became directors by 1941 in 243 firms in the machinery, shipbuilding, electrical equipment, and chemical, cement and glass, mining, metal, textile, food, and construction industries. Each person is counted only once, no matter how many firms had him as a director. The total number of directorships was 1,644. Of these, 530 directors (37.5 percent) had an educational background in the natural sciences and engineering (including a few in medical and agricultural sciences). Of this number, 257 (48.5 percent) had been graduated from the Engineering Department of the University of Tokyo or its predecessors; 63 (11.9 percent) from the Tokyo Institute of Technology; and 57 (10.8 percent) from the engineering departments of other Imperial Universities (Kyoto, Tohoku, Kyushu, Osaka, and Nagoya). Managers in these studies are limited to those in big companies that represent emerging modern industries; therefore, the significance of university graduates, particularly those of Tokyo graduates, is overvalued. There must have been many less well-educated entrepreneurs in small-scale or more traditional businesses, but no data are available.

Morikawa (1975) cited Hitachi as the most obvious case of the dominance of engineer-managers and Tokyo graduates. Hitachi had eleven directors until 1941, headed by the founder, Odaira Namihei. All except one, including Odaira, had been graduated from the Engineering Department of the University of Tokyo. It is noteworthy that, to a lesser extent, Tokyo graduates and engineers are still dominant at Hitachi's board of directors. In 1980, of the twenty-five directors, eleven were graduates from Tokyo's Engineering Department, four were from Tokyo's other departments (science, law, and economics), four were from the engineering departments of other national universities, one was from a technical school, and four were from commerce schools. In 1991, of the thirty-five directors, nine were from Tokyo's Engineering Department, five were from Tokyo's Law and Economics Departments, and fifteen were from the engineering departments of other universities (only one from a private university and the rest from national universities, including the Tokyo Institute of Technology).

One of Hitachi's original directors was Aikawa Yoshisuke, the founder of the Nissan Conglomerate, which comprised Nissan Motor, Hitachi, and other businesses in mining, steel, shipbuilding, fishing, and so forth. The Nissan Conglomerate, like other conglomerates (including *zaibatsu*), was disbanded under the influence of postwar economic reforms. Nevertheless, Hitachi and Nissan still cooperate in some business activities, because Nissan buys some of its auto parts from Hitachi, for example. However, the relationship is by no means strong, and neither of these two companies is among the ten largest shareholders of the other.

The Cases of Nissan and Toyota

Among Japanese automobile manufacturers, Nissan and Toyota are the oldest next only to Isuzu, although they were hardly the pioneers of the industry. Several pioneering efforts were made in the first decade of this century, whereas Nissan and Toyota started production in 1931 and 1935, respectively. The most prominent and persistent early effort was made by Hashimoto Masujiro. He studied at the Tokyo Institute of Technology and, after two years of working in a mining company, went to the United States for three years on a scholarship from the Japanese government, where he worked and studied in a steam-engine manufacturing company. In 1911, after coming back from the United States and working for a couple of Japanese companies, he established Kaishinsha with the intention of manufacturing automobiles. After three years of struggle, he succeeded in manufacturing a passenger car, Dat, using mostly domestic components. However, Kaishinsha suffered from competition with cheaper and more reliable Fords, General Motors (GM), and other imports, and the company could sell only seven Dats by 1917.

Another early effort was made by Kubota Gonshiro, who, without formal education, founded Kubota, which became the top maker of agricultural machinery and cast-iron pipes. With the cooperation of his brother Atsujiro, a graduate from

Osaka Koto Kogyo (now the engineering department of Osaka University), Kubota established Jitsuyo Jidosha in Osaka in 1919 to sell three-wheel cars (designed by an American, William Gorham). Gorham designed the plant, ordered equipment and some components from the United States, and hired more Americans to help guide inexperienced Japanese workers. Although the auto plant had the capacity to produce fifty units per month, the company could sell only 150 units in its first year. Gorham then designed a four-wheel model, but, against the competition from foreign models, the company could sell only about 100 units.

The passenger car business of both Hashimoto's Kaishinsha and Kubota's Jitsuyo Jidosha were eventually acquired by Tobata Casting, which had been founded by Aikawa Yoshisuke. Aikawa, after graduating from the engineering department of the University of Tokyo, went to the United States to learn black-hearted iron casting. He worked as an apprentice and in 1910, after returning to Japan, founded Tobata Casting to manufacture cast-iron tubing and other products using the technology he had learned. Because the products were suitable as components for cars, the company started supplying products to Ishikawajima Zosen (which was making trucks at the time), Kaishinsha, and the Japanese plants of Ford and GM. Tobata Casting thus accumulated knowledge about the automobile industry. After acquiring Kaishinsha and Jitsuyo Jidosha, Aikawa decided to sell a new, smaller model of a passenger car, named Datsun, which was developed by Gorham and his Japanese colleagues. In 1933, that business became Nissan Jidosha (Nissan Motor), as a subsidiary of the Nippon Sangyo holding company and Tobata Casting.

Morikawa (1975) listed the directors of Tobata Casting as Aikawa, Murakami Shosuke, Tsukamoto Usaburo, Yano Yoshiaki, Motogi Tadashi, Kudo Haruhito, and Fujita Seisuke. Tsukamoto and Motogi were classmates of Aikawa at Tokyo's Engineering Department (with mechanical engineering majors) and were invited to join the company from Nippon Seikosho (Japan Steel Works) and Niigata Tekkosho (Niigata Engineering), respectively. This is a good example of the use of a network of school graduates to attract talented people in a newly emerging company. Murakami, Yano, and Kudo had studied mechanical engineering at Kyoto, suggesting the use of another network, and Fujita, a graduate of the Science Department of Kyoto, was Aikawa's younger brother. The directors at Nissan were Aikawa, Yamashita Okiie, Asahara Genshichi, Watanabe Jusuke, Kudo (also a director at Tobata Casting), and Kubota Atsujiro, in addition to two others who had nontechnological backgrounds. Yamashita, Watanabe, and Asahara were all graduates from Tokyo, where the first two studied engineering and the latter studied science. Watanabe was Aikawa's classmate.

This brief history of Nissan illustrates two points. First, Aikawa's Nissan Group placed a heavy emphasis on technological aspects of business and hired many managers with science and technology backgrounds. This occurred not only at Tobata Casting and Nissan Motor, but also in other Nissan group companies, most notably Hitachi. Second, to find people with technological knowledge, Aikawa relied heavily on his school relationships. He used these relationships to locate available employees and to assess their potential.

Toyoda Kiichiro, the founder of Toyota Motor, was also a graduate of Tokyo's Engineering Department (with a mechanical engineering major). Kiichiro was a son of

Toyoda Sakichi, a famous inventor of automatic looms and a founder of Toyota Automatic Loom. (Sakichi was self-taught, did not trust the value of formal education, and apparently was unhappy about his son going to the University of Tokyo). After Sakichi's death, Kiichiro entered the carmaking business and recruited people with knowledge of related technologies.

Kiichiro recruited Suga Takatoshi, who had been working to develop an engine; Fukada Benzo, who had been running a tool factory; Ikenaga Higuma, who had been designing a vehicle; Ito Shogo, who had been developing a three-wheel car; and Ohno Shuji, who had been running a springmaking factory, suggesting that intercompany mobility was not especially low in prewar Japan. Although Toyota's company history (Toyota Motor, 1967) did not disclose these managers' educational background, except to say that Ito was Kiichiro's high school and university friend, all clearly had engineering knowledge. Kiichiro also recruited Saito Shoichi, a graduate from the Engineering Department of Tohoku University, and Toyoda Eiji, his cousin and a graduate from Tokyo's Engineering Department.

To solve technological problems and to ask for advice, Kiichiro often visited experts he met through his network of classmates. The most helpful was Kumabe Kazuo, with whom Kiichiro had written a graduation thesis and who then stayed at the university as an associate professor. Not only did Kumabe advise Kiichiro, but he also introduced his acquaintances. Thus, in 1937, when Toyota started a research and development department, Kiichiro asked seven professors, three (including Kumabe) from Tokyo, two from Tohoku, one from the Tokyo Institute of Technology, and one from the Tokyo Art College, to serve as consultants. Kumabe later joined Toyota and became a vice president.

Although the use of a school network to recruit people is less clear in Toyota's case than Nissan's, Toyota clearly benefited. The Engineering Department of the University of Tokyo seems to have played a central role in both cases. For the history of the Japanese automobile industry in general and, particularly, that of Nissan and Toyota, the most useful English reference is Cusumano (1985) (see also Odagiri and Goto, 1996). The prominence of Tokyo's Engineering Department in the early period of Japan's industrialization is hardly surprising. Knowledgeable scientists and engineers were scarce, and most were Tokyo graduates. In other industries, a similar reliance on the graduates of the Engineering Department of the University of Tokyo has been found.

In the rayon industry, for instance, almost all of its early engineers were direct or indirect students of Kawakita Yoshitatsu, a professor of organic chemistry at Tokyo, or Asahina Akito, a professor of applied chemistry at Osaka Koto Kogyo. These included Hisamura Seita and Hata Itsuzo, both Kawakita's students, who developed rayon technology for the first time in Japan in 1916 at Teijin. Other engineers were Hata's students at Yonezawa Koto Kogyo before he moved to Teijin or Kita's students. Kita Genitsu had studied with Kawakita and became a professor at Kyoto University's Engineering Department. Such engineers, employed in Asahi Kasei (Asahi Chemcial), Toyo Rayon (now Toray), Nippon Rayon (now Unitika), Kurashiki Rayon (now Kuraray), and other companies that followed Teijin, were instrumental in the development of the rayon industry in Japan, enabling Japanese firms to catch up technically with their rivals in the West (Uchida, 1983).

Search and Signaling

Uncertainty and incomplete information are major characteristics of labor markets. This is particularly true in the early stage of industrialization, when infrastructure and institutions are undeveloped. Incomplete information is evident at two levels. The first pertains to the question of which workers will apply for jobs or which employers will offer jobs; this is a problem of search. The second pertains to the evaluation of candidates who appear in a search; this is a question of quality. According to Spence (1974, p. 6):

> when the employer and potential employee confront each other in the market (the confrontation may be preceded by a considerable amount of search by either party or both), neither is certain about the qualities or characteristics of the service which the other is offering for sale. The potential employee may not know exactly what the job will be like, and the employer frequently does not know how effectively the job applicant will do the job if he or she is hired.

Employers, of course, try to estimate the quality of the applicants through various characteristics. Some of these, such as gender and race, are inborn and cannot be manipulated. Spence called these characteristics *indices*. There are also characteristics that can be manipulated by individuals. Dressing nicely to impress potential employers is one of these. Studying hard to get good grades is another. Spence called these manipulable characteristics *signals*.

When an employer wants to recruit a worker with a certain quality, say, with knowledge on how to fill in tax forms or how to manufacture automobile engines, he or she has to search among those seeking jobs and then estimate the candidates' quality using their signals and indices. A signal that has proved to be one of the most useful, reasonably accurate, and low-cost predictors of quality is education. A recommendation from trustworthy or influential persons is another, although if an acquaintance with such a person has occurred by accident or through family connections, it should be regarded as an index, according to Spence's terminology.

As long as signals are manipulable, rational employers must decide how much to invest in acquiring signals. They determine for how long and in which schools it is desirable to be educated. This decision is made by comparing the pecuniary and nonpecuniary costs of education to the benefits, which are estimated by assessing the wage scales (and other pecuniary or nonpecuniary gains) employers offer to people of different educational levels. If the costs are high (for example, if the tuition and foregone income during schooling are high or if one has to prepare hard to be admitted relative to benefits), fewer people will seek higher education. However, if few people finish higher education, their wages will be higher because of their scarcity, thereby increasing the benefits of education. Through this interrelationship, an equilibrium (or equilibria) may be found in which neither employer nor employee has any further incentive to adjust the balance. Spence has shown that multiple equilibria are a possibility and that overinvestment in education can occur in equilibria. What Dore (1976) called *qualification inflation* must be a direct consequence of this overinvestment.

An interesting question, then, is whether such overinvestment has taken place or is present in Japan. The answer depends both on the costs and benefits of education. On the cost side, the costs of education, including the lost income during schooling, plus the costs of preparation to gain admission have to be considered. On the benefit side, the wage differential according to level of education is obviously the most important factor. The answer also depends on the relative merit and accuracy of education as a signal, which in turn depends on the extent and speed of an employer's learning from the observed correlation between workers' educational background and their true productivity, as well as on the workers' perception of the extent of employers' learning. Finally, it also depends on the availability of other signals and indices to estimate applicant quality.

Until the first decade of this century, the cost of education was very high in Japan. The cost of continuing education for 15 to 20 years beyond the 4 years of compulsory education was prohibitively high for many parents, and tuition was by no means low. For example, after four years of compulsory *Jinjo Shogakko*, one moved on to four years of *Koto Shogakko*, five years of *Chugakko*, and three years of *Koto Gakko*, before getting into a university. Moreover, promotion examinations were not easy to pass at these schools (unlike present high schools in Japan), and many students failed to finish within these periods of time. Entrance examinations were also difficult at *Koto Gakko* and universities, and many students had to prepare a year or two, often going back to preparatory schools, before passing the examinations (Amano, 1992).

Kogakuryo and other practical schools founded by the Meiji government provided scholarships at first, but scholarships became very limited after the start of Tokyo Imperial University. As a result, the number of college graduates was small, and, as discussed previously, their contributions were large, particularly because of the technical knowledge they possessed. Their salary was accordingly high, whether in the private or public sector. In the government sector in 1894, college graduates earned 800 yen in the first year, whereas those from *Chugakko* earned only 12 yen. These salaries compare with the 4 yen farm workers generally earned and 8 yen carpenters earned (Fukaya, 1969, p. 214).

Naturally, as knowledge of college graduates' salaries spread, demand for university education rose. This trend accelerated as the average income level took off, owing to rapid industrialization of the country, which made investment in education tolerable to and even desirable for many. The result was *gakureki*-ism (or Dore's "diploma disease"), that is, an excessive emphasis on education to advance one's career. If *gakureki*-ism can be identified with what Spence called overinvestment in education, there may be two reasons why it became so prominent in Japan.

The first reason is the high demand for educated people, created in the course of Japan's industrialization, and the consequently high salary they earned. However, the income differential based on educational background has considerably narrowed since then and is probably smaller than in any other industrial country (Koike and Watanabe, 1979). Thus, a lag in the parents' and students' adapting belief in the value of education may have caused overinvestment, if it is overinvestment at all. The second reason may be the relative homogeneity of the population and the scarcity of signals and indices other than education. The relative homogeneity of students implies that the costs of struggling to score better than rival applicants on entrance examinations was tolerable for many.

Japan's high investment in education may have been the product of rational, historical, and demographic factors. This argument is somewhat but not entirely similar to Dore's (1976) thesis that the so-called diploma disease is more common and deep rooted in late-developing countries.

Because people from the same educational institutions get to know each other, not only among those in the same class or in the same year but also between the upper and lower classes, their school-mediated relationship has been often used to provide information about certain graduates or to recommend certain graduates to others. Education, as a consequence, was used extensively as a signal on its own, but also it produced a network of people that was useful in disseminating information and in issuing recommendations for those in search of jobs.

Education as a Source of Network or Nepotism?

Information is now reasonably abundant in the labor market. Not only does the Public Employment Security Office (*Shokugyo Antei Sho*) provide information to employers and job seekers, but private businesses also offer job information and job-matching services. As a result, college students looking for jobs usually receive a substantial amount of information from these sources and companies. At the same time, internal labor markets have developed within firms by which employers provide additional training to new recruits from universities. (For the historical development of the internal labor system, see Taira, 1970, or Levine and Kawada, 1980. For a treatment of the internal labor market system today and its impact on the behavior of firms, see Odagiri, 1992.)

Nonetheless, networks of professors, students, and graduates are still very important sources of information. Employers often ask professors to recommend suitable students, and students ask graduates of their universities who are now employed for information on job availability or working conditions. Such networks are used by employers and job seekers, and recommendations by the members of the network are taken as signals. The usefulness of such networks was even more important in the early stages of Japan's industrial development, when information was scarce and the supply of college graduates more limited. Even today, in some university departments, professors recommend their students to firms and even allocate them to various companies (Sakakibara and Westney, 1985). Such practice, often observed in science and engineering departments but rarely in humanities and social science departments, may be a product of historical development since the prewar era.

Using university-based networks to search and signal is rational, provided (as supposed in Spence's model) that employers revise their estimations of the productivity–education correlation based on experience with previously hired employees. Employers must reconsider the value of such signals with each new class of candidates. Similarly, students should revise their assessment of the wage–education correlation and then make decisions about the value of education. People are supposed to learn in a more or less Bayesian fashion.

In reality, however, people may fail to learn, or the learning may take place extremely slowly. For instance, they may simply assume that a graduate from College A is *x* times more productive than one from College B, even though, if they were to measure the real productivity of those hired in the past, they would find that the proportion is far less than x. Or employers may hire a graduate from College A, simply because they are also graduates from the same college and feel a kinship. *Gakubatsu*, or academic nepotism (Shinbori, 1969), can be observed among some of Japan's major firms and government agencies.

The extent of *gakubatsu* is usually measured by a disproportionately large share of graduates from a certain college, university, or department, such as the University of Tokyo (Mannari, 1974; Shinbori, 1969). Because these graduates may actually have higher average ability, it is extremely difficult to determine whether the share is disproportionately large in comparison to the rational or justifiable level. Distinguishing the role of schools as networks, signals, or sources of nepotism is indeed decidedly problematic.

Although this observation applies not only to Japan but also to other countries where graduates of Harvard, Oxford and Cambridge, the Haute Ecole, and the like are overrepresented as top executives and top government officials, several significant differences are found in this chapter concerning education as networks. Harvard and Oxford and Cambridge used to emphasize the study of pure science, whereas practical education was emphasized in many Japanese universities; the Haute Ecole were probably somewhere in between. In the United States, the Massachusetts Institute of Technology and many other universities started practical technical education in the late nineteenth century; at about the same time, others started offering business education. The first business school, Wharton, opened in 1881, and Harvard started its business school in 1908 (Chandler, 1990). The dominance of MBAs, particularly those from Harvard, among current U.S. business executives has been discussed in *Business Week* (1993).

Japan's need to catch up with the West technically and economically has been an important factor in the development of its educational system. Because of a shortage of advanced educational institutions and of the graduates of those institutions, higher education has played an important role as a source of network, signal, and nepotism. Network refers to the role of education in fostering close interpersonal relations among a group of students who have experienced the process of being educated together. Quite often, classmates have become colleagues in business and government service after graduation. Signal refers to the indication of achievement and talent suggested by advanced education. That is, students with talent, a certain amount of material wherewithal, and ambition often aspire to advance to higher levels of education. In a country with an insufficient number of well-educated citizens, advancing to higher levels of education sends a signal to the labor market: This person is valuable because he or she is a scarce and valuable resource. Finally, nepotism or favoritism shown to particular persons because of certain shared attributes is another feature of Japan's late-development emphasis on education. Graduates of the same schools were often hired and promoted preferentially in firms and government agencies. The widespread belief in the importance of old-school ties (*gakubatsu*) in career advancement would seem to support the notion of education as a source of nepotism. In sum, higher education in Japan, particularly during Japan's period of rapid industrialization, has been a source of network, signal, and nepotism. All have been important, and all have been present in the course of Japan's twentieth century modernization.

Note

This chapter was previously presented as a paper at the Network Conference, Institute of Asian Research, University of British Columbia, Canada, September 1993. I thank Howard Aldrich, Mark Fruin, and other participants of the conference, as well as Ronald Dore and Shin-ichi Yamamoto, for their comments.

References

Amano, I. *Gakureki no shakai-shi* [The Social History of *gakureki*]. Tokyo: Shincho Sha, 1992.
Business Week. "Portrait of a CEO." October 11, 1993, pp. 64–5.
Chandler, A. D., Jr. *Scale and Scope.* Cambridge, Mass.: Harvard University Press, 1990.
Cusumano, M. A. *The Japanese Automobile Industry.* Cambridge, Mass.: Harvard University Press, 1985.
Dore, R. P. *The Diploma Disease.* London: George Allen and Unwin, 1976.
Fukaya, M. *Gakureki shugi no keifu* [Pedigree of *gakureki*-ism]. Nagoya: Reimei Shobo, 1969.
Ishikawa, K. "Meiji-ki ni okeru kigyo-sha katsudo no toukei-teki bunseki [A Statistical Analysis of Entrepreneurial Activity in the Meiji Era]." *Osaka Daigaku Keizaigaku,* 23 (1974): 85–118.
Koike, K., and Y. Watanabe. *Gakureki shakai no kyozo* [The False Image of *gakureki* Society]. Tokyo: Toyo Keizai, 1979.
Levine, S., and H. Kawada. *Human Resources in Japanese Industrial Development.* Princeton, N.J.: Princeton University Press, 1980.
Locke, R. R. "Education and Entrepreneurship: An Historian's View." In J. Brown and M. B . Rose, eds., *Entrepreneurship, Networks and Modern Business.* Manchester: Manchester University Press, 1993, pp. 55–75.
Mannari, H. *The Japanese Business Leaders.* Tokyo: University of Tokyo Press, 1974.
Miyoshi, N. *Nippon kogyo kyouiku seiritsu shi no kenkyu* [A Study of the Early History of Engineering Education in Japan]. Tokyo: Kazama Shobo, 1979.
Morikawa, H. "Meiji-ki ni okeru senmon keiei-sha no shinshutsu katei [The Process of Emergence of Professional Managers in the Meiji Era]." *Business Review,* 21 (1973): 12–27.
Morikawa, H. *Gijutsu-sha* [Technicians]. Tokyo: Nihon Keizai Shimbun Sha, 1975.
Nippon Kagaku-Shi Gakkai, ed. *Nippon kagaku gijutsu-shi taikei, dai 8 kan* [The Series in the History of Science and Engineering in Japan, vol. 8]. Tokyo: Daiichi Houki Shuppan, 1964.
Odagiri, H. *Growth through Competition, Competition through Growth: Strategic Management and the Economy in Japan.* Oxford: Oxford University Press, 1992.
Odagiri, H., and A. Goto. *Technology and Industrial Development in Japan: Building Capabilities by Learning, Innovation, and Public Policy.* Oxford: Oxford University Press, 1996.
Sakakibara, K., and D. E. Westney. "Comparative Study of the Training, Careers, and Organization of Engineers in the Computer Industry in the United States and Japan." *Hitotsubashi Journal of Commerce and Management,* 20 (1985): 1–20.

Shinbori, M., ed. *Gakubatsu* [Academic Nepotism]. Tokyo: Fukumura Shuppan, 1969.

Spence, A. M. *Market Signaling: Informational Transfer in Hiring and Related Screening Processes.* Cambridge, Mass.: Harvard University Press, 1974.

Taira, K. *Economic Development and the Labor Market in Japan.* New York: Columbia University Press, 1970.

Toyota Motor Co. *Toyota Jidosha 30 nen shi* [The 30-Year History of Toyota Motor]. Toyota, Aichi, 1967.

Uchida, H. "Jinken oogon jidai [The Golden Age of Synthetic Fibre]." In H. Uchida (ed.), *Gijutsu no shakai-shi*, vol. 5. Tokyo: Yuhikaku, 1983, 151–198.

Uemura, M. "Meiji shoki Ookura-Sho no kinsei-teki keifu [The Origins of the Ministry of Finance in the Early Meiji]." *Osaka Daigaku Keizaigaku*, 23 (1974): 53–84.

Yuasa, M. *Nihon no kagaku gijutsu 100 nen shi* [The 100-year History of Science and Technology in Japan]. Tokyo: Chuo Koron Sha, 1980.

8

Making Things Clique

Cartels, Coalitions, and Institutional Structure in the Tsukiji Wholesale Seafood Market

THEODORE C. BESTOR

Tokyo's Tsukiji Central Wholesale Market is Japan's (and the world's) largest marketplace for fresh, frozen, and processed seafood, a market where more than 60,000 people come each day to buy and sell fish that will feed many of the Tokyo region's 22 million residents. Six days a week between 4 and 10 A.M., the rambling sheds at Tsukiji become a swirling maelstrom of frenetic motion and industrial-strength noise, high-tech electronics, and nearly preindustrial manual labor. Tsukiji stands at the center of a technologically sophisticated, multibillion dollar international fishing industry, and every day the market's auctions match international supply with the traditional demands of Japanese cuisine, made ever more elaborate by Japan's prosperity and the gentrification of culinary tastes. Boosters encourage the homey view that Tsukiji is "Tōkyō no daidokoro"—Tokyo's kitchen or pantry—but in this pantry over 628 million kilograms of seafood worth $5.3 billion changed hands in 1996 (Tōkyō-to Chūō Oroshiuri Shijō, 1997: 16–17). (By way of comparison, New York's Fulton Fish Market, the largest in North America, handled only 13% of the tonnage of Tsukiji's trade, valued at about $1 billion (*New York Times*, November 11, 1996, p. B4).) Despite the enormous scale of the marketplace as a whole, the bulk of Tsukiji's daily trade flows through tiny family businesses, the roughly 1,000 trading firms licensed to buy at Tsukiji's morning auctions and resell their purchases in the market's 1,677 stalls.

The social alliances, strategies, and maneuverings of these brokers, along with the institutional arrangements that enfranchise them and regulate their behavior as traders, are significant components of the social framework within which the economic life of the market is enacted. This chapter examines some organizational features of this marketplace that link and coordinate the actions of those brokers, known as *nakaoroshi gyōsha* (midlevel wholesalers) or simply as *nakaoroshi*, who buy at auction and resell within the marketplace to retailers, restaurateurs, and sometimes other wholesalers. In particular, I focus on the groups, networks, and coalitions formed by and among the midlevel wholesalers which enable this large but tightly circumscribed body of traders to operate as an orderly market.

The term "market" is inherently ambiguous, implying on the one hand abstract sets of economic phenomena and, on the other hand, specific social relationships and institutions within which economic transactions take place. When, as in the case of Tsukiji, these economic phenomena and social frameworks are simultaneously situated in a particular place—a marketplace—that is both spatially and legally bounded in very precise ways, the conceptual ambiguity becomes all the more pronounced. This, of course, reflects the reality that economic and social life are not separate things and that there is an interactive, mutually constitutive relationship between markets as economic process and markets as social institutions. In the customary usage of economists, "market" refers primarily to economic process. The social and institutional patterns that may sustain or facilitate or even create economic activity typically are regarded either as emergent properties of that activity itself or as imperfections that retard the full realization of economic process.

Certainly the institutions of the Tsukiji marketplace are shaped by particular functional and technical requirements inherent in the seafood trade and by the general principles of capitalism inherent in the wider Japanese economy. But the social institutions and organizational patterns that constitute the marketplace are not merely emergent properties of an abstract market mechanism. My analysis is predicated on a simple premise: Organizational patterns and institutional arrangements (and the cultural principles upon which such patterns and arrangements themselves are based) create frameworks for marketplace activity and, in so doing, configure the market—both as a specific set of bounded interactions among real actors and as economic processes per se. The economic life of the market is, to borrow Granovetter's (1985) terms, embedded in its institutional structure. It is not that institutions simply channel economic transactions that would happen nonetheless. Institutions define the players, the goods to be exchanged, the appropriate media of exchange, and the rules of transactions. In short, they create the conditions under which exchange can be envisioned and hence realized.

In this chapter I examine several interrelated aspects of the institutional arrangements that link, coordinate, or regulate the actions of Tsukiji's midlevel traders. As a whole, their social relationships may be viewed along a number of different dimensions, each highlighting a somewhat different general perspective on Japanese economic organization, for example, issues of vertical integration and coordination among firms, mutual reciprocity and long-term obligation, or government intervention. Here, I focus particularly on the creation of "horizontal" mutual interests in the institutional structure of the marketplace; the crystallization of those interests into formally organized groups; the mobilization of mutual interest and reciprocity as strategic responses to the institutional conditions of market life; and the effect of government actions on the formation of interest groups, in what might be called "the political economy of cliques."

To illustrate how these social features of the marketplace—constructed and reconstructed by cultural factors and institutional relations—create contexts within which the economic tasks of the market are formulated, my data and my analysis are presented ethnographically and historically. Although the issues dealt with here are as relevant to large-scale businesses as to small-scale ones, this study is situated in an economic universe of small-scale family firms. Thus an ethnographic approach is particularly appropriate for capturing the deeply embedded threads of dense social ties and social constraint that weave the fabric of Tsukiji

traders' economic existence. The frenzied whirl of activities and affiliations that
frame the daily lives of Tsukiji's traders does not neatly resolve into the discrete
themes I have outlined previously. This chapter therefore intercuts description
and analysis to untangle the multidimensional interplay between institutional
structure and economic life. I begin with an overview of activity in the market to
provide a context for subsequent sections in which I discuss the formation and dynamics of cliques, cartels, and coalitions in the institutional structure of the marketplace. I return, in the conclusions, to discuss the wider significance of the patterns of interest group organization that I identify in the following ethnographic
account based on extensive observations and interviews.

A Morning at the Auctions

Around 6 A.M. loud bells and buzzers begin to clatter across the Tsukiji marketplace. The work day is already several hours old; since midnight, employees and
subcontractors of the brokerage houses have been arranging, grading, labeling, and
rearranging the fish to be sold that morning. Hundreds of other market participants,
the midlevel wholesalers and their employees, have been inspecting lots: jabbing
frozen tunas with picks and rubbing slivers of flesh to feel the fat content; open-
ing styrofoam cases of salmon to check the consistency of multicrate lots; tasting
tiny dried sardines, smelling smoked smelt, or watching live sea bream as they
thrash around in flat wooden tubs.

The bells and buzzers don't bring this hubbub to an end; they merely signal that
its focus is about to shift to the auction arenas. At roughly 15- or 20-minute intervals, the several dozen auction pits scattered across the marketplace burst into life.
Each pit specializes in a specific commodity, and each has its regular community
of licensed traders. As a particular auction starts, the regulars take their places on
the rough wooden bleachers facing an auctioneer's stand, where fresh tuna, salted
salmon, or live shrimp are put up for bid.

The auctions proceed at a lightning pace; the throaty growl of auctioneers'
voices meeting the silent hand gestures of impassive buyers. An auctioneer can
roar through a dozen lots in only a minute or two, and an outsider is hard pressed
to tell who got each lot and for what. It all is a torrent of abbreviated jargon and
waving hands making quick, almost imperceptible gestures that signify prices offered. As the lots are cried, teams of assistant auctioneers feverishly scribble sales
results onto invoice slips. Auctioneers cultivate showmanship to rivet attention on
them, but their cadences are matter of fact, almost emotionless, rather than the-
atrical. The licensed traders flash finger signals to register their bids, but for them,
too, these are workaday performances, and their faces register little reaction to winning or losing a particular lot. From time to time, laughter sweeps the auction stand
when an auctioneer fumbles or a trader offers a bid that the others consider out-
landishly high. Once in a while anger flashes when someone feels an auctioneer
has ignored his bid. But, by and large, the traders quietly chat with friends, scru-
tinize their bidding notes, watch the crowd, and feign indifference as the lots they
want come up for bid.

Auctions are the core of the Tsukiji marketplace and all the 55 seafood markets
run under the national system of Central Wholesale Markets (*Chūō Oroshiuri*

Shijō). Auction sales are specified by national legislation as the "fundamental basis" of the market system, and the rules and regulations under which auctions must take place are spelled out in minute detail in local administrative regulations and the customary understandings that govern the activity in any marketplace. In the official administrative view, auctions ensure that transactions are "open, equal, and fair," and the extremely detailed rules surrounding auctions are intended to guarantee this.

Despite this legal sanction for uniformity in the interests of open competition, however, there is great variation in the ways in which auctions take place and even in whether auctions are held for specific categories of commodities. These variations, which are themselves spelled out in detail in the administrative regulations of the marketplace, are the product of disparate forces. Some variations, such as the designation of specific bidding techniques, originate in part from historical accretions of customary practice that have been institutionalized in the regulatory structure.

Other variations, such as distinctions in the handling of fresh, frozen, and processed seafood, reflect technical differences among specific types of commodities. Supply and price factors for aquacultural seafood products are generally stable, and so in these cases auctions are more important for allocating supplies among different buyers than for determining absolute price levels. Thus, in some shrimp auctions, for example, the winning bidder specifies how many cases he wants to take; the auctioneer then moves to a second round of bidding for the remaining cases, and so on, until all the cases have been bought.

Still other variations in auction practices reflect complex political accommodations among shifting alliances of producers, auction houses, auctioneers, licensed traders, trade buyers, and the consuming public at large. Supermarkets and small-scale retailers, for example, are constantly at odds with one another, and their rivalries carry over to midlevel wholesalers who specialize in serving one clientele or the other. Auction rules are affected, because to process seafood in large quantities and to stock counters for the day's business, supermarkets require longer lead times for deliveries than do small-scale retailers. Supermarkets and their allies press for earlier auction times or permission to make purchases without waiting for the auctions. Auction houses want to accommodate large-scale customers like supermarkets, but small-scale retailers and their midlevel wholesalers wield substantial political power over issues of market administration. The uneasy compromise is that wholesalers who supply supermarkets have conditional permission to remove carefully specified quantities and grades of products before the auctions begin each morning, at prices that are set at the highest levels registered in the day's bidding later on.

These examples demonstrate that the seemingly straightforward process of selling goods at auction is embedded, in practice, in complex social cotexts that define the universes of buyers and sellers and the relationships among them. These universes exert distinct pressures to modify or maintain the particular sets of relationships that any given auction arena embodies. Each auction arena at Tsukiji is therefore a separate and somewhat autonomous social system in which trading relationships are structured and integrated idiosyncratically, and in which economic advantage and disadvantage are differentially structured. The auction system as a whole forms the institutional context within which traders' mutual interests are identified and coalitions take form.

Constructing Identity and Mutual Interest

Much of the framework of firms' networks and affiliations can only be understood in terms of the occupational specializations that differentiate Tsukiji's 1,000 mid-level wholesalers (*nakaoroshi*). The differentiation of specializations is a product of both cultural and institutional factors and, in turn, generates mutual interests and social structures that further affect the institutional structure of the market-place as a whole.

Tsukiji's midlevel wholesalers stand at a fulcrum between primary producers and consumers. Their actions define the process through which relatively homo-geneous commodities (e.g., frozen tuna, farm-raised eels, or silver salmon) are repackaged both literally and figuratively into the array of foodstuffs restaurateurs or consumers can use. In trade jargon, the market and its *nakaoroshi* are centrally involved in "bulking and breaking." "Upstream" from the marketplace, products are assembled in larger and larger quantities of increasingly homogeneous charac-ter for auction at this and similar wholesale seafood markets. "Downstream" from the marketplace, however, customers do not demand large quantities of single commodities but small quantities of a wide array of dissimilar products. After all, only a rare retailer or restaurateur wants to offer only tuna, shrimp, or octopus; al-most no one can handle an entire 200-kilogram shipment of a single product. So, collectively and individually, one of the midlevel wholesalers' fundamental tasks is to make available to the market's customers a full array of appropriate seafood in appropriately sized packages.

It sounds like a simple task, and to state it this way makes it seem entirely ob-vious. However, given the volume of seafood arriving at Tsukiji each day (approx-imately 2.2 million kilograms) and the number of varieties of seafood handled in the course of a year (roughly 2,000), it requires an enormously complex organiza-tional effort each morning to enable a Tokyo *sushi* chef to stroll Tsukiji's aisles, se-lecting a handful of this, a fillet of that, and a kilogram of the other. Official mar-ketplace statistics report sales figures for 450 major categories of seafood, but many of these categories include five or six distinct varieties recognized in the trade. When asked about the total number of varieties, dealers shake their heads and guess "over 2,000."

Elsewhere (Bestor, in press) I have outlined in much greater detail the ways in which the market's daily activities are affected by Japanese food culture and culi-nary ideals that embody concepts of freshness, purity, domesticity, and timeliness. The important point here is that the occupational specializations of midlevel wholesalers are culturally constructed both by the categorizations relevant to pro-ducers and shippers, and by somewhat different sets of criteria that are relevant to consumers. For producers and shippers, categories of products are defined along such dimensions as methods and places of harvest, species or subspecies, methods of processing and transportation, scale of shipments, and so forth. On the other side of the market, categories are determined by culinary logic implicitly encoded by consumer preferences and demand, shaped by disparate concerns such as cost per serving, ease of preparation, seasonality, ritual appropriateness, and color sym-bolism. Of course, these two sets of culturally constructed criteria that frame the specializations of midlevel wholesalers are not necessarily congruent, wherein lies the challenge and sometimes the profit of the midlevel wholesalers' occupation.

But in addition to these cultural constructions, *nakaoroshi* specializations and their interactions with other traders are also socially constructed by the institutional framework of the marketplace. In particular, two closely related institutional features of the marketplace define *nakaoroshi* specializations. One is the system of auctions; the other is the system of licenses for market participants. Auctions are mandated for Tsukiji and the other similar seafood markets in the national system that operate under the authority of the national Ministry of Agriculture, Forestry, and Fisheries (MAFF). In such markets, there is an elaborate hierarchy of firms, many of which require licenses either from MAFF or from the marketplace administrators (in the case of Tsukiji, the Tokyo Metropolitan Government [TMG]) (see Figure 8-1). The business activities of these firms are carefully defined in and regulated by both national laws and municipal ordinances, which restrict market entry and access to the auctions, and therefore define the scope of activities that a firm may engage in within the marketplace as well as in related and unrelated fields of business outside the marketplace.

The Auction System

The Tsukiji marketplace contains several dozen distinct and spatially dispersed auction areas, each operating more or less independently of all others. Tsukiji's seafood auctions are run by seven large auction houses licensed to supply products to the marketplace. Their operations, which are highly regulated by municipal and national agencies, are fundamentally similar, although the seven firms vary widely in their volume and in the range of products they handle. Four are full-range auction houses that handle virtually all varieties of seafood, fresh, frozen, and processed; one handles most varieties of fresh and processed fish; two specialize only in dried, smoked, and other varieties of processed seafood. For each of the two dozen or more product categories each firm handles, each conducts its auctions separately, using licensed auctioneers (*serinin*) who are full-time, permanent employees of that auction house. Thus, in effect, perhaps a hundred distinct auctions are held each morning, with most commodity categories being the object of four, five, or seven distinct auction sequences (depending on the number of auction houses that handle a particular commodity).

Tsukiji's auction arenas are defined first and foremost by the different commodities they handle. Fresh tuna, frozen tuna, fresh fish from the waters near Tokyo versus fresh fish from the waters off Northern Honshū or the Sea of Japan, live fish, salted salmon, live shrimp, dried sardines, shark, or fresh sea urchin roe are but a few examples. At first glance, the categories seem wildly inconsistent and by no means mutually exclusive. Some are constituted around particular species of fish; others by the method of processing the fish have undergone. Some are organized around fish caught in particular locales; others represent particular quality grades or culinary uses. Fish do not end up by some automatic process in a particular auction arena. Instead, they are directed by routinized chains of decisions made by *serinin* who divert shipments to one of several possible auction arenas, based on their knowledge of the preferences and buying habits of the trading community of licensed buyers that frequents a particular auction arena.

From day to day the cast of characters at any arena is roughly the same, and each arena is a tight circle of familiar faces and established trading customs. All auc-

---

Figure 8-1 Who's Who at Tsukiji

REGULATORS

Ministry of Agriculture, Forestry and Fisheries [MAFF]—supervises Central Wholesale Markets (*Chūō Oroshiuri Shijō*) throughout the country, licenses fishing and some distribution activities, and authorizes municipal authorities to operate local Central Wholesale Markets.

Tokyo Metroplitan Government [TMG]—owns and maintains the marketplace's facilities, licenses some businesses within the marketplace, and provides overall regulatory supervision of the marketplace.

PLAYERS

Producers (*seisansha*) and **Consignors** (*ninushi*)—supply Tsukiji with seafood for sale on consignment by Tsukiji's auction houses. (Includes: domestic and foreign fishers, fishing cooperatives, fishing companies, trading companies, provincial seafood buyers, seafood processing firms, brokers, and wholesalers from other markets.)

Truckers and **Shippers**—deliver seafood to the market.

* **Unloaders** (*koage*)—receive consignments from truckers and unload, deliver, short, and arrange consignments within the marketplace for the several auction houses.

* **Auction houses**—*oroshiuri gyōsha* (wholesale traders) also known as *niukegaisha* (consignment companies)—receive seafood from producers and brokers on consignment for sale at daily auctions.

* **Auctioneers** (*serinin*)—conduct daily sales as employees of the auction houses.

* **Mid-level wholesalers** (*nakaoroshi gyōsha*)—purchase seafood at daily auctions and resell it at their stalls within the marketplace.

* **Authorized buyers** (*baibaisankasha*)—purchase seafood at daily auctions for use or resale outside the marketplace. Authorized traders are primarily large-scale users, such as supermarket chains, hospitals, commissaries, and food processors.

---

tions are conducted under standardized general regulations of the marketplace. However, each is governed by subtly different sets of rules that are based in part on the cumulative agreements among the seven large auction houses that supply the market and the midlevel wholesalers who constitute a trading community for a particular commodity.

Depending on the product to be sold, the techniques of the auction vary. Bidding may be by either a gestured or a written bid. In most cases, bidding is a one-shot affair, and simultaneous tying bids are broken not by a second round of bidding but by such mechanisms as *jan-ken-pon*—the child's hand game of rock–scissors–paper—that can be used to determine a winner among, for example, competing buyers in the fresh and live fish auctions. But in other trading communi-

Figure 8-1 (*continued*)

Trade buyers—purchase seafood from mid-level wholesalers within the marketplace. (Includes: retail fishmongers, buyers for supermarkets and department stores, fish processors, specialty wholesalers, restauranteurs, *sushi* chefs, caterers, and peddlers.)

* **Dock agents**—*kainihokansho* ('merchandise custodians'), colloquially called *chaya* ('teahouses')—receive trade buyers' purchases from mid-level wholesalers and hold them at loading docks for pick-up by trade buyers or by delivery services.

Delivery services—pick-up purchases from dock agents and deliver them to buyers' businesses throughout Tokyo.

Outer market dealers—have shops located in the outer marketplace (*jōgai shijō*) that supply retailers and restauranteurs but also welcome retail shoppers. Some outer market dealers have licenses as authorized traders and may participate in Tsukiji's auctions; others purchase their supplies from mid-level wholesalers like other trade buyers; still others obtain their supplies independent of the marketplace.

Retail customers—are discouraged from buying within the Tsukiji marketplace proper, but may shop freely in the outer marketplace.

*Specific licenses from MAFF or TMG required of these players

---

ties—centered, for example, around the tuna auctions—competing buyers can offer higher bids, if they act almost instantaneously.

Some commodities are sold at display auctions, where each lot is inspected as it goes up for bid [e.g., tuna, sea urchin roe, and *niboshi* (tiny dried sardines)]. In other auctions, the commodities are not on display. For some commodities, large-volume buyers are allowed to take products before the auctions start with the promise of matching the top price of the day for the privilege. For other commodities, the buyer must be present to bid. Some fish are sold piece by piece; others are sold by weight or by fixed units. Under some specified conditions, auctioneers have the option of suspending the auction and concluding negotiated sales. Under other conditions (and for some commodities), they do not.

In negotiations over trading rules the members of each trading community are represented by a specialized trade guild (*moyori gyōkai*, or simply *gyōkai*), of which there are presently sixteen, each representing a major commodity sector. (*Gyōkai* will be discussed in greater detail later.) Decisions about which commodity categories each auction arena handles, and hence the working definitions of the boundaries among the individual auction arenas, are constantly renegotiated within the formal institutions of market governance maintained among the sixteen specialized trade guilds, the auction houses, and the municipal authorities. This cartelization of decision-making under the guidance of government administrators is a hallmark of the institutional structure of the marketplace and a key to understanding the formation, persistence, and dynamics of interaction among and within trade groups at Tsukiji.

The Licensing System

Participating in the morning auctions requires a license from the marketplace administration, and approximately 1,400 wholesale firms hold licenses. These are
primarily the 1,000 *nakaoroshi* whose licenses authorize them to rent stalls and resell products inside the marketplace itself. In addition, about 400 "authorized buyers" (*baibaisankasha*) are allowed to bid at auctions but do not have stalls and cannot resell products within the marketplace. Generally, these buyers purchase on
behalf of restaurant chains, hotels, hospitals, schools, and other large-volume consumers.

When the present system was instituted in the 1950s, licenses were allocated on
the basis of a single stall holding. The marketplace contains 1,677 stalls, and so
there are 1,677 *nakaoroshi* licenses to participate in the auctions. The number of
stalls and licenses has remained constant since the late 1950s, but since the early
1970s, the marketplace administrators have allowed firms to expand to control two
or more stalls (and hence auction licenses) per firm. The pace of consolidation,
however, was rather slow until the 1990s, when, in the economic slump following
the collapse of the so-called bubble economy, many marginal traders went out of
business. Between 1991 and 1997 the total number of nakaoroshi firms at Tsukiji
declined from 1,101 to 968 (figures provided by Tō-Oroshi). There are still a couple of hundred *nakaoroshi* who operate only a single stall apiece, and a small
handful of firms operate as many as a dozen, but the vast majority of firms hold two
or three licenses and hence occupy two or three stalls.

Nothing in the licensing regulations or auction rules as such limits a *nakaoroshi*
to specialization in a particular kind of commodity or prohibits a firm from participating in any of the marketplace's many distinct auction areas. Nonetheless, the
licensing system reinforces the occupational specializations of mid-level wholesalers and the exclusivity of auction participation. Under the Tokyo Metropolitan
Government's rules, a *nakaoroshi* firm is allowed a single auction license for each
stall the firm leases. The auction license is concretely signified by an oblong plastic badge (roughly 4 inch × 8 inch) clipped to a baseball cap. Without the badge,
one cannot bid at an auction. A firm can rotate its badge(s) among its employees,
but obviously a badge cannot be used in more than one auction arena at the same
time. Because the auctions in the many categories of commodities are all held at
overlapping times, a single auction license generally restricts a midlevel wholesaler to participation in no more than two or three different auction arenas. Thus,
most *nakaoroshi* firms are virtually forced to specialize in only one or two main
commodity lines.

Mutual Interest and the Political
Economy of Cliques

These specialties are, of course, critical to the professional identity of *nakaoroshi*
and form the basis for some of the most strategically important institutions of the
marketplace: the sixteen guilds [*moyori gyōkai* or "customary trade groups" (see
figure 8-2)] organized by the midlevel wholesalers who handle specific commodities (e.g., shrimp, whale meat, pickled fish) or particular grades of products (e.g.,
sushidane—sushi toppings—the eclectic range of highest grade products demanded

Figure 8-2 Moyori Gyōkai (Trade Groups) of Mid-level Wholesalers

Sixteen trade groups (listed in descending order, according to size of membership). A *nakaoroshi* firm may belong to more than one trade group.

Members	Name	Commodities (and English Translation of Name)
335	**Ōmono Gyōkai**	–tuna and swordfish (Large Products Trade Group)
217	**Tokushumono Gyōkai**	–top grades of fish for the restaurant trade especially for *sushi* chefs (Special Varieties Trade Group)
161	**Enkaimono Gyōkai**	–fresh fish primarily for *sushi* and seasonal cuisine, from Japanese coastal waters distant from Tokyo; (Distant Coastal Water Products Trade Group)
96	**Kinkaimono Gyōkai**	–fresh fish primarily for *sushi* and seasonal cuisine, from Japanese coastal waters near Tokyo (Near Coastal Water Products Trade Group)
78	**Hokuyōmono Gyōkai**	–salmon and other North Pacific species (Northern Ocean Products Trade Group)
75	**Aimono Gyōkai**	–semi-processed but perishable fish (Mixed Products Trade Group)
66	**Enkangyo Gyōkai**	–salted and dried fish products (Salted and Dried Fish Trade Group)
63	**Ebi Kyōkai**	–shrimp (Shrimp Association)
56	**Neriseihin Gyōkai**	–*kamaboko* and other fish paste products (Fish Paste Products Trade Group)
28	**Tansuigyo Kumiai**	–eel and other fresh water fish (Fresh Water Fish Union)
25	**Enyōmono Gyōkai**	–pelagic products (Distant Ocean Products Trade Group)
22	**Tako Dōgyō Kumiai**	–octopus (Octopus Trade Group)
18	**Tōgeikai**	–whale meat (Eastern Whale Club)
7	**Ise-ebi Kumiai**	–domestic lobsters (spiny lobster) and other shrimp (Ise Shrimp Union)
7	**Tsukuwakai**	–boiled and pickled seafood products (Tsuku Harmony Club)
5	**Tōkakai**	–shark and other fish for processing into fish paste (Tenth Day Club)

1259	Total number of *moyori gyōkai* memberships
1068	Total number of *nakaoroshi* firms at time directory was published
1.18	Average number of memberships per firm

Source: Calculated from data in *Tōkyō-to Chūō Oroshiuri Shijō Suisanbutsu-bu Nakaoroshi Gyōsha Meibō 1990-Nenpan*, a commercial directory of *nakaoroshi* compiled as of May 20, 1990 (Nikkan Shokuryō Shinbunsha 1990).

by *sushi* chefs). These guilds range in membership from several hundred firms to as few as half a dozen. As mentioned previously, these *gyōkai* institutionally represent the trading communities that gather each morning at the various auction arenas. For *nakaoroshi*, these *gyōkai* are the most focused forum for the expression and elaboration of mutual interests among otherwise competitive firms.

These guilds settle disputes, set the terms of trade, and negotiate with the auction houses and the Tokyo Metropolitan Government administration over the operations of the auctions and the marketplace as a whole. The different auction rules and other conditions of trade established for each auction arena illustrate the kinds of negotiations in which *gyōkai* not only represent the mutual interests of the group against other actors, but by doing so also define the competitive environment existing among members of the group. Different kinds of bidding rules—secret versus public, one-shot versus incremental—clearly frame competitive relationships among *nakaoroshi* in different terms, as do decisions about such practices as the allotments of products that can be removed from auction with the promise that the buyer will simply match the high bid of the day.

As with many aspects of the cartelized governance of the marketplace, the regulatory impulses of these groups aim at preserving the claims of all members, rather than improving the competitive position of some members at the expense of others. This parallels the model of group decision-making proposed by Robert Marshall (1984), in which the outcomes of a potential decision must not jeopardize the individual positions of the parties to the decision. If the probable outcomes do not ensure parity, either the group will not make the decision, or individual defections or group fissioning occur. Thus, marketplace rules are aimed at preserving each member's position vis-à-vis the others. The goal is not to create a level playing field, but to maintain one in which existing bumps and potholes are preserved more or less intact.

Similarly, adjustment and calibration of the auction rules over time affect the relationship between *nakaoroshi* and auctioneers, subtly shifting the balance of market power between the two parties and shaping the kinds of information over pricing strategies and buying preferences that an auctioneer can accumulate. Elsewhere (e.g., Bestor, 1997, forthcoming) I have examined the information flows between auctioneers and producers on the one hand and between auctioneers and *nakaoroshi* on the other hand. The coordination of information flows by the auctioneer is a crucial aspect of vertical linkage and coordination between buyers and sellers at different levels in the distribution chain. Thus, even though the auctions are seemingly a spot market, producers, auction houses, auctioneers, and *nakaoroshi* are able to maintain stable long-term ties with preferred trade partners in a fashion that resembles patterns of obligatory or relational contracting. In this context, *gyōkai*—as closely knit cartels of like-minded buyers—stabilize the boundaries of trading communities and contribute to the consistency of information about pricing and buying preferences upon which these linkages of (apparent) vertical coordination depend.

Gyōkai also display a segmentary structure that characterizes other cartels throughout the marketplace. Organized around a common interest and enfranchised with both internal autonomy and considerable power over decisions that affect their interests, groups such as *gyōkai* rarely relinquish their rights over a particular trade niche, nor do they easily dissolve into larger groups. Once a *gyōkai*, always a *gyōkai*. Even though some contemporary *gyōkai* are the products of mergers and amalgamations, the preexisting *gyōkai* generally maintain a corporate identity and a controlling voice over those issues most directly involving their own original common interests.

Thus, for example, the *ōmono gyōkai* created by a merger of groups representing tuna and swordfish dealers still contains a distinct subgroup or caucus of swordfish dealers. Another case is the *tokushumono gyōkai*, formed by a merger of several specialized groups of dealers in high-quality seafood. Some specialize in supplying *sushi* chefs; others, inns and traditional restaurants (*ryōtei*); and still others, hotels and Western-style restaurants. Each specialty is still represented within the *gyōkai* by its own subgroup, along with other subgroups that cross-cut them, such as one for the blowfish (*fugu*) trade.

The persistence of even minicartels—and hence the segmentary structure of groups at Tsukiji—is both a wider characteristic of the institutional framework of the marketplace and a product of a particular style of indirect administration of economic affairs. This administrative mode is encouraged by government agencies that enfranchise groups with decision-making powers and internal autonomy over the administration of their particular market niches. Organizational consolidation therefore does not erase the differences among enfranchised privileges or prerogatives that spawned the interest groups in the first place. It is not simply that contemporary common interests continue to give segmentary units their cohesive framework. Rather, the definition of common interests and the organization of traders around those interests at some point in the past creates a kind of institutional lock-in that ensures that the group will continue to maintain common interests—even if only referential ones linked to past conditions in the marketplace—that mark its existence.

The sixteen highly specialized *moyori gyōkai* comprise a first level of the institutionalization of mutual interest among midlevel wholesalers. A second, higher-level horizontal organization is an all-inclusive federation—known as Tō-Oroshi (an abbreviation of Tōkyō Uoichiba Oroshi Kyōdō Kumiai, the Tokyo Fishmarket Wholesalers Federation)—to which all *nakaoroshi* belong. *Gyōkai* are segmentary—some contain cohesive subgroups that persist in their organization around common interests, whether contemporary or historically referential. At the same time, *gyōkai* are also segments of the structure of Tō-Oroshi. Tō-Oroshi was created over the past several decades by the mergers and amalgamations of various groups of *nakaoroshi* organized not only around commodity specializations, but also around licensing statuses that existed in the marketplace before and during World War II, before the current marketplace system was instituted in the 1950s. Even as these groups were gradually drawn into Tō-Oroshi, they have maintained their distinct organizational identities, either under the Tō-Oroshi umbrella as *gyōkai* or as quasiparallel organizations to some extent duplicating the roles that Tō-Oroshi now plays for all *nakaoroshi*.

For example, although all *nakaoroshi* now operate on an equivalent footing in the market hierarchy, during World War II, the forerunners of today's *nakaoroshi* were divided into categories based on the scale of customer demand. Some were responsible for supplying small-scale retailers, and others supplied large-volume customers (such as schools, hotels, and secondary processors). As the new market system was developed in the late 1940s and early 1950s, both groups of traders (and others) negotiated their entry into the new, relatively homogeneous status of licensed *nakaoroshi* from different starting positions. Although their licenses are now the same and their clienteles no longer differ dramatically, both groups nonetheless still maintain themselves as formally institutionalized bodies parallel to but somewhat autonomous from Tō-Oroshi (to which all of their members also belong).

Tō-Oroshi, the umbrella organization that encompasses all the *nakaoroshi* as individual members and recognizes the interests and existence of all the *gyōkai* and other segmental groups, has a professional staff of several dozen employees and plays several general roles that encompass a vast number of specific services. Tō-Oroshi provides financial, technical, and bureaucratic services for individual midlevel wholesalers and fosters good public relations for the wholesalers as a group. On a day-to-day basis, wholesalers are most often involved with Tō-Oroshi for the services it can provide them as individual firms, whether using its clearinghouse for settling accounts payable and receivable; consulting its staff over government licensing requirements, labor regulations, or tax obligations; or renting compartments in Tō-Oroshi's large freezer warehouse. Such services are available to members on an optional basis and are utilized more frequently by smaller firms than by larger ones.

Tō-Oroshi's public relations efforts are of minimal concern to most wholesalers, who correctly regard their trade as out of sight and hence obscure to the consuming public. Nonetheless, Tō-Oroshi is diligent in arranging for occasional visits by TV camera crews. Its officials attempt to explain that Tsukiji's high prices are not created by multiple layers of wholesalers, but reflect the realities of a business of wildly fluctuating supply and demand, rapid spoilage, and inevitable product shrinkage as whole fish are transformed into consumer-sized portions of high-quality seafood. Once a year or so, Tō-Oroshi sponsors a market open house for the public. In one recent year, the event featured the filleting of a 600-pound tuna from round fish into strips of *sashimi* to illustrate the fact that roughly 50 percent of the weight of a tuna sold at auction ends up as waste before *sashimi* reaches the consumers' plates. The point, of course, that Tō-Oroshi wanted to impress upon the scores of housewives present was that the consumer price per kilogram was therefore necessarily at least 100 percent above the auction price, even before any margins or overhead were figured for wholesalers and retailers.

Most importantly, Tō-Oroshi represents the collective interests of wholesalers in negotiations with the government's marketplace administrators, the brokerage houses that supply the market, and various other groups of actors throughout the marketplace hierarchy. This is not simply a matter of serving as a trade organization lobbying governmental agencies and politicians for favorable treatment (although Tō-Oroshi's activities, including its public relations efforts, carry an element of this). Rather, trade groups like Tō-Oroshi and the *moyori gyōkai* beneath it are central elements in the system of indirect administration that governs the marketplace. Significant decisions about market operations are made between and among officially recognized and enfranchised groups or cartels representing the various sectors of the marketplace's actors. At various times, examples of such decisions have included the allocation of licenses; the assignment of stalls; the classification of products and their allocation to particular auction arenas; the determination of rules for standardized settlement, clearance, and credit procedures; the negotiation of rights to purchase outside regular auction channels; and the determination of the days and hours of operation for the marketplace each year.

Thus, under the aegis of the marketplace administration, Tō-Oroshi (representing the midlevel wholesalers) negotiates agreements with the seven auction houses as a unit over the general conditions of auction sales. For example, Tō-Oroshi, along with the organization that represents the seven seafood auction houses, the vegetable wholesalers' federation, and a body representing the two auction houses that supply the produce division of the market, negotiates the hours of operation and scheduled closing days of the marketplace as a whole. In yet another example, Tō-Oroshi and the federation of "authorized buyers" (baibaisankasha) negotiate with the seven seafood auction houses over what proportions of a day's sales can be made to outside buyers. Tō-Oroshi and the vegetable wholesalers' federation also negotiate with the two federations that represent the loading dock operators who handle shipments destined for retailers and restaurateurs.

Each group or cartel is made up of diverse individual firms united not only by common interests—as nakaoroshi, seafood auction houses, authorized buyers, or loading dock operators—but also by the institutional structure of the marketplace administration. Within this structure, licensing requirements define membership and enfranchise the members of each group with specific rights, privileges, and obligations. Government administrators endow each group with broad powers to self-administer their collective affairs. The administrative structure of the marketplace as a whole rests on the assumption that cartels, each representing a particular sphere of economic activity, will jointly hammer out arrangements for coordination with a minimum of guidance from the marketplace administrators. As in the case of moyori gyōkai, enfranchised privilege leads to the segmentary structure of cartels, whereby rights and prerogatives granted to members of a specific group at some point in the past continue to be the basis for at least incipient divisions in the present.

The loading dock operators are a good example. There are about 250 of these, organized into three groups, all of whom perform the same tasks. Colloquially known as chaya (teahouses), the loading dock operators each have a regular clientele of retailers and restaurateurs for whom they receive goods from nakaoroshi and hold them for pick up later in the morning. A nakaoroshi will know, at least for his regular customers, to which chaya a purchase should be directed. Because the average restaurateur or retailer patronizes a number of nakaoroshi—anywhere from three or four to as many as a dozen—the chaya provide a convenient means of storing and consolidating purchases made throughout the marketplace.

Each group is the product of a different institutional evolution. One chaya group, established after World War II, is run by a federation of Tokyo retailers on behalf of its members. The other two chaya federations represent groups of freight agents that trace their firms' histories to the old Nihonbashi fish market—which functioned in the center of Tokyo from the mid-1600s until it was destroyed in the 1923 Kantō earthquake. One group is descended from land-based delivery agents, the other from ship chandlers. The term chaya, an abbreviated form of shiomachijaya ("tea houses for awaiting the tides"), harkens back to the days when boats tied up along the canals of Nihonbashi to make or accept deliveries.

As *chaya* were incorporated into the new market built after 1923 and their functions converged, the preexisting rights and monopolies of their somewhat different trades created separate starting positions for their evolution under the new market system. As in the persistence of *gyōkai* established under wartime conditions, the perception of separate pasts and different paths of structural accommodation that each group underwent to join the new market have left a lasting locked-in institutional structure of dual federations. Even as the loading dock operators have evolved out of historically distinct niches or identities and have converged toward what are now functionally identical roles in the market, the dynamics of group formation preserve earlier institutional distinctions.

Just as Tō-Oroshi is the product of decades of laborious effort to amalgamate different groups of *nakaoroshi*, each of whom regarded itself—and was regarded within the institutional structure of the marketplace—as possessing certain distinct rights and entitlements, the history of the Tsukiji marketplace repeatedly has demonstrated the difficulty of overcoming established rights. One of the most spectacular and protracted disputes began in the 1890s—when the municipal authorities first began to consider moving the fish market out of Nihonbashi—and was finally resolved during World War II. The issue, known as the *itafuneken mondai* (the "cutting board rights issue"), centered on land-use rights in the old Nihonbashi market, where large dealers rented space in front of their shops to lesser dealers to operate temporary stalls (see Tōkyō-to Chūō Oroshiuri Shijō 1958 and 1963). As discussions of constructing a new market began, the owners of this space demanded compensation for the loss of revenue they would suffer when their tenants were provided space by the municipal authorities in the proposed new market. This issue—and the fear of realignments in status that would be entailed within a new marketplace by the incorporation of disparate levels of dealers with what they considered distinct preexisting rights—created intractable opposition and stalled market relocation plans for decades.

The 1923 earthquake put to rest the issue of relocation per se, but even as Nihonbashi lay in smoldering ruins, one diehard faction of dealers resisted the move so strongly that the compensation issue remained as intractable as ever. In 1928, Nihonbashi dealers were responsible for a massive bribery scheme to influence the Tokyo City Council to provide compensation, provoking a scandal so severe that the Home Minister dissolved the council, and the following year the mayor resigned (Seidensticker 1990). Finally, in the early 1940s, the national government, using wartime powers, forced a settlement by agreeing to pay cash compensation to the old Nihonbashi dealers at one-tenth of the level originally demanded.

The history of the market has been almost constantly marked by disputes involving groups possessing—or arguing that they ought to possess—inherent rights based on previous government entitlements or recognition. Contemporary examples include the case of the Ōta Market, near Haneda Airport, which began operations in 1990 with several dozen seafood *nakaoroshi* relocated from Tsukiji and several dozen more relocated from a closed market at Ōmori. These *nakaoroshi* are represented by three separate organizations. One is a branch of Tō-Oroshi representing the wholesalers who were induced to move from Tsukiji; one is an organization of wholesalers from the old Ōmori marketplace who favored relocation to Ōta; and one is an organization of wholesalers also originally from Ōmori but who were opposed to the relocation. When the Ōta Market was created, it was originally planned to replace Tsukiji, but that move was blocked by opposition from Tsukiji dealers, retailers who favored the more convenient Tsukiji location, the ward government of Chūō-ku (where Tsukiji is located) that was concerned over the loss of tax revenues, and environmentalists concerned about the impact on Tokyo Bay's dwindling wetlands. As the combined opposition of these diverse allies stalled the planning process, estimated costs mounted to a point where the national and municipal governments realized the full project was financially prohibitive, but a scaled-back version was built.

The Ōta Market does, however, entirely replace the old Kanda Produce Market (formerly located next to Akihabara Station in central Tokyo), and the relocated Kanda vegetable *nakaoroshi* are similarly split between a faction who agreed to go along with relocation and those who were adamantly opposed. These groups are now also represented at Ōta by separate federations. Each group maintains its perspective on the economic rights and prerogatives that they possessed in their former locations, those that they possess in their new locations, and the obligations and entitlements that continue to be owed them by the municipal government now that they are relocated to Ōta.

Even among the Tsukiji relocatees in the Ōta branch of Tō-Oroshi, fault lines already exist for factional divisions around the issues of entitlements, reflecting the fact that the sixty-odd Tsukiji relocatees were induced to move to Ōta during three separate campaigns by the Tokyo Metropolitan Government. Those in the first wave were told that they would have to relinquish their Tsukiji stalls as soon as the Ōta market went into full operation. Those in the later two waves were allowed to retain varying degrees of participation in the Tsukiji market. And so members of the first two groups to move to Ōta feel their rights were unfairly curtailed.

Thus, differential governmental entitlements or enfranchisements contribute to the identification of group interests along factional lines that may recede but never disappear, and in this case may be created *de novo* by government policy. One key to understanding the basis for the preservation of institutional fissioning is that in these (and many other) cases, government bestowal or recognition of rights over particular economic activities of production or distribution is linked to implied acknowledgment that, when those rights are abrogated, compensation is warranted. Whether through government willingness to offer compensation or the ability of entrenched interest groups to block action until compensation is awarded, the net effect is the same. Government recognition of a cartel's rights over particular economic spheres carries with it the promise of future compensation should that cartel's interests be infringed.

Ad Hoc Alliances

Thus far, I have discussed the formation of interest groups as officially recognized bodies with routinized roles in the institutional structure of the marketplace. Other forms of social affiliation are also the basis for the creation of interest groups, many of them very loosely organized as ad hoc coalitions. Such groups may not be formally involved in the market's institutional framework, but they are spawned by the interplay of institutional forces in the marketplace and represent individual and collective strategic responses to the conditions of marketplace life. Two different cases illustrate the formation of such groups and the ways in which their existence is predicated on many of the same organizational dynamics that shape the formal groups that make up the institutional structure of the marketplace. The first example involves the allocation of space among *nakaoroshi*; the second focuses on the role of other social identities in creating alliances within the marketplace.

Allocational Equity and the Advantages of Microcoalitions

I mentioned previously that among the salient characteristics of the cartelization of governance at Tsukiji is the autonomy given to groups to administer those affairs that directly affect their membership and a corresponding tendency to aim toward some rough standard of equity among the members of the group. One of the most striking examples of this is found in the quadrennial lotteries run by Tō-Oroshi to reassign the 1,677 stalls among its members. Although the goal of equitable distribution of locational advantage over the long term is pursued by the institution as a whole through these lotteries, at the same time, microcoalitions of individual wholesalers form to maximize their advantages in the short term. Thus, this case illustrates ways in which the formal institutional dynamics of the marketplace set in motion forces that create other organizational strategies pursued at a lower level.

The 1,677 stalls for *nakaoroshi* occupy three enormous fan-shaped sheds, where rows upon rows of stalls jumble specialities with no apparent rhyme or reason. Even to a casual observer, clear differences among the stalls betray the locational advantages or disadvantages inherent in their placement, shape, and size. Stalls on the narrow front edge of the fan have easy access and attract buyers of small quantities of high-quality, *sushi*-grade fish. Wholesalers whose business is based on bulk sales to supermarket chains, however, find that the ideal location is the back edge of the sheds, furthest from the marketplace entrance for walk-in customers but more convenient to truck loading docks. Regardless of specialty, a location at the intersection of two aisles is always preferable to a midblock location where a customer must pass many other stalls to reach a particular shop.

Wholesalers themselves are acutely aware of the advantages and disadvantages of specific locations for their individual market niches. Every stall has its good and bad points, and most wholesalers can hold forth eloquently about the bad aspects of their stalls while grumbling about the unbeatable attributes of their competitors' locations.

Therefore, to impose some rough form of equality at least on the physical environment of business, every few years almost every *nakaoroshi* changes location as a result of the elaborate lottery system run by Tō-Oroshi, the *nakaoroshi* federation. The intent of the system is to equalize, over the long run, inequities created among stall holders by the physical circumstances of location. The effort is justified in the interests of equity among *nakaoroshi*, which is a principle at the heart of group dynamics, and of fairness, a concept legally embedded in the charter of the marketplace. There is, however, no legal requirement nor any administrative imperative to ensure fairness through stall rotations as such, and the system is carried out by Tō-Oroshi, which has administered the lotteries since the early 1950s. The lottery held in 1995 was the sixteenth such reallocation of stalls since 1951.

The details of the lottery system are highly complex and arcane (see Bestor, 1992, for a more detailed description). For the current discussion, only a few points about the system are necessary.

For the lottery, the market is divided into four major blocks, each containing between 250 and 480 stalls. Each block is intended to include roughly equivalent mixtures of good and bad locations. Each block has a general appeal, however, for particular sets of wholesalers, as mentioned earlier.

The lotteries are an elaborate undertaking, requiring months of planning through several stages. First, wholesalers file applications for one of the four major blocks. For administrative purposes, stalls (*tenpo*) are paired (into units called *koma*). Unless a *nakaoroshi* controls an even number of stalls, the wholesaler must find a partner or partners to file an application for one or more *koma*. That is, any number of wholesalers controlling any number of stalls may file a joint application in the lottery, as long as the total number of stalls they represent is an even number. Microcoalitions of three, four, five, or more wholesalers are not uncommon, representing various combinations of single- and multiple-stall holders.

Microcoalitions are formed, applications are filed, and after several preliminary lotteries to ensure that each block has precisely the proper number of applicants, the main lottery is held. The lottery does not assign specific locations but establishes a sequential order for filling locations. That is, an applicant group does not apply for particular locations that it either gets or doesn't through the luck of the draw, nor does it get to choose its preferred location based on some priority established by the lottery. Instead, each applicant group gets a number that indicates its relative position in a queue to fill a predetermined sequence of stalls. In a process rather like stringing different sized beads on a necklace, the final locations are not known until all applications have been picked. If the first applicant to draw a number pulled number 2 and the application was for five *koma* (ten stalls), the exact location of those stalls would not be clear until eventually some other applicant drew number 1. If the applicant group that drew number 1 controlled six stalls, then it would get stalls one through six, and the earlier applicant group would get stalls seven through sixteen. If an applicant drew number 50, the exact location of that sequence of stalls would not become clear until all the intervening lottery numbers (1 through 49) had been pulled and matched with the exact numbers of stalls that each applicant represented.

The lotteries are a momentous event; the outcome can radically affect a wholesaler's fortunes for years to come. Although hard figures are impossible to come by, many wholesalers estimate that the locational shift can affect their volume by as much as 10 to 15 percent either way. A good location can't save a failing business, and a bad location won't ruin a strong one, but middling operations can be seriously affected, and of course, no wholesaler can face a potential swing in volume of this magnitude with total equanimity. Volume aside, the stall rotations always mean a change in one's surroundings and social environment. Inevitably some established customers will simply find a more convenient shop and disappear; new neighbors may be helpful or difficult to get along with; one may end up surrounded by struggling stalls that diminish the appeal of one's own; perhaps one will be dwarfed by a giant firm that occupies ten or twelve stalls across the aisle; or a best friend or fiercest competitor may end up next door.

Overall, the lottery system aims to dampen the effects of locational advantage on average over time. But even as Tō-Oroshi aims for systemic equalization, for any stall holder the lottery clearly poses the risk of great fluctuations in the individual business. Needless to say, in the face of the lottery's enormous potential impact, wholesalers have devised many counterstrategies to try maximize their chances or minimize their risks.

On the maximizing side—for at least some wholesalers—the supernatural offers partial reassurance. Throughout the weeks and months leading to the lotteries, fortune tellers are consulted and geomancers are engaged to determine the best blocks and to advise on what route a wholesaler (or his particularly charmed representative) should take on the way to the lottery drawing. Amulets are obtained from favored shrines and temples, and unmarried daughters are carefully groomed to draw the family's fateful lottery slip. Many wholesalers belong to quasireligious pilgrimage groups (*kō*) constituted by trade specialty or hometown ties; each group is loosely centered on a shrine or temple that serves as the site for communal rituals and a convenient destination for occasional recreational outings. The *kō* organized by *unagi* dealers, for example, is centered on Takao-san, a holy mountain and pilgrimage site to the west of Tokyo. Several other *kō*—centered on the temple at Narita, the Asakusa Kannon, or other major pilgrimage sites in the Kantō region—are also active at Tsukiji, although their members are not necessarily all drawn from the same occupational specialities. Of course, many Tsukiji traders are individually active in *kō* that have no particular connection to the marketplace. During the season of the lotteries, these quasireligious affiliations take on a more urgent cast, as wholesalers seek intercession or oracular guidance from shrines and temples they ordinarily visit only for occasional weekends of relaxation and camaraderie.

On more mundane levels, risk minimizing is pursued by wholesalers who build lottery coalitions to be able to choose their neighbors and possibly arrange informal swaps of space. Wholesalers must choose a block in the early stages of the lottery, and so in that sense they can choose the broad block within which their stall will ultimately be located. Of course, they can do nothing to determine *where* within that block they may ultimately land. One way to minimize risk is by carefully choosing a group of partners with whom to make joint application in the lottery as a means of manipulating the microenvironment. The formation of such coalitions—made necessary by the administrative requirement that all stall assignments be in multiples of two—creates two possibilities. In the first place, it enables a wholesaler to choose his neighbors. One can avoid the risk of having one's greatest competitor right next door (though he may end up down the block or across the aisle). Also, one can arrange to have a congenial and complementary next-door neighbor. With luck, a properly selected next-door neighbor will refer some of his established clients.

The second advantage that may result from coalitions has to do with the physical placement of stalls. Even though a coalition cannot control where within a large block of several hundred stalls its application may land it—where on the necklace its particular bead will be—the larger the coalition, the greater the odds that the stalls it draws will include *some* better than average locations. It may not include, for example, a premier corner location, but it may include a corner of some kind. Among members of a coalition, internal deals can be reached for assignment of the specific stalls that each coalition member will ultimately occupy, because it is up to the coalition members to allocate among themselves the space that they are allocated through the lottery. For example, if a coalition includes five firms that together control fourteen stalls, it is certain—because the rows of stalls are intersected by aisles at eight- to twelve-stall intervals—that the coalition will end up with at least two (and possibly four) corner stalls, as well as a variety of midblock locations. The businesses of some coalition members may be less sensitive to location than others. A dried fish dealer who works mostly with standing orders from established customers may be quite content with a midblock location. Another coalition member may require the prominence and display space afforded by a corner. A *sushi* supplier with a large walk-in trade may enter a coalition precisely to be assured of getting a high-profile corner stall. Because the allocation of stalls within a coalition is left to its own deliberations, a variety of private deals are struck to seal these internal allocations.

Shared Affiliations and Other Identities

Microcoalitions for the purposes of the lottery are transitory, ceasing to have any real organizational meaning after the preliminary negotiations, the lotteries, and the final allocations of space. Of course, microcoalition members become close neighbors from one lottery until at least the next, and the ties among them remain active even if the coalition as such does not. Although some coalition partnerships are virtually permanent, others may be one-time affiliations. As individual businesses change over time, their needs for—and their appeal to—particular kinds of coalition partners may change dramatically.

In selecting partners for a lottery coalition, *nakaoroshi* are guided by many considerations, most importantly, the compatibility of specializations, appropriate scale, and reputation. In assessing reputation and the degree of trust and reliability one can place in a potential coalition partner and future neighbor, *nakaoroshi* can call upon many dimensions of personal affiliation, either to solicit known partners or to arrange introductions to appropriate but as yet unknown ones.

Kinship is a major factor in *nakaoroshi* networks, because intermarriage among *nakaoroshi* families is common. Thus, almost every *nakaoroshi* has at least a handful of other firms to whom some kin connection can be drawn. Fictive kinship, particularly through traditional patterns of master–apprentice relations, also creates dense networks that closely intertwine with those of consanguinial and affinal kinship. Older firms can trace either kinship or master–apprentice connections with dozens of other shops that over the generations have split from the main shop in a pattern known as *norenwake* ("dividing the curtain"). When a new business was established in this fashion, it was customary for a son or apprentice to take part of his master's shop name (*yagō*) for his business, symbolically dividing the shop curtain (*noren*) on which *yagō* were typically inscribed.

Many groups of shops tracing descent from a common ancestral shop continue to be identifiable by shop names (*yagō*) that contain a common element; for example, *Ise*hachi, *Ise*tomo, and *Ise*mata all trace their origins back to a now vanished shop, *Ise*nami. In the past generation or so, *norenwake* has become less common, but sending a son out to work in a friend's or a cousin's shop for a few years before

the son comes back into the family business is a frequent practice, creating somewhat similar (if less intense) patterns of affiliation among firms. These and other
personal ties among *nakaoroshi* are used not only in forming the microcoalitions
discussed previously, but also are frequently relied on for labor recruitment, customer introductions, and, perhaps most crucial on a day-to-day basis, emergency
sources of supply when one's inventory runs low or unusual conditions in the auctions prevent one from purchasing adequate stock.

Shared affiliations with native places are a common basis for identity in the
Tsukiji marketplace, both used conversationally to identify others and often reflected as well in stylized motifs adopted for shop names (*yagō*). In some cases, affiliations based on common place of origin are loosely institutionalized in *kō*, the
nominally religious pilgrimage groups mentioned previously that focus their de-
votional (and recreational) energies on a particular shrine or temple that symbol-
izes a particular locale. In other cases, native place ties are the basis for *kai*, or
clubs, for traders from a particular town or region.

One such group represents the several dozen wholesalers tracing their origins to
the Fukagawa district of Tokyo, just north of Tsukiji, where until a generation or
two ago fishers could still exploit the estuary of the Sumida River. Two groups
draw their members from old fishing communities 60 to 70 miles from Tokyo, one
from the Jōban coast to the northeast, the other from the deep water fishing port of
Chōshi due east on the Pacific Coast of Chiba. Yet a fourth group draws its members
from those who trace their ancestry to a region near Nagoya.

By and large, these organizations are informal; the networks of affiliation they
represent are affective rather than instrumental. They generally reflect occupational specializations only very loosely, although such networks certainly play a
role in providing introductions that are critical in labor recruitment. Identification
with native places is very strong in Japanese working class culture, but native
place ties play a relatively weak organizational role in most cases.

More crucial than affiliations based on place are those based on shared institutional experiences. Thus, colleges, senior and junior high schools, and even elementary schools spawn highly cohesive alumni groups and networks of "old boys"
whose interactions with one another continue for decades. At Tsukiji old boy networks shape recruitment of labor and, to some extent, marriages (for example, by
framing the contexts of introductions, selections of go-betweens, or definitions of
social fields in which inquiries about eligible partners may be carried out). Clearly
alumni ties—for example, from a particular fisheries high school or fisheries college—carry an element of native place, but school ties are much more highly focused on the experience of a particular school and its institutional culture as the
relevant frame of reference.

Native Places and "Middleman Minorities"

In some cases, native place ties per se have played a role in the emergence at Tsukiji of "middleman minorities" (Bonacich, 1973). These minorities are able to exploit existing, shared affiliations (in this instance, not ethnic, but regional) to create dense networks of information and exchange that enable members of the network

to dominate particular economic niches. This is particularly the case when the native place ties are organized around claims of collective entitlement, similar to the cases of cartels discussed previously.

The most prominent example at Tsukiji is what some market old-timers call the "Urayasu *renchū*" (the "Urayasu crowd"), so named for their native place, the old fishing port of Urayasu, located on the border between Tokyo and Chiba Prefectures just across the head of Tokyo Bay from where Tsukiji stands at the mouth of the Sumida River. Roughly 10 to 15 percent of the midlevel wholesaling firms at Tsukiji are regarded as Urayasu firms. Typically, they are in the shellfish business or related specialities (such as supplying *sushi* chefs), but the Urayasu firms also include high-profile tuna wholesalers who operate some of Tsukiji's largest and most prosperous companies.

Their emergence as a powerful—and none-too-well-loved—group at Tsukiji has occurred over the past generation or so, as fishers from Urayasu gradually transformed themselves into Tsukiji traders. For generations, Urayasu fishers had extensive connections to the wholesale and retail fish trade in Tokyo. Urayasu had been a major supplier of clams and other shellfish to Tokyo. Some Urayasu peddlers sold shellfish door to door in Tokyo; some Urayasu shellfish were sold directly to retail fishmongers in Tokyo; and some shellfish were sent directly to the Tsukiji seafood market. As shellfish harvesting came to an end in Urayasu in the 1960s (for reasons described below), many Urayasu fishers ended up at Tsukiji, first working as employees of midlevel wholesalers and then, as they acquired experience in the wholesale trade and purchased *nakaoroshi* licenses, becoming midlevel wholesalers themselves.

Technically, *nakaoroshi* licenses cannot be bought and sold at will. However, TMG regulations do allow the "transfer" of licenses under certain circumstances. Inheritance by a son—or by a daughter and an adopted son-in-law—are typical means of transferring a license. Outright sale is possible as long as the purchaser meets certain standards of capital and reputation and has previous experience working in the market for not fewer than five years (standards that must also be met in the case of inheritance). Licenses are therefore not available to total newcomers. In recent years, licenses have traded in the range between 150- and 200-million yen. Fishers from Urayasu had both the connections and the capital to acquire licenses.

The Urayasu case, however, is not simply one of like-minded people of similar origins carving out a common territory to dominate jointly. It also is a further example of ways in which government recognition of collective rights and subsequent compensation for the abrogation of those rights are fundamental factors in the formation and maintenance of interest groups.

During the 1950s and 1960s, the fishing industry in Tokyo Bay was almost eliminated. On the one hand, industrial pollution wiped out many fishing grounds. On the other hand, many areas of shallow water were filled in and reclaimed from the bay to create tracts for further industrial development. One such area included the waters and mud flats off Urayasu, long an important grounds for shellfish harvesting.

As the government pushed forward with land reclamation schemes for the Urayasu tide flats, negotiations began over compensation to the fishers for the loss of their ancestral fishing grounds and their contemporary livelihoods. In both

Japanese customary law and (since the nineteenth century) administrative law as well, Japanese fishers have rights of sea tenure (*gyogyōken*) to particular fishing grounds that are exercised collectively—nowadays by all members of a local fisheries cooperative (Gyogyō Kyōdō Kumiai). The fishers of Urayasu negotiated skillfully for compensation for the loss of their fishing grounds as the reclamation plans were developed, and when agreement was reached, Urayasu fishers received cash settlements as well as rights to some of the land being reclaimed.

The land-reclamation projects ended the shellfish business but left the Urayasu fishers with strong connections to Tsukiji—and the capital to pursue those ties further. Many Urayasu fishers did. Today somewhere between 100 and 150 firms at Tsukiji are controlled by people from Urayasu, and Urayasu people work in many more firms as well.

The subsequent success of Urayasu firms brings forth comments of grudging admiration from other Tsukiji traders in terms that make even virtue seem like dark conspiracy. Detractors grumble that the Urayasu wholesalers succeed because, as former fishers, they are willing to work hard and long under miserable conditions. Urayasu women and children are not accustomed to luxury, others complain, and they are willing to work in the stalls with the men. They are clannish and help each other out, and they have enormous amounts of capital.

The unspoken implication of the last point, of course, is that their capital is both unearned and undeserved, although it originated in the payments provided by the government to compensate for the loss of their preexisting fishing rights. Urayasu fishers, in fact, have benefited from a succession of extraordinary windfalls. With their original compensation payments, many acquired licenses at Tsukiji. Most already owned land in Urayasu, and many more invested in more with their compensation. As real estate values grew explosively throughout the 1980s, Urayasu landowners were able to finance other business ventures (for example, expansion at Tsukiji) through real estate loans readily available in what is now regarded as "the bubble economy" of the 1980s. Urayasu especially profited from the extension of a Tokyo subway line that made Urayasu one of the bedroom communities most convenient to central Tokyo. To gild the lily, Tokyo Disneyland was built in Urayasu in the late 1970s and early 1980s, bringing with it the development of luxury hotels. Land values rose still further. To the wondering eyes of other Tsukiji traders, Urayasu is indeed a magic kingdom.

In the Urayasu case, government recognition of collective rights and compensation for their loss played a fundamental, if probably unintended, role in stimulating the massive entry of Urayasu fishers into the Tsukiji market. As Urayasu traders have become a major bloc at Tsukiji, the collective interests of the past have continued to provide a basis for the identification of mutual interests in the present. This lock-in of collective interests and identity has contributed to the organization of an interest group that mobilizes Urayasu traders in the name of native place solidarity. This group is not accorded formal authority in the governance of the marketplace as a whole—on a footing comparable with a *gyōkai*, for example. Nevertheless, the Urayasu group wields considerable influence within Tō-Oroshi, as well as within the *gyōkai* representing specialities in which Urayasu traders have concentrated: *sushi* suppliers (*tokushumono*) and tuna (*ōmono*).

Summary and Conclusions

I have focused my analysis on the institutional dynamics of groups in the Tsukiji marketplace, specifically, the creation of horizontal mutual interests, the crystallization of those interests into formally organized groups, the mobilization of mutual interest and reciprocity in response to the institutional conditions of market life, and the role of government in the formation of interest groups.

These themes run through a diverse array of ethnographic and historical examples that illustrate how the economic tasks of the marketplace are embedded in complex institutional structures, themselves constructed and reconstructed by cultural factors and the dynamics of social relationships. The process whereby these institutional structures accord recognition to groups and create the conditions that give rise to group formation display a number of interrelated key features:

1. The government enfranchises categories of actors with common rights over property, information, or other resources, thereby constituting those actors as a group linked by their interests in these common rights. At the present time, such groups are defined in large part by the market's licensing requirements that distinguish particular categories of actors and bestow specific rights, privileges, and obligations on the members of each category as a group.

2. These groups are endowed with broad powers to administer autonomously those affairs that directly affect their own memberships. In pursuit of the common interests of their members, groups act as cartels.

3. The administrative structure of the marketplace as a whole rests on the assumption that officially recognized and enfranchised groups or cartels—each representing a particular sphere of economic activity—will jointly hammer out arrangements for coordination and governance of the market's operations with a minimum of guidance from the government's administrators. The result is not "administrative guidance," as the term is often used in analyses of the Japanese political economy, but rather should be seen as "administrative disinterest" in the decision-making process and its outcomes.

4. Almost by definition, cartels stabilize the boundaries of trading communities, and, through cartelized decision-making and negotiation, ensure high degrees of consistency among group members in the ways in which they exchange information, behave at auctions, and define desirable commodities. This consistency contributes to the stability of seemingly hierarchical linkages among groups at different levels in the market system.

5. Groups not only represent the mutual interests of the group against other actors through this cartelized decision-making system, but they also serve to define the competitive environment existing among members of this group.

6. The group's internal regulatory impulses to define relationships among members in this fashion—through negotiations with other groups and the transactional rules that result—tend to preserve the relative positions of all members according to some rough standard of equity rather than to improve the competitive position of some members at the expense of others.

7. Groups are organized in a segmentary structure. Once amalgamated or clustered into higher level organizations, preexisting groups retain a collective identity, cohesive internal organization, and controlling voice over those issues most di-

rectly concerned with their original common interests, even when the objective circumstances of that pre-existing common interest have radically changed. Groups rarely relinquish their rights over a particular trade niche, nor do they easily dissolve themselves into larger groups.

8. The persistence of groups, and hence the segmentary structure of higher level organizations, is a product of the particular style of indirect administration of economic affairs encouraged by government agencies that enfranchise groups with decision-making powers and internal autonomy over the administration of their market niches.

9. Organizational consolidation therefore does not erase the differences among enfranchised privileges or prerogatives that spawned the interest groups in the first place. It is not simply that contemporary common interests continue to give segmentary units their cohesive framework. Rather, the definition of common interests and the organization of traders around those interests at some point in the past creates a kind of institutional lock-in that ensures the group will continue to maintain common interests—even if only referential ones linked to past conditions in the marketplace—that mark its existence. That is, perceptions of separate pasts and distinct paths of structural accommodation have lasting impact on group identity and cohesion. Even as groups have evolved out of historically distinct niches or identities and have converged toward what are now functionally identical roles in the market, the dynamics of group formation preserve earlier institutional distinctions.

10. Enfranchised privilege leads to segmentary structure of cartels, whereby rights and prerogatives granted members of a group at some point in the past continue to be the basis for at least incipient divisions in the present. The collective interests of the past continue to provide a basis for the identification of mutual interests in the present.

11. Conflicts and disputes arise when changes in the overall structure of the market's operations threaten to eliminate or displace groups that possess—or argue that they ought to possess—inherent rights based on previous government entitlements or recognition. Thus, differential governmental entitlements or enfranchisements contribute to the identification of group interests along factional lines that may recede but never disappear.

12. The solution of such disputes is often achieved by government compensation for the loss of collective rights over particular economic activities or niches. This, in turn, reflects the apparent fact that government bestowal or recognition of rights to particular economic niches carries with it the implicit acknowledgment that compensation is warranted when the rights are withdrawn or abrogated. Government recognition of a cartel's rights over particular economic spheres carries with it the promise of future compensation should that cartel's interests be infringed.

13. This implicit expectation of compensation is one element in creating and preserving the segmentary structure of group organization. On the one hand, many groups maintain their common interests in awaiting compensation or redress of some sort for perceived losses of rights; on the other hand, other groups who have received compensation in the past are united by the common circumstances of the compensation. When issues concerning the scope or future legitimacy of the group's enfranchisement occur, negotiation of a compromise or compensation with

the group as a whole (via the group's internally constituted institutions), rather than with individual members, thereby confirms or reaffirms the primacy of the group first created by the government's enfranchisement. This is not a matter of cultural preference (i.e., elevation of the group over the individual). It is, rather, an issue of institutional structure similar to those surrounding common property rights in many other domains of Japanese society [see R. Marshall (1984) on rural decision-making].

14. Finally, the formal institutional dynamics of the marketplace set in motion forces that create other organizational strategies pursued at lower, less formal levels. The interplay of institutional forces in the marketplace creates conditions in which various de facto coalitions and alliances are formed as individual and collective strategic responses to market life, even though the resulting coalitions and alliances are not formally involved in or recognized by the market's institutional framework.

The Japanese anthropologist, Nakane Chie, in her famous formulation of Japanese social structure (Nakane, 1970), proposed a model of vertical social integration accomplished through the pervasive group orientation of Japanese social life (see Befu, 1980). The Tsukiji marketplace appears to conform to her model: groups or cartels are the significant components of the institutional structures of market governance at all levels. Nakane's model, however, posits group structure as the elaboration of hierarchical dyadic ties between superiors and subordinates, leaders and followers. The membership of a group, therefore, in her view is linked through the bundling of dyadic ties focused on a common leader or superior. Horizontal links among equals (i.e., among followers or subordinates) are weak or attenuated, and in the absence of the leader, the group would theoretically dissolve. The Tsukiji case, however, suggests that this view of group dynamics and group formation as an elaboration of individuals' structural role relationships ignores the process whereby groups are formed and coalesce around mutual common interests that provide strong and enduring horizontal linkages among relative equals. Although the groups that thus form may be marked internally by various hierarchical relationships (e.g., between leaders and followers, *senpai* and *kōhai*), common interests rather than hierarchical relationships give form and substance to the groups as active agents in the operations of the marketplace. The strong group orientation of the Tsukiji marketplace, therefore, is not simply the product of an overlay of cultural and social patterns external to economic process, but rather it is generated by the institutional system in which the economic activity of the market is embedded.

Note

Fieldwork at the Tsukiji marketplace and elsewhere in Japan was carried out during February–July 1989; January, July, and September–November 1990; May–June 1991; December–January 1991–92; May–June 1994; June–July 1995; and July–October 1997. Research in Japan as well as in the United States was made possible by the support of a number of organizations, including, at various times, the Japan Foundation, the Social Science Research Council, the U.S. Department of Education's Fulbright Program, the National Science Foundation (Grant number BNS 90-08696), the Abe Fellowship Program of the Center for Global Partnership, the New York Sea Grant Institute (Grant number R/SPD-3), the East Asian Institute and the

Center on Japanese Economy and Business, both of Columbia University, and the East Asia Program of Cornell University.

Special thanks go to the many people associated with Tsukiji who gave so generously of their time and knowledge about the marketplace and who made possible my access to it. The officers, members, and staff members of the Tōkyō Uoichiba Oroshi Kyōdō Kumiai and officials of the Tokyo Metropolitan Government's Bureau of Markets were particularly helpful both in providing access to unpublished documents and in their willingness to be interviewed. Victoria Lyon Bestor, Dorothy Bestor, and Dawn Grimes MacLellan all gave detailed readings of the manuscript and offered many suggestions for improvement. Of course, I am solely responsible for the statements of fact, interpretation, and opinion expressed here.

References

Befu, H. "The Group Model of Japanese Society and an Alternative." *Rice University Studies*, 66–1 (1980): 169–87.

Bestor, T. C. "Trading Places: Locational Advantage and the Culture of Equity in the Tsukiji Wholesale Fish Market." Paper presented at the annual meeting of the American Anthropological Association, San Francisco, 1992.

Bestor, T. C. "Visible Hands: Auctions and Institutional Integration in the Tsukiji Wholesale Fish Market, Tokyo." in Schon Beechler and Kristin Stucker (eds.), *Japanese Business*. Routledge. 1997.

Bestor, T. C. "The Raw, the Cooked, and the Industrial: Food Culture and Commodification in a Japanese Market." *Cultural Anthropology*, in press.

Bestor, T. C. *Tokyo's Marketplace: Culture and Trade in the Tsukiji Wholesale Seafood Market*. Forthcoming.

Bonacich, E. "A Theory of Middleman Minorities." *American Sociological Review*, 38–5 (1973): 583–94.

Granovetter, M. "Economic Action and Social Structure: The Problem of Embeddedness." *American Sociological Review*, 91–3 (1985): 481–510.

Marshall, R. *Collective Decision-making in Rural Japan*. Ann Arbor, Mich.: Center for Japanese Studies, University of Michigan, 1984.

Nakane, C. *Japanese Society*. Berkeley: University of California Press, 1970.

New York Times. November 11, 1996, pg. B4.

Nikkan Shokuryō Shinbunsha, *Tōkyō-to Chūō Oroshiuri Shijō Suisanbutsu-bu Nakaoroshi Gyōsha Meibō 1990-Nenpan*. Tokyo: Nikkan Shokuryō Shinbunsha, 1990.

Seidensticker, E. *Tokyo Rising*. New York: Knopf. 1990.

Tōkyō-to Chūō Oroshiuri Shijō. *Tōkyō-to Chūō Oroshiuri Shijō-shi* [History of the Tokyo Central Wholesale Market]. 2 vols. Tokyo: Tōkyō-to. 1958 and 1963.

Tōkyō-to Chūō Oroshiuri Shijō. *Tsukiji Shijō Gaiyō*. Tokyo: Tōkyō-to, 1997.

9

Patterns of Asian Network Capitalism

The Cases of Taiwan and South Korea

A passage from Perry Anderson's excellent essay on "The Asiatic Mode of Production" sets the tone for this chapter. After lengthy discussion of the literature on the Asiatic mode of production, Anderson (1974, p. 549) concluded with the following "procedural lesson":

> Asian development cannot in any way be reduced to a uniform residual category, left over after the canons of European evolution have been established. Any serious theoretical exploration of the historical field outside . . . Europe will have to supersede traditional and generic contrasts with it, and proceed to a concrete and accurate typology of social formations and State systems in their own right, which respects their very great differences of structure and development. It is merely in the night of our ignorance that all alien shapes take on the same hue.

In this insightful passage, Anderson identified two mistakes that Western theorists frequently make.

The first mistake is to view all non-Western societies—and here we are talking about the Asian ones, in particular—either at lesser versions of models seen more clearly in the West or as residual categories. In this latter role, such non-Western societies sometimes take the form of a reverse or mirror image of what has occurred in the West. This kind of thinking is a mistake, because Asian societies have developed according to their internal and intersocietal dynamics and follow the trajectories that these historical patterns provide.

The second procedural error is to conclude, after viewing from the distant cultural vantage point that we call the West, that all Asian societies are alike. Analyzing European development, we would never seriously argue that all European states or all European economies are alike, that in the end there are no differences between France and Spain or England and Ireland, just to pick two sets of neighboring countries. Yet, even today, when we should know better, good and well-intentioned scholars search for the Asian model of development or the model of Asian management. This kind of thinking is also an error, because there are, in-

deed, very great differences among Asian societies, differences that made consequential differences in the patterns of historical change, including the incorporation of capitalism.

Network- and Firm-Based Economies

In this chapter, I concentrate on the second lesson. In an effort to demonstrate the
organizational variation among Asian economies, I examine some macroscopic differences in the economic organization of Taiwan and South Korea, both of which
substantially differ from Japan. But before I begin this examination, I want to touch
on one major point of difference that exists between Asian and Western economies
at a more general level. This point of difference sets the background to my discussion of the economies of Taiwan and South Korea. As Nicole Biggart and I (Biggart
and Hamilton, 1992; also see Whitley, 1992) have described elsewhere, Asian
economies, although greatly different from one another, are broadly similar in that
their organization structure rests on very prominent interfirm relationships. Many
other analysts (Fruin, 1992; Gerlach, 1992; Hamilton, 1991a; Whitley, 1992) have
also noted the prominence of Asian business networks but have generally done so
in the course of examining only one country.

Although many differences exist within each region of the world, I still argue,
from a typological point of view, that the organizational structure found in Asian
economies rests on relational networks. In contrast, the organizational structure
found in Western economies rests on the legal, and to some extent the economic,
individuation of economic actors, which are usually firms. Right away, many read-
ers may think of numerous Western examples to the contrary, such as all those networks created by corporate interlocks in the United States and Europe (Scott, 1991)
or all the production networks created through the spread of subcontracting systems, the flexible specialization described so well by Piore and Sabel (1984). For
Asia, one might recall all those large firms whose names seem so familiar today—
the Sonys, the Toyotas, and the Hyundais of Asia—and all the property across the
world that they own. There are, of course, networks in Western economies and
firms in Asian economies, but my point here is what takes precedence in determining economic structure. Is it the firm, or is it the network in which the firm is
embedded? My answer is that Asian economies are network based, whereas Western economies are firm based.

Let me quickly draw some differences between these types of economies. First,
in network-based economies, relational bonds among people (e.g., owners, workers, suppliers) are of paramount importance. Such relational bonds precede business and structure it; accordingly, such bonds contain strong normative elements
and form qualitatively different links for different types of people. For instance, regional bonds, such as those formed between people coming from the same home
town, identify, in normative terms, a particular type of relationship and a particular type of morality that is intrinsic to that relationship (Fei, 1992). But whatever
the tie, relational bonds always connote something qualitative and moral about the
interaction among those joined by network ties.

By contrast, in firm-based economies, firm boundaries are extremely important.
Western firms are known by their boundaries. Exactly who owns what and who

controls it weigh on Western minds a great deal. Inputs and outputs, profits and losses, or whatever accounting jargon one elects to use, all have, as a part of their structural grammar, some aspect of firm boundaries as necessary dividing lines. In sociological terms this division is understandable because the importance of firm boundaries derives from the fact that such dividing lines separate two types of authority, neither of which prevails in Asia in the same way. Inside the organization, in principle at least, we govern people uniformly through a command structure, as symbolized by a line-and-block chart, that is set up expressly for that purpose. Outside and among organizations, again in principle at least, we govern actors, whether firms or individuals, by having them follow their best interests.

Conceptually, this "control through free will" is accomplished in three ways. First, we establish an environment of constraints, which we call laws or the legal framework. Second, we govern particular forms of interaction between otherwise free actors by means of contracts; these contracts stipulate decisions and bind free will. Finally, people are governed by exercising "their own good sense," which is what Adam Smith meant by the term "market"; people who have been socialized to accept a given rationality for action will act the same in situations that are structured to solicit that rationality. A stock market is a perfect example.

Network-based economies, however, do not have such hard boundaries and do not have theoretically autonomous, individuated actors. Asian countries all have laws and recognize legal contracts, but in none of the Asian countries is these laws and contracts as salient or as enforced as they are in the West. In fact, the more I study Asian economic organization, the more I realize how very difficult it is to draw clearly defined boundaries anywhere and how impossible it is to impute individual rights to economic actors. In Asian settings, ownership and control are often very ambiguous and diffuse, and purposefully so. Therefore, it is hard to tell where one firm ends and another begins.

That briefly sketches a dimension of difference between Eastern and Western economic structure. I return to this contrast in my conclusion, but for now I will stress that Taiwan and South Korea are both network-based economies. I now explain the differences in the economic network structures of these two societies.

Differences in Industrial Structure

Having described the general organizational structure, now let me describe the issue that guides this chapter: Taiwan and South Korea are two rapidly industrializing economies. They are located in the same part of the world, about two hours' flight time from each other. They have developed in roughly the same years at roughly the same rates. They have had similar historical influences, both having been socially and culturally dominated first by China and then, in the colonial period, by Japan. Both have used similar economic policies to develop, first supporting a strategy of import substitution and then adopting an aggressive strategy of export-led industrialization. In all these background variables, Taiwan and South Korea are as nearly the same as could be imagined between any two countries today. Yet—and this is the problem for analysis—the industrial structure of the economies in these two countries differs radically. How can we explain these differences?

The first step is, of course, to demonstrate that there is sufficient empirical justification for this question to merit an explanation of the differences. These points have already been developed in other articles (Feenstra et al., 1993; Hamilton and Biggart, 1988; Hamilton and Feenstra, 1995; Hamilton et al., 1990; Orrù et al., 1991), so I will not present a prolonged demonstration of differences at this point, but rather simply summarize previous works.

Our point of observation is not the rates of economic growth, but rather the organizational patterns of that growth. The rates of economic growth are almost identical between Taiwan and South Korea, but the organizational patterns of the economy and the trajectories of development are very different. One of the clearest ways these organizational differences can be demonstrated is through a discussion of economic concentration of large business groups.

Business groups are networks or clusters of legally independent firms. In Korea, such large business groups dominate the economy. These groups are called *chaebol*, or "money cliques." There are also business groups in Taiwan, called *qiyejituan*, but they are much less prominent than their counterparts in South Korea. Table 9-1 shows general characteristics of both sets of business groups. As aggregated here, the *chaebol* are much larger than Taiwan's business groups. The differences increase, as presented in the next three tables.

Table 9-2 indicates that the top *chaebol* form a very large percentage of the total sales for the South Korean economy, whereas Taiwan's business groups, although still important, are much less dominant. Table 9-3 breaks that down still further, by showing the dominance of business groups across broad economic sectors in the two societies. Here we see that with the exception of banking and mining, *chaebol* control a very large portion of each sector across the economy, whereas Taiwan's business groups are heavily concentrated only in manufacturing. Table 9-4 further refines the analysis by breaking down the manufacturing sector into twenty major categories, which roughly correspond to the three-digit industrial classification code. Here we see yet more clearly that *chaebol* dominate industrial production. They account for more than 50 percent of the total sales in five sectors and between 25 and 50 percent in eight other sectors. In Taiwan, however, only in textiles do business groups account for more than 50 percent of the total sales, and only in three other sectors do they control between 25 and 50 percent of the total sales.

These tables show that the organizational networks represented by *chaebol* dominate the South Korean economy. By contrast, Taiwan's business groups seem to be much less significant. We should remember that these economies have roughly equal export levels, with the edge going to Taiwan, even though it has only one-half the population of South Korea. According to the General Agreement on Tariffs and Trade (GATT, 1988), Taiwan accounts for 2.2 percent and South Korea 1.9 percent of the entire world's merchandise exports. Taiwan also has a higher per capita income.

Economic Organization and Embedded Networks

Tables 9-2, 9-3, and 9-4 demonstrate some important differences between the economic organization of the societies, but without specifying those differences. What are these differences?

Table 9.1 East Asian Business Groups Comparative Statistics.

	South Korean Chaebol (1983)					Taiwan Business Groups (1983)				
	Top 5	Top 10	Top 20	Top 30	Top 50	Top 5	Top 10	Top 20	Top 50	Top 96
Total Sales (($U.S. millions)[a]	35,3602	47,317	58,187	64,509	70,772	5,084	7,488	10,444	14,027	15,842
Total Assets ($U.S. millions)[a]	24,872	33,772	44,078	49,611	56,391	5,547	9,660	13,744	17,902	19,763
Total Firms	123	202	328	412	552	90	180	283	494	743
Firms per Business Groups (by interval)	25	16	13	8	7	18	18	10	6	5
Total Workers	322,876	425,872	550,458	688,385	798,976	85,719	164,129	220,413	289,787	330,098
Workers per Business Group (by interval)	64,575	20,599	12,457	13,793	5,530	17,144	15,682	5,628	1,908	876
Workers per firm (by interval)	2,625	1,304	989	1,641	780	952	871	546	321	162

Sources: For South Korea, Ilbo Hankook (1985); for Taiwan, China Credit Information Service (1985).

[a] Exchange rate per $U.S.: Japan, 233 yen; Korea, 772; Taiwan, 40 NT$.

Table 9-2. Business Group Concentration Ratios (Percentages).

	Total Nonfinancial Sales to GNP Ratio	Value-Added Contribution to GNP	Manufacturing Sales Ratio	Manufacturing Employment Ratio
Taiwan (1983)[a]				
Top 20 Groups	17.6	—	14.1	8.3
Top 96 Groups	27.3	—	19.0	13.0
Korea (1983)[b]				
Top 20 Groups	— (76.2)[c]	—	35.3	16.2
Top 50 Groups	87.2 (92.6)[c]	19.7	45.4	22.9

[a]*Sources*: China Credit Information Service (1983); Republic of China (1983); Republic of China (1987); and Republic of China (1986).

[b]Daily Economic News (1986); Management Efficiency Research Institute (1985); Bank of Korea (1986); Chu (1985); and Lee (1985).

[c]Ratio of total sales (including Finance and Insurance) to GNP.

The clearest way to answer this question is to compare the business group networks in the two locations. These groups are not only organized differently as networks, but networks are also integrated differently within their respective economic environments; that is, they represent different types of industrial structures.

South Korean business groups vigorously compete with each other for dominance in the economy. *Chaebol* do not cooperate well with other Korean businesses, large or small, and they form export-oriented, vertically integrated networks that attempt to create economic self-sufficiency. This practice has been called "one-setism" in the literature on the Japanese economy (Gerlach, 1992). In contrast, Taiwan's business groups form economic alliances with other Taiwanese businesses, large and small, and form diverse, interlinked patterns of networks

Table 9-3. Business Group Shares by Broad Economic Sector.

Sector	Korea (1983 Sales Share of Top 50 *Chaebol*)[a]	Taiwan (1983 Sales Share of 96 Largest Groups)[b]
Mining	10.6	0.0
Manufacturing	45.4	19.0
Construction	66.0	5.6
Transport & Storage	23.1	1.8
Banking & Financial Services	—	5.8
Trading & Commerce	—	4.1

[a]Management Efficiency Research Institute (1986) and Bank of Korea (1987). For Construction and Transport & Storage, the figure is the percentage rate of *chaebol* sales to industry gross output.

[b]For Construction, the 1983 total sales figure used to calculate the ratio was estimated using reported index numbers for building construction and the transactions figures in the 1984 Input–Output Tables for Taiwan. Total sales figures for the other sectors come from the 1983 industrial census. For the Transport & Storage and Banking & Financial Services sectors, revenue figures are used. *Sources*: China Credit Information Service (1983); Republic of China (1983); Republic of China (1985); and Republic of China (1987).

Table 9-4. Business Group Shares by Manufacturing Sector (Percentages).

Sector	Korea (Top 50 *Chaebol*)[a]	Taiwan (96 Largest Enterprise Groups)[b]
Food Products	33.7	26.3
Beverage & Tobacco	27.6	3.8
Textiles	38.4	50.7
Garments & Apparel	12.6	12.0
Leather Products	15.2	9.1
Lumber & Wood Products	31.5	4.0
Pulp & Paper Products; Printing & Publishing	6.7	20.1
Chemical Materials	54.3	42.4
Chemical Products	24.0	8.4
Petroleum & Coal Products	91.9	0.0
Rubber Products	76.8	13.0
Plastic Products	0.1	5.4
Non-Metallic Mineral Products	44.6	47.6
Basic Metal	28.0	7.8
Metal Products	26.7	6.0
Machinery	34.9	3.6
Electrical & Electronic Products	50.9	22.7
Transportation Equipment	79.0	23.6
Precision Machinery	14.0	0.0
Miscellaneous Industrial Products	5.2	10.7

[a]Calculated from 1983 sales data for each *chaebol*-member firm and 1983 industrial census data. *Sources*: Daily Economic News (1986); Management Efficiency Research Institute (1985); and Economic Planning Board (1985).

[b]Calculated from 1983 sales data for each Group-member firm and 1983 industrial census data. *Sources*: China Credit Information Service (1983) and Republic of China (1983).

that solicit broad-scale economic cooperation from most participants. Vertical integration is rare, big businesses do not export final products, and economic self-sufficiency is nowhere in evidence.

To understand how these business groups fit into their respective economies, four types of interfirm networks must be understood. Interfirm networks are any stable, but not necessarily long-term, linkages among firms. The four analytically distinct types of interfirm networks are

1. ownership networks (i.e., firms linked through common ownership);
2. production networks (i.e., firms linked by production sequences);
3. capital networks (i.e., firms and individuals linked by capital and investments);
4. distribution networks (i.e., firms linked by the distribution of commodities).

Although I discuss four types, other types are possible, such as firms linked through common labor networks. A Chinese example of personnel networks for firms and professions is recruitment through ties of common regional origins, or *tongxiang guanxi*. The focus of analysis here is to examine how these four types of interfirm networks work empirically in both societies and then to contrast these network configurations between the two locations.

In South Korea, all four types of networks tend to overlap. The only exception to this in the past has been the capital networks. Because the Korean government owned the banks and tightly controlled the financial system, the state was able to control access to capital and carefully allocated, as loans, investment capital to specific *chaebol* for specific projects (Kim, in press; Zeile, 1993). Recently, there are some signs of changes, as many of the top *chaebol* are trying to arrange their financing from non-state, usually international, sources and have also been trying to create their own internal financial institutions, such as tax-exempt foundations.

Chaebol are networks of firms defined by their common ownership. In the simplest terms, this common ownership is family ownership. Uniformly, all *chaebol* are owned and controlled by individuals, *haejang*, who are also patriarchal heads of powerful families. This practice contrasts sharply with Japanese business groups, which are jointly owned through public stock holdings by the firms that make up the business group. In South Korea, however, the stock market in the past has not been the primary source of capital, and stock ownership, even with an expanding stock market, does not define who owns the *chaebol*. Instead, the *chaebol* were largely the creation of entrepreneurs, who borrowed money from state banks at favorable rates to establish firms in areas targeted for development by state planners (Kim, in press). Based on our figures, in 1983 the debt ratio for the top fifty *chaebol* was 453 percent. The debt ration for *chaebol*-member firms in manufacturing was 370 percent, slightly more than the 360 percent for all Korean manufacturing firms. This figure contrasts with what is considered the very high debt ratio of 324 percent for Japanese manufacturing firms, 158 percent for Taiwan manufacturing firms, and the moderate level for U.S. manufacturing corporations of 104 percent (Zeile, 1993). Put simply, *chaebol* firms are financed through low cost loans given to the *haejong*, and, as those firms have expanded and prospered with increasing development, the *haejong* and selected family members have retained both ownership and control over all the firms in the *chaebol*.

The Korean state has become worried about the growing economic power of the biggest *chaebol* and is trying to force them to be less vertically integrated and more diversified in their ownership through the stock market. However, the government has had with only mixed success. In 1990, only about 25 percent of the business groups' firms were listed on the stock market. Moreover, with the equity raised through the stock market, the *chaebol* have been able to increase their holdings by starting or buying firms in areas related to their production. In addition, the government is also attempting to limit cross-ownership of firms within the *chaebol* by reducing the cross-investments in business groups, but again the success has been mixed (Kim, in press).

How do these ownership networks that constitute the *chaebol* boundaries overlap with the firms that are linked through production and distribution sequences? In South Korea, the production and distribution networks are largely coterminous with the *chaebol* boundaries. In fact, *chaebol* represent extensive sets of vertically integrated firms that center around several large core firms. As shown elsewhere (Hamilton and Feenstra, 1995), the Korean *chaebol* have, on average, very high rates of "one-setism," what we call rates of internalization; they supply their intermediate inputs and distribute their products through their trading companies. As a consequence of this industrial strategy, the *chaebol* are strongly diversified across numerous industrial sectors.

Table 9-5. Korea's Top Five *Chaebol*, 1983.[a] Distribution of Group-member Firms by Industrial Sector.

Sect/Group	Hyundai	Samsung	Lucky-GS	Sunkyung	Daewo
Finance & Insurance	2	2	4		3
Trade	2	2	2	2	1
Fishery & Forestry					
Mining				1	
Construction	5	2	2	1	
Food & Beverage		2			
Textiles		2		2	
Garments & Apparel					2
Leather Products					2
Lumber & Wood Prd.					
Pulp & Paper		1			
Chemicals		1	1		1
Petroleum Products			1	1	1
Rubber Products					
Plastic Products					
Glass + Cement	2	1			
Basic Metal	3		1		1
Metal Products	3				
Machinery	2	3	6	1	2
Electrical	1	1	5	1	2
Transport. Mach.	5	2		1	3
Precision Instr.	1				
Other Manuf.	2	2	1		1
Real Estate		1			
Storage & Trans.	1			2	1
Serv. Industry	3	7	1	1	4
Total Number of Firms	32	29	24	14	24

[a]Complied from Management Efficiency Research Institute (1985).

Drawing on the work of Zeile (1993), table 9-5 shows the diversification for the top five *chaebol*, and table 9-6 shows Zeile's measurements of this diversification. In this table, 1 represents maximum diversification, and 0 represents minimum diversification. The larger the *chaebol*, the more the diversification. The same relationship also is true for our measurement of the rates of internationalization (Hamilton and Feenstra, 1995): The larger the *chaebol*, the higher the rates of internalization.

Indeed, at the top of the heap, such *chaebol* as Hyundai and Daewoo are huge networks of firms fiercely competing with one another domestically for largely the same international markets. Each of these large groups has sets of firms that make such similar export products as cars, electronics, ships, and clothes. Leading to those final products, the *chaebol* have their own construction companies, oil refineries, and chemical plants that contribute to the production of those commodities. They have trading companies to market the products, shipping companies to haul the products, and insurance companies to insure the products and the process itself. A distinctive feature of this system of production is that, unlike the arrangement in Japan or Taiwan, there are very limited (and then only short-term) sub-

Table 9.6 Indices of Manufacturing Diversification for Korean *Chaebol*.

Sales Rank	Name	Number of Manufacturing Activities	H^*	S^*	S_w^*	V^*
1.	Hyundai	13	0.772	0.601	0.541	0.405
2.	Samsung	9	0.757	0.582	0.466	0.378
3.	Lucky/Goldstar	10	0.644	0.457	0.446	0.284
4.	Sunkyung	6	0.161	0.086	0.701	0.701
5.	Daewoo	12	0.817	0.710	0.639	0.633
6.	Ssangyong	7	0.567	0.467	0.523	0.523
7.	Kukje	7	0.619	0.416	0.733	0.591
8.	Hanguk Huayak	7	0.654	0.541	0.780	0.370
9.	Hanjin	1	0.0	0.0	0.0	0.0
10.	Hyosung	14	0.817	0.670	0.770	0.662
	Average for Top 10 *Chaebol*	8.6	0.581	0.453	0.560	0.455
	(Standard Deviation in Parentheses)	(3.86)	(0.280)	(0.236)	(0.232)	(0.213)
	Average for Top 20 *Chaebol*	6.6	0.472	0.351	0.437	0.321
	(Standard Deviation in Parentheses)	(3.81)	(0.283)	(0.244)	(0.271)	(0.238)
	Average for Top 50 *Chaebol*	4.7	0.384	0.277	0.320	0.243
	(Standard Deviation in Parentheses)	(3.16)	(0.254)	(0.216)	(0.251)	(0.220)

Diversification indices defined:

$$H^* = 1 - \sum_{i=1}^{h} a_i^2$$

where $a_i = \dfrac{\text{Sales by Group in Manufacturing Sector } i}{\text{Total Manufacturing Sales by Group}}$

$S^* = 1 - S$

where $S = \dfrac{\text{Sales in Group's Leading Manufacturing Sector}}{\text{Total Manufacturing Sales by Group}}$

$S_w^* = 1 - S_w$

where $S_w = \dfrac{\text{Number of Employees in Group's Leading Manufacturing Sector}}{\text{Total Number of Employees in Group's Manufacturing Activities}}$

$V^* = 1 - V$

where $V = \dfrac{\text{Number of Group Employees in all Sectors Vertically Relocated to Group's Major Manufacturing Sector}}{\text{Total Number of Manufacturing Employees in Group}}$

contracting relationships between *chaebol* and non-*chaebol* firms. The ownership, production, and distribution processes are internalized within the *chaebol* themselves, and what cannot be internalized in the domestic economy is handled through joint ventures with non-Korean businesses, mainly with U.S. and Japanese companies. But in Korea, as the *chaebol* expand into new product areas, they start new firms, buy other firms, and compete against all comers. This pattern of expansion and ruthless competition has earned the *chaebol* the label "octopus legs."

How do these network patterns contrast with Taiwan's business group networks? It is difficult to imagine a greater contrast. The tip of the iceberg can be seen by comparing the characteristics of manufacturing sectors in relation to business group participation in that sector. Table 9-7 shows that diversification of the Tai-

Table 9-7. Taiwan's Top Five Business Groups.[9] Distribution of Group-member Firms by Industrial Sector.

Sect/Group	Formosa Plastics	Linder Intern.	Tainan Spinning	Yue Loong Motors	Far Eastern
Finance & Insurance		3	3		1
Trade & Commerce		2	3		4
Fishery & Forestry			3		
Mining					
Construction		2	1		1
Food & Beverage			3		
Textiles	5		10	2	2
Garments & Apparel	1		2		
Leather Products	1				
Lumber & Wood Prd.	2				
Pulp & Paper					
Chemicals	2		1		
Petroleum Products	1				
Rubber Products					
Plastic Products	3				
Glass & Cement			2	1	2
Basic Metal				1	
Metal Products					
Machinery					
Electrical			1		
Transport. Mach.				4	
Precision					
Other Manuf.					
Real Estate			4	3	1
Storage & Trans.	1				1
Serv. Industry	2	4			
Total Number of Firms	18	12	33	11	15

[a]Compiled from China Credit Information Service (1985).

wan's five largest business groups is much less significant than is the diversification in South Korea's largest business groups.

As already discussed, *chaebol* concentrate in capital-intensive sectors but are highly diversified, so *chaebol* firms produce both intermediate products, such as steel and chemicals, and final products, such as cars and TV sets. Taiwan's business groups are also located in capital-intensive sectors, but they predominate in sectors characterized by producing intermediate products not made for export. This is a significant finding because Taiwan's economy is predominantly an export economy. In fact, in 1985, Taiwan's exports, as a percentage of GNP, were 51 percent as compared with South Korea's 37.5 percent and Japan's 16.4 percent for the same calculation. South Korea's and Japan's biggest business groups dominate their export sectors. Yet, in Taiwan, the country with the world's highest percentage of exports to total output, the biggest businesses produce intermediate goods sold domestically.

How can this paradox be explained? The business endeavors in Taiwan that have been able to grow large relative to other businesses in Taiwan are upstream producers for the thousands of small- and medium-sized firms that have sprung up around every easily assembled consumer fashion that has appeared in the last 20 years, everything from trail bikes to computers. In Taiwan, a gold-rush effect is operating.

In a gold rush, everyone joins the stampede to dig for gold, and although a few people strike it rich by finding gold, the ones who make the most money are the ones who supplied the miners with what they wanted. The same is true in Taiwan. Everyone is trying to get into the manufacturing game; everyone wants to be an entrepreneur; everyone wants to be the *laoban* (a boss). According to the *Free China Review* (1988), that desire is almost a reality; in Taiwan, with a population of nearly 20 million, there are 700,000 businesses, all of which have their *loaban*. This is one *laoban* for every fifteen persons, and if we count only adults, one *laoban* for every eight persons. I should note, however, that this figure is an overstatement because our research shows that many successful entrepreneurs own more than one business. Still, the general point is true: Being a *laoban* is almost commonplace.

The clearest demonstration of this gold-rush effect is in textiles. This is the only manufacturing sector in which business groups produce more than 50 percent of the total sales. But as seen in Table 9-4, business groups only account for 12 percent of the total sales in the Garment and Apparel sector. Business groups produce the fabrics, not the clothes; the next step is done by countless small factories working on consignments from major retail outlets. This same process is repeated in almost every sector and for almost every large business group. Table 9-8 quantitatively demonstrates this lower degree of diversification, relative to the measures for Korea found in table 9-6.

To illustrate this point further, by far the biggest group in Taiwan is Formosa Plastics, one of the world's largest producers of plastics. Until recently, a large part of the total production was used locally by thousands of small, independent firms in the manufacture of export products. In the mid-1980s, business group firms accounted for 42.4 percent of the total sales of Chemical Material sector, but only 5.4 percent of the Plastic Products sector. The explosion of small firms has also occurred around the manufacture of bicycles, electronic items such as TVs, and most recently, computers. These small firms primarily produce for the export market instead of large firms. The Taiwan government calculates that firms having fewer than 300 employees account for nearly 50 percent of Taiwan's total manufacturing output, a figure that would be much higher if only exports were considered (*Free China Review*, 1988). This point is further brought home by the contrast with South Korea. According to the Biggs' calculations (1988a, pp. 3–4), in Taiwan between 1966 and 1986 "the number of reported firms increased by 315 percent . . . and the average firm size expanded 15 percent." In the same time, the reverse process occurred in South Korea, where "average firm size jumped by 300 percent and its firms grew in number by only 10 percent."

How is it possible for all those small- and medium-sized firms to produce so much? Most firms in Taiwan's business groups are small- and medium-sized firms. Where did the investment capital come from for these firms? As in South Korea, in Taiwan the stock market neither defines ownership nor is an important source of investment capital. Unlike South Korea, however, Taiwanese firms are not financed through loans from government-owned banks or from international sources,

Table 9-8. Taiwan's Business Group Diversification Indices (Mean and Standard Deviation).

	S^*	$S_w{}^*$	Firms
Top 10	0.301	0.319	18.000
	(0.190)	(0.237)	(8.406)
Top 20	0.242	0.232	
	(0.203)	(0.232)	(8.106)
Top 30	0.225	0.318	12.500
	(0.186)	(0.205)	(7.224)
Top 50	0.250	0.291	9.880
	(0.188)	(0.205)	(6.567)
All	0.218	0.255	7.740
	(0.189)	(0.204)	(5.543)

$S^* = 1 - S$

where S = $\dfrac{\text{Sales in Group's Leading Manufacturing Sector}}{\text{Total Manufacturing Sales by Group}}$

$S_w{}^* = 1 - S_w$

where S_w = $\dfrac{\text{Number of Employees in Group's Leading Manufacturing Sector}}{\text{Total Number of Employees in Group's Manufacturing Activities}}$

such as the World Bank. Instead, according to Biggs (1988a), capital investment comes from two main sources. First, the largest portion, about 45 to 55 percent, comes from accumulated profits that were then reinvested to expand existing firms and to start new firms. The smaller the firms, the more likely that the owners supplied the capital themselves. Second, the next largest portion, about 30 percent of the total, comes from the unregulated curb market, from family, friends, and acquaintances (Biggs, 1988a,b; Lee, 1990).

Understanding these sources of investment allows us a better understanding of who owns Taiwan's firms. When matched with what else we know about Chinese business practices, it seems clear from our data that in the Chinese context there are two important types of ownership. First, ownership and control of businesses are in the hands of families. Kao Cheng-shu and his colleagues in Taiwan, with whom I worked collaboratively, have determined that eighty-three of the top ninety-seven business groups can be strictly classified as family-owned business groups (Peng, 1989). Sixty-one of those business groups have multiple family members classified among the core people in the group, and most of those family members (81 percent, fifty-three out of the sixty-seven) are of three types: fathers and sons, brothers, or brothers and their sons.

A second type of ownership, which we call *guanxi* ownership, is also important. All the largest businesses are also limited partnerships. Limited partnerships in the Chinese context are not equivalent to those found in the West. By long convention ("Chinese Partnerships," 1887, p. 41), "every Chinese partnership is represented by one individual, who is solely responsible to the outside world for the solvency of his firm." The Chinese practice of partnership is similar to having "silent partners" who do not participate actively in making business decisions, but who earn profits on their capital investments. More important in the Chinese context, these silent partners are usually either more distant family members or members of the owners' personal network of acquaintances, which in Chinese would be called *guanxi* networks. In a database made from the list of Taiwan's ninety-six largest business groups compiled by the China Credit Information Service (1983), I found that every one of the 743 firms in the 96 business groups lists a number of co-owners. Not counting duplications, and there are many, more than 5,000 names of co-owners are listed for the 743 firms. The network analysis of these data clearly shows that there are substantial interlocked clusters within business groups, but relatively few across business groups (Orrù, Biggart, Hamilton, 1997).

These *guanxi* owners are the sources of investment capital that have financed Taiwan's industrialization, but we should recognize that this network clustering of *guanxi* owners represents more than just capital; rather, it represents a type of capitalism. This becomes clear when we look at production networks. On the surface, the whole process of production in Taiwan seems to run against our notions about economies of scale. How is it possible for all those small- and medium-sized firms to produce so much and such complex products? The answer is that production sequences are neither internalized within firms nor within Taiwan's business groups. They are "externalized." If we look at the networks of firms linked by the production of commodities, we see that extensive cooperative networks exist among many independent firms. These cooperative networks seem to come in two types.

First, there are extensive subcontracting relationships between relatively large and relatively small firms. The small firms make some parts that the larger, usually middle-sized firms manufacture. I once visited the second largest hydraulic jack company in Taiwan, which is a modest firm of about 200 employees. The owner's orders fluctuated a lot, so that during times when he had many orders, many basic metal parts of the jacks would be made by other small, independent firms; when the orders slackened, he would make many parts in his own factory.

The second type of cooperative network is just as or maybe more common. This network is called the satellite-assembly system, and it consists of many different and usually independent firms, each producing some parts of a final product, which are in turn assembled by other firms. Taiwan is the world's largest producers of bicycles for export, and yet there are no huge, vertically integrated bicycle plants, but rather many different satellite assembly systems. From this example, we might correctly think that quality control would be a problem and that R&D would be difficult. But R&D is not a major problem, because most of Taiwan's products are made to someone else's specifications. Not many people, except those who have lived in Taiwan, can name a single company in Taiwan or a brand name of a single Taiwanese product. The reason is that around 70 percent of all Taiwan-made products coming to the United States enter under a U.S. brand name or as a component of a product having a U.S. brand name, and many other products are too insignificant to have well-known brand names.

In the hydraulic jack company I mentioned previously, the owner had one small room that was devoted, he said, "exclusively to R&D." But in his showroom where he met with customers, he had a display cabinet, which he rolled open to my view. The opened door revealed row after row of cartons, each of which bore a different brand name. There were more than twenty-five different U.S. and European companies that, using their own names, sold his entire line of jacks. K-Mart and Grand Auto were both represented, and he explained that, after applying the distinctive paint and labels, the only way one could tell whether a jack was made by his company was the "k" stamped into the metal underneath the jack. Sears' TV sets, Target's stereos, and parts of IBM's PCs are all made this way. Someone else does much of the R & D, and it seems that quality is controlled through *guanxi* ties. If one produces substandard goods, one's contract is not in jeopardy, because normally there are no legally binding contracts between subcontractors. Rather, one's honor or, more accurately, one's face is in jeopardy. In other words, just as much as *guanxi* ties form the foundation of Taiwan's capital resources, *guanxi* ties also cement the system of production. This is different from the Korean case.

What about distribution networks? Here, too, *guanxi* figures in but is less important. Until recently, Taiwan businessmen had few contacts outside Taiwan, and they did not need the contacts because distribution was handled by Macys, Marshalls, K-Mart, and 10,000 different U.S. firms who sent buyers to the East. In addition, a very large percentage of the total exports from Taiwan was handled through Japanese trading companies.

Conclusion: The Social Sources of Economic Networks

As we dig deeper into the network structures of the economies of Taiwan and South Korea, we begin to realize that the organizational differences between them are both numerous and large, and both economies, in turn, differ greatly from the extensive networks found in the Japanese economy.

Economists are reluctant to acknowledge the independent effects of social structure on economic organization. Instead, most theorists of economic organization (Scherer and Ross, 1990; Schmalensee and Willig, 1989; Williamson, 1985, 1991) argued that economic processes, such as efficiency and competition, create economic organization. Our own analysis of East Asian economies (Hamilton and Biggart, 1988; Hamilton and Feenstra, 1995; Orrù et al., 1991) points in a different direction, toward the importance of Granovetter's (1985, 1994) embeddedness thesis that economic actions are embedded in social relationships and social institutions. Social relationships and social institutions also interact with economic opportunity and economic power to create path-dependent trajectories, which are in turn altered by such economic processes as competition and efficiency.

Asian capitalism, represented here by the economies of Taiwan and South Korea, was constructed on social institutions that existed before, and has continued to develop and change since the onset of industrialization. In both countries, the governments and key entrepreneurs took ideas, policies, technology, and organizational practices from Japan and the West, but in both places these borrowings led to new innovations, because what was borrowed was incorporated in and altered by an established way of life (see Westney, 1987). In South Korea, capitalistic entrepreneurs, including government officials, built on a tradition of "great families" (usually called clans in the Korean literature) that were encompassed in a strong patrimonial state (Biggart, 1990). In the dynastic period preceding Japanese colonialization, these families competed with each other and with state officials for political patronage and economic power. These families were able to maintain themselves by developing a form of primogeniture in a strongly Confucian, patrilineal society (Deuchler, 1992). When capitalist opportunities presented themselves after World War II, particularly after the Korean War, those mobilizing the society for industrialization used their understanding of the Korean state and society to generate their own political and economic advantage. This understanding, in the form of political patronage of key individuals and family groups, led to the reemergence of a group of elite families. The families changed, but the patterns of social structure remained in place, and initial economic success continued to feed and to accelerate the formation of a capitalist order that was and still is dominated by networks centering on large, family-owned groups. The networked groups hotly compete with each other and with the state for control of the economy. This type of network structure recreates a modern form of patrimonialism (Biggart, 1990), what might be termed "neo-patrimonial capitalism."

In Chinese societies, from the late imperial times, aristocratic institutions supporting the great families who had existed in earlier dynasties had long been destroyed and were replaced with institutions (such as the unrestrictive civil service examinations) supporting a much more fluid society than that existing in Korea (Ho, 1964; Hamilton, 1991b). Privilege arose from education, office holding, and land owning, but none of these privileges could automatically be passed intact to one's heirs, because inheritance is partible, with each son, in principle, getting an equal share of the father's estate. As these lineage conventions institutionalized, Chinese society grew highly mobile, and mobility strategies centered on alliances within and between patrilineages, which cut across class lines. As the control of the economy passed from wealthy elites to the more mobile and less privileged segments of society, a form of petty commercial capitalism developed in the late imperial times. When Western industrial capitalism was introduced in Chinese societies in the nineteenth and twentieth centuries, the most economically mobilized were the peasant and merchant groups, who used existing forms of interrelationships to take advantage of economic opportunities. These interrelationships created a form of capital and resource mobilization that rested on norms of making nonlineage alliances, norms that required reciprocation and continual maintenance (Fei, 1992; Hwang, 1987; King, 1991; Yang, 1989). Individuals could secure modest amounts of capital and other resources by developing non-family alliances. These alliances became institutionalized as *guanxi* networks in various types of associations among fellow regionals, friends, and distant relatives. I call the parochial, household-based capitalism that developed from these networks "*guanxi* capitalism." These are the foundations upon which Taiwan's economy of family-owned, small, medium-sized, and large firms has been built.

This point about the social sources of Taiwan's and South Korea's economic organization is related to the contrast between Asian and Western societies that I mentioned in the first part of this chapter. It would be a serious mistake to conclude that the economic systems that have developed in Taiwan or South Korea are simply variants of a capitalist model that is best represented by—or is present in its truest form—in Western countries. In the modern world, capitalism is not a singular phenomenon, and we should not see it as simply a type of economic formation having essential characteristics. Rather, many different types of economic and social configurations can and do participate in the world economy. In the 1850s, and 1860s, when Karl Marx was writing *Das Kapital*, England certainly represented a capitalist model, but well into the last decade of the twentieth century, we should see a proliferation of ways to participate in the global marketplace.

Notes

I thank William Zeile for assistance with the tables and Nicole Beggart, Gary Gereffi, and Mark Fruin for comments on an earlier draft.

References

Anderson, P. *Lineages of the Absolutist State.* London: New Left Review, 1974.

Bank of Korea. *Economic Statistics Yearbook, 1986.* Seoul, 1986.

Biggart, N. W. Institutionalized Patrimonialism in Korean Business. *Comparative Social Research,* 12 (1990): 113–33.

Biggart, N. W., and G. G. Hamilton. "On the Limits of a Firm-based Theory to Explain Business Networks: The Western Bias of Neoclassical Economics." In N. Nohria and R. G. Eccles, eds., *Networks and Organizations: Structure, Form, and Action* (pp. 471–490). Cambridge, Mass.: Harvard Business School Press, 1992.

Biggs, T. S. "Financing the Emergence of Small and Medium Enterprise in Taiwan: Heterogeneous Firm Size and Efficient Intermediation. Employment and Enterprise Policy Analysis Project." EEPA Discussion Paper, No. 16. Cambridge: Harvard Institute of International Development, 1988a.

Biggs, T. S. "Financing the Emergence of Small and Medium Enterprise in Taiwan: Financial Mobilization and the Flow of Domestic Credit to the Private Sector." Employment and Enterprise Policy Analysis Project. EEPA Discussion Paper, No. 15. Cambridge: Harvard Institute of International Development, 1988b.

China Credit Information Service (Zhonghua Zhengxinso), comp. *Taiwan diqu jitua qiye yanjiu, 1983–1984* (Business Groups in Taiwan, 1983–1984). Taipei: China Credit Information Service, 1983.

China Credit Information Service (Zhonghua Zhengxinso), comp. *Taiwan diqu jitua qiye yanjiu, 1985–1986* (Business Groups in Taiwan, 1985–1986). Taipei: China Credit Information Service, 1985.

"Chinese Partnerships: Liability of the Individual Members." *Journal of the China Branch of the Royal Asiatic Society,* N. S. 22 (1887): 41.

Chu, C. *Chaebol kyugjeron* (Economics of the Chaebol). Seoul: Cheonghum Munhwasa, 1985.

Daily Economic News. *Firm Directory of Korea for 1985.* Seoul, 1986.

Deuchler, M. *The Confucian Transformation of Korea: A Study of Society and Ideology.* Cambridge, Mass.: Council on East Asian Studies, Harvard University, 1992.

Economic Planning Board, Republic of Korea. *Report on Industrial Census for 1983.* Seoul: Economic Planning Board, 1985.

Feenstra, R. C., T. H. Yang, and G. G. Hamilton. "Market Structure and International Trade: Business Groups in East Asia." Working Paper Series, National Bureau of Economic Research, No. 4536. Cambridge, Mass.: NBER, 1993.

Fei, X. T. *From the Soil: The Foundations of Chinese Society.* Trans., Introduction, and Epilogue by G. G. Hamilton and Z. Wang. Berkeley: University of California Press, 1992.

Free China Review, 38–11 (November 1988): p. 10.

Fruin, W. M. *The Japanese Enterprise System: Competitive Strategies and Cooperative Structures.* Oxford: Clarendon Press, 1992.

General Agreement on Tariffs and Trade. *International Trade*. Geneva: GATT Sec-
    retariat, 1988.
Gerlach, M. *Alliance Capitalism: The Strategic Organization of Japanese Business*.
    Berkeley: University of California Press, 1992.
Granovetter, M. "Business Groups." In N. Smelser and R. Swedberg, eds., *Hand-
    book of Economic Sociology*. Princeton, N.J.: Princeton University Press, 1994,
    pp. 453–75.
Granovetter, M. "Economic Action and Social Structure: The Problem of Embed-
    dedness." *American Journal of Sociology*, 91 (1985): 481–510.
Hamilton, G. G., ed. *Business Networks and Economic Development in East and
    Southeast Asia*. Hong Kong: Centre of Asian Studies, University of Hong Kong,
    1991a.
Hamilton, G. G. "The Organizational Foundations of Western and Chinese Com-
    merce: A Historical and Comparative Analysis." In G. G. Hamilton, ed., *Busi-
    ness Networks and Economic Development in East and Southeast Asia*. Hong
    Kong: Centre of Asian Studies, University of Hong Kong, 1991b, pp. 48–65.
Hamilton, G. G. "Why No Capitalism in China?" *Journal of Developing Societies*,
    2 (1985): 187–211.
Hamilton, G. G. and N. W. Biggart. "Market, Culture, and Authority: A Comparative
    Analysis of Management and Organization in the Far East." *American Journal
    of Sociology*, 94 (Supplement) (1988): S52–S94.
Hamilton, G. G., and R. Feenstra. "Varieties of hierarchies and markets." *Industrial
    and Corporate Change*, 4 (1995): 1.
Hamilton, G. G., W. Zeile, and W. J. Kim. "The Network Structures of East Asian
    Economies." In S. R. Clegg and S. G. Redding, eds., *Capitalism in Contrasting
    Cultures*. Berlin: de Gruyter, 1990, pp. 105–129.
Ho, P. T. *The Ladder of Success in Imperial China*. New York: Wiley, 1964.
Hwang, K. K. "Face and Favor: The Chinese Power Game." *American Journal of So-
    ciology*, 92 (1987): 944–74.
Ilbo Hankook. *Pal Ship O nyndo hankook ui 50 dae jae bul* (The 50 Top Chaebol
    in Korea). Seoul, 1985.
Kim, E. M. *Big Business, Strong State: Collusion and Conflict in South Korean De-
    velopment*. Albany: State University of New York Press, in press.
King, A.Y.C. "*Kuan-hsi* and Network Building: A Sociological Interpretation."
    Daedalus, 120–2 (1991): 63–84.
Lee, S. Y. *Money and Finance in the Economic Development of Taiwan*. London:
    Macmillan, 1990.
Lee, Y. K. "Conglomeration and Business Concentration, the Korean Case." In *In-
    dustrial Policies of the Republic of Korea and the Republic of China*. Seoul:
    Korea Development Institute, 1985, pp. 181–202.
Management Efficiency Research Institute. *Korea's Fifty Major Groups for 1983 and
    1984*. (In Korean). Seoul: Management Efficiency Research Institute, 1985.
Management Efficiency Research Institute. *Financial Analysis of Korea's Fifty
    Major Groups for 1986*. (In Korean). Seoul: Management Efficiency Research
    Institute, 1986.
Orrù, M., N. W. Biggart, and G. G. Hamilton. "Organizational Isomorphism in East
    Asia. In W. Powell and P. DiMaggio, eds., *The New Institutionalism in Organi-
    zational Analysis*. Chicago: Chicago University Press, 1991, pp. 361–89.
Orrù, M., N. W. Biggart, and G. G. Hamilton. *The Economic Organization of East
    Asian Capitalism*. Thousand Oaks, Calif.: Sage, 1977.

Peng, H. J. *Taiwan qiye yezhu de 'guanxi' jiqi huanbian, yige shehuixue de fenxi* (Relationships Among Taiwan Business Owners and their Changes: A Sociological Analysis). Ph.D. dissertation, Tunghai University, 1989.

Piore, M. J., and C. F. Sabel. *The Second Industrial Divide: Possibilities for Prosperity.* New York: Basic Books, 1984.

Republic of China. *Report on Industrial and Commercial Surveys, Taiwan Area.* Taipei: Directorate-General of Budget, Accounting and Statistics, 1983.

Republic of China. *Input–Output Tables, Taiwan Area.* Taipei: Directorate-General of Budget, Accounting and Statistics, 1985.

Republic of China. *Yearbook of Labor Statistics.* Taipei: Directorate-General of Budget, Accounting and Statistics, 1986.

Republic of China. *Taiwan Statistical Data Book, 1987.* Taipei: Council of Economic Planning and Development, 1987.

Scherer, R. M., and D. Ross. *Industrial Market Structure and Economic Performance,* 3rd ed. Boston: Houghton Mifflin, 1990.

Schmalensee, R., and R. D. Willig, eds. *Handbook of Industrial Organization.* 2 vols. Amsterdam: North-Holland, 1989.

Scott, J. "Networks of Corporate Power: A Comparative Assessment." *Annual Review of Sociology,* 17 (1991): 181–203.

Westney, E. *Imitation and Innovation: The Transfer of Western Organizational Patterns to Meiji Japan.* Cambridge, Mass.: Harvard University Press, 1987.

Whitley, R. *Business Systems in East Asia.* London: Sage, 1992.

Williamson, O. E. "Comparative Economic Organization: The Analysis of Discrete Structural Alternatives." *Administrative Science Quarterly,* 36 (June 1991): 269–96.

Williamson, O. E. *The Economic Institutions of Capitalism.* New York: Free Press, 1985.

Yang, M. M. H. "The Gift Economy and State Power in China." *Comparative Studies in Society and History,* 31–1 (January 1989): 40–41.

Zeile, W. J. *Industrial Targeting, Business Organization, and Industry Productivity Growth in the Republic of Korea, 1972–1985.* Ph.D. diss., Department of Economics, University of California, Davis, 1993.

10

Japanese Corporate Boards and the Role of Bank Directors

PAUL SHEARD

Banks occupy an important place in the loose networks of large firms that characterize the Japanese brand of capitalism. Most listed firms in Japan have an identifiable connection to one of the ten or so major commercial banks. Many firms are affiliated with one of the six bank-centered groupings, most clearly the case when they belong to the group presidents' club. Keizai Chosa Kyokai (1993) identified 635 (60 percent) of the 1,053 first-section–listed firms in 1991 as being affiliated with one of the six bank-centered groups and 140 (13 percent) as being affiliated with one of the nine other city or long-term credit banks. Only 93 firms (9 percent) were found not to be affiliated with a bank or parent company. President club membership is much more exclusive: In 1991, only 175 (8 percent) of the 2,086 listed firms belonged to one of the six clubs (Toyo Keizai Shinposha, 1991). Even if the affiliation is not this clear-cut, most firms have a "main bank" relationship (as do group-affiliated ones), meaning that the bank maintains the leading position in loan shares and other banking business with the firm and that the bank and firm maintain a significant interlocking shareholding relationship. [See Aoki et al. (1994) for more discussion of the main bank system and Sheard (1994b) on bank-firm interlocking shareholdings.]

Such group and main-bank ties have attracted much interest recently, mainly from two different angles. One angle is in the context of Japan's economic conflicts with the United States and other trading partners, where the term *keiretsu* has gained prominence. *Keiretsu*, it is claimed, impede access to the Japanese market and facilitate predatory behavior (e.g., dumping) in the international market [see Lawrence (1993), Saxonhouse (1993), and Sheard (1991, 1992), for example]. The second angle is in the context of attempts to understand the sources of Japan's competitive success, perhaps learn from this, and apply the lessons elsewhere. Here attention has focused on the nature of supply networks (so-called vertical *keiretsu*) and the Japanese system of corporate governance (the main bank system), where "corporate governance" refers to the way in which the capital market monitors and exercises control over corporate management. [As regards the former, see, for example, Fruin (1992), Sako (1992), and Smitka (1991), and for the latter see Aoki and

Patrick (1994), Hoshi (1994), and Sheard (1994b).] Both angles share the perspective that the institutions of Japanese capitalism are distinctive and deserving of detailed analysis, but they differ when it comes to interpretation.

This chapter adds to the analysis of bank–firm ties as it relates to the Japanese system of corporate governance. Recently, there has been increased academic and policy interest in the role of large banks and other intermediaries in capital market monitoring and corporate governance. Economists traditionally saw the takeover mechanism as exerting both ex ante and, when that failed, ex post discipline on management teams. [See Manne (1965) for an early statement and Jensen and Ruback (1983) for elaboration.] Takeovers were seen as an important part of the "market for corporate control," the stock market-based arena in which actors competed for the rights to manage corporate resources. Now researchers and practitioners realize that various mechanisms exist for coping with the agency and control problems associated with the pursuit of economies through the modern corporate form (Holmstrom and Tirole, 1989). A focus of increasing interest has been the role played by "incumbent" agents of corporate control who occupy strategic prior positions in the firm (large shareholders, banks, boards) as opposed to "new entrants" (corporate raiders, takeover agents, green-mailers) who react to arbitrage opportunities created by decentralized activity in the stock market [see, for example, Coffee (1991), Gilson (1990), Morck et al., (1989), and Stiglitz (1985)].

The role played by "main banks" in the corporate governance of large Japanese firms exemplifies this point. Although an Anglo-American-style takeover mechanism largely fails to be active in Japan, large banks maintain significant equity and loan positions in client firms, monitor their finances and at times intervene in the management of these firms. This is particularly so in financial distress when intervention by the main bank seems closely to approximate the disciplinary and allocative functions attributed to the takeover and bankruptcy mechanisms [see, for example, Sheard (1989, 1994c) and for careful empirical studies Kaplan (1994), Kaplan and Minton (1994), and Morck and Nakamura (1992)]. Attention has focused on the role of the main bank as a kind of "delegated monitor" for the capital market as a whole and the fact that the whole system of corporate governance is buttressed by extensive share interlocks among coalitions of inside "stable shareholders" (*antei kabunushi*) [see, for instance, Aoki et al. (1994), Prowse (1990), and Sheard (1994a,b)].

As well as maintaining close financial ties, banks supply executives to the boards of client firms. This process occurs most visibly in extraordinary times when the bank launches a rescue-cum-reorganization operation in a distressed firm. Banks, however, also frequently supply mid- and late-career executives to client firms in the normal course of events. Such bank executive placements are usually seen as one important element of the close bank-firm links thought to characterize Japanese corporate organization and are not limited to cases of poor performers. For instance, the influential publication *Keiretsu no kenkyu* uses director placements, along with equity, lending, and historical ties, to classify listed firms into various affiliated groups (Keizai Chosa Kyokai, 1993).

Until recently, however, there has been little systematic investigation of the role of bank executive placements on Japanese corporate boards and its relation to other aspects of bank-firm ties. Recent studies by Kaplan and Minton (1994), Morck and Nakamura (1992), Lincoln et al. (1992, 1993) start to redress this gap in the literature (see also Taki, 1992). This chapter adds to the growing empirical literature on the determinants of bank executives serving on Japanese corporate boards.

The main task in the chapter is to examine whether director ties are systematically related to variables that relate to the role of banks in corporate monitoring and governance. Japanese bankers, perhaps eager to avoid the charge that they attempt to exercise influence over independent corporations, sometimes suggest that bank "director dispatches" (*yakuin hakken*) are of little or no consequence. It would be of interesting to know, however, whether bank executive placements are integral to the role of banks in capital market monitoring and corporate governance, or whether they are unrelated to those presumed roles. This question has relevance for the ongoing policy debate in Japan relating to perceived weakness in the way that the capital market oversees corporate managers; it is also relevant to similar debates in the United States and elsewhere, because the Japanese system of corporate governance is increasingly cited as a benchmark of comparison, if not a model to be emulated [see, for instance, Aoki and Patrick (1994), Coffee (1991), Gilson and Roe (1993), Grundfest (1990), and Roe (1993)].

In the first section of this chapter, I analyze the composition of Japanese corporate boards and the place of outside directors on them, focusing in particular on directors who have entered from banks. The next section describes a probit regression analysis of the determinants of bank executives being present on Japanese corporate boards and explains the variables used and why they are included. The next section presents the empirical results of the study. In the final section I discuss the implications of the analysis.

Composition of Japanese Corporate Boards

In Japan board members are the top executive officers of the corporation and in most cases work full-time for the firm. They fall into two categories in their background: (a) directors who have worked for the firm for a long period, in many cases since entering the workforce as graduates, and have been promoted up through the ranks and (b) directors who have entered from outside the firm in mid- or late career either directly as directors with executive duties or in senior management positions with a view to being promoted to the board in due course. It is convenient to term the former "inside directors" and the latter "outside directors," although this usage differs somewhat from that in the U.S. literature, in which an outside director refers to a part-time director, typically having multiple board memberships, who is not an officer of the firm (Black, 1992; Kaplan, 1994). In this chapter, "outside" refers to the background of the director, rather than his or her current status. Most outside directors are full-time managers of the firm who no longer have a formal employment relationship with the firm or bank that arranged their entry to the firm. Even though they are no longer employed by the original firm, relocating executives may still have retirement benefits vested with the firm, and, under the Japanese "lifetime" employment system, can be expected to continue to identify strongly with the interests of the source firm. In the sample used for data analysis, of the 2,095 bank executives identified as being corporate board members, 1,905 were full-time corporate directors. Only 190 (9.1 percent) held part-time appointments, and most of these (84 percent) were in the "lowest" director and auditor positions.

Table 10-1. Composition of boards of directors of listed Japanese firms by position and background, 1991

| Position | Inside firm | Background of Board Member | | | Total |
| | | Outside firm | | | |
		Bank[a]	Other firm[b]	Government[c]	
Chairman[d]	678	68	296	61	1103
	(61.5)	(6.2)	(26.8)	(5.5)	(100.0)
President	1328	131	561	66	2086
	(63.7)	(6.3)	(26.9)	(3.2)	(100.0)
Vice-pres.	1010	122	215	77	1424
	(70.9)	(8.6)	(15.1)	(5.4)	(100.0)
Senior exec.	2651	285	490	141	3567
dir. (*Senmu*)	(74.3)	(8.0)	(13.4)	(4.0)	(100.0)
Exec. dir.	5843	434	1013	271	7561
(*Jomu*)	(77.3)	(5.7)	(13.7)	(3.4)	(100.0)
Managing[e]	14368	555	2656	265	17844
dir.	(80.5)	(3.1)	(14.9)	(1.5)	(100.0)
Auditor	3936	500	1312	149	5897
	(66.7)	(8.5)	(22.2)	(2.6)	(100.0)
Total	29849	2095	6508	1030	39482
	(75.6)	(5.3)	(16.5)	(2.6)	(100.0)

Source: Toyo Keizai Shinposha (1991), *Kigyo keiretsu soran* [Corporate affiliations annual], Tokyo, Toyo Keizai Shinposha, p. 90.

[a]city, long-term credit, trust, and regional banks

[b]including insurance companies, other financial institutions, and miscellaneous categories

[c]government ministries and agencies

[d]including 87 vice-chairmen

[e]including 325 director-advisors

Table 10-1 provides information on the composition of corporate boards in Japan by position and inside/outside director status. In 1991, the 2,086 firms listed on Japanese stock exchanges had 39,482 directors, an average of 18.9 per firm. Three-quarters (75.6 percent) of all directors were inside directors, and one-quarter (24.4 percent) were outside directors who entered firms from banks (5.3 percent of all directors), other firms (16.5 percent), and government ministries and agencies (2.6 percent).

Table 10-2 provides information on the kinds of positions that outside directors occupy. Japanese boards typically comprise a rank hierarchy of positions: statutory auditor (*kansayaku*), managing director (*torishimariyaku*), executive director (*jomu*), senior executive director (*senmu*), vice-president (*fuku-shacho*), president (*shacho*), and chairman (*kaicho*), with the president being the chief executive. The auditor is not a director as such but an officer charged with oversight of the discharge of duties by the directors. In most cases (95 percent according to one comprehensive survey), the auditor attends meetings of directors (Tokyo Bengoshikai Kaishahobu, 1986), and in about one-half of the cases receives regular reports from directors (Shoji Homu Kenkyukai, 1989). In most cases (81 percent) the auditor is

Table 10-2. Indexes of distribution of board positions by background status[a]

Position	Outside/ total	Outside/ inside	Bank/ total	Bank/ insider	Bank/ other firm
Chairman	1.57	1.94	1.14	1.43	0.71
President	1.49	1.77	1.19	1.41	0.73
Vice-president	1.19	1.27	1.61	1.72	1.76
Exec. director	1.06	1.07	1.51	1.53	1.81
Managing dir.	0.93	0.91	1.06	1.06	1.33
Director	0.80	0.75	0.59	0.55	0.27
Auditor	1.37	1.53	1.60	1.81	1.18

Source: Compiled from table 10-1.

[a]Each index is constructed as the ratio of the respective category's fraction of directors in that position

an internally promoted employee of the corporation, most commonly having been a director (28 percent of such cases) or a departmental or section chief (28 percent); the most common source of auditors entering from outside the firm is financial institutions (38 percent of such cases) and parent firms (20 percent) (Shoji Homu Kenkyukai, 1989).

Outside directors compared to inside directors are relatively more concentrated in the senior management positions of vice-president and above and as auditors (table 10-2). Bank directors, compared to inside directors are proportionately more concentrated in senior management positions, particularly executive director and vice-president, and as auditors. Relative to outside directors from other firms, bank directors are proportionately more concentrated in senior management positions below president, particularly executive director and vice-president. Bank directors are most underrepresented in the most common managing director position (45 percent of board positions).

Table 10-3 shows the distribution of bank–firm director ties by major bank, both on a stock and flow (new supply) basis. In 1993, about 4 percent of total listed firm directors were former (or current) executives of the twelve banks shown. In that year, there were 185 instances of bank executives becoming directors or auditors of listed firms. In most cases (93 percent), this process involved the executives leaving employment with the bank and entering the firm as full-time executives; in 7 percent of the cases, the executives held part-time appointments jointly with their bank position. Because some firms receive more than one executive, 10 percent is an upper limit on the proportion of listed firms that received a new bank executive in that year. Although there is some variation, the 10 years' series of data shows a fairly stable pattern of bank executives leaving the banks in late career to take up director or auditor positions in listed firms.

What kind of bank executives enter the board of nonfinancial corporations? Of 751 directors of first-section-listed firms in 1991 who had entered from the seven major bank sources (as listed in table 10-3), 279 (37 percent) reached the rank of director or above in the bank; 126 (17 percent) entered from the position of bank branch manager (Keizai Chosa Kyokai, 1993).

The flow of executives is almost entirely from banks to corporate clients; there is almost no flow in the reverse direction. The twelve large banks shown in table

10-3 had 538 directors in 1991, of which all but 18 were internally promoted "inside directors." Most of these (twelve) came from the Bank of Japan or the Ministry of Finance; four were from other financial institutions. Tokai Bank was the only bank to have outside directors from nonfinancial corporations, having two such part-time directors (one from Toyota, the bank's top shareholder) (Toyo Keizai Shinposha, 1991).

Table 10-4 presents the results of an analysis of the relationship between the presence of directors from outside the firm and ownership and financing ties between the firm and the source of outside directors. Specifically, for each listed firm, outside sources of directors were identified, and the total shareholding in the firm and total share of loans to the firm of those source firms were computed. Although outside directors form a minority of directors overall (albeit a substantial one), most firms have outside directors on their board. These outside directors come predominantly from firms with leading financial ties to the firm.

Table 10-4 shows that 92 percent of all listed firms have one or more outside directors; only 163, or 8 percent of listed firms, have boards comprised only of insiders. Moreover, outside directors come mainly from leading shareholders and lenders. In only 192 (8.9 percent) of the 1,792 cases in which outside directors were present does the director connection appear unrelated to financial ties, in the sense that one or more source firms did not appear as a top twenty shareholder or principal lender to the firm. One in four listed firms had outside directors from firms that held more than 30 percent of the firm's shares; one in two had directors from firms that held more than 10 percent. On the lending side, one in five listed firms had outside directors from firms (principally banks) that supply more than 30 percent of loans; 42 percent had directors from firms that supplied more than 10 percent.

Close to one-half (46 percent) of all listed firms have outside directors from firms (mainly banks) that held shares in the firm (as a top twenty shareholder) and were listed as a principal supplier of loans. More than one in five listed firms (23 percent) have outside directors from firms that held more than 10 percent of shares and supplied more than 10 percent of loans. These data strongly suggest that the flow of senior executives between firms in Japan is closely associated with ownership and financing ties, a pattern that would not be expected if late entries to senior management occurred in the context of an open, competitive managerial labor market.

Table 10-5 illustrates the issue from the bank's perspective. It presents the results of an analysis of the financial links that banks maintain with the firms to which they supply directors. Specifically, every listed firm director identified as a former (or current) bank executive was checked as to whether the bank held shares in or supplied loans to that firm. Table 10-5 provides strong evidence that the flow of executives from banks to corporate boards occurs between banks and firms that have close financial and shareholding ties.

At the end of the 1990 financial year, 1,320 cases of former (or current) executives serving on listed firm boards could be identified (Table 5). In 87 percent of cases, the bank was listed as a principal lender to the firm; in 8 percent of cases the firm had no borrowings, and in only 5 percent of cases did the firm have borrowings but not from the source bank. In 57 percent of cases, the bank had the largest loan share, and in 79 percent of cases, it was one of the top three lenders. In 10 per-

Table 10-3. Stock and flow of bank executives on boards of listed Japanese firms: major banks, 1983–92[a]

Name of bank	Year									
	1983	1984	1985	1986	1987	1988	1989	1990	1991	1992
DKB	187	177	183	187	195	204	202	229	239	236
	28	15	na	13	12	15	27	24	31	26
Mitsubishi	156	151	169	172	165	170	171	181	178	183
	22	13	na	13	23	23	17	20	20	15
Fuji	143	146	144	152	161	168	175	173	176	183
	18	17	na	11	21	16	15	14	18	17
Sakura[b]	142	132	141	153	150	153	150	165	182	181
	16	6	na	11	21	12	16	20	27	22
Sanwa	114	109	132	133	130	142	153	168	171	177
	15	5	na	10	20	13	23	19	21	16
Sumitomo	133	130	141	152	148	161	167	188	178	170
	14	8	na	18	13	18	16	26	23	15
IBJ	171	162	151	156	149	143	141	138	149	143
	18	8	na	16	13	13	18	11	25	6
Tokai	94	93	100	101	94	117	126	137	144	142
	na	7	na	8	na	14	20	13	18	13
Asahi[c]	79	79	76	82	77	80	81	82	77	81
	na	11	na	na	na	na	5	13	8	14
Daiwa	70	63	68	69	65	67	71	71	75	80
	9	2	na	na	na	na	4	9	9	11
LTCB	45	44	51	53	51	56	62	76	76	78
	9	4	na	8	na	na	13	11	7	23

	50	56	53	55	58	61	60	60	56	55
Tokyo	7	12	na	na	na	9	9	5	6	7
Total	1384	1342	1409	1465	1443	1522	1559	1668	1701	1709
(as % of all directors)	(4.6)	(4.4)	(4.5)	(4.6)	(4.4)	(4.5)	(4.3)	(4.4)	(4.3)	(4.3)
	156	108	na	108	123	110	183	185	211	185
(as % of all listed firms)[d]	(8.8)	(6.0)	(na)	(5.9)	(6.5)	(5.7)	(9.2)	(9.1)	(10.1)	(10.1)

Source: Compiled from Toyo Keizai Shinposha (various issues); *Kigyo keiretsu soran* [Corporate affiliations annual], Tokyo; Toyo Keizai Shinposha.

na   not available

[a]Upper row: total number of former or current executives of a bank on a listed firm's board as of July of that year lower row: number of executives of bank who became director or auditor of a listed firm during that year

[b]Formerly Mitsui Taiyo-Kobe Bank; pre-merger series combined

[c]Formerly Kyowa-Saitama Bank; pre-merger series combined

[d]Because some firms receive more than one director this is an upper bound on the proportion of listed firms that received a bank executive onto their board in that year.

Table 10-4. Distribution of listed firms in Japan according to total shareholdings and total loan shares in firm of firms identified as being outside source of full or part-time directors, 1991

Total shareholding of source firm(s) (%)	Total loan share of source firm(s) (%)											No outside directors	Row total	Cumulative percentage total
	90 < ≤ 100	80 < ≤ 90	70 < ≤ 80	60 < ≤ 70	50 < ≤ 60	40 < ≤ 50	30 < ≤ 40	20 < ≤ 30	10 < ≤ 20	0 < ≤ 10	0			
70 < ≤ 80	1	0	0	0	0	0	0	0	0	0	3		4	0.2
60 < ≤ 70	0	0	2	1	0	1	1	0	2	1	36		44	2.5
50 < ≤ 60	1	1	2	0	6	9	8	7	8	2	100		144	9.8
40 < ≤ 50	0	0	2	0	3	3	13	12	11	1	100		145	17.2
30 < ≤ 40	1	1	2	4	5	6	12	15	6	7	88		147	24.8
20 < ≤ 30	3	0	2	1	4	14	18	27	28	7	108		212	35.6
10 < ≤ 20	3	2	9	11	24	22	44	55	39	10	100		319	51.9
5 < ≤ 10	1	2	2	5	20	20	24	35	17	23	64		213	62.8
0 < ≤ 5	2	4	2	5	15	24	51	77	66	16	104		366	81.5
0	0	0	0	0	0	0	1	1	0	4	192		198	91.7
No outside directors												163	163	
Column total	12	10	23	27	77	99	172	229	177	71	895	163	1955	
Cumulative percentage total	0.6	1.1	2.3	3.7	7.6	12.7	21.5	33.1	42.2	45.9	91.7	100.0		

Source: Compiled from Toyo Keizai Shinposha (1991); *Kigyo keiretsu soran* [Corporate affiliations annual], Tokyo; Toyo Keizai Shinposha, pp. 102–590.

cent of cases, the bank was the number one shareholder, and in 56 percent, it was the number one shareholder among banks. In 50 percent of cases, the bank was one of the top three shareholders, and in 86 percent of cases, it was one of the top three shareholders among banks.

In 88 percent of cases, the bank was either a top three lender or top five shareholder, and in 65 percent of cases, it was both a top three lender and a top five shareholder (Table 5). In only 32, or 2 percent, of cases, the bank was neither a top 20 shareholder nor lender to the firm.

This analysis provides a general picture of bank-firm ties through the supply of executives to corporate boards. The data confirm two points in particular: banks extensively supply executives to corporate boards, and the flow of executives is far from random, as might be expected were it purely a manifestation of final (from the bank's point of view) employment separation and arms-length rehiring in the competitive managerial labor market. Rather, the flow occurs between banks and firms with close financial (equity and loan) ties.

Researchers of corporate governance have argued that managers in Japan are relatively autonomous, given that most promotions are made from an internal pool of managers and the external takeover mechanism is not active. They have also argued that a form of insider corporate governance system, latent in normal times but triggered particularly by worsening corporate performance, checks and disciplines managerial excesses. [For this line of argument, see Aoki (1989), Aoki et al. (1994), Kaplan (1994), Kaplan and Minton (1994), Lincoln et al. (1993), and Sheard (1994b, 1994c).] The data on outside directors presented here is consistent with this characterization, as it shows institutional owners and financiers of firms to be substantially "represented" on corporate boards.

Factors Behind Flow of Bank Personnel to Boards

Two broad economic hypotheses concerning bank executives on corporate boards can be identified. One hypothesis focuses on the managerial labor market in Japan, the other on monitoring and corporate governance. The managerial labor market hypothesis explains bank executive placements as reflecting the operation of the mid- to late-career managerial labor market in Japan. The major banks are among the most prestigious of corporate employers in Japan. Competition among graduates for entry to these banks is intense, but competition for promotion to senior management positions in the banks is even more so. Managers who by their late forties to early fifties are not likely to reach the board of the bank, or having reached lower director levels are not likely to reach much higher, are liable to have their employment terminated with the bank. However, the bank assists them to find reemployment with its corporate customers. Firms, for their part, may value the human resources that the bank executive embodies, particularly specialist financial or banking expertise. The movement of a bank executive into the board of a corporation then represents a labor market "match."

The monitoring/governance hypothesis focuses on the role of director placements in facilitating monitoring and active intervention in top management by banks. Specifically, it suggests that, by placing directors, banks are better able to

Table 10-5. Distribution of bank executives on boards according to bank's shareholding and loan share rank for all listed firms in Japan, 1991

Shareholding rank (top) / Among banks (bottom)	Loan share rank in firm of bank having executive on firm's board												Firm has no borrowings	Row total	Cumulative percentage total
	1	2	3	4	5	6	7	8	9	10	lower than 10	no loans to firm			
1	81	11	6	3	2	-	1	-	-	-	-	2	3	109	9.8
	535	80	26	14	8	4	1	-	-	-	-	18	55	741	56.1
2	181	39	12	4	2	2	1	-	-	-	1	5	22	269	28.6
	158	71	25	5	4	4	1	-	-	-	1	10	21	300	78.9
3	185	36	15	7	2	4	-	-	-	-	-	8	28	285	50.2
	31	25	10	9	2	-	-	-	-	-	1	9	9	98	86.3
4	147	38	10	5	1	1	1	-	-	-	-	9	14	226	67.4
	15	5	17	5	4	1	1	-	1	-	-	-	6	55	90.5
5	68	19	8	2	3	1	-	-	-	-	1	10	9	121	76.6
	2	4	8	3	2	3	-	-	3	-	-	2	1	29	92.7
6	41	16	7	5	2	2	-	-	-	-	-	3	7	83	82.9
	3	3	2	2	-	1	-	-	-	-	2	1	2	16	93.9
7	12	9	13	4	2	-	-	-	-	-	-	-	5	45	86.2
	1	1	3	2	-	-	-	1	1	1	-	1	3	13	94.8
8	8	8	5	3	-	1	-	-	1	-	1	1	1	28	88.3
	1	-	-	-	-	-	-	-	-	-	1	1	-	2	95.0
9	9	5	2	2	3	2	-	-	1	-	2	-	3	29	90.5
	-	-	1	-	1	1	1	-	-	-	1	-	-	4	95.3
10	5	-	7	2	1	1	-	1	-	-	1	1	-	19	92.0
	1	-	-	-	-	-	-	-	-	-	-	-	-	1	95.4

														total
11-20	4	4	-	1	1	2	-	-	1	-	-	-	-	
not listed in top 20ᵃ	4	4	1	4	4	2	5	5	2	1	4	27	46	60
Column total	751	193	93	44	22	20	5	2	5	4	10	68	103	1320
total	751	193	93	44	20	5	4	2	5	4	10	68	103	1320
Cumulative percentage	56.9	71.6	78.6	81.9	83.6	85.1	85.5	85.6	86.0	86.3	87.1	92.2	100.0	
total	56.9	71.6	78.6	81.9	83.6	85.1	85.5	86.0	86.3	87.1	92.2	95.5	100.0	

Source: Compiled from Toyo Keizai Shinposha (1991), *Kigyo keiretsu soran* [Corporate affiliations annual], Tokyo, Toyo Keizai Shinposha, pp. 102–590.

ᵃIn some cases top ten shareholders.

gather information and keep an eye on corporate management in normal times and actively intervene to restructure firms in times of financial distress. From the firm's viewpoint, accepting bank directors in normal times represents a form of voluntary disclosure (Diamond, 1985). Information is disclosed to the main bank, not to the public. In times of financial distress, banks may dismiss or demote some top executives when they intervene, but in as much as it improves the firm's management and future prospects, bank intervention may be seen as key to the firm's survival and be welcomed by employees (Sheard, 1994c).

Although it is useful conceptually to distinguish them, these are not necessarily competing hypotheses. Instead, the mechanisms involved may be complementary. Bank director placements may facilitate both the operation of the top executive managerial labor market and the bank's role in monitoring and corporate governance. They may also be integral to the bank's incentive and promotion system. When a bank places an executive with a client firm, it may "kill three birds with one stone." Namely, it gets rid of one of its "lifetime" employees and creates a vacancy in its promotion hierarchy that can be used to induce the next round of internal competition, it supplies human resources to a firm that values them, and it facilitates its information links with that firm. The relative importance of the three factors may vary from case to case.)

Bankers may perceive the last point more in terms of maximizing their commercial advantage than in terms of monitoring. To economists, "monitoring" means "taking a costly action to improve the amount or reliability of information"; however, bankers do not gather information for its own sake but rather as an input to their business transactions. Having a former colleague in the firm may make it easier for executives in the bank to do financial business with the firm. It does this by improving the information available to the bank, because the bank acts on this information. Aoki et al. (1994) noted that, by operating a large part of the settlement business of its client firms, the main bank can monitor day-to-day cash-flow movements, allowing the bank to detect deteriorating performance and emerging financial difficulties ahead of time. Bankers are more likely to perceive the monitoring of settlement accounts as a strategy to maximize their commercial advantage in selling a range of banking services to the firm rather than as monitoring. But the two are complementary: the information that the bank acquires about cash flows and uses to position itself favorably in its commercial dealings with the firm can also be used to assess the firm's financial position and the level of the bank's risk exposure.

The fact that the labor market and informational effects are complementary makes it difficult to distinguish them empirically, particularly at the level of firm data, as in the analysis here. However, it is possible to test a limiting form of the labor market hypothesis, namely, that the movement of bank executives into firms reflects labor market matches that are unrelated to, or at least not driven by, bank–firm relational considerations. Under this hypothesis, we should not find strong effects on variables that most strongly proxy bank–firm relations, such as financial dependency variables.

The analysis is complementary to recent papers by Kaplan and Minton (1994) and Morck and Nakamura (1992), but differs in a number of ways. These researchers investigated the determinants of new bank appointments to corporate boards. Kaplan and Minton used a sample of the largest (by sales) 119 publicly traded industrial firms for 1980–88 and found that the likelihood of a new bank appointment to the board is negatively related to stock performance and low earnings, and positively related to the borrowings-to-asset ratio and the largest lender's loan share. They also found that corporate appointments were strongly related to share ownership and outside appointments coincide with abnormally high executive turnover. Morck and Nakamura used a sample of the largest 383 manufacturing firms for 1981–87 and found that the likelihood of bank intervention is negatively related to various measures of firm performance and positively related to loan exposure. They also found that accounting performance improves following bank intervention. The results of both studies confirm the view that bank and intercorporate relations substitute for the absence of a more active external market for corporate control in Japan (Sheard, 1989).

In this study I treated firms having one or more bank directors as being qualitatively different from firms that do not have bank executives on their boards. Rather than focus on new placements per se, the presence of a former (or in some cases concurrently serving) bank executive on the board is viewed as a characteristic of the firm. This cross-sectional approach is taken to investigate a wider set of determinants of bank executive presence over a larger sample, namely, all non-financial firms listed on the first section of the Tokyo and other stock exchanges (up to 940 firms). A data set of 1,064 first-section-listed firms was compiled (1,149 for some variables), but in the regressions, the largest sample size is 940, because data were unavailable for certain variables and observations. Of course, the stock and flow approaches are closely related: For a firm to have a bank director, there must have been an entry event in the past. However, there are some important differences. A flow approach, as in Kaplan and Minton and Morck and Nakamura, seems to be suited to investigating the bank-intervention hypothesis—the ex post monitoring role of banks in Aoki et al.'s (1994) terms. In the case of zero observations (no new placement), however, it does not distinguish between firms that already have a bank executive and those that do not. The cross-sectional approach makes this distinction and so seems better suited to asking questions about why some firms have bank executives on their boards and others do not. This inquiry also extends to consideration of the ex ante and interim monitoring roles of banks.

Whether a bank executive is present on a firm's board is a zero–one event. The dependent variable in the probit regression was one if the firm had a former (or concurrently serving) bank executive on its board in 1991 and zero otherwise. Three models, corresponding to different definitions of the dependent variable, were estimated. DEPVAR(1), the broadest definition of bank presence on the board, was 1 if Toyo Keizai Shinposha's (1991) *Kigyo keiretsu soran* listed the firm as having a former or concurrently serving bank executive on its board in a position of director (*torishimariyaku*) or above (including auditor) as of mid-1991. In the sample of 1,064 listed firms, 55 percent were identified as having a bank executive on the board; 45 percent as not. DEPVAR(2) restricted attention to cases in which one or more bank executives were in a position of executive director (*jomu*) or above (34.4 percent) and DEPVAR(3) restricted attention to cases in which one or more bank executives was a senior executive director (*senmu*) or above (25.2 percent). The aim was to see whether there are different influences, depending on the importance of the bank director in the managerial hierarchy. In the latter two models, to avoid possible misspecification in the dependent variable, a restricted sample was used, in which firms having bank directors but not at the level specified in the dependent variable were eliminated. There was, then, in the restricted-sample regressions a 0 for the dependent variable indicated a firm without any bank directors, and a 1 was a firm with at least one bank director of the rank of executive director, for DEPVAR(2), or senior executive director, in the case of DEPVAR(3). For forty firms, the only bank director(s) concurrently served. When the dependent variables were amended to exclude these cases, the regression results were qualitatively very similar to the ones reported.

The following explanatory variables were included. LEVERAGE was measured as the percentage ratio of total borrowings to total assets. Banks are argued to be information intermediaries that specialize in monitoring the lower tail of the distribution of profit state outcomes. All other items being equal, firms with higher borrowings face a higher probability of having to default on or renegotiate hard budget contraints (debt repayments), and the banks' supply of monitoring services should be high. If the supply of executives to corporate boards contains a monitoring component, the probability should rise with the amount of bank debt. The expected sign, then, was positive, and a strong effect of this variable was expected under the monitoring/governance hypothesis.

The literature on Japanese corporate governance has emphasized the fact that banks can hold equity, up to a limit of 5 percent (unless an exemption is sought), as well as supply loans. There is clear evidence that top lenders also tend to be top shareholders, particularly in the case of the main bank but also for other principal lenders. It is widely felt that bank shareholdings of this kind facilitate main bank interventions in cases of financial distress and help to minimize the kinds of agency costs and conflicts of interest between equity- and debtholders discussed in the U.S. finance literature. [For arguments along these lines, see, for instance Aoki et al. (1994), Prowse (1990, 1992), and Roe (1993), and for empirical evidence on main bank shareholding, see Flath (1993) and Sheard (1989, 1994b,d).] BANK-SHARE was the percentage total shareholding of financial institutions and a measure of the role of banks in the equity side of the firm. By including this variable, we could see whether bank director links are driven more by loan or equity relations.

Other ownership variables were also tried: FIRMSHARE, the percentage shareholding of non-financial domestic corporations; DIRECTORSHARE, the shareholding ratio of directors; and INSIDESHARE, the percentage total shareholding of individuals (among the top twenty shareholders) who were identified as being members of the founding family (including shareholdings of associated nonlisted firms and foundations). TOPSHARE and FIRMSHARE were highly correlated (0.72), and only TOPSHARE was retained. DIRECTORSHARE and INSIDESHARE were highly correlated (0.67), and both were with INSIDEOWNER (0.57 and 0.73, respectively). However, only INSIDEOWNER proved to be significant.

The focus on bank shareholding is most appropriate when banks or other financial institutions (notably insurance companies) occupy the top shareholder positions. In many cases, however, a large block of a firm's shares (e.g., more than 10 percent) is held by one or more large parent firms, such as a large listed industrial or trading company. Whether there is a large blockholder present is an important aspect of corporate governance and influence on the role played by banks. Indicative of this are some statistics from the sample: 580 firms (50.5 percent) had direc-

Table 10-6. Distribution of listed Japanese firms according to size of top share-holder's shareholding and top lender's loan share, 1991

Range	Top shareholder's shareholding[a]	Top lender's loan share[b]
less than 3%	0.2	0.2
3% or more, less than 4%	1.5	0.2
4% or more, less than 5%	12.3	0.1
5% or more, less than 10%	44.0	3.5
less than 10%	58.0	3.9
10% or more, less than 20%	16.4	27.9
20% or more, less than 30%	11.9	29.1
30% or more, less than 40%	5.2	13.7
40% or more, less than 50%	3.9	5.5
50% or more	4.7	7.0
no borrowings		12.8
Total	100.0	100.0

Source: Compiled from data set.

unit: per cent fraction of firms falling in category.

[a]Sample of 1149 firms listed on first section of Tokyo and Osaka stock exchanges.

[b]Sample of 1108 firms (data unavailable for 41 firms).

tors who had entered from the top shareholder, and in 61.5 percent of the 338 cases in which the president was from outside the firm, the source was the top share-holder.

Table 10-6 presents evidence on the distribution of listed firms in the sample by the size of the largest shareholding. It shows that qualitatively there are two kinds of listed firms: firms with relatively diversified top shareholding positions (although still concentrated by U.S. standards; see Prowse, 1992), in most cases the top shareholder being a financial institution, and firms that are affiliated with a large parent-firm blockholder. Specifically, although 14 percent of listed firms had a top shareholder with less than 5 percent (mostly 4–5 percent) and another 44 percent between 5 and 10 percent, for 25.7 percent of listed firms, the top share-holder had a 20 percent or more holding. For 42.1 percent, the top shareholder had a holding of 10 percent or more (Table 10-6).

TOPSHARE was the top shareholder's percentage shareholding. Banks may supply directors even if a dominant shareholder is present, but in general, and as suggested by Kaplan and Minton's (1994) results, monitoring by banks and the dominant shareholder should be substitutes. The expected sign was negative, if bank director placements served a monitoring or an intervention purpose.

PROFIT, measured as the percentage ratio of operating income to total assets for the financial year in which the latest entry of a bank executive occurred, was a measure of return on assets and was included to capture the effect of poor performance or financial distress. Case studies, theory, and the two quantitative studies cited earlier suggest that banks dispatch executives as on-the-spot monitors, discipliners, and troubleshooters when client firms are in financial difficulty. The expected sign was negative, and a strong effect was expected under the monitoring hypothesis. This variable allowed one version of the labor market hypothesis to be tested, because it suggested a positive sign on the coefficient. If, as is sometimes suggested, members of the bank executive elite descend into lucrative preretirement director slots as part of a cozy top executive cartel, poorly performing firms should not be a favored destination.

An innovation of this study is to take into account a key governance aspect of firms that has tended to be overlooked in the literature: whether an inside owner figure is present. An entrepreneurial owner–manager figure is present in many large firms in Japan. In the sample of 1,064 first-section-listed firms, it was possible to identify the presence of an inside owner in 36 percent of cases. This does not mean that a single family figure runs the firm and controls its decision-making. In some cases, the inside owner may be quite marginal in the firm's corporate decision-making and control. However, in 25 percent of cases, the president was an inside owner and in 16 percent of cases, the chairman was. Moreover, in 12 percent of cases, the top shareholder was an inside owner.

Rather than explicitly consider inside-owner controlled firms, researchers have focused on alleged differences in financial structure by focusing on the (perhaps overdrawn) "group-affiliated" versus "independent firm" dichotomy, in which the definitions follow the Keizai Chosa Kyokai listings or some variant thereof. Starting with Nakatani (1984), there is now an extensive line of studies in this vein, including Hoshi et al. (1990, 1991), Lawrence (1991), Prowse (1992), and Weinstein and Yafeh (1992). One problem with this approach is that it is not clear what economic behavior the "independents" category captures, because it is not generated directly from first principles but rather falls out as a residual category—those firms not found to belong to a particular group. In fact, Keizai Chosa Kyokai (1993) defines these firms as "affiliation unknown" (*fumei*), rather than as "independent," which has a somewhat different and stronger connotation. From a theory of the firm or corporate governance viewpoint, one tangible measure of independence is the presence of an inside owner. (The absence implies a greater degree of separation of ownership and control). Rather than rely on an indirect residual category, it is preferable to obtain a direct measure of inside family ownership or control. An innovation in this study was to measure this dimension of independence directly and control for its effects. INSIDEOWNER was a dummy variable that was 1 when the top shareholder was a founding entrepreneur or a member of the founder's family. (In many cases a nonlisted firm or foundation is used as the vehicle for this shareholding.)

Two possible effects from this variable were anticipated. One, coming from the firm side, is that a firm subject to strong incumbent control by an owner–manager may resist external monitoring and perceived intrusion by its banks. In keeping with the intuitive notion of "independence" discussed previously, an "owner"-controlled firm may be prone to keep a more arms-length stance vis-à-vis its banks. A second effect going in the opposite direction, coming from the bank's side, is that banks may be more intent on monitoring such firms because of a possible greater risk of misappropriation of internal resources and free cash flow (Jensen, 1986) or of internal control failures (so-called *wanman keiei*, literally "one-man management," effect). Given that a bank can only send an executive if the firm agrees, however, it might be expected that the first effect would dominate, suggesting a negative sign on the coefficient.

Because INSIDEOWNER was a dummy variable, a negative sign would indicate a shift in the intercept of the regression, that is, an overall lowering of the likelihood of bank directors independent of the particular values taken on by the other explanatory variables. However, interactive effects may be important also; that is, the slopes of the other coefficients may be affected by the presence of INSIDE-OWNER. Variables constructed as the product of INSIDEOWNER and other explanatory variables could capture such effects.

One such variable of particular interest is PROFIT*INSIDE, which was the product of PROFIT and INSIDEOWNER. The idea was to investigate whether, in the case that an inside owner is present, the presence of a bank director is sensitive to the performance of the firm. Significance of this variable would provide evidence that the way in which bank director presence varies with profitability—a key aspect of contingent corporate governance—differs between the two sets of firms, those with active or residual entrepreneurial/family influence and those without. Interactive variables other than PROFIT*INSIDE were tried but found not to be significant.

A priori, however, the expected sign on this variable is unclear. A negative sign would indicate that, relative to other firms, the presence of a bank director is more sensitive to corporate profitability; a positive sign indicates that it is less sensitive. Plausible explanations exist for either result. A negative sign, combined with a negative sign on INSIDEOWNER, would be consistent with the view that firms with inside owners try to maintain more independence from banks, but their capacity to do so depends on the strength of their relative bargaining position, which is closely correlated with financial health, as measured by profitability. A positive sign might indicate that the contingent corporate governance aspect is muted in the case of inside-owner firms. This might be because, whereas other firms readily accept bank director intervention when performance deteriorates, firms with residual inside ownership guard their independence more fiercely. From the bank side, it might reflect the fact that banks are less likely to perform their ex post intervention role or are more discriminating in doing so.

Two variables were constructed to capture the presence of a major supplier of loans. LOANSHARE(1) was defined as the percent of total loans supplied by the top lender. TOPLENDER was defined as the percentage ratio of borrowings from the top lender to total assets. Higher values of LOANSHARE(1) indicate a higher degree of exclusivity or "dependence" in the bilateral relationship (particularly on the firm's side), which might increase the likelihood of the bank supplying a director. On the other hand, if the main bank system operates according to the delegated monitoring hypothesis, the loan share of the top lender should not be an important factor per se. What matters more is the banks' total financial exposure, captured by LEVERAGE. TOPLENDER measured the importance of the top lender relative to total assets. LOANSHARE(1) could be quite high even though TOPLENDER was low, if the firm had few borrowings but obtained these from a few sources, or even a single source. In fact, TOPLENDER was also the interactive variable LOANSHARE(1)*LEVERAGE. Morck and Nakamura (1992) did not find an effect for TOPLENDER and dropped it from their regressions.

LOANSHARE(1) measured the importance of the top lender relative to all lenders. Another measure of relative exclusivity is the importance of the top lender relative to other top lenders. To measure this effect, LOANSHARE(2–3), the combined loan share of the second and third top lenders, was included. There are two possible effects to consider. On the one hand, larger values would indicate the presence of other important lenders, and one or more of these might also supply directors. This possibility is suggested by the following statistics from the sample of all first-section-listed firms (1,149 firms): in 68 percent of cases in which the firm was identified as having one or more bank directors, the directors came from a single bank; in 25.3 percent of cases, directors came from two banks; and in 6.6 percent of cases, directors came from three or more. A positive sign would be expected under this line of reasoning.

On the other hand, larger values of LOANSHARE(2-3) could indicate that firms were attempting to achieve more diversification in major lending sources. Firms pursuing such an "independent" strategy would tend not to accept former bank directors into their senior management ranks; this would suggest a negative sign. The coefficient on LOANSHARE(2) may also speak to the delegated monitoring hypothesis. A positive sign would be consistent with the notion that the banks monitor independently, whereas a negative sign would be more consistent with the delegated monitoring notion.

ASSETS, the total assets of the firm, was included as a measure of firm size. Size of the firm might have an influence on whether bank executives sit on the board, although on theoretical grounds the sign of this effect is ambiguous. All other items being equal, the larger the firm, the more likely that bank executives will be present, particularly under the monitoring hypothesis. Larger firms also will tend to be parent firms to other listed and nonlisted subsidiary firms. If, as suggested by Kaplan and Minton's (1994) results, there is an effective division of labor among large operating firms and banks in corporate governance, which TOPSHARE aimed to capture, then banks would be expected to have more director links to larger firms, because these firms stand at the pinnacle of corporate groups and are not subject to parent firm monitoring. Although large parent firms oversee and intervene when necessary in the management of their listed affiliates, banks might be expected to monitor these large parent firms [see Sheard (1987, p. 70) for an earlier argument along these lines relating to the risk-sharing aspect of ownership and corporate group relations]. Viewed in this light, ASSETS would be expected to have a positive sign. On the other hand, larger firms, as long as their performance is adequate, might be better able to keep banks at arms length, suggesting that a negative sign on ASSETS might be expected. Another argument, related to the reemployment hypothesis and also suggesting a negative effect, is that larger firms may have accumulated better internal managerial resources and would be in less need of acquiring the human capital services of former bank executives.

The age of the firm may influence the probability of a bank executive being present. FIRMAGE, the year that the firm was established, was included to test for such an effect. Older firms might be thought to have accumulated better managerial resources; in terms of the human resource hypothesis, then a negative sign would be expected. By the same token, banks are more likely to have already accumulated considerable information about older firms, and older firms will have established more reputational capital, suggesting a negative sign based on the monitoring hypothesis (Diamond, 1991). The year that the firm was first listed on the stock exchange was also used to test for firm-age effects, but this variable was highly correlated (0.56) with FIRMAGE, and including both in the regressions resulted in both having low t-statistics and neither being significant.

Bank–firm director ties are perceived as strong among firms associated with an enterprise grouping, such ties being thought of as one of the defining features of a grouping, together with shareholding, lending, commercial, and historic ties. [See, for example, the definition employed by Keizai Chosa Kyokai (1993)]. The presidents' club is often taken in the literature as defining the core membership of the loosely knit intermarket enterprise groupings. To test for such an effect, dummy variables were included for membership of the presidents' clubs of the six major enterprise groupings. The idea was to test whether group association was a factor explaining director ties or whether any effects go away after controlling for other relevant variables. Finally, industry dummy variables were included to control for industry-specific effects.

Results of Regression Analysis

Regression results corresponding to the three versions of the dependent variable are reported in table 10-7. Estimation was carried out using the Probit option in TSP. The standard errors were computed from analytic second derivatives. t-statistics robust to heteroscedasticity in the error term were generally very close to those reported, and use of these would not have altered significance judgments. Overall, the models performed reasonably well, although much variation clearly remained unexplained. For the full model, the R^2 was 19 percent, and the pseudo-R^2 was 15 percent (Davidson and MacKinnon, 1993). The R^2 rose to 27 percent (and pseudo-R^2 to 23 percent) when the dependent variable was restricted to the presence of bank executives in senior director positions, and better results were produced in terms of the percent of correct predictions of the model.

For all three versions of the dependent variable, the coefficients for LEVERAGE, TOPSHARE, INSIDEOWNER, LOANSHARE(1), and PROFIT were significant, usually at the 5 percent level at least and often at the 1 percent level, and the signs were as expected. The coefficient on ASSETS was also consistently significant, and the sign was negative. FIRMAGE was significant at the 5 or 10 percent level and had the expected sign. LOANSHARE(2–3) was not significant in the full model but became significant in the restricted samples; the sign was negative. BANKSHARE and TOPLENDER were of the expected sign but were not significant.

Firms are more likely to have former bank executives on their boards the more they rely on bank borrowings, the larger the loan share of the top lender, and the greater the discrepancy in loan shares among top lenders. Firms are less likely to have former bank executives on their boards when there is a dominant large shareholder, when there is residual family involvement in management and ownership, and when the firms are larger, older, and more profitable. Overall, the most significant variables were LEVERAGE, TOPSHARE, and PROFIT. This is consistent with the monitoring/governance hypothesis and confirms Kaplan and Minton's (1994) results. Basically, banks tend to supply executives when financial (lending) exposure is high (ex ante or interim monitoring, in Aoki et al.'s [1994] terms) or profitability low (ex post monitoring), but they do not when a dominant nonfinancial shareholder is present. A plausible explanation is that monitoring is performed by the parent firm in those cases.

The negative coefficient on ASSETS has a noteworthy implication, when viewed

Table 10-7. Probit regressions for presence of one or more bank executives on board of listed Japanese firms, 1991

Variable	7.1	7.2	7.3
CONSTANT	−0.230	−0.551	−0.845*
	(−0.618)	(−1.274)	(−1.759)
LEVERAGE	0.0133***	0.0176***	0.0202***
	(2.578)	(3.151)	(3.282)
TOPSHARE	−0.0321***	−0.0364***	−0.0413***
	(−6.697)	(−6.370)	(−6.225)
INSIDEOWNER	−0.636***	−0.611**	−0.888***
	(−2.560)	(−2.247)	(−2.816)
LOANSHARE(1)	0.00710**	0.00907***	0.00837**
	(2.109)	(2.408)	(1.949)
LOANSHARE(2-3)	−0.00484	−0.00691*	−0.00956**
	(−1.322)	(−1.649)	(−2.000)
ASSETS	−0.155**	−0.262***	−0.230**
	(−2.296)	(−2.665)	(−2.188)
PROFIT	−0.0490***	−0.0682***	−0.0776***
	(−3.495)	(−4.103)	(−4.136)
FIRMAGE	0.00483*	0.00593**	0.00582*
	(1.623)	(1.741)	(1.533)
TOPLENDER	0.0231	0.0172	0.0185
	(1.140)	(0.784)	(0.708)
PROFIT*INSIDE	0.0624*	0.0644	0.0689
	(1.772)	(1.593)	(1.458)
BANKSHARE	0.00177	0.000627	0.000309
	(0.377)	(0.115)	(0.0513)
MITSUI	−0.698**	−0.820*	−1.158**
	(−2.0790)	(−1.899)	(−2.255)
MITSUBISHI	1.234***	0.245	0.350
	(3.113)	(0.415)	(0.555)
SUMITOMO	−0.941**	−0.634	−0.616
	(−2.483)	(−1.590)	(−1.459)
FUYO	0.412	0.606*	0.646*
	(1.274)	(1.700)	1.653)
SANWA	0.453	0.700**	0.535
	(1.633)	(2.310)	(1.547)
DKB	0.451*	0.641**	0.619**
	(1.804)	(2.280)	(2.0448)
log likelihood	−551.7	−419.3	−332.2
R^2	0.191	0.233	0.269
psuedo-R^2	0.152	0.140	0.233
% correct predictions	68.6	70.1	75.7
observations	940	767	678

Notes: t-ratios in brackets; industry dummies included but not reported

***significantly different from zero at 1% confidence level

**significant at 5% level

*significant at 10% level

(one-sided or two-sided test as appropriate)

in tandem with the result for TOPSHARE. It seems to be at odds with the notion of a hierarchical nesting of monitoring relations: banks specializing in the monitoring of large parent firms that in turn assume direct responsibility for their affiliates. Banks are more likely to supply directors to relatively smaller (listed) firms that are not affiliates of larger firms (but less so when there is family control), according to the results. On a priori grounds, banks should be more interested in monitoring larger firms, both because of the scale effect (their scarce resources are best allocated where the returns to monitoring are highest) and because large firms tend not to be affiliates of (therefore monitored by) parent firms. The result may suggest that, although the above is true, large firms are better able to keep banks at bay. Alternatively, larger firms may be better run, for instance, because of more effective internal mutual monitoring among managers (Fama, 1980); or, consistent with the labor market hypothesis, they may have less need for outside managerial resources because they attract better managerial personnel to start, or because of scale effects in the accumulation of internal managerial resources.

Two further points are important. First, banks monitor through a variety of means; director placements are only one method. Second, there is still the effect of PROFIT: even though large firms may be less likely to be subject to internal monitoring in normal times, the intervention effect in financial crisis is still at work, consistent with what Kaplan and Minton (1994), Morck and Nakamura (1992), and Hoshi et al. (1990) found and with the results in the case study literature (Sheard, 1985, 1989, 1994c).

When an interaction effect between ASSETS and PROFIT was also tested, some support for this notion was found. Among the three specifications of the dependent variable, ASSETS remained significant only for DEPVAR(1). The coefficient on the interactive variable ASSETS*PROFIT was negative in sign. It was significant at the 5 percent level for DEPVAR(2) and at the 10 percent level for DEPVAR(3), but not significant for DEPVAR(1). The results suggest that it is not size per se but its interaction with the firm's performance that is important. Profitable large firms are less likely to have bank directors, but unprofitable large ones are more likely, perhaps because intervention is more likely to be triggered in such cases.

The failure of BANKSHARE to be significant is noteworthy. It seems to suggest that banks send directors as lenders rather than as shareholders. One interpretation might be that it is large debt exposure that gives banks both the most incentive to monitor and the means to do so.

The insignificance of TOPLENDER is also noteworthy. Along with the results for LEVERAGE and LOANSHARE(2–3), it seems to provide some indirect evidence for the delegated monitoring hypothesis. This says that the main bank monitors on behalf of other lenders as well for itself either by agreement or by default (given the local public good nature of monitoring, as the largest creditor, the main bank's monitoring provides beneficial spillovers for other creditors). In the majority of cases in which firms have bank directors only one bank is involved, but the share of total bank lending in assets rather than the share of the largest bank (almost always the bank supplying the director) seems to drive the bank–firm director link. The negative significant sign on LOANSHARE(2–3) is consistent with this idea. Larger loan shares of the next largest lenders work against the firm's having bank directors; more discrepancy in leading loan shares, when there is a major lender in relative as well as absolute loan share terms, works for the firm's having bank directors.

The results for inside ownership are interesting. A number of measures were developed, including whether an inside owner is present on the board or on the share register and whether the president or chairman is an inside owner. In preliminary regressions, all these measures were tried, including a measure of insider shareholding, but the only one that proved to be significant was INSIDEOWNER, capturing whether the top shareholder is an inside owner. Intuitively, this variable can be seen as indicating qualitatively a strong form of internal control (occupying the top shareholder position). The other dummy variable measures identified wider sets of firms and may have picked up quite a few firms in which there is in fact little or no residual family control. The result suggests that, when a firm is under fairly strong family control, banks are less likely to be able to (or feel the need to) conduct inside monitoring. It is consistent with the conventional wisdom that inside owners try to keep banks, literally, at arms length.

An interesting result is the positive sign on the interactive variable PROFIT*INSIDE; it was significant in the DEPVAR(1) regression but not when the dependent variable was defined more narrowly. Combined with the result for INSIDEOWNER, it suggests both that firms with inside owners are less likely to have bank executives on their boards and that this likelihood is less sensitive to profitability. The positive sign means that the tendency not to have bank executives on the board is accentuated when profitability is low but muted somewhat when profitability is high.

As noted earlier, this finding might reflect a combination of two forces. On the firm side, relative to other firms, those with inside owners resist bank intervention and the intensification of external control that this implies when performance is poor, but they are less prone to do so when they are performing well (when the attenuation of internal control associated with accepting an outside director itself is likely to be low). On the bank side, it may suggest that the banks are more discriminating in performing their ex post intervention role when it comes to more independent-oriented firms.

INSIDEOWNER was significant in all of the regressions, usually at the 1 percent level, whereas PROFIT*INSIDE was significant only under the broadest definition of director presence. The main effect of inside ownership seems to be that it reduces the likelihood of bank director presence (the intercept) rather than alter the slopes of other coefficients. To test this more thoroughly, various tests were conducted of structural change in the intercept and slopes between the two samples of firms with inside ownership (as defined by INSIDEOWNER) and those without. A likelihood ratio test that the intercept and slope coefficients on all variables (except the presidents' club and industry dummies) differed between the two samples was rejected at the 1 percent level. This result suggests that the basic model is applicable to both samples and vindicates the approach used here of treating inside ownership as an additional effect within a single model. On the assumption that other slope coefficients did not vary, a test for no structural change in the intercept and on the slope coefficient of PROFIT was rejected at the 5 percent level for DEPVAR(1) and at the 1 percent level for DEPVAR(3), but it was accepted for DEPVAR(2). Overall, then, the results suggest an interesting qualitative difference in the role that banks play in corporate governance depending, on whether a form of residual entrepreneurial or family control is in evidence.

Some interesting results were obtained for the presidents' club variable. In a regression not reported, a single dummy variable for membership of a presidents' club was included, but it was significant (and positive) only in the case of DEP-VAR(1), and only then at the 10 percent level. A dummy variable for membership of one of the three groups with strongest prewar ties (Mitsui, Mitsubishi, and Sumitomo) was tried also. It was not significant for DEPVAR(1) and was significant at the 1 percent level, but negative in sign, for DEPVAR(2) and DEPVAR(3). Thus, contrary to the conventional wisdom, once other relevant factors were controlled for, membership of a presidents' club seemed to have no effect or to decrease the probability of a firm having a bank director in the case of the three groups usually thought to exhibit the most cohesion.

To investigate the presidents' club effect further, dummies for each of the presidents' clubs were included separately. Interestingly, the separate presidents' club dummies were sometimes significant but with mixed signs. In the full model (7.1), for instance, the coefficients on the Mitsui and the Sumitomo dummies were significant at the 5 percent level but negative in sign. In contrast, the coefficients on the Mitsubishi and DKB dummies were positive in sign and significant at the 1 percent level for the former and the 10 percent level for the latter. Somewhat surprisingly, being in the Sumitomo or Mitsui presidents' club reduces the likelihood of the firm having a bank director, whereas Mitsubishi "crosses lines" to behave more like the newer postwar groupings. For the restricted sample models, however, the Mitsubishi and Sumitomo dummies were no longer significant, whereas the Fuyo group dummy became significant, as did the Sanwa dummy for model 7.2. The Mitsui and DKB dummies, however, showed consistently significant effects across all regressions, although the signs were opposite.

The results suggest that viewing (bank) director dispatch ties as being a characteristic of group affiliation or group cohesion may be misplaced. For two major groups the opposite was found: being in a Mitsui or Sumitomo presidents' club actually reduced the likelihood of having a bank executive on the board. This finding does not mean that these banks are less active as suppliers of bank executives to the senior management ranks of listed firms. Indeed, Table 10-3 shows Mitsui (Sakura) and Sumitomo to be comparable in stock and flow terms to Mitsubishi, Sanwa, and Fuji (DKB stands out). Rather, they may be more likely to supply directors to firms to which they act as the main bank, firms that are not in the closest group ranks as measured by presidents' club membership. Overall, the results support the view that bank–firm director ties reflect the operation of the broader "main bank system" (as reflected in the results on financial and ownership variables), rather than narrower enterprise group relations.

As for industry effects, a number of industry dummy coefficients had positive signs and were significant in the three models, most notably the construction industry. The highly regulated nature of the construction industry and scope for managerial moral hazard may lead to enhanced supervision by banks; alternatively, by giving them more director positions, construction companies may allow banks to share in their lucrative managerial rents.

Conclusions

Conventional wisdom has it that the board of directors in Japan is quite different in make-up and function from its Anglo-American counterpart. Whereas a board of directors in the United States or Britain is the representative instrumentality of stockholders, in Japan it is the operational superstructure of incumbent management. [On the role of the board in corporate governance in the United States, particularly U.S.-style "outside directors," see Kaplan and Reishus (1990), Shivdasani (1993), and Weisbach (1988).] The juxtaposition of various institutional features— a highly internalized managerial labor market, the lack of an active takeover market, the pervasiveness of interlocking shareholding, a low level of individual shareholding, and the perfunctory nature of annual stockholders meetings—has led many observers to doubt whether top corporate management in Japan faces any meaningful capital market oversight or discipline.

A different perspective appears in the literature on Japanese corporate governance. Despite apparent institutional differences, the Japanese system has its own set of mechanisms for dealing with the agency problems associated with the separation of ownership and control in modern business enterprise. These "insider-based" mechanisms involving banks, boards, and blockholders arguably perform the functions as the more "market-oriented" mechanisms associated with an active market for corporate control (Aoki, 1988, 1994; Aoki et al., 1994; Kaplan, 1994; Kaplan and Minton, 1994; Morck and Nakamura, 1992; Sheard, 1989, 1994b,c). The data and analysis presented in this chapter are consistent with this latter view. Although the majority of Japanese directors have risen through the ranks of the "lifetime employment" managerial hierarchy, one quarter are entrants from outside the firm.

The data presented here show that these "outside directors" come mainly from the principal banks and firms that own or lend to the firm. It is tempting, but probably too simplistic, to characterize this situation as one in which the owners and financiers of Japanese firms are extensively "represented" on their boards. However, the data caution against the equally simple view that the top managers of Japanese corporations are free to pursue their goals without supervision, checks, or intervention from those agents in the capital market with the largest direct financial stakes. If we view the ability to influence the selection of top management as a key dimension of corporate governance, the fact that one in four directors has entered from outside the firm and that 41 percent of presidents have (Toyo Keizai Shinposha, 1992, mainly from parent firms and leading financiers, suggests, contrary to much of the popular rhetoric, that Japanese listed corporations are subject to quiet, but perhaps quite effective, governance forces).

Two hypotheses were put forward as potential explanations of the extensive flow of executive personnel from leading banks to the top ranks of Japanese corporate management. One, it reflects the executive managerial labor market at work. Two, it facilitates bank monitoring and the implementation of intervention strategies triggered by deteriorating corporate performance. These two economic functions are quite complementary, so the empirical analysis did not pit one hypothesis against the other. In fact, the two functions may be more than complementary; at times they may be two sides of the same coin. When a bank arranges for a manager to enter a troubled client firm as a senior executive, it is both intervening in the firm, a manifestation of corporate governance, and supplying a key managerial resource, an aspect of the managerial labor market.

The empirical results suggest that there is more to the bank director phenomenon than the operation of a market for recycling early-retiring bank executives. The probability of a firm having a former bank executive in its senior management or as an inside auditor is systematically related to financial, ownership, and governance-related variables. Less profitable, higher leveraged, younger firms and firms with a prominent leading bank lender are more likely to have bank directors. Larger firms and those with leading shareholders and inside owners are more likely not to. Bank executives entering corporate boards late in their career seems to be one important element in the Japanese system of corporate control. Further research is required to understand more fully the processes at work and how effective they are. This study points to the value of such an endeavor.

This chapter adds to the empirical literature on the role of banks in corporate monitoring and governance in Japan by analyzing the role of bank executives on Japanese corporate boards. Japanese corporate boards comprise the top executive officers of the corporation, and the majority of directors are internally promoted managerial employees. However, data were assembled showing that new entrants to the board, defined in this chapter as outside directors, come mainly from firms and banks with leading equity and lending positions in the firm. A probit model of whether a firm has bank executives on its board or not was estimated for all first-session-listed firms. It was found that firms were more likely to have bank executives on their board the more they relied on bank borrowings, the larger the loan share of the top lender, and the greater the discrepancy in loan shares among top lenders. Firms were less likely to have executives on their board when there was a dominant shareholder, there was residual family control over management, and they were larger, older, and more profitable. Overall, the results suggest that the movement of executives from banks to corporate boards is integral to the operation of the secondary top executive managerial labor market in Japan and closely related to the role of banks in capital market oversight and governance.

Note

This chapter is based on Sheard (1994e), a study I undertook as a Visiting Scholar at the Institute for Monetary and Economic Studies at the Bank of Japan. I thank the Bank of Japan for providing excellent research support and for kindly allowing me to incorporate material from that study in this chapter. I wrote the chapter while International Cooperation (Osaka Gas) Associate Professor in the Faculty of Economics at Osaka University. Support from the Osaka Gas research fund at Osaka University is gratefully acknowledged. I also thank Howard Aldrich, Richard Beason, Jim Lincoln, Colin McKenzie, Yoshiro Miwa, Hiroyuki Odagiri, John Ries, Tom Roehl, Hiroo Taguchi, Adrian Tschoegl, David Weinstein, Tetsufumi Yamakawa, and participants in presentations at the Association of Japanese Business Studies annual conference, the Bank of Japan, Finance Forum, and the University of British Columbia for helpful comments. Keiichi Ebisawa, Kenichi Iriyama, and Kazuo Tsuda provided helpful insights into Japanese banking practices.

References

Aoki, M. *Information, Incentives, and Bargaining in the Japanese Economy*. Cambridge: Cambridge University Press, 1988.

Aoki, M. Towards an Economic model of the Japanese Firm. *Journal of Economic Literature*, 28 (1989): 1–27.

Aoki, M. "Monitoring Characteristics of the Main Banks System: An Analytical and Historical View." In M. Aoki and H. Patrick, eds., *The Japanese Main Bank System: Its Relevancy for Developing and Transforming Economies*, pp. 109–41. Oxford: Oxford University Press,1994.

Aoki, M. and H. Patrick, eds. *The Japanese Main Bank System: Its Relevancy for Developing and Transforming Economies*. Oxford: Oxford University Press, 1994.

Aoki, M., H. Patrick, and P. Sheard. "The Japanese Main Bank System: An Introductory overview." In M. Aoki and H. Patrick, eds. *The Japanese Main Bank System: Its Relevancy for Developing and Transforming Economies*. Oxford: Oxford University Press, 1994, pp. 3–50.

Black, B. S. "Agents Watching Agents: The Promise of Institutional Investor voice." *UCLA Law Review*, 39/4 (1992): 811–93.

Coffee, Jr., J. C. "Liquidity versus Control: The Institutional Investor as Corporate Monitor. *Columbia Law Review*, 91 (1991): 1277–1368.

Davidson, R., and J. G. MacKinnon. *Estimation and Inference in Econometrics*. New York: Oxford University Press, 1993.

Diamond, D. W. "Optimal Release of Information by Firms." *Journal of Finance*, 40/4 (1985): 1071–94.

Diamond, D. W. "Monitoring and Reputation: The Choice between Bank Loans and directly placed debt." *Journal of Political Economy*, 99 (1991): 689–721.

Fama, E. "Agency Problems and the Theory of the Firm." *Journal of Political Economy*, 88/2 (1980): 288–307.

Flath, D. "Shareholding in the Keiretsu, Japan's Financial Groups." *Review of Economics and Statistics*, 75/2 (1993): 249–57.

Fruin, W. M. *The Japanese Enterprise System: Competitive Strategies and Cooperative Structures*. Oxford: Clarendon Press, 1992.

Gilson, S. "Bankruptcy, Boards, Banks, and Blockholders." *Journal of Financial Economics*, 27/2 (1990): 355–87.

Gilson, R. J. and M. J. Roe. "Understanding the Japanese Keiretsu: Overlaps between Corporate Governance and Industrial Organization. *Yale Law Journal*, 102/4: 871–906.

Grundfest, J. A. "Subordination of American Capital." *Journal of Financial Economics*, 27 (1990): 89–114.

Holmstrom, B. R., and J. Tirole. "The Theory of the Firm." In R. Schmalensee and R. D. Willig, eds., *Handbook of Industrial Organization*, vol. 1 Amsterdam: North-Holland, 1989, pp. 61–133.

Hoshi, T. The Economic Role of Corporate Grouping and the Main Bank System." In M. Aoki and R. Dore, eds., *The Japanese Firm: The Sources of Competitive Strength* Oxford: Clarendon Press, 1994, pp. 285–309.

Hoshi, T., A. Kashyap and D. Scharfstein. "The Role of Banks in Reducing the Costs of Financial Distress in Japan." *Journal of Financial Economics*, 27/1 (1990): 67–88.

Hoshi, T., A. Kashyap and D. Scharfstein. "Corporate Structure, Liquidity, and Investment: Evidence from Japanese Industrial Groups." *Quarterly Journal of Economics*, 106 (1991): 33–60.

Jensen, M. C. "Agency Costs of Free Cash Flow, Corporate Finance, and Takeovers." *American Economic Review*, 76 (1986): 323–29.

Jensen, M. C. and R. S. Ruback. "The Market for Corporate Control: The Scientific evidence." *Journal of Financial Economics*, 11 (1983): 5–50.

Kaplan, S. N. "Top Executive Rewards and Firm Performance: A Comparison of Japan and the United States." *Journal of Political Economy*, 102/3 (1994): 510–46.

Kaplan, S. N. and B. A. Minton. "Appointments of Outsiders to Japanese Boards: Determinants and Implications for Managers." *Journal of Financial Economics*, 36 (1994): 225–58.

Kaplan, S. N., and D. Reishus. "Outside Directorships and Corporate Performance." *Journal of Financial Economics*, 2 (1990): 389–410.

Keizai Chosa Kyokai. *Nenpo keiretsu no kenkyu: Daiichibu jojo kigyohen (Corporate Affiliation Annual Directory: First-section Listed-firm Edition)*. Tokyo: Keizai Chosa Kyokai, 1993.

Lawrence, R. Z. "Efficient or Exclusionist? The Import Behavior of Japanese Corporate Groups." *Brookings Papers on Economic Activity*, 1 (1991): 311–41.

Lawrence, R. Z. "Japan's Different Trade Regime: An Analysis with Particular Reference to *keiretsu*." *Journal of Economic Perspectives*, 7/3 (1993): 3–19.

Lincoln, J. R., M. L. Gerlach and C. Ahmadjian. "*Keiretsu Networks and Corporate Performance in Japan*. Mimeo. Berkeley: University of California, 1993.

Lincoln, J. R., M. L. Gerlach, and P. Takahashi. *Keiretsu* Networks in the Japanese Economy: A Dyad Analysis of Intercorporate Ties. *American Sociological Review*, 57/5 (1992): 561–85.

Manne, H. "Mergers and the Market for Corporate Control." *Journal of Political Economy*, 73 (1965): 110–20.

Morck, R., and M. Nakamura. "*Banks and Corporate Control in Japan*." Mimeo. Edmonton: University of Alberta, 1992.

Morck, R., A. Shleifer, and R. Vishny. "Alternative Mechanisms for Corporate Control." *American Economic Review*, 9 (1989): 842–52.

Nakatani, I. "The Economic Role of Financial Corporate Grouping." In M. Aoki, ed., *The Economic Analysis of the Japanese Firm*. Amsterdam: North-Holland, 1984, pp. 227–58.

Nihon Keizai Shinbunsha. *1980 nenban kaisha nenkan: jojo gaishaban* (1980 Annual Corporation Reports: Listed Firm Edition). Tokyo: Nihon Keizai Shinbunsha, 1979.

Nihon Keizai Shinbunsha. *1982 nenban kaisha nenkan: Jojo gaishaban* (1982 Annual Corporation Reports: Listed Firm Edition). Tokyo: Nihon Keizai Shinbunsha, 1981.

Nihon Keizai Shinbunsha. *1984 nenban kaisha nenkan: Jojo gaishaban* (1984 Annual Corporation Reports: Listed Firm Edition). Tokyo: Nihon Keizai Shinbunsha, 1983.

Nihon Keizai Shinbunsha. *1986 nenban kaisha nenkan: Jojo gaishaban* (1986 Annual Corporation Reports: Listed Firm Edition). Tokyo: Nihon Keizai Shinbunsha, 1985.

Nihon Keizai Shinbunsha. *1988 nenban kaisha nenkan: Jojo gaishaban* (1988 Annual Corporation Reports: Listed Firm Edition). Tokyo: Nihon Keizai Shinbunsha, 1987.

Nihon Keizai Shinbunsha. *1990 nenban kaisha nenkan: Jojo gaishaban* (1990 Annual Corporation Reports: Listed Firm Edition). Tokyo: Nihon Keizai Shinbunsha, 1989.

Nihon Keizai Shinbunsha. *Nikkei kaisha joho [kikan]'92-I shinshungo* (Nikkei corporate information, 1992 edition I). Tokyo: Nihon Keizai Shinbunsha, 1991.

Prowse, S. D. "Institutional Investment Patterns and Corporate Financial Behavior in the United States and Japan." *Journal of Financial Economics*, 27 (1990): 43–66.

Prowse, S. D. "The Structure of Corporate Ownership in Japan." *Journal of Finance*, 47/3 (1992): 1121–40.

Roe, M. J. "Some Differences in Corporate Structure in Germany, Japan, and the United States." *Yale Law Journal*, 102/8 (1993): 1927–2003.

Sako, M. *Prices, Quality and Trust: Inter-firm Relations in Britain and Japan.* Cambridge: Cambridge University Press, 1992.

Saxonhouse, G. R. "What Does Japanese Trade Structure Tell Us about Japanese Trade Policy?" *Journal of Economic Perspectives*, 7/3 (1993): 21–43.

Sheard, P. Main banks and structural adjustment in Japan. "Pacific Economic Papers," No. 129. Canberra: Australia-Japan Research Centre, Australian National University, 1985.

Sheard, P. "How Japanese Firms Manage Industrial Adjustment: A Case Study of Aluminum." *Pacific Economic Papers* No. 151. Canberra: Australia-Japan Research Centre, Australian National University, 1987.

Sheard, P. "The Main Bank System and Corporate Monitoring and Control in Japan." *Journal of Economic Behavior and Organization*, 11 (1989): 399–422.

Sheard, P. "The Economics of Japanese Corporate Organization and the 'Structural Impediments' Debate: A Critical Review." *Japanese Economic Studies*, 19/4 (1991): 30–78.

Sheard, P. "*Keiretsu* and Closedness of the Japanese Market: An Economic Appraisal." ISER Discussion Paper No.273. Osaka: Institute of Social and Economic Research, Osaka University, 1992.

Sheard, P. "Reciprocal Delegated Monitoring in the Japanese Main Bank System." *Journal of the Japanese and International Economies*, 8/1 (1994a): 1–21.

Sheard, P. "Interlocking Shareholdings and Corporate Governance." In M. Aoki and R. Dore, eds., The Japanese Firm: Sources of Competitive Strength. Oxford: Clarendon Press, 1994b, pp. 310–49.

Sheard, P. "Main Banks and the Governance of Financial Distress." In M. Aoki and H. Patrick, eds., The Japanese Main Bank System: Its Relevancy for Developing and Transforming Economies. Oxford: Oxford University Press, 1994c, pp. 188–230.

Sheard, P. "Long-termism and the Japanese Firm." In M. Okabe, ed., *The Structure of the Japanese Economy.* New York: Macmillan Press, 1994d, pp. 25–52.

Sheard, P. "Bank Executives on Japanese Corporate Boards." *Bank of Japan Monetary and Economic Studies*, 12/2 (1994e).

Shivdasani, A. "Board Composition, Ownership Structure, and Hostile Takeovers." *Journal of Accounting and Economics*, 16, 167–198, 1993

Shoji Homu Kenkyukai. *Kansayaku seido no unyo: seido unyo ni kansuru anketo chosa no bunseki* (Operation of the Statutory Auditor System: Analysis of a Questionnaire Study Regarding Operation of the System). Tokyo: Shoji Homu Kenkyukai, 1989.

Smitka, M. J. *Competitive Ties: Subcontracting in the Japanese Automobile Industry.* New York: Columbia University Press, 1991.

Stiglitz, J. E. Credit Markets and the Control of Capital. *Journal of Money, Credit, and Banking,* 17, 133, 52, 1985.

Taki, A. *Ginko ni yoru yakuin haken no keizai bunseki* (An Economic Analysis of Director Despatches by Banks). Paper presented to Japan Economics and Econometrics Association conference, Kyushu University, Fukuoka, 1992.

Tokyo Bengoshikai Kaishahobu. *Torishimariyakkai ketsugi jiko no handan kijun (Standards of Judgment for Decision Items at Director Meetings).* Tokyo: Shoji Homu Kenkyukai, 1986.

Toyo Keizai Shinposha. *Shukan toyo keizai rinji zokan kigyo keiretsu soran 1984 nenban* (Special Issue of Weekly Oriental Economist: Directory of Corporate Affiliations 1985). Tokyo: Toyo Keizai Shinposha, (1983).

Toyo Keizai Shinposha. *Shukan toyo keizai rinji zokan kigyo keiretsu soran 1985 nenban* (Special Issue of Weekly Oriental Economist: Directory of Corporate Affiliations 1985). Tokyo: Toyo Keizai Shinposha, 1984.

Toyo Keizai Shinposha. *Shukan toyo keizai rinji zokan deta banku kigyo keiretsu soran 1986 nenban* (Special Issue of Weekly Oriental Economist: Directory of Corporate Affiliations 1986). Tokyo: Toyo Keizai Shinposha, 1985.

Toyo Keizai Shinposha. *Shukan toyo keizai rinji zokan deta banku kigyo keiretsu soran 1987 nenban* (Special Data Bank Issue of Weekly Oriental Economist: Directory of Corporate Affiliations 1987). Tokyo: Toyo Keizai Shinposha, 1986.

Toyo Keizai Shinposha. *Shukan toyo keizai rinji zokan deta banku kigyo keiretsu soran 1988 nenban* (Special Data Bank Issue of Weekly Oriental Economist: Directory of Corporate Affiliations 1988). Tokyo: Toyo Keizai Shinposha, 1987.

Toyo Keizai Shinposha. *Shukan toyo keizai rinji zokan deta banku kigyo keiretsu soran 1989 nenban* (Special Data Bank Issue of Weekly Oriental Economist: Directory of Corporate Affiliations 1989). Tokyo: Toyo Keizai Shinposha, 1988.

Toyo Keizai Shinposha. *Shukan toyo keizai rinji zokan deta banku kigyo keiretsu soran 1990 nenban* (Special Data Bank Issue of Weekly Oriental Economist: Directory of Corporate Affiliations 1990). Tokyo: Toyo Keizai Shinposha, 1989.

Toyo Keizai Shinposha. *Shukan toyo keizai rinji zokan deta banku kigyo keiretsu soran 1991 nenban* (Special Data Bank Issue of Weekly Oriental Economist: Directory of Corporate Affiliations 1991). Tokyo: Toyo Keizai Shinposha, 1990.

Toyo Keizai Shinposha. *Shukan toyo keizai rinji zokan DATA BANK kigyo keiretsu soran 1993 nenban* (Special Data Bank Issue of Weekly Oriental Economist: Directory of Corporate Affiliations 1993). Tokyo: Toyo Keizai Shinposha, 1992.

Toyo Keizai Shinposha. *Shukan toyo keizai rinji zokan DATA BANK kigyo keiretsu soran 1992 nenban* (Special Data Bank Issue of Weekly Oriental Economist: Directory of Corporate Affiliations 1992). Tokyo: Toyo Keizai Shinposha, 1991.

Weinstein, D., and Y. Yafeh. "Japan's Corporate Groups: Collusive or Competitive? An Empirical Investigation of *keiretsu* behavior. Mimeo. Cambridge: Harvard University, 1992.

Weisbach, M. S. "Outside Directors and CEO Turnover." *Journal of Financial Economics,* 20 (1988): 431–60.

Appendix

List of variables

Dependent Variables

DEPVAR(1): 1 if one or more former or concurrently serving bank executives is a director or statutory auditor (*kansayaku*) of the firm; 0 otherwise (where "bank" refers to any city, trust, long-term credit, or regional bank, but does not include government financial institutions, insurance companies, agricultural financing cooperatives, or other financial institutions).

DEPVAR(2): 1 if one or more former or concurrently serving bank executives is a director of the rank of executive director (*jomu*) or above; 0 otherwise (where "above" includes senior executive director, vice-president, president, vice-chairman, and chairman).

DEPVAR(3): 1 if one or more former or concurrently serving bank executives is a director of the rank of senior executive director (*senmu*) or above; 0 otherwise.

Explanatory Variables

LEVERAGE: percentage ratio of total bank borrowings to total assets.

TOPSHARE: percentage shareholding of number one shareholder.

LOANSHARE(1): percentage share of total borrowings supplied by number one lender (0 if no borrowings) (Government financial institutions are excluded from the definition of top three lenders, but their loans are a component of total borrowings.)

ASSETS: total assets of the firm (million million yen).

PROFIT: percentage ratio of operating income (*eigyo rieki*) to total assets for the financial year in which the bank executive entered the firm or the most recent executive entered, in the case that more than one bank executive is on the board.

FIRMAGE: year in which the firm was established (1900 normalized to 0).

LOANSHARE(2–3): percentage share of total borrowings supplied by number two and number three lenders combined (0 if no borrowings).

TOPLENDER: percentage ratio of borrowings from number one lender to total assets [=LEVERAGE*LOANSHARE(1)].

PROFIT*INSIDE: interactive variable constructed by multiplying PROFIT by INSIDEOWNER.

BANKSHARE: percentage ratio of total shares of firm held by financial institutions.

Dummy Variables

INSIDEOWNER: number one shareholder identified as "founding family figure."

MITSUI: member of Mitsui group presidents' club (*Nimoku-kai*).

MITSUBISHI: member of Mitsubishi group presidents' club (*Kin'yo-kai*).

SUMITOMO: member of Sumitomo group presidents' club (*Hakusui-kai*).

FUYO: member of Fuyo (Fuji Bank) group presidents' club (*Fuyo-kai*).

SANWA: member of Sanwa group presidents' club (*Sansui-kai*).

DKB: member of DKB (Daiichi Kangyo Bank) group presidents' club (*Sankin-kai*).

Unless otherwise stated, all other variables are for the 1990 financial year (FY), usually end of March 1991. Data on the dependent variables are current as of July 1991.

Descriptive Statistics of Variables[a]

Dependent Variables

	0	1	*n*
DEPVAR(1)	479	585	1,064
DEPVAR(2)	698	366	1,064
DEPVAR(3)	796	268	1,064

Explanatory Variables

Continuous Variables

	Mean	Standard deviation	Minimum	Maximum
LEVERAGE	0.170	0.174	0.000	0.936
TOPSHARE	14.843	13.395	2.300	72.030
LOANSHARE(1)[b]	23.666	17.790	0.000	100.000
ASSETS	0.352	0.896	0.00333	11.088
PROFIT[c]	4.634	4.0798	−25.032	53.445
FIRMAGE	38.213	16.601	−31.000	85.000
LOANSHARE(2-3)[d]	23.374	13.510	0.000	66.667
TOPLENDER[b]	4.236	5.0456	0.000	52.764
PROFIT*INSIDE[c]	0.711	2.367	−7.108	21.659
BANKSHARE	41.204	13.627	1.565	78.344

Dummy Variables

	0	1
INSIDEOWNER	937	127
MITSUI	1,045	19
MITSUBISHI	1,042	22
SUMITOMO	1,048	16
FUYO	1,041	23
SANWA	1,028	36
DKB	1,026	38

[a] *n*=1,064, unless otherwise stated

[b] *n*=1,025

[c] *n*=985

[d] *n*=1,016

Data Sources

Data for the dependent variables, bank borrowings and loan shares, shareholdings of the top shareholder, and membership of a presidents' club, and for the construction of industry dummy variables were obtained from Toyo Keizai Shinposha (1991).

Data on the total shareholdings of financial institutions and total assets for 1990 FY and operating income from 1985 FY were obtained from the NEEDS-Kigyo zaimu (Corporate Financial) electronic database. Data on total assets before 1990 FY and operating income before 1985 were obtained from Nihon Keizai Shinbunsha (1979, 1981, 1983, 1985, 1987, 1989).

Data on the presence of an inside owner were obtained from Toyo Keizai Shinposha (1991), and Nihon Keizai Shinbunsha (1991).

Data on the year firms were established were obtained from Nihon Keizai Shinbunsha (1991).

Data on the year that the bank executive became a corporate director were obtained from Keizai Chosa Kyokai (1993).

11

To Sue or *Keiretsu*

A Comparison of Partnering in the United States and Japan

JEFFREY H. DYER

But if pure *keiretsu* are un-American, the United States can still learn from them. By collaborating on research and production, *keiretsu* members regularly deliver new products ahead of lone-wolf rivals. . . . U.S. companies can no longer ignore these advantages . . . In short, there's a pressing need for U.S. manufacturers to develop something similar to *keiretsu* (*Business Week*, January 27, 1992).

Since the 1980s, the advantages and disadvantages of the Japanese *keiretsu* have been hotly debated in the popular press and by academics. Proponents of *keiretsu*-style alliances argue that interfirm alliances are key to Japanese business success and are something to be emulated. Opponents call for the dismantling of the *keiretsu* because they do not allow for open, free market competition. But both proponents and opponents of *keiretsu* relationships agree on one issue: *Keiretsu* relationships are substantially different from the traditional arms-length relationships that have tended to characterize interfirm relationships in the United States. Moreover, both sides agree that understanding the dynamics of *keiretsu* relationships—how and why they work—is extremely important.

To assess the relative efficiency advantages of alliances, such as the Japanese *keiretsu*, requires a framework that distinguishes the advantages and disadvantages of different institutional arrangements designed to govern exchange. The emerging field of transactional cost economics (TCE) has proven to be a useful model for explaining the boundaries of economic institutions as well as the variety of institutional arrangements employed to "govern" exchange (Coase, 1937; Williamson, 1985). Indeed, it has been the only paradigm to address directly the following key question: What are the relative efficiencies of different institutional arrangements that can be employed to govern exchange? In particular, markets (arms-length relationships) and hierarchies (vertical integration) have received significant attention as alternative modes of governance at two ends of the spectrum. However, the markets-and-hierarchies paradigm has been criticized because it is limited in its ability to explain "hybrid" or "network" institutional arrangements—

like the Japanese *keiretsu*—that are neither purely market nor purely hierarchy (Perrow, 1986; Powell, 1990). This is unfortunate because partnerships/alliances are increasingly used as an organizational form for competitive advantage and are mushrooming in an unprecedented fashion (Anderson, 1990; Powell, 1990). Anderson (1990) noted that more alliances have been announced since 1981 than in all prior years combined.

Williamson (1991, p. 269) acknowledged that "transaction cost economics has been criticized because it deals with polar forms—markets and hierarchies—to the neglect of intermediate or hybrid forms." He (1991) addressed those criticisms by attempting "to identify and explicate the key differences that distinguish three generic forms of economic organization—market, hybrid, and hierarchy." Williamson suggested that hybrid governance falls between market and hierarchical governance in terms of asset specificity and is governed by "neoclassical contracts" as opposed to "classical contracts" (as with markets) or "organization fiat" (as with hierarchy). He also argued that under a high degree of uncertainty, hybrids become "nonviable." However, although the current TCE model is useful for explaining the extreme forms of governance (markets and hierarchies), its current application, even after Williamson's (1991) paper, seems to fall short in explaining hybrid/ network governance. Indeed, the weaknesses of the transaction cost model become evident when one explores such phenomena as Japanese vertical *keiretsu* relationships. *Keiretsu* relationships are characterized by recurrent transactions of a highly specific nature in an uncertain environment—and yet the transactions are not governed by hierarchy, as the TCE model would predict. Moreover, as shall be described, Japanese *keiretsu* transactors do not employ neoclassical contracts to exert governance over the exchange. These empirical anomalies are of particular interest because preliminary evidence suggests that *keiretsu* relationships are more efficient than the market and hierarchical governance structures employed by competing U.S. firms (Nishiguchi, 1989; Womack et al., 1990; Dyer, 1996).

Different literatures use different terms to refer to nonmarket, nonhierarchical transaction relationships. In this chapter, I refer to hybrids, networks, and alliances as representative of transaction relationships that are not governed purely by prices or classical contracts (as with markets) or by organization fiat (as within hierarchies). Virtually all empirical studies testing transaction cost propositions have focused on comparing internal (hierarchical) transactions with external (market) transactions (Masten, 1984; Monteverde and Teece, 1982; Walker and Poppo, 1991; Walker and Weber, 1984). Few, if any, researchers have explicitly focused on comparing hybrid or network forms of governance with market forms.

One reason is that there is no easy way to distinguish a "market" transaction relationship from a "hybrid" transaction relationship. Williamson (1985) noted that the "study of extreme instances often provides important leads to the essentials of the situation." The supplier–purchaser relationship within the Japanese *keiretsu* represents such an "extreme" case, which provides important insights into hybrid governance. As Asanuma (1985a, p. 3) observed: "*keiretsu* affiliations and the subcontracting relationship in Japan . . . fall into neither the pure market [n]or fully integrated hierarchy categories."

In this chapter, I examine the differences between hybrid/network and market governance in the automotive industry in the United States and Japan. More specifically, I describe the results of a study comparing a sample of *keiretsu* and non-*keiretsu* relationships in the Japanese auto industry with samples of supplier relationships in the United States that are identified as "most like a *keiretsu* relationship" and "arms-length relationships." Two fundamental issues are addressed:

1. To what extent are there differences in asset specificity between Japanese transactors and U.S. transactors? Between Japanese *keiretsu* (partner) relationships and nonpartner (independent) relationships?

2. If significant differences in asset specificity exist, do transactors that are highly cospecialized control opportunism in ways that are significantly different than less specialized transactors? To what extent do *keiretsu*-style relationships exist in the United States?

Asset specificity is of primary importance because: (1) investments in transaction-specific assets boost productivity and create interfirm dependency, and (2) the current TCE model predicts that differences in asset specificity are what fundamentally determine the efficient form of governance (e.g., market, hybrid, hierarchy). The prediction, of course, is that hybrid/network transactions will be characterized by a higher level of asset specificity than market transactions in both countries. Moreover, if partner suppliers in Japan are more specialized to automakers than partner suppliers in the United States (as anecdotal evidence suggests they should be), TCE theory would predict that these Japanese transactors must have developed stronger safeguards to protect against the hazards of opportunism. Understanding the specific characteristics of *keiretsu* relationships—both how they create value and how they are governed—is critical if competing firms have any hope of emulating, or dismantling, them.

The chapter is organized as follows. The first section provides a review of the TCE literature on the nature of firm boundaries and choice of governance. Next is a description of the research method employed to compare hybrid and market transaction relationships in the United States and Japan. The third section includes reports of the findings on differences in asset specificity between hybrid and market transactors in the United States and Japan. Finally, I describe the informal and formal mechanisms employed in Japanese *keiretsu* relationships that reduce cooperation and control opportunism.

Choosing among Governance Structures: A Review

Proponents of the TCE perspective view the "transaction" as the unit of analysis and consider markets and firms as "governance structures" designed to govern and permit efficient exchange between transactors. The purpose of governance structures is to provide, at minimal cost, the coordination, control, and trust that are necessary for transactors to believe that engaging in the exchange will be of benefit to them (Palay, 1985; Williamson, 1985).

Coase (1937) was the first to recognize that markets and firms are alternative ways of organizing economic exchanges. Coase's fundamental insight was that firms exist because it is costly to use the price mechanism, meaning that there are costs associated with determining the value of each activity in an exchange. Williamson (1975) further argued that markets fail, and hierarchies take their place, because of transaction costs that make market transactions inefficient. He proposed that transaction costs arise for four reasons: (1) a person's bounded rationality, (2) uncertainty about the future, (3) the possibility of opportunistic behavior, and most important, (4) *asset specificity*. (Asset specificity refers to durable investments in assets that are specialized to a particular transaction.) At the core of Williamson's (1979, 1985) model is the assertion that differences in asset specificity determine the relative efficiency of various discrete forms of governance. Williamson (1985, p. 30) stated that "transaction cost economics further maintains that the most critical dimension for describing transactions is the condition of asset specificity."

Economists have long recognized that "resource owners increase productivity through cooperative specialization" (Alchian and Demsetz, 1972, p. 777). Indeed, in advanced modern economies, the value chain or production network has become characterized by a highly developed interfirm specialization, such that individual firms engage in a narrow range of activities that are embedded in a complex chain of input-output relations with other firms. As Perry (1989, p. 213) noted, "Gains from trade are enhanced by investments in assets which are specialized to their exchange."

However, the benefits of increased specialization cannot be achieved without a cost. When transactors make investments in specialization, transaction costs arise because of the fear of opportunism. Hill (1995:121) summarized the argument as follows:

> When specialization boosts productivity, the owner of the specialized resource can charge more for that resource than the owner of a less specialized resource. The existence of such a quasi-rent creates an incentive to invest in specialization. However, this incentive is tempered by the fact that the more specialized a resource becomes, the lower its value in alternative uses. The contingent value of a specialized resource exposes its owner to a greater risk of "hold-up" than the owner of a generalized resource. . . . Given this possibility, the resource owner might never make the specialized investment and the gains from specialization will be lost (p. 121).

Thus, when considering an exchange, transactors are faced with two important choice variables: (1) What level of specialized investments will optimize joint output (maximize the gains from trade)?, and (2) Given the desired level of specialized investments, what safeguard(s) should be employed to protect against the hazards of opportunism?

Within the TCE perspective, Williamson treated opportunism as a constant feature of human nature, ruling it out as an explanation for the variance in transaction governance forms (Lincoln, 1990). This assumption is the fundamental weakness of the TCE framework's ability to explain hybrid/network forms of governance. Indeed, there is substantial evidence that opportunistic tendencies vary considerably by transactor and by the transaction characteristics (Argyle, 1991; Light, 1972). The key to the TCE perspective is that transaction costs will not exist without asset specificity *and opportunism*: "The lack of trust is the quintessential cause of transactional costs" (Jarillo, 1988, p. 34).

Recent empirical studies by game theorists using the prisoner's dilemma game (PDG) have demonstrated that opportunism varies depending upon the identity of the exchange partner (see Axelrod, 1984, for a description of the PDG). For example, researchers in one study found that there are more cooperative (C) choices if

(1) subjects are already friends, (2) they are similar to each other, or (3) if they are simply told that they are similar to or are members of the same group. Researchers also found that husbands and wives make 100 percent C choices, compared with 65 percent for friends and 22 percent for strangers (Argyle, 1991).

Although Williamson (1991) explicitly recognized that differences in asset specificity influence governance selection, he did not consider how differences in opportunistic tendencies will influence government selection. He argued that transactors must defend against opportunism because ex ante they cannot costlessly determine which other transactors are opportunistic. Thus, opportunism is assumed in all cases, and third-party dispute resolution mechanisms—either legal or organizational—are required to control opportunism. However, this assumption ignores the important reality that transactors have a variety of options for screening those with nonopportunistic intent. Alternative means of safeguarding transactions have been offered. These include informal safeguards, such as trust or embeddedness (Sako, 1991; Smitka, 1991; Gulati, 1995; Uzzi, 1997) and reputation (Weigelt and Camerer, 1988), as well as formal safeguards such as financial hostages (Klein, 1980) and cospecialized investment hostages (Klein, 1980; Williamson, 1983).

This is a critical issue because hybrid or network forms of governance rely on transactors' abilities to control opportunism without resorting to contracts. Indeed, the distinguishing characteristic of effective network governance is that the exchange is forged around investments in specialized assets that create economic value. However, the relationship is not plagued by opportunistic behavior because of various informal and formal safeguards that are employed to reduce the probability that either party will behave opportunistically. When each party to an exchange can be assured that the other party will not attempt to behave opportunistically, asset specificity ceases to pose significant transactional difficulties. Hence, the notion of "controlling opportunism" is critical in assessing whether hybrid governance can be effectively substituted for markets or hierarchies.

In summary, when we study or examine transaction relationships, it is important to focus on two key transaction dimensions: asset specificity and methods of controlling opportunism (control mechanisms).

Research Method

In this section, I describe the research setting, sample, and measures used empirically to examine how hybrid/network governance works in practice in the United States and Japan.

Research Setting

The auto industry was deemed appropriate as a research setting for studying hybrid governance in the United States and Japan for three reasons. First, the automobile industry is the largest industry in both countries, and the United States and Japan have more than one major producer. Second, some evidence suggests that Japanese automakers and their suppliers make greater relation-specific investments than do U.S. automakers and their suppliers (Asanuma, 1989; Clark and Fujimoto, 1991; Nishiguchi, 1994). If this is true, we can examine whether differences in asset specificity are accompanied by differences in contractual safeguards. Finally, the automobile is a complex product with thousands of parts that must work together as a system. Each automaker works with a large number of suppliers who produce approximately 40 to 70 percent of the components for a car. Because each component is part of the total system (or subsystem), mutual adjustment and coordination are required on the part of suppliers and automakers to produce a well-functioning system/product. Thus, this is an industry setting in which transaction-specific investments are likely to be important because suppliers and automakers are interdependent.

Sample and Data Collection

The sample consisted of two Japanese automakers (Nissan and Toyota), all three U.S. automakers (Chrysler, Ford, and General Motors), and a sample of their suppliers. The unit of analysis was the supplier–automaker relationship. Each automaker purchasing department manager selected a sample of fifty domestic supplier relationships. In selecting this sample of fifty, each automaker was asked to select a sample of twenty-five "supplier partners with whom you work most closely" and a sample of twenty-five "most typical arms-length supplier relationships." When identifying "partner" suppliers, U.S. automakers were asked to select suppliers that they believed were "most like a *keiretsu* relationship." This method of sampling was designed to allow for a comparison between the "partner" sample of suppliers and the "arms-length" sample.

I interviewed sales and engineering vice presidents at fifty suppliers (twenty Japanese and thirty U.S.), during which a survey was developed. The survey was then sent to the supplier executive identified by the automaker's purchasing department as most responsible for managing the day-to-day relationship (usually the supplier's sales vice president or the sales account manager). Usable responses were received from seventy-four Japanese suppliers (74 percent response rate) and eighty-two U.S. suppliers (55 percent response rate), with roughly equal response from "partner" and "arms-length" suppliers.

Operational Measures of Specialized Assets

Williamson (1979) identified site, physical, and human asset specificity as distinct types of transaction-specific investments. Operational measures of each of these types of asset specificity were included in this study.

Site-specific investments.   Site specificity refers to transactors locating facilities (e.g., plants) so that they are largely dedicated to a particular transactor. Following Nishiguchi (1994), site specialization was operationalized as the distance (miles) between the supplier plant (manufacturing the highest volume component) and the automaker plants producing small and midsize vehicles. The closer the plant, the more specialized it was.

Physical asset specificity.   Physical asset specificity refers to transaction-specific capital investments in customized machinery, equipment, tools, dies, and so forth.

It is difficult to "measure" the extent to which a piece of equipment is customized to a particular customer (unless it is 100 percent specialized). In this study, physical asset specialization was operationalized as the percentage of the supplier's total capital equipment investments that would have to be scrapped if the supplier were prohibited from conducting any future business with the automaker. This percentage was estimated by supplier sales and engineering vice presidents. Physical asset specificity was assumed to increase with an increase in the percentage of capital investment that could not be redeployed.

In addition, Schonberger (1982) found that physical asset specialization increases with an increase in the frequency of deliveries (e.g., use of just-in-time delivery). Interviews with suppliers revealed that tailoring their delivery systems and making frequent deliveries to a customer required substantial planning and investment in customized information-processing systems, materials-handling systems, order-processing systems, flexible manufacturing, and so forth. Thus, we would expect that as the frequency of deliveries increases, so does physical asset specificity.

Human asset specificity.   Supplier–automaker human asset cospecialization was operationalized in three ways:

1. The annual "person-days" that the supplier–automaker spent in face-to-face contact in 1991. This variable (FACE) includes face-to-face contact between supplier sales and engineering personnel and automaker purchasing and engineering personnel. The assumption behind this measure is that as the number of days of face-to-face contact increases, so does human asset specificity. To normalize for the volume of exchange between the supplier and automaker, FACE was divided by the supplier's sales (in millions of dollars) to the automaker. Thus, if one supplier had 1,000 person days of face-to-face contact and $100 million in sales to the automaker, the ration of FACE/SALES would be 1,000/100, or 10. This would be equivalent to a supplier with 10 times the absolute face-to-face contact, or 10,000 person days of contact, and $1,000 million ($1 billion) in sales to the automaker (10,000/1,000, or 10).

2. The average number of colocated or "guest" engineers (GUEST). Guest engineers are supplier engineers who become a part of the design team and are colocated with automaker engineers. Greater human asset specialization is expected the more engineers are colocated (dedicated) to the automaker. Again, to normalize for the volume of exchange, the number of guest engineers was divided by the supplier's sales (in millions of dollars) to the automaker.

3. Measures of information sharing were developed to measure the extent to which suppliers and automakers shared relevant task-related information. More specifically, the degree of information sharing between the supplier and automaker was operationalized by measuring the extent to which suppliers shared confidential/proprietary technical information and information on their production costs. Supplier respondents reported the extent to which they shared this type of information on a seven-point Likert-type scale (1 = "Not at all" to 7 = "To a very great extent"). In addition, supplier respondents indicated the extent to which they received information and assistance from the automaker to lower their production costs, improve their quality, and improve their delivery and inventory-management systems. Again, respondents indicated the extent to which they received

Table 11-1. Summary of Asset Specificity Operational Measures.

Variables	Description
SITE	The distance in miles between the supplier plant and automaker plants.
PHYSICAL	Percent of supplier's total capital equipment investment which is not redeployable to other customers.
DELIVERY	The average number of deliveries per week.
FACE	Total annual "person/man days" of face-to-face contact between supplier salesmen and engineers and automaker purchasing personnel and engineers.
FACE/ SALES	Total annual "person/man days" (FACE) divided by the supplier's sales to the automaker (in millions of dollars).
GUEST	The average number of supplier colocated or "guest" engineers.
GUEST/ SALES	The number of supplier guest engineers divided by the supplier's sales (in millions of dollars) to the automaker.
TRUST	The extent to which the supplier trusts the automaker with confidential information (Likert scale).
PRODCOST	The extent to which the supplier shares detailed information on their production costs (Likert scale).
COASTASST	The extent to which the automaker shares information with the supplier to assist them in cost reduction (Likert scale).
QUALASST	The extent to which the automaker shares information with the supplier to assist them in quality improvement (reduce defects) (Likert scale).
DELASST	The extent to which the automaker shares information with the supplier to assist them in improving their delivery and inventory management systems (Likert scale).

cost, quality, and delivery assistance on a seven-point Likert-type scale. (See table 11-1 for a summary of the asset specificity variables.)

Results: U.S./Japan Differences in Asset Specificity

Differences in asset specificity for the different samples are reports as sample means in table 11-2. Following is a summary of the key U.S./Japanese differences in supplier–automaker asset specialization.

Greater Site Specialization in Japan

Japanese *keiretsu* suppliers' (*kankei kaisha*) plants were, on average, only 41 miles from automaker plants, whereas U.S. partners were 413 miles from automaker plants. Independent supplier (*dokuritsu kaisha*) plants were farther away than *kankei kaisha* plants, but they were still only 125 miles away versus 589 miles for U.S. "arms-length" suppliers.

Some may argue that Japan is smaller than the United States, and therefore we should expect the plants to be closer in Japan. Perhaps this is a reasonable argument. However, I found that *kankei kaisha* transplants in the United States were, on average, only 87 miles from "parent" company plants in the United States. Al-

Table 11-2. Sample Means on Asset-Specificity and Information Sharing
Measures.

	U.S. Suppliers- U.S. Automakers		Japanese Suppliers- Japanese Automaker	
	Arms-length $N = (32-46)$	Partner $N = (32-46)$	Arms-length $N = (38-48)$	Partner $N = (31-45)$
Asset Specificity				
Site Specificity				
Distance between plants (in miles)	589	413	125[b]	41[a]
Physical Specificity				
Percent of total capital equipment not redeployable	15%	17%	13%	31%[a]
Deliver frequency	3.3	9.6	32.2[b]	32.4[b]
Human Specificity				
Annual "person days" of face-to-face contact	1,169	1,385	3,181[b]	7,270[a]
"Person Days"/Sales	7.7	9.0	11.6[b]	12.7[a]
Guest Engineers	0.45	0.47	2.3[b]	7.2[a]
Guest Engineers/Sales	.0029	.0031	.0084[b]	.012[a]
Information Sharing				
Supplier trusts automaker with confidential information	3.1	3.3	5.3[b]	6.2*
Supplier shares detailed data on cost structure	4.5	4.3	4.3	5.9*
Automaker shares information to assist the supplier with cost reduction	2.1	1.9	2.6[b]	4.2*
Automaker shares information to assist the supplier with quality	2.9	3.1	3.0	4.4*
Automaker shares information to assist suppliers with delivery	2.1	2.3	2.7	4.2*

Tests of group differences are one tailed *t*-tests assuming unequal variances.

[a]Significantly different from all other populations (p<.01).

[b]Significantly different from U.S. populations (*p*<.01).

Note: The sample size (*N*) ranges for each variable because all respondents did not answer all questions. The range of sample sizes is listed below each of the four sample groups.

though this is farther away than their plants in Japan, it is still significantly closer than U.S. supplier plants. Moreover, *absolute differences do matter*. A supplier plant that is 40 miles away has significant economic advantages over a plant that is 400 miles away, regardless of the country in which it is located.

Greater Physical Asset Specialization in Japan

Roughly 31 percent of a *kankei kaisha*'s total capital investments were so specialized to the parent firm that they would have to be scrapped if they were prohibited from doing any future business with that customer. In contrast, U.S. suppliers and *dokuritsu kaisha* indicated that only about 15 percent of their investment was nonredeployable. It is interesting to note that partner suppliers in the United States were no more specialized than arms-length suppliers. It is also interesting to note that *dokuritsu kaisha* were similar to U.S. suppliers in terms of the level of reported physical asset specificity. These findings are consistent with previous studies in which researchers found that Japanese suppliers take more responsibility for the detailed engineering of parts and are more likely than U.S. suppliers to develop unique parts for their customers.

For example, Clark and Fujimoto (1991) found that 38 percent of U.S. automakers' parts were "off the shelf" parts, whereas only 18 percent of Japanese automaker parts were "off the shelf." Similarly, Nishiguchi (1993) found that when a U.S. supplier develops a component for a U.S. customer, the same auto component is fitted into 8.3 car models. In contrast, Japanese suppliers sell the identical part for only 5.71 models, indicating higher customization of Japanese auto parts for car models. This greater customization occurs despite the fact that Japanese suppliers indicated more total customers (16.3 regular customers) than did U.S. suppliers (3.6 regular customers).

Greater Human Asset Specialization in Japan

Japanese suppliers and automakers make significantly greater investments in human cospecialization than do U.S. suppliers and automakers. Most noteworthy is the fact that Japanese *kankei kaisha* engaged in 7,270 person days of face-to-face contact and *dokuritsu kaisha* 3,181 person days of contact, compared to only 1,384 and 1,168, respectively, for their U.S. supplier counterparts. Thus, Japanese suppliers and automakers engaged in three to seven times more absolute face-to-face contact with automakers than did their counterparts. When adjusted for sales volume, the differences are smaller but still significant. Japanese suppliers also colocated significantly more guest engineers than did their counterparts.

Moreover, Japanese suppliers were much more likely to share key task-related information with automakers on their methods of production and their production costs. They were also much more likely to trust the automaker with confidential information (e.g., technical). Finally, Japanese automakers were reported as providing more information and assistance to suppliers to support them in reducing costs, increasing quality, and improving delivery.

These findings suggest that interfirm human asset cospecialization between Japanese automakers and their suppliers is significantly greater than between U.S. automakers and their suppliers. Thus, it is not surprising that the automotive value chain in Japan is more effective at coordinating the production of a complex product with many process steps. Greater interfirm human-asset cospecialization gives Japanese transactors the ability to disseminate knowledge rapidly throughout the value chain (particularly tacit knowledge) and respond quickly to changes in the environment. Indeed, greater overall specialization in the production network (value chain) of Japanese automakers allows for productivity gains that are not possible in the less specialized production networks of their competitors. Perhaps this at least partly explains why Japanese automakers are able to develop cars of higher quality and with lower costs and shorter new-model cycle times than do their U.S.

Table 11-3. Auto Industry Performance Differences, United States versus Japan.

	United States	Japan
1. Quality		
Problems Reported Per 100 Vehicles Sold[a]	133	94
2. New Model Cycle Time		
Average Major Model Change Frequency (1982−87)[b]	8.1 years	4.6 years
3. Efficiency/Cost		
Cost of Parts and Assembly for a Compact Car (1985)[c]	$5,200	$3,480
Inventory Costs[d]		
• Automaker Inventory/Sales	8.8%	3.5%
• Supplier Inventory/Sales	10.7%	7.8%
4. Profitability		
Automaker Pretax Return on Assets (Avg. 1982−91)[d]	3.7%	9.3%
Supplier Pretax Return on Assets (Avg. 1988−92)[d]	4.65	5.5%

Sources:

[a]J.D. Power, 1990−92; defects per 100 vehicles for all models for GM, Ford, and Chrysler, compared with Nissan and Toyota.

[b]Clark and Fujimoto (1991).

[c]Bain & Company Study, January, 1985, reported in Dyer and Ouchi (1993).

[d]From annual reports; 10-year average inventory to sales ratio and pretax ROA (1982−91) for GM, Ford, and Chrysler compared to Toyota and Nissan. Supplier inventory and profit data are from Dyer (1996).

counterparts (See Table 11-3 for a summary of performance differences between Japanese and U.S. automakers.)

The Case for Noncontractual Controls: Partnering in Japan

From a TCE perspective, Japanese *kankei kaisha* relationships are troubling because they raise the following key issue: Given the high levels of asset specificity that characterize these relationships, why aren't these interfirm relationships unstable and troubled by opportunism? Are the opportunistic tendencies of the transactors controlled because they have written effective neoclassical contracts that serve to check opportunism and facilitate adaptation? According to received theory (Williamson, 1991), this should be the case.

However, an examination of *keiretsu* relationships and their legal contracts reveals that *kankei kaisha* and automakers do not rely on contracts to control opportunism. Asanuma's (1985a, 1989) study of legal contracts in the automobile and the electronic industries revealed that they typically employ a "standard contract," which is a short document that outlines the general obligations of the parties and effectively acts as a "constitution" for the relationship. This contract does not specify exact prices, quantities, or delivery schedules, which are determined later by the "mutual consent" of the parties. It does typically specify a standard duration (e.g., 4 years), but the contract is automatically renewed at the end of the duration unless either party wants to renegotiate. In the words of a Nissan purchasing manager, these contracts have "no real termination date."

Table 11-4. Differences in Contracting in the Auto Industry, United States versus Japan.

	U.S. Automakers		Japanese Automakers	
	Arms-length	Partner	Arms-length	Partner
Contract Types				
1. "Classical" Contract	25%	19%	0%	0%
•Fixed price				
•Fixed quantity				
•Fixed duration				
2. "Neoclassical" Contract	59%	48%	0%	0%
•Variable price				
•Variable quantity				
•Numerous contingency clauses (variation based on formula)				
•Fixed duration				
3. "Relational" Contract	16%	39%	100%	100%
•Negotiated price				
•Estimated quantities				
•Automatically renewed or no termination date				
Avg. Contract Duration (Years)	2.4	4.7	3.0 Yr. Rolling[a]	3.0 Yr. Rolling[a]

[a]Automatically renewed after three years unless one party wants to renegotiate the agreement (one Japanese automaker employed a 2-year standard, the other a 4-year standard).

In the law and economics literature, this type of contract is described as a "relational contract" because few details of the agreement are actually written in the contract (Macneil, 1978). A more standard type of contract (a classical contract) is characterized by predetermined prices and quantities that are set for a fixed duration. The entire relationship and set of obligations of the parties are written "within the four corners of the document" (Macneil, 1978). Finally, a neoclassical contract is more flexible than a classical contract because it has numerous contingency clauses that provide some flexibility in the event that market conditions change (Macneil, 1978; Williamson, 1991).

In this study, purchasing agents at the automakers were asked to identify which type of contract was employed with each supplier. A description of each type of contract (classical, neoclassical, and relational) was given, and the purchasing manager was asked to identify which of these three descriptions most accurately characterized the contract. The results are presented in table 11-4. These results suggest that Japanese automakers rely completely on relational contracts with their Japanese suppliers, whereas U.S. automakers rely primarily on classical and neoclassical contracts.

If Japanese automakers and their affiliated suppliers do not rely on neoclassical contracts to control opportunism (as received theory suggests they should), on what do they rely? Dore (1983, p. 463) suggested that "opportunism may be a lesser danger in Japan because of the explicit encouragement and actual prevalence, in the Japanese economy of what one might call moralized trading relationships of mutual goodwill." The Japanese are simply more benevolent and are less oppor-

Table 11-5. Measures of Noncontractual Safeguards, United States versus Japan.

	U.S. Suppliers– U.S. Automakers		Japanese Suppliers– Japanese Automakers	
	Arms-length	Partner	Arms-length	Partner
Social Knowledge/Trust				
Percent of supplier top management team (*yakuin*) who are former automaker employees[c]	5%	3%	1%	27%[a]
Total number of former automaker employees[d]	1.8	.7	1.1	12.6[a]
Annual "person days" of face-to-face contact	1,169	1,385	3,181[b]	7,270[a]
Number of years doing business	40	42	40	41
Financial Hostages				
Percent of supplier stock owned by the automaker	0%	.5%	2%	23%[a]

Tests of group differences are one-tailed *t*-tests assuming unequal variances.

[a]Significantly different from all other populations (p<.01).

[b]Significantly different from U.S. populations (*p*<.01).

[c]U.S. suppliers were asked how many of their top ten executives in the firm were former employees of the automaker.

[d]In Japan, former employees were transferred to the supplier. In the United States, these individuals left the automaker to accept a job at the supplier.

tunistic, presumably for cultural reasons. Perhaps this is true to some extent, although previous researchers have found that Japanese transactors are also quite opportunistic. Nishiguchi (1989) found that following World War II, subcontractors in Japan were often abused by large customers, which led them to appeal to the government for assistance. Light (1972) found similar opportunistic behavior by Japanese individuals in the banking industry in the United States. Although Japanese transactors may be less opportunistic, on average, than U.S. transactors, opportunism is still of concern among Japanese transactors.

My study of *kankei kaisha*–automaker relationships suggests that these relationships involve a complex set of self-enforcing informal and formal controls. For a comparison of the extent to which hybrid and arms-length transactors employ informal and formal safeguards to control opportunism, consider the data presented in table 11-5. These data suggest that *kankei kaisha* relationships employ a broader variety of safeguards than do *dokuritsu kaisha* or supplier relationships. An entire chapter could be devoted to exploring the control mechanisms that bond Japanese partnering firms. However, the most important bonding mechanisms that facilitate partnering in the Japanese automobile industry are briefly examined here.

Development of Extensive Interfirm Social Knowledge/Trust

Three important practices employed by Japanese automakers and their *kankei kaisha* cultivate extensive interfirm social knowledge and trust. These practices are lifetime employment, interfirm career paths, and substantial face-to-face contact.

Stable/lifetime employment.   Much has been written about the Japanese employment practice of long-term employment within one firm (Ouchi, 1980; Fruin, 1983). This key practice fosters the development of social knowledge and trust among individuals both within the firm as well as across firms. As Dore (1983, p. 466) noted, "There are *real* personal relations between the purchasing manager of Toyota and the manager/owner of a subcontracting firm" (emphasis in original). The importance of these relationships should not be underestimated. Numerous studies indicate that as communication persists over time, individuals develop idiosyncratic and valuable knowledge about each other. Furthermore, over time, individual attitudes converge, cohesiveness increases, and specialized language and personal trust develop. Indeed, Ouchi (1980, p. 138) observed that "instability of employment, which upsets the long socialization period necessary, is the chief enemy of this (clan) form of control." Hence, it is not surprising that the Japanese have been able to develop substantially greater social knowledge and trust across firms, given the practice of lifetime employment within firms.

Interfirm career paths.   Another way that *kankei kaisha* and Japanese automakers build interfirm social knowledge and trust is by employing interfirm career paths in which employees are transferred across firms. Gerlach (1987, p. 132) found that "employee transfers, both temporary (usually two years) and permanent, are common among business partners, particularly between banks and their client firms and between large manufacturers and their subcontractors." Cusumano (1985) described how executive transfers were particularly important in the auto industry because they "usually preceded technical assistance, loans, or exclusive procurement contracts." Cusumano's study indicates that these transfers preceded additional partner-specific investments on the part of the automakers. However, none of these previous studies provides data on how widespread this practice is in Japan. My study at Nissan indicates that on average 30.6 percent of the executives at Nissan's *kankei kaisha* are former Nissan employees (see table 11-6). Thus, more than 30 percent of the top executives at Nissan's *kankei kaisha* are former Nissan employees. This practice plays an important role in helping Nissan and its suppliers build interfirm trust and work cooperatively.

Moreover, in addition to employee transfers, the *kankei kaisha* had an average of 7.2 guest engineers (compared to 0.5 guest engineers for the U.S. sample) colocated with the automaker engineers at their technical centers. Guest engineers become a part of the design team and are given desks in the same room with the automaker's engineers. Guest engineers may work at the automaker's technical center for as long as 1 to 2 years and thus are more likely to develop greater social knowledge/trust.

Substantial face-to-face contact.   Finally, *kankei kaisha* and automakers have a tremendous amount of face-to-face contact. The *kankei kaisha* in my sample had an average of more than 7,270 person days of face-to-face contact per year with automakers (including guest engineers). Conversely, U.S. "partner" suppliers had an average of 1,384 person days of face-to-face contact with automakers. Thus, *kankei kaisha* had more than five times the face-to-face contact with automakers, compared to U.S. suppliers, even when one does not include employee transfers. This is significant because face-to-face contact is much more important than other forms of contact for transactors to develop mutual social knowledge and trust (Argyle, 1991). Undoubtedly, this finding partially explains why Japanese suppliers indicated that they were much more likely to trust the Japanese customers with confidential information than did their U.S. counterparts.

Efficient Market for Reputation in Japan

Williamson (1991, p. 291) argued that "improved reputation effects attenuate incentives to behave opportunistically in interfirm trade—since the immediate gains from opportunism in a regime where reputation counts must be traded off against future costs." Thus, mechanisms that improve the efficiency of the market for reputation should reduce opportunism. The evidence suggests that the market for reputation is more efficient in the Japanese auto industry for two reasons: bank-centered enterprise (*keiretsu*) groups and supplier associations. The *keiretsu* groups are important institutions that regulate business activity and alliances through the creation of high-level executive councils, which provide a forum for interaction among group firms, and structure exchange networks—specifically debt, equity, directorship, and trade networks. The *keiretsu* group, especially the main bank, is a significant provider of capital for firms within the *keiretsu* and may act as a third-party arbitrator in cases in which there are trade disputes. *Keiretsu* groups can impose real economic sanctions (e.g., withdrawing capital or business) on a firm that behaves inappropriately in a trading relationship.

Moreover, if a firm exploits a trading partner, it quickly develops a negative reputation. In the automotive and other major industries, suppliers have formed supplier associations that share ideas on how to work more effectively with the "primary" firm and act as an "information clearinghouse" (Odaka et al., 1988). Nishiguchi found that managers at Japanese automotive and electronic firms were unwilling to "fire" or deal harshly with subcontractors because they didn't want to develop a negative reputation. Developing such a reputation would, in the words of one Japanese manager, make it "extremely difficult to find other subcontractors when business picks up who can achieve the same quality standards" (Nishiguchi, 1989, p. 286). Furthermore, Fruin (1992) observed that supplier associations are a vehicle through which automakers can damage the reputation of suppliers by publicly reporting on their suppliers' performance. Naturally, mechanisms that increase the efficiency with which one firm can damage the reputation of another will reduce the probability that a firm will exploit a trading partner.

Financial Hostages

Many Japanese firms, instead of vertically integrating, will either swap stock or take significant minority ownership positions in key suppliers. For example, Nissan owns an average of 33 percent of the stock of its *kankei kaisha*, whereas they own only 2 percent of *dokuritsu kaisha* stock (see table 11-6). Williamson (1985) claimed that companies need "credible commitments" if they are to make partner-specific investments and that an arrangement akin to an "exchange of hostages"

Table 11-6. Nissan Relationships with Supplier Partners.

Company	Percent of Direct Sales to Nissan (%)[a]	Percent of Shares Owned by Nissan (%)	Executives Transferred from Nissan	Size of Supplier Management Team	Percent of Supplier Management from Nissan (%)	Major Products
Yamato Kogyo	83	34	5	10	50	Boby panels, fuel tanks
Yamakawa Ind.	77	34	4	12	33	Auto instruments
JECS	77	54	6	9	67	Electronic fuel injection parts
Calsonic	77	33	7	13	54	Radiators, heaters, air conditioners
Atsugi Unisia	76	31	6	17	35	Engine parts, steering, suspension
Yorozu Mfg.	75	35	4	12	33	Body parts
Kansei	70	36	9	13	67	Plastic parts, measuring parts
Ohi Seisakusho	67	34	3	12	33	Door locks, door hinges
Fuji Tekko	65	34	2	12	17	Transmissions, axles
Hashimoto Forming Ind.	62	25	4	14	29	Moldings, radiator grills
Tsuchiya Manufacturing	56	67	5	10	50	Air cleaners, filters
Kinugwa Rubber Ind.	54	24	4	11	36	Body parts
Kasai Industries	53	25	3	12	25	Door trim, sun visors
Nihon Plast	52	30	5	13	38	Instrument parts, steering wheels
Ikeda Bussan	51	43	2	12	17	Seats, interior components
Niles Parts	49	40	2	12	17	Electronic controllers
Ichiko Industries	49	20	2	19	11	Headlamps, mirrors
Kiryu Machine	46	59	5	8	63	Disk brakes, drum breaks
Tokyo Sokuhan	41	49	3	6	50	Auto parts, measuring instruments
Kokusan Kinzoku Kogyo	40	25	3	9	33	key sets, auto parts
Tochigi Fuji Sangyo	39	21	3	12	25	Auto parts, door locks

Kato Hatsujo	38	17	0	10	0	Springs, fasteners
Clarion	32	13	0	15	0	Car radios, car stereos
Marui Industries	30	25	4	11	36	Emblems, knobs
NDC	28	70	5	10	50	Bearings, bushings
Keeper	25	12	1	10	10	Oil seals, valve seals, bushings
Saga Tekkohsho	23	33	3	10	30	Bolts
Sanoh Ind.	13	10	0	13	0	Breaks, fuel tubes
Dalkin Manufacturing	6	34	NA	NA	NA	Clutches
Average	50	33	100	327	30.6	

[a]Does not include sales to Nissan through other companies (subcontractors).

Source: Nissan Purchasing Department, 1990.

can act as a credible commitment. Stock ownership in Japanese trading relationships represents credible commitments that firms have made to each other. For example, in the automotive industry, stock ownership represents a credible collateral bond for the supplier, who needs such a bond as an incentive to make the partner-specific investments required by automakers.

Specialized Investment Hostages

Japanese auto suppliers develop unique parts for their customers and make greater investments in specialized assets. In particular, more than 90 percent of *kankei kaisha* executives in my sample claimed that they do *not* receive a separate payment for their investment in highly customized tools, dies, molds, and jigs; these items are so highly customized (because they "touch the part") that they would need to be scrapped if the automaker cut off orders to the supplier. In contrast, more than 90 percent of U.S. suppliers said they do receive a separate payment from U.S. automakers to buy the tools, dies, and molds. *Kankei kaisha* executives indicated that, on average, 31 percent of their total investment in capital equipment could not be redeployed to produce components for other customers. U.S. supplier executives indicated that only about 15 percent of their capital equipment investment could not be redeployed. Moreover, *kankei kaisha* manufacturing plants are built close to the customer and are largely dedicated to a specific customer. The average distance between a *kankei kaisha* plant and automaker plant is 41 miles in Japan, and more than 60 percent of output is dedicated to a specific customer. Conversely, U.S. partner supplier plants are, on average, 413 miles from their primary customer plants, and only 35 percent of output goes to the primary customer. Thus, specialized capital investments by Japanese suppliers make them highly dependent on the automakers with the real possibility of opportunistic exploitation.

However, automakers are also dependent on *kankei kaisha* to an important degree. Most *kankei kaisha* parts are "black box," meaning that the automaker provides only very general specifications and the supplier does all the detailed functional specifications and blueprints. Consequently, suppliers have much more knowledge about the design and manufacture of the part than does the automaker. Because *kankei kaisha* black-box parts are highly customized to a specific model, the automaker is highly dependent on the supplier. If the supplier does not perform as desired, it would be very difficult for the automaker simply to shift business to another supplier, given the customized nature of the product and the fact that the supplier owns the tools, molds, and dies. Moreover, some *kankei kaisha* claim that they do not provide all the specific functional details to the automakers when they submit their design drawings for approval. They will intentionally leave out certain important details. (In fact, the term "black box" was used because the supplier engineers would literally blacken a box on the blueprints to prevent sharing proprietary information.) Thus, Japanese suppliers try to protect proprietary designs and technology, thereby making it difficult for the automaker to change suppliers quickly. The result is that the automaker is also quite dependent on the supplier. As one *kankei kaisha* executive observed, "They can't really move business away from us very easily. They need us for our skills just as we need them." Because U.S. suppliers are less likely to have done the product design and have property rights to the design, they do not have the same kind of leverage as

Japanese suppliers. Clark and Fujimoto (1991) found that whereas 62 percent of Japanese automakers' components were black box, only 18 percent of U.S. automaker components were black box.

Under these conditions the parties are highly *inter*dependent, and the specialized investments made by each party create a composite profit (rent) stream only if the transactors continue working together. If the relationship is terminated, each party loses some portion of the rents. Thus, these specialized investments create interdependence, which, in turn, creates incentives to cooperate (Fruin, 1992).

Conclusion

An examination of hybrids in Japan suggests that legal contracts are not necessary to control opportunism. Evidence from this study suggests that the legal centralism assumption that market exchange would be possible without some third-party enforcer to impose sanctions on opportunistic parties is incorrect. A neoclassical contract (third-party enforcement) is but one means of assuring that transactors do not behave opportunistically. Japanese transactors, notably *kankei kaisha* and automakers, rely on trust, reputation, financial hostages, and cospecialized investment hostages to safeguard specialized investments. Indeed, they rely on multiple noncontractual safeguards that, when used in combination, are highly effective at controlling opportunism. Thus, a *keiretsu* relationship requires the development of a complex web of self-enforcing safeguards that elicit cooperation and create interfirm trust. U.S. automotive transactors have not demonstrated a similar ability to make credible, noncontractual interfirm commitments. Rather, they rely largely on legal contracts (or suing) to control opportunism within the exchange relationship. This implies that although U.S. automotive firms do know how to *sue* (use legal contracts), they do not know how to *keiretsu* (develop trust through a mix of noncontractual safeguards). Because legal contracts are relatively ineffective at safeguarding specialized assets, especially under conditions of uncertainty, U.S. suppliers rationally refuse to make investments that are highly specialized to a particular automaker. Thus, U.S. automotive transactors forego the benefits of specialization that Japanese transactors are able to achieve.

This research offers evidence that Japanese suppliers and automakers make greater investments in specialized assets than do their U.S. counterparts. Moreover, given that we expect transactors to "increase productivity through cooperative specialization," this may explain why Japanese automakers have been able to produce higher quality cars in faster development times and with lower costs. This study also offers evidence that "partner" suppliers in Japan make greater specialized investments in their automaker customers than do independent suppliers. Interestingly, "partner" suppliers in the United States were not significantly more specialized to automakers than were "arms-length" suppliers. The primary difference between U.S. partner suppliers and arms-length suppliers was simply in the length of the contract. Partner suppliers received contracts of much longer duration (4.7 years versus 2.4 years), which apparently was reflective of a good relationship. These data suggest that *keiretsu*-style relationships are either nonexistent or extremely rare among U.S. automakers and suppliers.

Finally, my research suggests that to create a specialized production network like the vertical *keiretsu*, transactors must first develop effective self-enforcing safeguards that build interfirm trust. To create an efficient production network requires that transactors within the network make investments in performance-enhancing specialized assets. However, without trust (credible interfirm commitments), transactors rationally refuse to make the investments and, thus, will forego the benefits of specialization. Japanese production networks realize the benefits of specialization because these transactors know how to make credible interfirm commitments. If a specialized production network is critical for competitive advantage, these data do not bode well for U.S. transactors. They suggest that U.S. automotive transactors must learn how to develop *keiretsu* relationships (or something similar to a *keiretsu*-style relationship), or else continue to forego the benefits of a highly specialized production network.

Note

The National Association of Purchasing Management (NAPM) and Center for International Business and Education Research (CIBER) are gratefully acknowledged for their support of this research.

References

Alchian, A., and H. Demsetz. "Production, Information Costs, and Economic Organization." *American Economic Association*, 62–5 (1972): 777–95.

Anderson, E. "Two Firms, One Frontier: On Assessing Joint Venture Performance." *Sloan Management Review*, 31–2 (1990): 19–30.

Argyle, M. *Cooperation: The Basis of Sociability*. New York: Routledge, 1991.

Asanuma, B. "The Contractual Framework for Parts Supply in the Japanese Automotive Industry." *Japanese Economic Studies*, 13–4 (1985a): 54–78.

Asanuma, B. "The Organization of Parts Supply in the Japanese Automotive Industry." *Japanese Economic Studies*, 13–4 (1985b): 32–53.

Asanuma, B. "Manufacturer–Supplier Relationships in Japan and the Concept of Relation-Specific Skill." *Journal of the Japanese and International Economies*, 3 (1989): 1–30.

Axelrod, R. *The Evolution of Cooperation*. New York: Basic Books, 1984.

Clark, K. B., and T. Fujimoto. *Product Development Performance*. Cambridge, Mass.: Harvard Business School Press, 1991.

Coase, R. H. "The Nature of the Firm." *Economica*, 4 (1937): 386–405.

Cusumano, M. A. *The Japanese Automobile Industry: Technology and Management at Nissan and Toyota*. Cambridge, Mass.: Harvard University—The Council on East Asian Studies, 1985.

Dore, R. "Goodwill and the Spirit of Market Capitalism." *British Journal of Sociology*, 34–4 (1983): 459–82.

Dyer, J. "Towards a Theory of Hybrid Governance: Insights from the Japanese *keiretsu*." Working paper. The Wharton School of the University of Pennsylvania, Philadelphia, 1993.

Dyer, J. "Specialized Supplier Networks as a Source of Competitive Advantage." *Evidence from the Auto Industry. Strategic Management Journal*, 17, 4 (1996): 271–292.

Dyer, J., and W. Ouchi. "Japanese Style Partnerships: Giving Companies a Competitive Edge." *Sloan Management Review*, 35–1 (1993): 51–63.

Fruin, W. M. *Kikkoman: Company, Clan, and Community*. Cambridge: Harvard University Press, 1983.

Fruin, W. M. *The Japanese Enterprise System*. New York: Oxford University Press, 1992.

Gerlach, M. "Business Alliances and the Strategy of the Japanese Firm." *California Management Review*, 30–1 (1987): 126–42.

Gulati, R. "Does familiarity breed trust? The implications of repeated ties for contractual choice in alliances," *Academy of Management Journal*, 38, (1995), 85–112.

Hill, C. "National Institutional Structure, Transaction Cost Economizing, and Competitive Advantage: The Case of Japan." *Organization Science*, 6, 2 (1995): 119–131.

Jarillo, C. J. "On Strategic Networks." *Strategic Management Journal*, 9 (1988): 31–41.

Klein, B. "Transaction Cost Determinants of "Unfair" Contractual Arrangements." *American Economic Review*, 70, 2 (1980): 356–362.

Klein, B., R. G. Crawford, and A. A. Alchian. "Vertical Integration, Appropriable Rents, and the Competitive Contracting Process." *Journal of Law and Economics*, 21 (1978): 297–326.

Light, E. *Ethnic Enterprise in America*. Berkeley: University of California Press, 1972.

Lincoln, J. "Japanese Organization and Organization Theory." In B. M. Staw and L. L. Cummings, eds., *Research in Organizational Behavior*, vol. 12. Greenwich, Conn.: JAI Press, 1990, pp. 255–94.

Macneil, I. R. "Contracts: Adjustment of Long-term Economic Relations under Classical and Neoclassical, and Relational Contract Law." *Northwestern University Law Review*, 72 (1978): 854–905.

Masten, S. E. "The Organization of Production: Evidence from the Aerospace Industry." *Journal of Law and Economics*, 27 (1984): 403–17.

Monteverde, K., and D. J. Teece. "Supplier Switching Costs and Vertical Integration in the Automobile Industry." *Bell Journal of Economics*, 13 (1982): 206–13.

Nishiguchi, T. "Strategic Dualism: An Alternative in Industrial Societies." Ph.D. diss. Nuffield College, Oxford University, 1989.

Nishiguchi, T. *Governing Competitive Supplier Relations: New Auto-Industry Evidence*. Paper, the MIT/IMVP Annual Sponsors' Briefing, 1993.

Nishiguchi, T. *Strategic Industrial Sourcing*. New York: Oxford University Press, 1994.

Odaka, K., O. Keinosuke, and F. Adachi. *The Automobile Industry in Japan: A Study of Ancillary Firm Development*. Tokyo: Kokusaibunken, 1988.

Ouchi, W. G. "Markets, Bureaucracies, and Clans." *Administrative Science Quarterly*, 25 (1980): 124–41.

Palay, T. "Avoiding Regulatory Constraints: Contracting Safeguards and the Role of Informal Agreements." *Journal of Law, Economics, and Organization*, 1–1 (1985): 155–75.

Perrow, C. *Complex Organizations: A Critical Essay*, 3rd ed. New York: Random House, 1986.

Perry, M. K. "Vertical Integration." In R. Schmalensee and R. Willig, eds., *Handbook of Industrial Organization*, vol. 1. New York: Elsevier-North Holland, 1989, pp. 185–255.

Powell, W. W. "Neither Market nor Hierarchy: Network Forms of Organization." In B. M. Staw and L. L. Cummings, eds., *Research in Organizational Behavior*, vol. 12. Greenwich, Conn.: JAI Press, 1990, pp. 295–336.

Sako, M. "The role of 'trust' in Japanese Buyer–Supplier Relationships." *Ricerche Economiche*, 45–2/3 (1991): 449–74.

Schonberger, R. *Japanese manufacturing techniques*. New York: Free Press, (1982).

Smitka, M. J. *Competitive Ties: Subcontracting in the Japanese Automotive Industry*. New York: Columbia University Press, 1991.

Uzzi, B. "Social structure and competition in interfirm networks: The paradox of embeddedness." *Administrative Science Quarterly*, 42, (1997), 35–67.

Walker, G., and L. Poppo. "Profit Centers, Single-source Suppliers, and Transaction Costs." *Administrative Science Quarterly*, 36 (1991): 66–67.

Walker, G., and D. Weber. A Transaction Cost Approach to Make-or-buy." *Administrative Science Quarterly*, 29 (1984): 373–391.

Weigelt, K., and C. Camerer. "Reputation and Corporate Strategy: A Review of Recent Theory and Applications." *Strategic Management Journal*, 9 (1988): 443–54.

Williamson, O. E. *Markets and Hierarchies: Analysis and Antitrust Implications*. New York: Free Press, 1975.

Williamson, O. E. "Transaction–Cost Economics: The Governance of Contractual Relations." *Journal of Law and Economics*, 22 (1979): 223–61.

Williamson, O. E. "Credible Commitments: Using Hostages to Support Exchange." *American Economic Review*, 73–4 (1983): 519–35.

Williamson, O. E. *The Economic Institutions of Capitalism*. New York: Free Press, 1985.

Williamson, O. E. "Comparative Economic Organization: The Analysis of Discrete Structural Alternatives." *Administrative Science Quarterly*, 36 (1991): 269–96.

Womack, J., D. Jones, and D. Roos. *The Machine That Changed the World*. New York: Harper, 1990.

12

Governance, Managed Competition, and Network Organization at a Toshiba Factory

W. MARK FRUIN

During the 1980s, a decade of increased trade, foreign direct investment, and internationalization of the Japanese economy, between 73 and 83 percent of the production value of the Yanagicho Works (one of the Toshiba Corporation's multifunction, multiproduct Knowledge Works) was sourced from suppliers (Fruin, 1997). This occurred despite elevated internationalization in the form of foreign direct investment (FDI) in three overseas branch factories and a decided dependency on literally hundreds of suppliers for most of the value-added content, quality, and price/performance appeal of Yanagicho's products.

Such continuity and dependency at the factory level of organization suggest that Japan's industrial firms, like Toshiba, are only as good as their suppliers. This competitive reality has transformed assembler–supplier relations from traditional notions of asymmetrical exploitation of small firms by large ones into something more akin to partnerships or strategic business alliances. For Yanagicho, relations with key suppliers—how manufacturers respond to, join, and combine with core suppliers—are pivotal to manufacturing success. Given the strategic significance of suppliers, their large numbers, their value-added manufacturing contribution, and the proliferation of new products, processes, and technologies in today's electronics industry, the governance structures and strategies that are adopted by assemblers and suppliers are well worth further study and examination. This chapter argues that a network form of organization and a strategy of "managed competition" are the logical outcomes of the high-levels of assembler–supplier interdependency at the Yanagicho Works.

The Visible Hand and Supplier Relations

Any alliance implies both autonomy as well as interdependence. That is, partners decide when to share risks and rewards by investing jointly in various forms of asset specificity. In the Japanese electronics industry, such partnerships are *not* typically based on and secured by equity exchange (unlike the auto industry, for example). Perhaps the Japanese electronics industry is too fast moving, or perhaps a plethora of small- and medium-sized firms makes large firms' equity investments unnecessary. Whatever the reasons, instead of equity-based, tangible asset specificity, intangible asset specificity or knowledge sharing is increasingly favored.

Sharing knowledge is absolutely strategic. It is not entrusted to the invisible hand of the marketplace. Instead, a calculated, forward-looking, decidedly managerial attitude drives decisions of what to share, when to share, how to share, and with whom to share knowledge. In hardware-based partnering, such as when fixed costs in telecommunications and transportation systems are shared, the costs of network activity can be estimated with considerable accuracy because they are related to economies of scale in investment and frequency of use. Costs of membership, operation, and even disintegration are easily estimated (Oniki, 1992, pp. 397–410).

However, in sharing knowledge and know-how, costs and rewards cannot be easily determined. Thus, the visible hand of management takes over even more in situations in which intangible assets link organizational actors. A visible hand defines rewards and incentives precisely because transactions are motivated by what is invisible. Thus, knowledge-based networks need to be managed with an eye toward measuring value by something other than standard formulas, such as calculations for estimating returns on investment (ROI) or returns on equity (ROE), the coin of the realm when tangible assets are shared or exchanged. Instead, the value of intangible assets are calculated according to the speed and effectiveness with which know-how can be traded, mobilized, and acted upon. Such relational qualities of know-how are associated with market-share expansion and fast-to-market strategies, neither of which is well served by net present value estimations (Stalk and Hout, 1990; Fruin, 1995).

Because knowledge sharing is hard to define and even harder to enact, a variety of interfirm governance mechanisms, such as supplier associations, supplier grading schemes, exchanges of engineering and managerial personnel, and dedicated training programs for the diffusion of technology and know-how—like Total Quality Management (TQM) and Total Productivity Management (TPM) seminars and forums—have appeared. All of these—associations, schemes, seminars, forums, training programs, campaigns, and other forms of information exchange and knowledge sharing—are designed to help partners organize, manage, coordinate, enhance, and reinforce mutually beneficial relations in the absence of any clearcut market-based means for doing so.

The salience and importance of such mechanisms and arrangements are roughly proportional to the degree of partnership asset specificity. That is, the greater the asset specificity is (especially, intangible asset specificity) and the more important partner relations are, the more attention is given to managing the growth and governance of those relations. As asset specificity has increased in Japan, most notably in the high economic growth decades of the 1960s, 1970s, and 1980s, so has an emphasis on effective, equitable, vital partnership and supplier relations, and on the speed with which such relations can be activated for competitive purposes. Hence, a notable growth in asset specificity (both tangible and intangible) can be traced to rapid economic growth and increased velocity in assembler–supplier transactions. This growth has propelled Toshiba and other major firms into *network forms of organization* as a means of sustaining high levels of equity, learning, and competitive performance (Williamson, 1975, 1985; Fruin and Nishiguchi, 1993).

Invisible Assets

In a fairly typical year, 1988, nearly four-fifths of the production value of the Yanagicho Works, one of Toshiba's twenty-seven factories in Japan (including three branch factories at that time), was sourced from suppliers. Two hundred thirty-two of these suppliers sold $42 million of parts, components, subassemblies, and services to the Yanagicho Works, constituting about two-thirds of the value of the factory's output. Another 500 suppliers sold an additional $6.9 million to the factory (personal communications, Purchasing Department, Yanagicho, 1989). The value of supplier goods from all 732 suppliers, as a percentage of total manufacturing output, was 78 percent in 1988.

In 1988, the outsourced high-tech communications and information-processing products included photocopiers, automatic mail-sorting devices, SuperSmart IC cards, and high-speed laser printers. Product life cycles were short—often impossibly so, as little as six months in a few instances. Profit margins were slim, between 1 and 4 percent. Sharing of information and technology between assemblers and suppliers was intense, often resulting in little or no differences with respect to product design, development, and manufacturing capabilities.

About one-half of the 232 key or core suppliers to Yanagicho's Kyoryokukai, or Supplier Association. Out of 232 suppliers, 164 provided ordered goods or *gaichuhin*, whereas the remaining 68 made purchased goods or *konnyuhin*, following Asanuma's (1985, 1989) classification scheme. There were also *kanren kigyo* suppliers, or firms that are part of the Toshiba interfirm network at the corporate level of organization (as opposed to the factory level of affiliation). Ordered or *gaichuhin* goods are custom ordered; that is, suppliers provide finished components and products against the functional specifications of assemblers. Extreme examples of customization and cospecialization are so-called "black box" parts, in which assemblers are not informed how suppliers met assemblers' functional specifications. In the motor vehicle industry in Japan, black box parts run two to one as compared with other parts (Clark and Fujimoto, 1991). Suppliers' proprietary parts or assemblers' detail-controlled parts are the "others."

Central to the comanagement process is the Kyoryokukai or the governance system uniting Yanagicho and its core suppliers. Because Toshiba does not lend capital to or own shares in suppliers of either ordered or purchased goods (except in extremely rare cases, and not at all in Yanagicho's case), the Kyoryokukai is the primary organizational means for Yanagicho to ensure that its relations with suppliers are going well. "Going well" means that its investments in suppliers are secure and well placed, and that its 73–83 percent dependence on suppliers for parts, components, assemblies, and services is well considered. In sum, the Kyoryokukai is Yanagicho's primary means of governing its treasure of tangible and intangible assets with suppliers. Given high levels of asset interdependence and a need for fail-safe coordination, it is almost predictable that an extraorganizational body would be created and empowered with the means to ensure interunit communication and exchange (Van de Ven and Walker, 1984; Oliver, 1990).

Managed Competition and the
Supplier Association

The Yanagicho Works is located just outside Tokyo in the city of Kawasaki. Thirteen different product lines are made and managed there today. Since its founding in 1936, Yanagicho has developed and manufactured literally dozens of different product lines (Fruin, 1992). As distinct from a "mass production" factory, the Yanagicho Works finds its mission in product and process innovation—in marrying new process technologies to existing product lines and designing and developing new products with existing technologies.

To some degree the variety of product lines at the Yanagicho Works is a general feature of the Japanese electronics industry. Large firms produce a full line of products, and because there is variety in the scale of production as well as in the degree of technological maturity, major firms produce large numbers of fairly diverse products. In 1991, in fact, Toshiba made 11,500 different kinds of products (personal communication, Tetsuya Yamamoto, Senior Manager, Logistics, Toshiba Corporation, Tokyo, April 3, 1992). Factories like the Yanagicho Works are the reason why Toshiba can be so prolific.

Photocopiers and nonimpact printers are by far the most important products at Yanagicho, accounting for roughly one-half of the value of the facility's entire output. The labor-saving equipment department, itself a rather broad product area encompassing ATMs and ticket-taking and cash-handling equipment, brings in about 27 percent. Optoelectric image systems, utility meters and gauges, compressors, speciality peripherals, and parts account for increasingly smaller portions of the value-added recipe.

Given Yanagicho's diverse range of products, 700 to 800 suppliers, and high value of outsourced parts, components, and subsystems, good supplier relations are much more difficult to achieve in fact than in theory. Developing, maintaining, and enhancing interdependent capabilities means pursuing a dynamic balance between cooperation and competition in assembler–supplier relations across a considerable swath of product and process capabilities. The most important relations—those with ordered-goods suppliers—become strategic alliances in which complementarity and partnering find expression in processes of organizational learning that join and strengthen assembler–supplier capabilities. For such interdependent capabilities to have meaning, take shape, and be manageable, however, they require a form, something with boundaries, something that can be governed.

The Kyoryokukai meets the need. As Yanagicho's formal means of interacting with suppliers, it is a site- and relation-specific, organization-centered governance system designed to enhance the interactive capabilities of suppliers within one another and the factory. Suppliers are an integral part of a strategy to offer a full line of products in many different market segments and to lower the costs and risks associated with this full-line strategy. Manufacturers intensify their foci on particular product and market niches by recruiting other enterprises, usually smaller and less well-endowed enterprises, to complement and complete their efforts. To the degree that manufacturers excel with this strategy, much of the credit must be assigned to the creative management of suppliers, that is, to the Supplier Association, the structure and process of interfirm governance, and patterns of learning that buttress, sustain, and extend supplier relations.

The Supplier Association was established in its present form in 1982. It existed previously as the Seisanbukai or Manufacturing Association, but the Seisanbukai was less active in its meetings and interactions than the present Supplier Association, and it did not stand on nearly as equal a footing with the factory as today's Supplier Association. There are 164 ordered-goods firms in the Association, or 71 percent of all core suppliers. Although participation in the Association is voluntary, most firms join at the invitation of Yanagicho's Purchasing Department.

Given the incredible complexity of designing, developing, and manufacturing thirteen different product lines within one factory facility, the 164 ordered-goods suppliers in Kyoryokukai are certainly a major reason for Yanagicho's success. But the dependence is not just in one direction: Just as Yanagicho depends on its key suppliers, the suppliers depend on Yanagicho for employment, sales, technological guidance, managerial aid, and logistical support. In the aggregate, more than 1,300 firms and 59,000 people populate Toshiba's supplier network, and these figures that do not include others engaged in transportation, shipping, and distribution.

Ultimately, what Toshiba does not need it will not buy, and therein comes the risk for suppliers—a risk not fully shared by Toshiba or other big firms. They can decide on their own the degree to which they make or buy, and there are always concerns within large firms that they may outsource too much and fail to employ their own workers fully. However, effective communication and information exchange within supplier associations may substantially reduce the risk of underemployment, and this is a major concern for everyone involved but especially for the key suppliers of ordered goods.

Also, if Yanagicho depends too heavily on suppliers for particular products and services, Yanagicho may lose its creative edge in the product-development process. Eventually, that shift will result in reduced sales and lowered levels of employment for everyone. Even if the organizing presence of Yanagicho dominates its supplier network, Yanagicho cannot be profitable without an active and mutually beneficial supplier network. In sum, although Yanagicho (Toshiba) decides the balance of cooperation/competition among and between suppliers, it is also manifestly evident that Yanagicho needs its suppliers as much as they need Yanagicho.

Toshiba-Style Contracts

For negotiating that balance, there are no Western-style contracts that fix clearly the terms of performance, namely, price, quality, and delivery, in advance. Yanagicho sets schedules for the delivery of specific quantities of specific items at specific destinations on specific dates. In theory, the prices for such "contracts" are negotiated every six months, but in practice, they are renegotiated every month (Kawasaki and McMillan, 1987).

Schedules are fixed monthly, detailing daily deliveries of predetermined amounts at set prices for the next month. In general, prices remain fixed regardless of fluctuations in volume during the month. Rather than specify firm prices for parts to be delivered beyond the monthly schedules, agreements specify rules by which prices for various components (suppliers' labor, materials, and energy costs) may be altered between monthly negotiations. Negotiations for setting prices and fixing the duration of contracts occur according to the changing needs of Yanagicho and the market. Because designs, products, and models are changing more or less constantly in the electronics industry, prices are being renegotiated more or less continuously. At a minimum, prices are renegotiated monthly, depending on the part/assembly in question and the volume being purchased.

Western-style contracts, in contrast to Japanese-style contracts, traditionally place little or no premium on the process of lowering production costs and developing increasingly better relations with suppliers based on cospecialization or property-rights sharing. Prices remain fixed for the duration of the contract, generally six months in North American practice; more often than not, the same price point is used for negotiating the second six-month period. Japanese-style contracts have opposite effects. For the short run, between price negotiations, suppliers are allowed to keep whatever production cost reductions they realize; in the long run, both parties benefit from reductions in production costs, given norms of coexistence and coprosperity. The ongoing success of suppliers in lowering costs is one of the motivating factors, in addition to the number of design and model changes, that forces frequent price negotiations. Ultimately, buyers get less expensive parts, and suppliers increase their business.

Put another way, in exchange for bearing some risk of unpredictable production-cost increases, buyers benefit from the efforts of suppliers to lower costs. One could argue with this conclusion based on how economic rents (profits) are distributed. Given the valuation problems associated with sharing intangible assets, it would be extremely difficult to prove. Given the relatively low levels of exit from the supplier associations, one has to assume that the distribution of profits is sufficient to sustain supplier membership.

Thus, despite the small numbers of buyers, their monopsonic powers, and the arbitrary determination of the timing and content of economic contracting, Japanese price negotiations are characterized by regular, long-term, market-based transactions. More or less constant negotiation and renegotiation of price and delivery terms underpin a philosophy of coexistence and coprosperity, and the practice of long-term continuity allows for short-term indeterminacy in actual transactional terms. Whatever was not quite right during the most recent negotiations will be balanced during the next. This process of cooperation on the one hand and competition on the other colors the character of assembler–supplier relations at Yanagicho, in Toshiba, and more broadly in the Japanese electronics industry.

The Purchasing Department as Entrepreneur

Processes of negotiation, prices paid to suppliers, and the overall management of assembler–supplier relations are handled by purchasing departments (*shizaibu*) at various levels in Toshiba. The corporate purchasing department sets policies and procedures for the entire company through two corporate-level committees, the Manufacturing Strategy Committee and the Supplier Strategy Working Group. These bodies determine the basic posture and degree of (inter)dependence with suppliers; their work is probably more important to the long-term health and well being of Toshiba than any other committee at the corporate level.

Toshiba is organized into numerous product groups, within which divisions and business units are found. Each division and business unit has a Supplier Management Committee that sets the policy directions and structures within which supplier networks are created, upgraded, and managed. Finally, every manufacturing unit has its own local purchasing department, which is charged with administering and overseeing factory–supplier interactions.

Throughout Toshiba, the point of balance between manufacturing in-house and using outside suppliers is strategically important. Outside suppliers have across-the-board lower manufacturing costs; also, labor, land, and overhead expenses are typically lower. Once one relies on suppliers for the manufacture and assembly of products, however, the know-how associated with the design, production, and packaging of those products may be lost to Toshiba. An ideal point of balance is somewhere between taking full advantage of the economies of specialization offered by small, focused suppliers and not losing the knowledge and experience accumulated by achieving economies in-house.

Nonetheless, there are transaction costs associated with managing supplier networks as well as potentially large costs associated with a loss or transfer of proprietary know-how. Unless the partnership binding assemblers and suppliers is effectively managed, transaction costs can easily offset the lower manufacturing costs that originally motivated the search for outside suppliers. Transaction costs can balloon, for example, if technically demanding parts and processes are outsourced to less capable suppliers, and thus, a great deal of management and engineering oversight is required.

Competition and Managed Partnerships

In 1986, the internal transfer value of Yanagicho's output reached approximately $65 million ($1 = 150 yen), of which 64.9 percent, or $42 million were goods purchased from core suppliers. The average for all Toshiba factories in that year was 65 percent, although the value varies according to product line and size of factory (personal communication, Purchasing Department, Yanagicho Works, 1987). Based on 1986 data, the process and means by which Yanagicho partners with and manages its key suppliers are discussed next. Given the thoroughness and rigor with which these processes are accomplished, the overall importance attached to assembler–supplier relations can easily be appreciated.

Of the roughly $42 million contracted by the Purchasing Department with Association suppliers, 4 percent went for basic materials, like carbon black and hydraulic fluids; 33 percent was expended on purchased goods, such as integrated circuits and other standardized components; and 63 percent was spent on ordered goods. Software development expenses, earmarked either for products or production processes, are not included in these totals, because they are included within administrative overhead for the factory as a whole. But it should be noted that both on- and off-site software costs are among the most rapidly rising for the factory. The breakdowns for all supplies purchased as well as for ordered goods alone are shown in figures 12-2 and 12-3.

In some cases, whole assemblies come from suppliers, and the efforts of the factory are directed toward final integration of subassemblies, testing and quality control, a blending of software and hardware. As one department head told me, "sup-

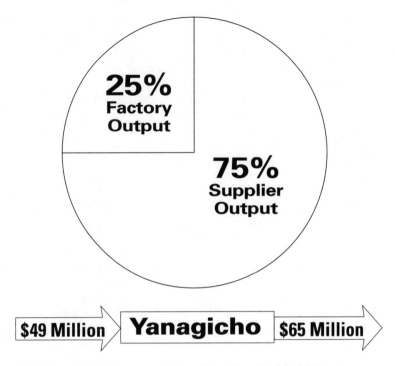

Figure 12-1 Yanagicho: Factory and Supplier Valued-Added Output

pliers are an extension of our own production lines." To be so tightly connected to the Yanagicho Works, the Purchasing Department must expend considerable time and effort in training suppliers how to perform their functions—how to deliver low cost goods of high quality on time.

"The Age of Selection"

Supplier management occurs within what is called the "Age of Selection" (*senbetsu no jidai*). The need for a system to manage suppliers at the factory level of organization first appeared during the 1960s as demand outstripped the capacity of factories to fill orders; in response, factories cultivated suppliers for their extra productive capacity. Sourcing parts and assemblies from suppliers enabled firms/factories to reduce in-house tooling, engineering, and design costs at a time when investment for these were severely constrained (Nishiguchi, 1994). The first postwar period of locating, training, and cultivating suppliers was generally known as the age of "nurturing excellent subcontractors" at Toshiba.

Since the late 1970s, however, an intensification of domestic competition and a movement of production overseas have led to less effort invested in developing good suppliers. Instead, techniques for distinguishing the good from the average are administered from the outset, and there is little tolerance for suppliers who

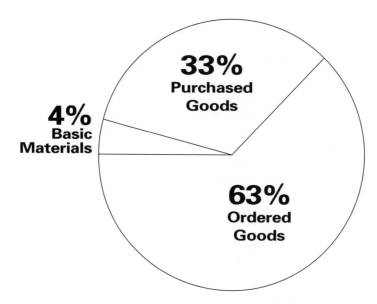

Figure 12-2 Goods Purchased from Suppliers

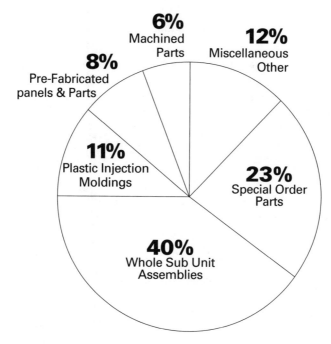

Figure 12-3 Breakdown of Ordered Goods

cannot make the grade early. The economy has been increasingly geared toward the production of high-value–added goods, and assemblers as well as suppliers must conform. Under the leadership of President Iwashita Futao, who assumed leadership of Toyota during the height of the Oil Crises in 1976, *sentaku keiei*, or "selective management," became a watchword (Fruin, 1992, pp. 243–7).

A new "Age of Selection" practiced by the Yanagicho Purchasing Department was really an outgrowth of President Iwashita's "selective management" policy and a Total Productivity (TP) campaign initiated in 1985. The Purchasing Department believes that the number of suppliers will necessarily decline in today's tougher conditions, leading to a decline in absolute numbers–even while the relative value of supplier activities will likely increase. In fact, however, the number of suppliers has grown slightly in recent years. This trend appears to reflect an increase in the number of product lines manufactured by Yanagicho rather than a heightened division of labor among existing suppliers. The number of *gaichuhin* suppliers has grown as follows:

in 1983, 146 suppliers; 1984, 153; 1985, 160; 1986, 162; 1987, 163.

In 1988, however, the Purchasing Department trimmed the number of ordered-goods suppliers in the Association to 151 in an effort to ensure the quality of core suppliers. Subsequently, the numbers have been further cut to 143 in 1989 and 131 in 1990. However, although core suppliers in the Association have been weeded, the total number of suppliers of both ordered and purchased goods has grown.

Assembler–Supplier Relations

To react successfully in an "age of selection," both Yanagicho and its suppliers have made changes. For Yanagicho, it has meant a new personnel rotation policy, so that all production departments move key persons through the purchasing function, thereby acquainting them with supplier management methods and problems. Before the factory can effectively manage suppliers, however, there is a complicated process of deciding which parts, components, subassemblies, and assemblies to make in-house and which to source from suppliers. This decision is not as simple as it may sound, however, because Yanagicho believes that there are six advantages to outsourcing (see figure 12-4).

Obviously, managing suppliers is more than a simple matter of identifying wage rate and manufacturing cost differentials. Indeed, every part, product, and process in the Yanagicho Works is scrutinized according to a complex scheme that situates the part, product, and process somewhere along a continuum of high-to-low desirability of in-house manufacture. The parts and products that fall clearly on one or another end of the continuum are not a problem; when they fall somewhere in the middle, however, another elaborate evaluation is required.

The second order make-or-buy decision illuminates strategic as well as tactical elements. At the first level of decision-making, clear-cut cost or technological advantages lie with either the factory or its suppliers. But a majority of cases are not so clear-cut. Table 12-1 lists some issues in clarifying second order make-or-buy decisions.

In addition to fairly elaborate judgments of cost differences between the factory and its suppliers based on detailed capacity-utilization calculations, additional

Figure 12-4 Advantages to Subcontracting

suppliers can respond more quickly to market and technological change

alliances with suppliers promote progress in the industry

suppliers have lower wage costs

suppliers have fewer labor restrictions

suppliers have special technological strengths in the case of certain manufacturing
processes

suppliers may have unused manufacturing capacity

considerations include estimates of wage costs, overtime, and fringe benefits for personnel, operating costs, repair costs, setup costs, depreciation costs, and insurance costs, as well as finance costs for materials, plant and equipment. Finally, because a decision of what to make or to buy is itself part of an overall strategy of how, when, and where to attack the marketplace, the Yanagicho's Purchasing Department must keep in mind numerous basic considerations. Although it may be possible to quantify many of these decision points, most variables are highly subjective and depend heavily on a sense or feel for products and markets.

Yanagicho wants to keep its personnel, plant, and equipment utilized to the fullest extent; thus, keeping in-house those products and manufacturing processes that have long production runs will be profitable and have high value-added content. This often comes down to identifying the so-called key components of products, those parts and components that differentiate Toshiba products from all others. At Yanagicho, for example, these key components are the drums for photocopiers, the casings for ATM machines, and the flat batteries and stainless steel boards for IC cards. Yanagicho is reluctant to let anyone else make these, and as a consequence, criteria that define key components must be applied in all instances of outsourcing. The strategic value of key components is such that Yanagicho will make them in-house, even at a comparative cost disadvantage.

Generally, a supplier's manufacturing costs (based on existing equipment and facilities) are remarkably lower, even with a healthy markup, than Yanagicho's costs (the costs for doing the same job with new equipment). For this reason alone, everything possible is outsourced as long as Yanagicho's personnel are efficient and equipment is running full and steady. After determining what should be made in-house and what outsourced, Yanagicho seeks at least two suppliers for every part and component that it sources. This fundamental rule of supplier management, a two-vendor policy, protects the factory from a variety of possible shortcomings, such as an interruption in the flow of needed parts and components and a ballooning beyond expectation of the costs of supplied goods. Having two suppliers for the same part greatly minimizes these risks, and it also serves as a standard for comparing suppliers on matters of quality, cost, delivery, and managerial competence.

Comparative statistics are gathered by the Purchasing Department. The factory employs a six-part, 100-point scheme for ranking suppliers, and then it further segregates them into four different groups for differential attention and control. The 100-point ranking scheme is reproduced in figure 12-5.

Table 12-1. To Make or to Buy.

Decision Category	Check Point	In-House	Supplier
QUALITY			
Who has higher quality?	•defect rate •plant facilities •technical level		
Who has better quality monitoring management?	•level of routine quality control •level of work standards •inspection audit documentation		
Who has more experience and capability?	•years of experience •number of skilled workers (jukurenko)		
DELIVERY			
Who is more dependable?	•record on deliveries •efforts to improve deliveries •facilities location		
Who has a more cooperative attitude?	•efforts to improve delivery schedule •efforts to improve design specs		
Who has a better arrangement for managing deliveries	•delivery management capabilities •following deliveries system & efforts •balance of delivery & manufacturing abilities		
OTHER CONSIDERATIONS			
Amount of excess manufacturing capacity?			
Number of underutilized workers?			
Need for specialized training of workforce?			
Any increase in indirect staff?			

This information may be graphed according to a conventional scatter diagram for easier illustration and comparison, with quality as the *x*-axis, for example, and technology or quality level along the *y*-axis. The aim of such comparisons, of course, is to increase supplier reliability, quality, delivery, and technical proficiency. Yanagicho expects better suppliers to follow the factory's lead in improving performance and to stay in touch with the factory's internal efforts to lower costs, improve quality, and generally advance the design and manufacture of products. Illustrative of the tighter fit that the factory seeks with its better suppliers is the 30 points out of 100 that were awarded for supplier delivery performance.

Comparative figures on supplier performance are gathered for each major product group. Although some suppliers may provide parts and components for several different product lines, most will be specialized in just one or a few parts, components, or subassemblies. Depending on the nature of what is supplied, the level of acceptable performance can vary widely with regard to quality, cost, or delivery. The standard for timing on deliveries, for example, can vary from 1 hour to 72 hours at Yanagicho, depending on the scheduled rates of production for particular products. In general, supplier schedules are fixed three months in advance even though minor adjustments are made right up to the current month.

Figure 12-5 Standards for Ranking Excellent Suppliers

Item	Content		Evaluation						
1. Quality	Reject rate &	Rank:	1	2	3	4	5	6	7
	attitude toward	Points:	20	18	16	12	8	4	2
2. Delivery		Rank:	1	2	3	4	5	6	7
		Points:	30	25	20	15	10	5	0
3. Technological		Rank:	1	2	3	4	5	6	7
Level		Points:	10	8	6	4	2	1	0
4. Value	VA cooperation;	Rank:	1	2	3	4	5	6	7
Analysis	VA suggestions: quality & number	Points:	10	8	6	4	2	1	0
5. Evidence of	CD drop/quarter	Rank:	1	2	3	4	5	6	7
Cost Down	CD drop/product	Points:	20	16	12	8	4	2	0
6. Cooperativeness		Rank:	1	2	3	4	5	6	7
		Points:	10	8	6	4	2	1	0

Part of the cooperative–competitive balance between factory and suppliers is a tacit understanding that the factory will neither attempt to hire away the supplier's best people nor steal a supplier's innovations in production and delivery. A large share of the motivation of suppliers to lower costs and improve quality and delivery is the knowledge that such improvements will increase their profit margins at the expense of contractors, at least until the next major renegotiation of the terms of price and delivery. Thus, suppliers work hard to lower costs and thereby improve their margins within the life cycle of models and products.

The considerable effort expended on appraising suppliers does not go wasted. Using the standards for ranking suppliers discussed previously, the Purchasing Department has designed a method of grouping suppliers into five categories according to the degree of effort that must be exercised in managing them. The standards are listed in table 12-2.

Comprehensive pricing and performance appraisals of the factory and suppliers occurs every three years on a rolling average. However, models and products are changing constantly, and so average pricing and performance measures are hard to come by. All suppliers are informed officially of their performance rankings once a year, but, in fact, weekly and even daily reports are tallied on the quality, cost, and reliability of parts, components, and subassemblies. The results of these tallies are shared informally with suppliers as needed. Lists of "good" and "bad" suppliers, that is, those that are doing well or poorly according to the factory's performance criteria, are posted publicly. Also, information on a supplier's performance is available at monthly Kyoryokukai meetings.

In addition, all Toshiba factories publish listings of their better suppliers (those falling into Categories I and II, from table 12-2), and the information is circulated widely with the firm. When a factory wants to do business with another plant's already established supplier, its Purchasing Department is expected to check first with the Purchasing Department of the factory having prior claim on a supplier. Sharing information on suppliers allows a review of the financial, technical, man-

Table 12-2. Toshiba's Categories for Ranking Suppliers.

Group I	Superlative suppliers that require little or no oversight; the group on which the future of the factory rests.
Group II	Suppliers which are excellent in their respective fields, even if they require some direction and advice otherwise.
Group III	Potentially good suppliers but needing considerable training and help at present.
Group IV	Suppliers who will lose orders during the next model change or mid-term negotiations, unless they make more effort.
Group V	The group of suppliers with whom transactions should be regularly reduced.

ufacturing, and managerial circumstances of a potential supplier, possibly ensuring that a supplier is not outstripping its resources and capacities by contracting with a new factory.

As a rule, suppliers falling somewhere in the middle grade require help in three areas: technical support, advice on how to lower costs, or information to improve general managerial skills. Yanagicho will gladly offer help in these areas, at no cost to suppliers, as long as suppliers appear willing and able to learn. Training of this sort can take place with the dispatch of personnel directly from Yanagicho as well as on-the-job training within Yanagicho itself. It can also occur through training sessions sponsored by the Supplier Association. At one point in 1986, the distribution of key suppliers according to the fivefold ranking scheme was as follows: Suppliers in Group I: 20; Group II: 16; Group III: 17; Group IV: 37; Group V: 2.

The consequences of this ranking scheme become immediately obvious when the value of the goods supplied to the factory is disaggregated by group classification. Not surprisingly, the higher the ranking (Groups I, II, and III), the more parts and components supplied to Yanagicho. Relative rankings and value of transactions are shown in table 12-3.

Obviously, higher ranking suppliers get more work and make more money. There are fifty-three suppliers in the first three ranks (or 58 percent of the total suppliers), yet they produce 87 percent of the value of ordered goods. More impressively, twenty suppliers in Group I provide nearly 60 percent of Yanagicho's ordered parts and supplies. In short, more competitive suppliers interact more cooperatively and profitably with the Yanagicho Works.

Table 12-3. Ranking and Value of Transactions for Ninety-Two Suppliers and the Yanagicho Works

Rank	Number	Percent (%)	Value of Transaction (in 1,000,000 yen)	Percent (%)
I	20	21.7	20,484	58.1
II	16	17.4	1,752	5.0
III	17	18.5	8,436	23.9
IV	37	40.2	4,320	12.3
V	2	2.2	240	0.7
Totals	92	100.0	35,232	100.0

Notwithstanding that some suppliers will increase their business whereas others will flounder, the link between Yanagicho and its ordered-goods suppliers is not countercyclical; that is, less work is not contracted during a recession or an economic downturn. Basically, core suppliers are expected to bear an equal share in any decline or rise in factory orders, and the Purchasing Department tries to make sure that everyone shoulders an equal burden. At least, this appears to have been true for the 1980s and 90s. (This is the informal assessment of the Purchasing Department at Yanagicho.)

It is not for a lack of effort that some suppliers disappear. The factory will send out technicians and specialists to suppliers to improve their performance. Product and process information are freely given, and suppliers are welcomed to the factory for on-site training experience. But most suppliers are small, the majority with ten to twenty employees, and less than a million yen in assets. Many are family-based firms. Generational changes in leadership and management are common causes of at least temporary difficulty and occasional failure. Sometimes suppliers are stuck in old technology, or they are reluctant to make meaningful changes, and the factory gradually disengages from these suppliers. Also, software as opposed to hardware contributes an increasingly higher value-added share to many products today, and software development is done in house as much as possible rather than outsourced. Depending on the importance and amount of software associated with different product lines, therefore, some suppliers find themselves with an ever shrinking slice of the pie.

Network Organization and Managed Competition

Even though assembler–supplier relations in the Japanese electronics industry are highly sequenced, structured, and strategically driven, the mechanisms of control and coordination are neither the "arms-length" haggling of the marketplace nor the administrative fiats of firms. They are neither markets nor hierarchies, as Powell (1990) declares. Supplier Associations are network forms of organization.

Network forms join otherwise independent actors in voluntary, mutually beneficial, cooperative activities. These adjectives describe assembler–supplier relations at Yanagicho, especially the relations between the factory and its best ordered-goods suppliers. Voluntary, mutually beneficial, and cooperative relations are realized within an organizational context of order and predictability that allows for bargaining, voice, and exit (Helper, 1991).

Organizational boundaries are neither completely open nor completely closed; they are "permeable" (Fruin, 1992). Permeable boundaries, a large number of actors, a mix of market-like and hierarchy-like features, and a managed entry and exit of suppliers culminate in an organizational design that can only be described as a network organization. (Note that this is less of a rational choice model than a range-of-choices model.)

Toshiba has no financial stake in any of Yanagicho's suppliers, except for a few corporate affiliates (*kanren kigyo*) that coincidentally are factory suppliers. Moreover, only 7 percent of 232 core suppliers are dependent on the factory for more than 70 percent of their business, and only 10 percent, or 23 firms, for more than

50 percent of their business. (These figures are based on a 1988 survey of members in the Supplier Association as conducted by the Purchasing Department of the Yanagicho Works.) Hence, contractual safeguards do not appear to regulate transactional flow across the permeable boundaries of the network; factory and suppliers are *not* interdependent in the traditional, neoclassical sense of such transactions.

If not investments and contracts, what then? Instead, governance with a particular eye toward an effective management of "mutually held" assets has evolved. The specific assets in question are knowledge, know-how, and the embodied capabilities that are realized in a network form of assembler and supplier relations. The nature and value of the assets are defined by specific investments in interdependent capabilities and resources jointly undertaken by an assembler (the Yanagicho factory) and its group of suppliers. Most significantly, as interdependent assets they are co-owned and comanaged.

Managed Competition and Network Organization

Co-ownership and comanagement require a form of organization different from either market-based, price-bargaining arrangements or vertically/quasivertically integrated firms. Neither is well suited to the long-term partnering and highly complex and perishable asset-specificity that motivate assemblers and suppliers in the fast-moving electronics industry. Instead, network forms of organization promote a dynamic balance of cooperation and competition, innovation and interdependency that can be observed at the Yanagicho Works and more broadly throughout Japanese industry. The resulting combination of highly focused factories and networks of suppliers fosters a dynamic tension and balance in assembler–supplier partnerships that I call in this chapter "managed competition."

Network strategies economize on transaction costs (partnering transforms some portion of transaction costs into learning or experience costs) yet maximize the independence and autonomy of individual actors (suppliers and assemblers may choose the degree and amount of cospecialization, a range-of-choices model). By economizing on transaction costs and by amplifying learning through a voluntary sharing of resources, network organizations encourage efficient and effective resource utilization. Herein lies the importance of supplier grading schemes, training seminars, resident engineering programs, and all the other activities that animate supplier associations. These are roughly proportional to the degree of asset-specific cospecialization, and hence, they are tied to the prevalence and performance of network forms of organization.

High levels of asset-specific cospecialization necessitate particularly intense, frequent multilateral information exchange that, in turn, constitute a basis for collective action. Because network organizations represent a deliberate attempt to internalize externalities (that is, to cooperate with actors and actions that are outside of one's organizational sphere), the greater the degree of externalities, the greater the effort to establish governance mechanisms to encompass the need for communications, coordination, and control. The mutual processing of information through such governance mechanisms is obviously pivotal to reducing transaction costs. Where levels of asset specificity and information processing are less well developed, less robust coupling and governing mechanisms will suffice.

In Yanagicho's case, however, suppliers cannot provide what the factory wants without the active collaboration, detailed orders, design advice, and technical and managerial assistance of the factory. Even more important, the factory's Purchasing Department seeks only the best efforts of the best suppliers. Those that do not measure up are edged out. Attitude, action, and performance are all carefully assessed. Once contracts are secured, suppliers are required to make transaction-specific investments to meet and maintain supply agreement conditions. The best suppliers are partners in a division of labor that shares risks and rewards, but that worthy symmetry is earned by suppliers' strict attention to manufacturing detail and internal costs as well as a willingness to compete against other suppliers.

Managed competition of this sort infuses and enriches supplier networks, yet it is manifest only in the context of a governance system that joins and motivates assemblers and suppliers. That is the function of the Supplier Association, the visible hand of management. Good management allows Yanagicho to choose interorganizational goals and aims in process rather than as fixed structures or policies. In the contemporary, fast-moving electronics industry, such abilities make all the difference to long-term, competitive survival and performance. In a world where Toshiba buys as much as 90 percent of the value of its photocopiers from suppliers, the sourcing of parts, components, subassemblies, fully assembled products and services from suppliers, affiliates, and subcontractors is absolutely strategic. As Yanagicho is Toshiba's principal factory for the assembly of photocopiers (including such brands as 3M, Harris, and Lanier photocopiers), site-specificity in photocopier design and manufacture is tightly coupled with Yanagicho's relation-specific efforts in developing, managing, and organizing a network of suppliers.

Toshiba and Yanagicho are tied to suppliers in various and complex ways, and suppliers are dependent on assemblers not only for orders but also for the transfer of design know-how, process information, product specifications, and general performance data. Yanagicho's Purchasing Department invests considerable time and energy in managing the Supplier Association because the factory depends heavily on the parts, components, and subassemblies that come from suppliers. Effective orchestration of "inside" and "outside" resources is the competitive key.

An efficient interface and an effective boundary spanning strategy between the factory and outside suppliers are absolutely crucial. By nurturing a factory-centered supplier network of some 800 to 900 suppliers, Yanagicho is simultaneously solving two basic problems of business: how to get the best prices for products and services, and how to get the correct products and services. Both solutions are available in a network of suppliers that is at once responsive to factory needs and, at the same time, replete with its own capabilities and choices. Though not an economist's ideal market of many buyers and sellers, there is information sharing (responsiveness) as well as choice (multiple sourcing). Because the system mimics the marketplace, both the best prices and the best products are part of Toshiba and Yanagicho's story of managed competition and supplier network organization.

Note

The data in this chapter were collected during five years of fieldwork (1986–91) at the Toshiba Corporation and one of its Kawasaki City factories, the Yanagicho Works. Although most data were collected during summer field visits to Japan, I spent most of the 1990–91 academic year in Tokyo as a Fulbright scholar.

References

Asanuma, Banri. "Transactional Structure of Parts Supply in the Japanese Auto-
    mobile and Electric Machinery Industries: A Comparative Analysis." Techni-
    cal Report No. 1, Socio-Economic Systems Research Project. Kyoto: Kyoto Uni-
    versity, July 1985.

Asanuma, Banri. "Manufacturer–Supplier Relationships in Japan and the Concept
    of Relation-Specific Skill," *Journal of the Japanese and International Econom-
    ics*, 3 (1989): 1–30.

Clark, Kim, and Takahiro Fujimoto. *Product Development Performance*. Cam-
    bridge, Mass.: Harvard Business School Press, 1991.

Fruin, W. Mark. *The Japanese Enterprise System*, Oxford: Oxford University Press,
    1992.

Fruin, W. Mark. *Knowledge Works*. New York: Oxford University Press, 1997.

Fruin, W. Mark. "Competing the Old-Fashioned Way: Localizing and Integrating
    Knowledge Resources in Fast-to-Market Competition." In J. Liker, J. Ettlie, and
    J. Campbell, eds. *Technology and Management: America and Japan*. New
    York: Oxford University Press, 1995.

Fruin, W. Mark, and Nishiguchi Toshihiro. "Supplying the Toyota Production Sys-
    tem." In Bruce Kogut, ed., *Country Competitiveness*. New York: Oxford Uni-
    versity Press, 1993.

Gerlach, Michael. *Alliance Capitalism*. Berkeley: University of California Press,
    1992.

Helper, S. "An Exit-Voice Analysis of Supplier Relations." In R. Coughlin, ed.,
    Morality, Rationality and Efficiency: New Perspectives on Socio-Economics,
    New York: M. E. Sharpe, 1991, pp. 355–72.

Kawasaki, Seiichi, and John McMillan. "The Design of Contracts: Evidence from
    Japanese Subcontracting." *The Journal of Japanese and International Econ-
    omies*, 1–3 (1987): 327–49.

Nishiguchi, Toshihiro. *Strategic Industrial Sourcing*. New York: Oxford University
    Press, 1994.

Oliver, Christine. "Determinants on Interorganizational Relationships: Integration
    and Future Directions." *Academy of Management Review*, 15–2 (1990): 241–65.

Oniki, Hajime. "On the Cost of Deintegrating Information Networks." In C. An-
    tonelli, ed., *The Economics of Information Networks*. Amsterdam: Elsevier
    Science Publishers, 1992.

Powell, Walter W. "Neither Market nor Hierarchy: Network Forms of Organization."
    Research in Organizational Behavior, 12 (1990): 295–336.

Stalk, George, and Thomas M. Hout. *Competing Against Time*. New York: The Free
    Press, 1990.

Van de Ven, Andrew H., and G. Walker. "The Dynamics of Interorganizational Co-
    ordination." *Administrative Science Quarterly*, 29–4 (1984): 598–621.

Williamson, Oliver E. *Markets and Hierarchies: Analysis and Antitrust Implica-
    tions*, New York: Free Press, 1975.

Williamson, Oliver E. *Economic Institutions of Capitalism*, New York: Free Press,
    1975.

13

The Limits of Autarky

Regional Networks and Industrial Adaptation
In Silicon Valley and Route 128

ANNALEE SAXENIAN

The competitive advantages of regional clusters have become the focus of scholarly and policy attention. Once only the province of economic geographers and regional scientists, the work of Krugman (1991) and Porter (1990) has spurred widespread interest in regions and regional development. These newcomers have ignored an already extensive and sophisticated literature on the dynamics of industrial localization (see, for example, Scott, 1988a,b; Storper, 1989; Vernon, 1960). Yet, like their predecessors, they share a reliance on external economies to explain the advantages that are derived from the spatial of clustering of economic activity.

In this chapter I compare California's Silicon Valley and Route 128 in Massachusetts to suggest the limits of the concept of external economies and propose an alternative, network approach to analyzing regional economies. The common notion of external economies is based on an assumption that the firm is an atomistic unit of production with clearly defined boundaries. By drawing a sharp distinction between what occurs inside and what occurs outside the firm, scholars overlook the complex and historically evolved relations between the internal organization of firms and their connections to one another and the social structures and institutions of a particular locality. The network perspective helps explain the divergent performance of apparently comparable regional clusters, such as Silicon Valley and Route 128, and provides important insights into the local sources of competitive advantage. This comparison also illuminates important parallels between the organization of production in Silicon Valley—which itself is increasingly part of the Pacific Rim—and the fast-growing economies of Asia.

The Limits of External Economies

Marshall (1920) developed the notion of "external economies of scale" to refer to the sources of productivity increase that lie outside of individual firms. In the classic view, producers derive external benefits by sharing the fixed costs of common resources, such as infrastructure and services, skilled labor pools and specialized suppliers, and a common knowledge base. In addition, some theorists distinguish external economies that depend on the size of the market, including such factors as a labor pool and specialized supplier base (pecuniary external economies) from those that involve spillovers of knowledge between firms (technological external economies). When these factors of production are geographically concentrated, firms gain the additional benefits of spatial proximity, or "agglomeration economies." Once established in a locality, such an advantage becomes self-reinforcing through a dynamic process of increasing returns (Arthur, 1990; Krugman, 1991, Scott, 1988b; Storper, 1989).

Students of regional development typically treat Silicon Valley and Route 128 as classic examples of the external economies that are derived from industrial localization. They are seen as cumulatively self-reinforcing agglomerations of technical skill, venture capital, specialized input suppliers and services, infrastructure, and spillovers of knowledge associated with proximity to universities and informal information flows (see, for example, Castells, 1989; Hall and Markusen, 1985; Krugman, 1991; Porter, 1990; Scott, 1988b). Some researchers have compared the two areas to the nineteenth-century industrial districts described by Marshall (Piore and Sabel, 1984).

Yet this approach cannot account for the divergent performance of the two regional economies. In spite of their common origins in postwar military spending and university-based research, Silicon Valley and Route 128 have responded differently to intensified international competition. Both regions faced downturns in the 1980s. Although Silicon Valley recovered quickly from the crisis of its leading semiconductor producers, Route 128 was very slow to reverse a decline that began in the early 1980s. The rapid growth of a new wave of start-ups and the renewed dynamism of established companies such as Intel and Hewlett-Packard were evidence that Silicon Valley had regained its former vitality. Along Route 128, by contrast, start-ups failed to compensate for continuing layoffs at the Digital Equipment Corporation (DEC) and other minicomputer companies. By the end of the 1980s, Route 128 producers had ceded their long-standing dominance in computer production to Silicon Valley.

Regional data underscore this divergence. Between 1975 and 1990, Silicon Valley firms generated some 150,000 new technology jobs—triple the number created along Route 128, even though both areas enjoyed roughly the same employment levels in 1975. Figure 13-1 illustrates this difference.

In 1990, producers based in Silicon Valley exported more than $11 billion in electronics products, almost one third of the nation's total, compared to Route 128's $4.6 billion (Saxenian, 1994). Finally, Silicon Valley was the home of thirty-nine of the nation's one hundred fastest-growing electronics companies, whereas Route 128 claimed only four. By 1990, both Southern California and Texas had surpassed Route 128 as locations of fast-growing electronics firms (see figure 13-2).

These rankings are based on five-year sales growth rates, but the list is not limited to small firms. Multibillion dollar companies such as Sun Microsystems, Apple Computers, Intel Semiconductor, and Hewlett-Packard all ranked among the fastest-growing enterprises in 1990.

The concepts of agglomeration and external economies cannot explain why clusters of specialized technical skills, suppliers, and information produced a virtuous and self-reinforcing dynamic of increasing industrial advances in Silicon

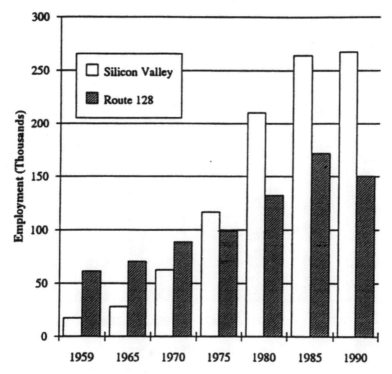

Figure 13-1 Total High Technology Employment, Silicon Valley, and Route 128, 1959–1990

Valley, while producing relative decline in Route 128. These theories account for regional stagnation or decline through imprecise references to "diseconomies" of agglomeration or the acculturation of negative externalities. Yet if such diseconomies are related to the overall size of a regional cluster, the degree of congestion, or the costs of production, growth should have slowed in the more densely populated Silicon Valley long before Route 128. The simple fact of spatial proximity evidently reveals little about the ability of firms to respond to the fast-changing markets and technologies that now characterize international competition.

The distinction between internal and external economies is based on the assumption that the firm is an atomistic unit of production with clearly defined boundaries. Treating regions as collections of autonomous firms has even led some observers to conclude that Silicon Valley suffers from excessive, even pathological, fragmentation (Florida and Kenney, 1990). Proponents of this argument overlook the complex of institutional and social relationships that connect the producers in its fragmented industrial structure. Researchers who adopt the broadest interpretations of technological external economies recognize that firms learn from each other through flows of information, ideas, and know-how (Storper, 1989), but they do so only by denying the theoretical distinction between internal and external economies, between what is inside and what is outside the firm.

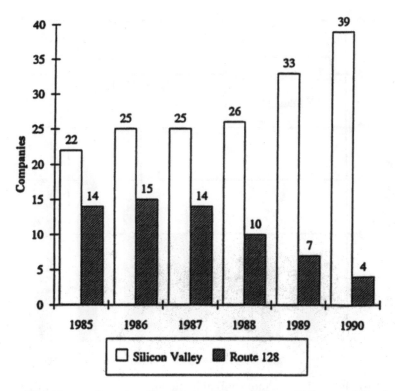

Figure 13-2 Fastest Growing Electronics Firms, Silicon Valley, and Route 128, 1985–1990

A Network Approach to Regions

Far from being isolated from what lies outside them, firms are embedded in networks of social and institutional relationships that shape, and are shaped by, their strategies and structures (Granovetter, 1985). The network perspective helps illuminate the historically evolved relationships between the internal organization of firms and their connections to one another and to the social structures and institutions of their particular localities (Nohria and Eccles, 1992b; Powell, 1987).

A network approach can be used to argue that, despite similar origins and technologies, Silicon Valley and Route 128 evolved distinct industrial systems in the postwar period. The differences in productive organization have been overlooked by economic analysts or treated simply as superficial differences between "laid back" California and the more "buttoned-down" East Coast. Far from superficial, these variations demonstrate the importance of the local social and institutional determinants of industrial adaptation.

Silicon Valley has a regional network-based industrial system that promoted learning and mutual adjustment among specialist producers of a complex of related technologies. The region's dense social networks and open labor markets encourage entrepreneurship and experimentation. Companies compete intensely, while at the same time they learn from each other about changing markets and technologies through informal communications and collaborative practices. Loosely linked team structures encourage horizontal communication among firm divisions and with outside suppliers and customers. The functional boundaries within firms are porous in the network-based system, as are the boundaries between firms and between firms and local institutions such as trade associations and universities.

The Route 128 region, in contrast, is dominated by autarkic (self-sufficient) corporations that internalize a wide range of productive activities. Practices of secrecy and corporate loyalty govern relations between firms and their customers, suppliers, and competitors, reinforcing a regional culture that encourages stability and self-reliance. Corporate hierarchies ensure that authority remains centralized and information tends to flow vertically. Social and technical networks are largely internal to the firm, and the boundaries between firms and between firms and local institutions remain far more distinct in this independent firm-based system.

Regional Networks and Industrial Adaptation

Understanding regional economies as networks of relationships rather than as clusters of atomistic producers, and thinking of the regions as examples of two models of industrial systems—the regional network-based system and the independent firm-based system—help illuminate the divergent trajectories of the Silicon Valley and Route 128 economies during the 1980s.

In the language of this volume, we can see that Silicon Valley's system of regional networks—which enhance, rather than replace, market competition—have proven more adaptive than the hierarchical model that dominates Route 128. Silicon Valley's superior performance cannot be attributed to differentials in real estate costs, wages, or tax levels. Land and office space were significantly more costly in most of Silicon Valley than in the Route 128 region during the 1980s; the wages and salaries of production workers, engineers, and managers were higher (Sherwood-Call, 1992), and there were no significant differences in tax rates between California and Massachusetts (Tannenwald, 1987).

Nor can the differences in regional performance be traced to patterns of defense spending. Route 128 has historically relied more heavily on military spending than has Silicon Valley, and hence is more vulnerable to defense cutbacks; however, the downturn in the Massachusetts electronics industry began in 1984, when the value of prime contracts to the region was still increasing. Although defense spending cannot account for the timing of the downturn in the region's technology industry, the military spending cutbacks that began in the late 1980s exacerbated the difficulties of an already troubled regional economy.

Route 128's difficulties lie in the rigidities of its local industrial system. The independent firm-based system flourished in an environment of market stability and slowly changing technologies because extensive integration offered the advantages of scale economies and market control (Chandler, 1977). It has been overwhelmed, however, by changing competitive conditions. Corporations that invest in dedicated equipment and specialized worker skills find themselves locked into obsolete technologies and markets, and their self-sufficient structures limit their ability to adapt in a timely fashion. The surrounding regional economy in turn is deprived of resources for self-regeneration because large firms tend to internalize most local supplies of skill and technology.

Regional network-based industrial systems like that of Silicon Valley, in contrast, are well suited to conditions of technical and market uncertainty. Producers in these systems deepen their capabilities by specializing while engaging in close, but not exclusive, relations with other specialists. Network relations promote a process of reciprocal innovation that reduces the distinctions between large and small firms and between industries and sectors (DeBresson and Walker, 1991). Evidence from the industrial districts of Europe suggests that the localization of know-how and information encourages the pursuit of diverse technical and market opportunities through spontaneous regroupings of skill, technology, and capital. The region, if not all the firms in the region, is organized to innovate continuously (Herrigel, 1993; Best, 1990; Sabel, 1988). The small-firm networks that characterize Taiwan's fashion footwear and personal computer industries similarly provide flexibility and responsiveness to fast-changing markets (Hsing, 1993; Levy and Kuo, 1991).

The competitive advantages of network organizational forms are reflected in the experience of Japanese industry as well. Japanese producers of electronics and autos, for example, rely on extensive networks of small- and medium-sized suppliers, to which they are linked through ties of trust and partial ownership. Although Japan's large firms may have often exploited suppliers in the past, many firms increasingly collaborate with them, encouraging them to expand their technological capabilities and organizational autonomy (Nishiguchi, 1989). Like their Silicon Valley counterparts, these Japanese producers tend to be geographically clustered and depend heavily on informal information exchange as well as more formal forms of cooperation (Aldridge, 1993; Kanai, 1993; Friedman, 1988; Imai, 1989).

As the case of Japan suggests, there are large-firm as well as small-firm variants of network-based systems (Dyer, 1993; Fruin, 1992, 1993). Large corporations can integrate into regional networks through a process of internal decentralization. As independent business units are forced by competition to achieve the technical and productive standards of outsiders, they often rely on external institutions that facilitate knowledge sharing and collaboration with suppliers and customers.

Of course, all economic activity does not cluster within a single regional economy. Firms in network systems serve global markets and collaborate extensively with distant customers, suppliers, and competitors. Technology firms, in particular, are highly international. However, the most strategic relationships are often local because of the importance of timeliness and face-to-face communication in complex, uncertain, and fast-changing industries (Nohria and Eccles, 1992a, Fruin, 1997).

Regional Network versus Firm-Based Systems

In the rest of this chapter I use a set of paired comparisons to illustrate the differences in the organization and adaptive capacities of Silicon Valley's regional network and Route 128's independent firm-based industrial systems. The comparison of Apollo Computers and Sun Microsystems—both 1980s generation start-ups competing in the emerging workstation market—demonstrates how small firms benefit from the open flows of information, technology, and know-how in a network system. The comparison of the Digital Equipment Corporation (DEC) and Hewlett-Packard Co. (HP)—the leading computer systems producers along Route 128 and in Silicon Valley, respectively—in turn shows how regional networks can facilitate the reorganization of large firms.

Clearly, these cases alone cannot encompass the experience of two complex regional economies. For an extended treatment of the origins and evolution of the two regional economies, see Saxenian (1994). Nor can the focus on individual firms fully portray the myriad decentralized relationships in a regional network-based system. Indeed, the resilience of Silicon Valley's network system lies precisely in the fact that it does not depend upon the success of any individual firm. However, these comparisons illustrate the social and institutional dimensions of productive organization that are overlooked in the concept of external economies and the competitive advantages of regional networks in the current economic conditions.

Start-Ups: Apollo Computer and
Sun Microsystems

The largest wave of start-ups in Silicon Valley's history began in the late 1970s and accelerated during the 1980s. The region was home to scores of new ventures that specialized in everything from workstations and semicustom semiconductors to disk drives, networking hardware and software, and computer-aided engineering and design. These start-ups contributed to the diversification of the regional economy away from its original concentration in semiconductors and into a complex of computer-related specialists.

In contrast with the upsurge of entrepreneurial activity in Silicon Valley, the pace of start-ups along Route 128 slowed during the 1980s. Massachusetts experienced lower rates of new high-tech firm formation between 1976 and 1986 than either New England or the United States as a whole (Kirchoff and McAuliffe, 1988). In addition, the performance of companies founded during the 1980s was disappointing. Nothing in the Route 128 experience matched the spectacular successes of the 1980s generation of Silicon Valley start-ups such as Sun Microsystems, Conner Peripherals, and Silicon Graphics. By the end of the decade, public companies that were started in Silicon Valley during the 1980s collectively accounted for more than $22 billion in sales, whereas their Route 128 counterparts had generated only $2 billion (Standard & Poor's, 1992).

Investment decisions reflected this divergence. Annual venture capital investments in Northern California during the 1980s were double or triple those in Massachusetts. Over the course of the decade, Massachusetts-based companies received some $3 billion in venture capital, or 75 percent of the total raised in the region, whereas firms in Northern California received $9 billion, or 130 percent of the total capital raised locally (see figure 13-3). Silicon Valley companies were consistently awarded at least one-third of the nation's total venture capital pool.

By 1992, 113 technology enterprises located in Silicon Valley reported revenues exceeding $100 million, compared to 74 companies in Route 128. Moreover, the great majority of Silicon Valley's $100 million enterprises were started during the 1970s and 1980s, whereas those in Route 128 were overwhelmingly started prior to 1970 (CompTech, 1993).

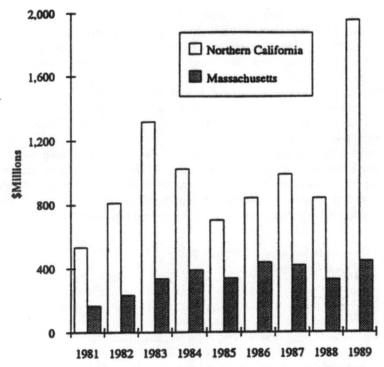

Figure 13-3 Venture Capital Investment, Northern California and Massachusetts, 1981–1989

The comparison of Apollo Computer and Sun Microsystems demonstrates how the autarkic structures and practices of Route 128's independent firm-based system created disadvantages for start-ups in a technologically fast-paced industry. Apollo pioneered the engineering workstation in 1980 and initially was enormously successful. By most accounts, the firm had a product that was superior to that of its Silicon Valley counterpart, Sun Microsystems (which was started two years after Apollo, in 1982). The two firms competed neck and neck during the mid-1980s, but in 1987 Apollo fell behind the faster-moving, more responsive Sun and never regained the lead. By the time Apollo was purchased by Hewlett-Packard in 1989, it had fallen to fourth place in the industry, whereas Sun led the industry with more than $3 billion in sales (Bell and Corliss, 1989).

Apollo's founder, 46-year-old William Poduska, one of Route 128's few repeat entrepreneurs, had worked for Honeywell and helped to found Prime Computer before starting Apollo. Not only was Poduska himself well steeped in the culture and organizational practices of the region's established minicomputer firms, but the entire Apollo management team had moved with him from Prime. This history contrasts with that of the typical Silicon Valley start-up, in which talent was typically drawn from a variety of different firms and even industries, representing a mix of corporate and technical experience.

Not surprisingly, Apollo's initial strategy and structure reflected the model of corporate self-sufficiency of the region's large minicomputer companies. In spite of its pioneering workstation design, for example, the firm adopted proprietary standards and chose to design and fabricate its own central processor and specialized integrated circuits. Although it sourced components such as disk drives, monitors, and power supplies, Apollo began with a proprietary operating system and architecture that made its products incompatible with other machines.

Sun, in contrast, pioneered open systems. The firm's founders, all in their twenties, adopted the UNIX operating system because they felt that the market would never accept a workstation custom designed by four graduate students. By making the specifications for its systems widely available to suppliers and competitors, Sun challenged the proprietary and highly profitable approach of industry leaders IBM, DEC, and HP, which locked customers into a single vendor of hardware and software.

This strategy allowed Sun to focus on designing the hardware and software for its workstations and to limit manufacturing to prototypes, final assembly, and testing. Unlike the traditional vertically integrated computer manufacturers, Sun purchased virtually all its components off the shelf from external vendors and subcontracted the manufacture and assembly of their printed circuit boards. (In the late 1980s, Sun began assembling some of its most advanced printed circuit boards internally.) The firm even relied on outside partners for the design and manufacture of the reduced instruction set computing (RISC)-based microprocessor at the heart of its workstations and encouraged its vendors to market the chip to its competitors.

Although specialization is often an economic necessity for start-ups, Sun did not abandon this strategy even as the firm grew into a multibillion dollar company. As Sun's Vice President of Manufacturing, Jim Bean, asked in the late 1980s, why should Sun vertically integrate when hundreds of Silicon Valley companies invest heavily in staying at the leading edge in the design and manufacture of integrated circuits, disk drives, and most other computer components and subsystems? Relying on outside suppliers greatly reduced Sun's overhead and ensured that the firm's workstations contained state-of-the-art hardware.

This focus also allowed Sun rapidly to introduce complex new products and continuously alter their product mix. According to Bean: "If we were making a stable set of products, I could make a solid case for vertical integration" (Whiting, 1987). Relying on external suppliers allowed Sun to introduce an unprecedented four major new product generations during its first five years of operations and to double the price–performance ratio each successive year. Sun eluded clonemakers through its sheer pace of new product introduction. By the time a competitor could reverse engineer a Sun workstation and develop the manufacturing capability to imitate it, Sun had introduced a successive generation.

As a result, the Sun workstations, although vulnerable to imitation by competitors, were also significantly less expensive to produce and sold for half the price of the proprietary Apollo systems (Bulkeley, 1987). Sun founder and CEO Scott McNealy described the advantage for customers:

We were totally open with them and said, "We won't lock you into anything. You can build it yourself if we fail," whereas our competition was too locked up in this very East Coast minicomputer world, which has always been proprietary, so that encouraging cloning or giving someone access to your source code was considered like letting the corporate jewels out or something. But customers want it (Sheff, 1989, p. 50).

It quickly became apparent that customers preferred the less expensive, non-proprietary Sun workstations. However, Apollo, like the Route 128 minicomputer producers, was slow to abandon its proprietary operating system and hardware. As late as 1985, the firm's management refused to acknowledge the growing demand for open standards and even turned down the offer of a state-of-the-art RISC microprocessor from Silicon Valley-based MIPS Computers. Apollo finally committed 30 percent of its research and development budget to RISC development in 1986, but the effort became an economic burden, and the chip they ultimately developed internally was no faster than the chip they could have bought two years earlier from MIPS.

Sun's innovative computing strategy was inseparable from the firm's location in the sophisticated and diversified technical infrastructure of Silicon Valley. Apollo, in contrast, responded sluggishly to industry changes in part because of a more limited regional infrastructure. According to Jeffrey Kalb, an engineer who worked for DEC in Route 128 for many years before moving to Silicon Valley to start the MasPar Computer Corp.:

> It's hard for a small company to start in Route 128 because you can't get stuff like IC's and disk drives fast. Route 128 is dominated by large, vertically integrated firms that do everything themselves. In Silicon Valley, you can get anything you want on the market.
>
> You can get all those things in Route 128 sooner or later, but the decisions are much faster if you're in Silicon Valley. From the East Coast, interacting with the West Coast is only possible for 3–4 hours a day because of the time difference, and you spend lots of time on the phone. It's no one thing, but if you get a 20–30% time to market advantage by being in Silicon Valley, that's really significant (Kalb, 1991).

Apollo's other major misstep was in its 1984 choice of a President and CEO to replace Poduska. Following the tradition of the large Route 128 companies, they hired a long-time East Coast corporate executive who had worked his way up the ranks at General Electric and then become the President of GTE Corporation. The 53-year-old Thomas Vanderslice was asked to bring "big-company organizational skills" to fast-growing Apollo and help the firm to "grow up." He couldn't have had a more different background than the twenty-something graduate students and computer whizzes who had founded Sun Microsystems two years earlier (Beam and Frons, 1985).

The media played up the superficial differences between Apollo and Sun: the buttoned down, conservative Apollo executives alongside the casually attired, laid-back founders of Sun. It made for great journalism: Vanderslice enforced a dress code and discouraged beards and moustaches at Apollo, and Sun threw monthly beer bashes and employees showed up on Halloween in gorilla suits. Whereas Vanderslice was chauffeured to work daily in a limousine, an April Fool's Day prank at Sun involved placing founder Bill Joy's Ferrari in the middle of the company's decorative pond.

However, the important differences between the two firms lay in their management styles and organization: Vanderslice brought in a traditional, risk-averse management team who focused on imposing financial and quality controls, cutting costs, and diversifying the firm's customer base. Former Apollo employees describe him as an archetypical "bean counter" who established formal decision-making procedures and systems in the firm at a time when flexibility and innovation were most needed.

This commitment to formality, hierarchy, and long-term stability—which typified most large Route 128 companies—could not have offered a greater contrast with the "controlled chaos" that characterized Sun (Weiss and Delbecq, 1987). Like many Silicon Valley companies, Sun developed decentralized organizational forms in its efforts to preserve the flexibility and enthusiasm of a start-up even as it grew. Corporate strategy was generated by discussions among representatives of autonomous divisions rather than dictated by a central committee, and Sun's culture encouraged informal communications, participation, and individual initiative (Levine, 1988).

In the late 1980s, when Sun surpassed Apollo in both sales and profitability, more than a dozen Apollo managers defected to their West Coast rival. They joined other experienced and ambitious engineers from ailing Route 128 companies who recognized that opportunities to join or start technologically exciting new ventures lay not in New England, but along the increasingly crowded freeways of Northern California. As skilled engineers moved west, the advantages of Silicon Valley's network-based industrial system multiplied.

Large Firms: Digital Equipment and Hewlett-Packard

The successes of the 1980s generation start-ups were the most visible sign that Silicon Valley was adapting faster than Route 128, but changes within the two regions' largest firms were equally important. Established producers in Silicon Valley began to decentralize their operations, creating interfirm production networks that built on that region's social and technical interdependencies and strengthened its industrial system. By institutionalizing long-standing practices of informal cooperation and exchange, they formalized the process of collective learning in the region. Local firms redefined themselves by participating in local production networks, and the region as a whole organized to create new markets and sectors.

Adaptation in the Route 128 economy, by contrast, was constrained by the autarkic organization and practices of its leading producers. Focused inward and lacking dynamic start-ups from which to draw innovative technologies or organizational models, the region's large minicomputer firms only slowly adjusted to the new market conditions. By the end of the decade, they were struggling to survive in a computer industry that they had once dominated.

Although it is difficult to develop accurate and useful measures of vertical integration, one indication of the greater reliance of Route 128 firms on internal production is the lower sales per employee figures shown in table 13-1 for the leading Route 128 firms and their Silicon Valley counterparts.

The comparison of DEC and HP during the 1980s highlights the differing relationship of large firms to the region in network and firm-based industrial systems. By 1990 both were $13 billion companies and the largest and oldest civilian employers in their respective regions. (Lockheed Missile and Space and Raytheon Corporation were the largest private employers in Silicon Valley and Route 128, respectively. But both were military contractors with limited commercial business.)

Table 13.1. 1990 Sales Per Employee: Silicon Valley and Route 128 ($ thousands)

Silicon Valley		Route 128	
Apple	$382.26	Prime	$128.7
Sun	214.6	Wang	123.7
Silicon Graphics	200.0	Data General	114.8
HP	143.8	DEC	104.4

Source: "The Electronic Business 200," Electronic Business (July 22, 1991): 43–49; Annual 10-K company reports.

Both DEC and HP were vertically integrated producers of proprietary minicomputers with shared origins in an earlier era of computing. Yet the companies responded differently to comparable competitive challenges. HP gradually opened up by building a network of local alliances and subcontracting relationships while strengthening its global reach. DEC, in spite of its formal commitment to decentralization, retained a substantially more autarkic organizational structure and corporate mindset.

The transformations in the computer industry during the 1980s placed a premium on speed and focus. Computer markets were forced to develop and bring new products to market faster than ever before, often in a matter of months. Harold Edmonson, HP Vice President of Corporate Manufacturing, claimed in 1988 that one-half of the firm's orders in any year came from products introduced in the preceding three years (Edmondson, 1988). At the same time, the cost of developing new products increased as they became more technologically complex. Innovation in all segments of the industry—from microprocessors, logic chips, and system and applications software to disk drives, screens, input–output devices, and networking devices—meant that it was more and more difficult for a single firm to produce all these components, let alone remain at the forefront of the underlying technologies.

This increasingly competitive environment posed a challenge for established computer makers like DEC and HP. By 1990, however, HP had successfully managed the transition from minicomputers to workstations with open systems, whereas DEC remained dependent on its proprietary VAX line of minicomputers. As a result, even though both enjoyed 1990 revenues of $13 billion from electronics products, HP earned $771 million, while DEC lost $95 million.

Variations in corporate performance always have multiple causes, but the firms' organizational structures and their relationships to their respective regions help explain these differences. DEC maintained clear boundaries between itself and other companies or institutions in the region. This was, in part, a result of extensive vertical integration: The firm designed and manufactured internally virtually all software and hardware components for its computers. Moreover, DEC's corporate culture rewarded secrecy and corporate loyalty; departed employees were typically treated like pariahs and cut off from the corporate "family" (Rifkin and Harrar, 1990). As a result, the technical and social networks that mattered were all internal, and there were few opportunities for collaboration, learning, and exchange with other local firms.

HP was both less dominant in Silicon Valley and more open to the surrounding economy. DEC dominated the Route 128 region in a way no firm did in Silicon Valley. With more than 30,000 Massachusetts employees in 1990, DEC accounted for almost 20 percent of regional high-technology employment, whereas HP's 20,000 Silicon Valley employees represented only 8 percent of the regional total. HP benefited from a long history of participation in the region's rich associational life and fluid labor markets. Continuous and open exchange about everything from the latest start-ups to technical breakthroughs allowed local technologies and market trends (Vedoe, 1990).

HP's decentralized divisional structure also offered an ideal training ground for general managers. Former HP executives were responsible for starting more than eighteen firms in Silicon Valley between 1974 and 1984, including such notable successes such as Rolm, Tandem, and Pyramid Technology (Mitchell, 1989). A 16-year veteran of DEC who moved to HP described how the firms' autonomous divisions preserve opportunities for entrepreneurship:

> Running a business at the division level, you get a chance to be a general manager. You get a chance to learn . . . to be creative. . . . There are a lot of new divisions springing up [within HP], new ideas springing up, brand new businesses, and old divisions that couldn't make it anymore transform themselves into new businesses (Porter, 1993, p. 3).

In contrast, DEC's matrix organization—which represented only a partial break from traditional functional corporate hierarchies—stifled the development of managerial skill and initiative in the Route 128 region. The matrix demanded continuous negotiations to reach consensus, and despite the addition of cross-functional relations among product groups, final authority remained highly centralized (Schein, 1985). As a result, aside from Data General, it is difficult to identify successful spin-offs from DEC.

Both DEC and HP began the 1980s with the bureaucracy and internal conflicts typical of large firms. Both missed opportunities and made false starts in workstation and RISC markets, and both had difficulty keeping up with newer, more agile competitors. Yet HP quickly became the leading producer in the fastest-growing segments of the market. By 1990, HP controlled 31 percent of the $8 billion RISC computer systems market—a market in which DEC still had no presence. HP also boasted a 21 percent share of the $7.2 billion workstation market and 13 percent of the $33 million UNIX computer systems market, compared to DEC's 16 percent and 8 percent, respectively. In addition, HP controlled 66 percent of the market for desktop laser printers and 70 percent of the market for inkjet printers (Nee, 1991).

Hewlett-Packard reinvented itself by investing heavily in RISC microprocessor technology and the UNIX operating system well before most established computer companies recognized the importance of open standards. By betting the future of the computer division (which accounted for 53 percent of HP revenues) on RISC systems in 1985 and by undertaking internal reorganizations that unified and rationalized the firm's disparate computer divisions and component technologies, HP positioned itself advantageously for emerging markets (Yoder, 1991). In 1990, for example, the firm created an independent team to develop a RISC workstation. The ultimate product, the Series 700 workstations, was far ahead of the rest of the industry, and it allowed HP quickly to become one of the world's biggest sellers of

UNIX systems. A financial analyst for Salomon Brothers assessed the situation: "They [HP] have done an excellent job of identifying trends in the computer market such as UNIX, RISC, and PCs. No other major computer company has done a better job of positioning. . . . They are the one company I can count on surviving. HP has a better base today than IBM or DEC" (Greene, 1990, p. 27).

HP's ability to identify market trends early reflected the firm's openness to external changes and a Silicon Valley location that gave it easy access to state-of-the-art information markets and technologies. This flexibility contrasts sharply with DEC's prolonged denial of the growing demand for personal computers and UNIX-based systems. In the words of a former DEC marketing manager: "DEC had its head in the sand. They didn't believe that the world would really change. . . . They got focused on the internal evolution of the company rather than on the customer or markets" (Vedoe, 1990). As late as 1985, DEC CEO Olsen referred to personal computers as "snake oil" (Harrar and Rifkin, 1990).

DEC was plagued by ongoing internal conflicts and a series of costly course reversals in its efforts to enter the workstation and open systems markets. The firm's strategy remained confused and inconsistent, even after the defection of large customers such as GE and AT&T forced Olsen to authorize a shift to open systems and away from the vision of a single proprietary VMS operating system and VAX architecture for all DEC systems (DeNucci, 1990).

DEC's research lab in Silicon Valley developed state-of-the-art RISC and UNIX technologies in the early 1980s, but is discoveries with virtually ignored by headquarters, which continued to favor the highly profitable VAX–VMS system (Comerford, 1992). Insiders claim that DEC's Palo Alto lab contributed more to other Silicon Valley firms such as Sun and MIPS than it did to DEC, because their findings quickly diffused to other Silicon Valley firms through technical papers and local industry forums (Basche, 1991; Furlong, 1991).

DEC finally decided to build its own RISC-based workstation in 1986, following conventional wisdom within the firm that the RISC microprocessor should be designed and built in-house. It was not until 1992, however, after a series of costly reversals, that the firm finally introduced its own RISC processor, Alpha (Comerford, 1992). By this time, DEC controlled only 13 percent of the workstation market (McWilliams, 1992).

The contrast between DEC's Palo Alto Lab and its East Coast operations is instructive. Engineers who worked at both emphasize how different the two were: DEC East was internally focused, whereas DEC Palo Alto was well integrated into Silicon Valley's social and technical networks. According to Joe DeNucci, a former employee:

> DEC definitely relates differently to the regional economy in Silicon Valley than in Route 128. DEC is the largest employer in Route 128 and you come to think that the center of the universe is North of the Mass Pike and East of Route 128. The thinking is totally DEC-centric: All the adversaries are within the company. Even the non-DEC guys compete only with DEC.
>
> DEC Palo Alto is a completely different world. DEC is just another face in the crowd in Silicon Valley; the adversaries are external, firms like Intel and Sun. It forces a far more aggressive and "prove-it" mind set (DeNucci, 1991).

He described his years with the DEC engineering and development group in Palo Alto:

> We had an immense amount of autonomy, and we cherished the distance from home base, from the "puzzle palace," and from the "corridor warriors" and all the endless meetings. It was an idyllic situation, a group of exceptionally talented people who were well connected to Stanford and to the Silicon Valley networks. People would come out from Maynard and say "this feels like a different company." The longer they stayed, the more astounded they were (DeNucci, 1991).

Tom Furlong, who headed a DEC workstation division in Maynard before moving west in 1985, described the newly formed Workstation Group in Palo Alto as a typical Silicon Valley start-up. The group's autonomy from headquarters allowed members to take full advantage of the local knowledge available within the regional economy. At the same time, the group benefited from the financial backing and reputation of a large, well-established corporation. By 1990, Furlong was the manager of a 275-person group. He compared his experience working in the two locations:

> It would be very difficult for me to do what I'm doing here within DEC on the East Coast. I'm a fairly autonomous business manager out here, with all the functions necessary to success reporting to me and the freedom to use outside suppliers. Back East, I would have to rely on DEC's internal suppliers and functional groups for everything.
> We're like a start-up organization here. We're not really significant to DEC, we're only contributing $.5 billion to them, but we have the advantages of their resources and name (Furlong, 1991).

He explained the consequences of these organizational differences for new produced development:

> The same job of bringing a new workstation to market takes two times as long in the East Coast and many more people than it does here. In Maynard, I had to do everything inside the company. Here I can rely on the other companies in Silicon Valley. It's easier and cheaper for me to rely on the little companies in Silicon Valley to take care of the things I need, and it forces them to compete an be more efficient. At DEC, the commitment to internal supply and the familiar environment means that bad people don't get cut off. I had to depend on all sorts of inefficient people back at DEC East (Furlong, 1991).

The Workstation Group did not achieve this independent position without resistance: "It was a huge embarrassment to them that we had to rely on external suppliers such as MIPS. DEC takes great pride in being vertically integrated, in having control over its entire system" (Furlong, 1991).

DEC was ultimately unable to assimilate the lessons of its geographically distant Palo Alto group, in spite of their technical advances, and in 1992 transferred it back to the Maynard headquarters. Furlong and other members of the workstation team left DEC to work for Silicon Valley companies.

HP began the decade with a comparable level of vertical integration to DEC, but it soon recognized that it could not continue to produce everything in-house. In the late 1980s, HP began outsourcing most sheet metal fabrication, plastics, and machining for its computer systems. The firm also consolidated the management of some fifty disparate circuit technology units into two autonomous divisions, Integrated Circuit Fabrication and Printed Circuit Board Fabrication. These divisions were organized as internal subcontractors for the company's computer systems and instrument divisions. They were forced to compete with external vendors for HP's business and were expected to remain competitive in technology, service, and cost to sell successfully to outside customers.

HP also built alliances with local companies that offered complementary technologies. During the 1980s, the firm created partnerships with Octel Communications for voice–data integration, 3Com for local area network-manager servers, and Weitek for semiconductor design. An HP manager explained the acquisition of a 10 percent stake in Octel: "In the business and office processing environment, no one company can develop everything on its own, so we're increasingly looking at forming alliances to meet our customers' needs" (Tuller, 1988, p. 113).

The partnership between HP and semiconductor design specialist Weitek illustrates how a large firm benefited from Silicon Valley's networks. Tiny Weitek, which lacked manufacturing capacity of its own, was the leading designer of ultra-high-speed "number crunching" chips for complex engineering problems. In 1987, HP opened its state-of-the-art fabrication facility to Weitek for use as a foundry, hoping to improve the performance of the Weitek chips in its workstations. Realizing that the manufacturing process at the foundry Weitek used slowed down the chips, the HP engineers suggested fully optimizing the Weitek designs by manufacturing them with HP's more advanced fabrication process. This culminated in a three-year agreement that allowed the firms to benefit directly from each other's technical expertise.

The arrangement assured HP of a steady supply of Weitek's chips and allowed them to introduce their new workstation faster than if they had designed the chip in-house. It provided Weitek with a market, the legitimacy of a close association with HP, as well as access to a state-of-the-art foundry. Moreover, the final product represented a significant advance over what either firm could have produced independently. This partnership allowed each firm to draw on the other's distinctive and complementary expertise to devise novel solutions to shared problems.

HP opened itself to outside influences during the 1980s, creating a model of a large firm that is internally decentralized and horizontally linked to networks of other specialists. DEC's dominant and isolated position in Route 128, by contrast, hindered its efforts to shift to new technologies or a new corporate form. Saddled with an autarkic organizational structure and located in a region that offered little social or technical support for a more flexible business model, DEC's difficulties worsened.

In 1992, DEC CEO and founder Ken Olsen was forced to resign after the company reported a $2.8 billion quarterly loss—the biggest in computer industry history. One year later, HP surpassed DEC in sales to claim the position as the nation's second largest computer company, after IBM. As a final irony, in 1993 DEC moved a design team for its new Alpha microprocessor from the East Coast to Palo Alto to immerse Alpha engineers in the Silicon Valley semiconductor community. According to industry analyst Ronald Bowen of Dataquest: "Digital is finding the support network of other companies is very, very limited back East. In effect, what's been happening is the people who work on the East Coast spend a lot of time flying to San Jose anyway" (Nash and Hayes, 1993, p. 1).

Conclusion

This comparison of Silicon Valley and Route 128 highlights the analytical leverage gained by treating regions as networks of relationships rather than as collections of atomistic firms. By transcending the theoretical distinction between what lies inside and what lies outside the firm, this approach offers important insights into the structure and dynamics of regional economies. It directs attention to the complex networks of social relationships within and between firms and between firms and local institutions.

The Silicon Valley experience also suggests that network forms of organization flourish in regional agglomerations. Proximity facilitates the repeated, face-to-face interaction that fosters the mix of competition and collaboration required in today's fast-paced technology industries. Yet the case of Route 128 demonstrates that geographic clustering alone does not ensure the emergence of regional networks. Competitive advantage derives as much from the way that skill and technology are organized as from their presence in a regional environment.

Note

A previous version of this chapter was presented as a paper at the Vancouver Network Conference, sponsored by the Institute of Asian Research, University of British Columbia, Whistler, B.C., September 10–12, 1993.

References

Aldrich, H. and T. Sakano. "Unbroken Ties: Comparing Personal Business Networks Cross-Nationally." Paper presented at the Vancouver Network Conference, Whistler, B.C., September 1993.

Arthur, B. "Positive Feedback in the Economy." *Scientific American*, 262–2 (1990): 92–9.

Basche, T. Vice President, Sparcstation Group, Sun Microsystems, personal communication, 1991.

Beam, A., and M. Frons. "How Tom Vanderslice is Forcing Apollo Computer to Grow Up." *Business Week*, March 25, 1985, pp. 96–8.

Bell, A., and E. Corliss. "Apollo Falls to the West." *Mass High Tech*, April 24, 1989, pp. 1, 9.

Best, M. *The New Competition: Institutions of Industrial Restructuring*. Cambridge, Mass.: Harvard University Press, 1990.

Bulkeley, W. M. "Culture Shock: Two Computer Firms with Clashing Styles Fight for Market Niche." *Wall Street Journal*, July 6, 1987, p. A1.

Castells, M. *The Informational City: Information Technology, Economic Restructuring, and Urban–Regional Process*. Oxford: Blackwell, 1989.

Chandler, A. D. *The Visible Hand: The Managerial Revolution in American Business*. Cambridge, Mass.: Belknap, 1977.

Comerford, R. "How DEC Developed Alpha." *IEEE Spectrum* (July 1992): 2631.

CorpTech. *Technology Company Information: Regional Disks*. Woburn, Mass.: Corporate Technology Information Services, 1993.

DeBresson, C., and R. Walker, eds. "Special Issue on Networks of Innovators." *Research Policy*, 20–5 (1991).

DeNucci, J. Vice President, Entry Systems Group, MIPS Computer Systems, personal communication, 1990.

Dyer, J. "The Japanese Vertical *keiretsu* as a Source of Competitive Advantage." Paper, Vancouver Network Conference, Whistler, B.C., September 1993.

Edmondson, H. Vice President of Corporate Manufacturing, Hewlett Packard Corporation, personal communication, 1988.

Florida, R., and M. Kenney. "Silicon Valley and Route 128 Won't Save Us." *California Management Review*, 33–1 (1990): 68–88.

Friedman, D. *The Misunderstood Miracle: Industrial Development and Political Change in Japan*. Ithaca, N.Y.: Cornell University Press, 1988.

Fruin, M. *The Japanese Enterprise System*. Oxford: Oxford University Press, 1992.

Fruin, M. "The Visible Hand and Invisible Assets: Network Organization and Supplier Relations in the Electronic Industry in Japan." Paper presented to the Vancouver Network Conference, Whistler, B.C., September 1993.

Fruin, W. M. *Knowledge Works*. New York: Oxford University Press, 1997.

Furlong, T. RISC Workstation Manager, DEC Palo Alto, personal communication, 1991.

Granovetter, M. "Economic Action and Social Structure: The Problem of embeddedness." *American Journal of Sociology*, 91–3 (1985): 481–510.

Greene, T. "Can HP Find the Right Direction for the '90s?" *Electronic Business*, January 22, 1990, pp. 26–9.

Hall, P., and A. Markusen. *Silicon Landscapes*. Boston: Allen & Unwin, 1985.

Herrigel, G. "Large Firms, Small Firms, and the Governance of Flexible Specialization: The Case of Baden-Wurtemmberg and Socialized Risk." In B. Kogut, ed., *Country Competitiveness*. New York: Oxford University Press, 1993.

Hsing, Y. "The Work of Networks in Taiwan's Fashion Shoe Industry." Paper presented at the Vancouver Network Conference, Whistler, B.C., September 1993.

Imai, K. "Evolution of Japan's Corporate and Industrial Networks." In B. Carlsson, ed., *Industrial Dynamics*. Boston: Kluwer, 1989.

Kalb, J. President, MasPar Computer Corporation, personal communication, 1991.

Kanai, T. "Entrepreneurial Networking Organizations: Causes, Taxonomy, and Paradoxes." Paper, Vancouver Network Conference, Whistler, B.C., September 1993.

Kirchoff, B., and R. McAuliffe. "Economic Redevelopment of Mature Industrial Areas." Report prepared for Technical Assistance and Research Division, Economic Development Administration, U.S. Department of Commerce, Washington, DC: GPO, 1988.

Krugman, P. *Geography and Trade*. Cambridge, Mass.: MIT Press, 1991.

Levine, J. B. "Sun Microsystems Turns on the Afterburners." *Business Week*, July 18, 1988, pp. 114–18.

Levy, B., and W. Kuo. "The Strategic Orientation of Firms and the Performance of Korea and Taiwan in Frontier Industries." *World Development*, 19–4 (1991): 363–74.

McWilliams, G. "Crunch Time at DEC." *Business Week*, May 4, 1992, pp. 30–33.

Mitchell, J. "HP Sets the Tone for Business in the Valley." *San Jose Mercury News*, January 9, 1989, pp. 10.

Nash, J., and M. Hayes. "Key DEC Project Moving to Palo Alto." *Business Journal (San Jose and Silicon Valley)*, July 19, 1993, pp. 1, 17.

Nee, E. Back to Basics at Hewlett-Packard. *Upside* (June/July 1991): 38–78.

Nishiguchi, T. "Strategic Dualism: An Alternative in Industrial Societies." Ph.D. Diss., Nuffield College, Oxford University, 1989.

Nohria, N., and R. Eccles. "Face-to-Face: Making Network Organizations Work." In N. Nohria and R. Eccles, eds., *Networks and Organizations: Structure, Form and Action*. Cambridge, Mass.: Harvard Business School Press, 1992a.

Nohria, N., and R. Eccles. *Networks and Organizations: Structure, Form, and Action*. Cambridge, Mass.: Harvard Business School Press, 1992b.

Piore, M., and C. Sabel. *The Second Industrial Divide: Possibilities for Prosperity*. New York: Basic Books, 1984.

Porter, M. *The Competitive Advantage of Nations*. New York: Free Press, 1990.

Porter, P. "Executive Interview: HP's Gary Eichorn Tackles Enterprise Computing." *Mass High Tech*, August 23, 1993, p. 3.

Powell, W. "Neither Market nor Hierarchy: Network Forms of Organization." In B. Staw, ed., *Research in Organizational Behavior*. Greenwich, Conn.: JAI Press, 1987.

Rifkin, G., and G. Harrar. *The Ultimate Entrepreneur: The Story of Ken Olsen and Digital Equipment Corporation*. Rocklin, Calif.: Prima Publishing, 1990.

Sabel, C. "Flexible Specialization and the Reemergence of Regional Economies." In P. Hirst and J. Zeitlin, eds., *Reversing Industrial Decline?: Industrial Structure and Policy in Britain and Her Competitors*. Oxford: Berg, 1988.

Saxenian, A. *Regional Advantage: Culture and Competition in Silicon Valley and Route 128*. Cambridge, Mass.: Harvard University Press, 1994.

Schein, E. *Organizational Culture and Leadership*. San Francisco: Jossey-Bass, 1985.

Scott, A. *Metropolis: From the Division of Labor to Urban Form*. Berkeley, Calif.: University of California Press, 1988a.

Scott, A. *New Industrial Spaces: Flexible Production Organization and Regional Development in North America and Western Europe*. London: Pion, 1988b.

Sheff, D. "A New Ballgame for Sun's Scott McNealy." *Upside* (November/December 1989): 46–54.

Sherwood-Call, C. "Changing Geographic Patterns of Electronic Components Activity." *Economic Review (Federal Reserve Board of San Francisco)*, 2 (1992): 25–35.

Standard and Poor's. Compustat PC+ database, 1992.

Storper, M. "The Transition to Flexible Specialization in the U.S. Firm Industry: External Economies, the Division of Labor, and the Crossing of Industrial Divides." *Cambridge Journal of Economics*, 13 (1989): 273–305.

Tannenwald, R. "Rating Massachusetts' Tax Competitiveness." *New England Economic Review* (November/December 1987): 335–345.

The Top 100 Exporters. *Electronic Business* (March 16, 1992): 4–42.

Tuller, D. "HP Plans to Buy 10% Stake in Octel." *San Francisco Chronicle*, August 12, 1988, pp. 1B.

Vedoe, C. Manager, Workstation Marketing, Sun Microsystems, personal communication, 1990.

Vernon, R. *Metropolis 1985*. Cambridge, Mass.: Harvard University Press, 1960.

Weiss, J., and A. Delbecq. "High Technology Cultures and Management: Silicon Valley and Route 128." *Group and Organization Studies*, 12–1 (1987): 39–54.

Whiting, C. "For Flexible, Quality Manufacturing Don't Do It Yourself." *Electronic Business* (March 15, 1987): 46–47.

Yoder, S. "A 1990 Reorganization at Hewlett-Packard Already is Paying Off." *Wall Street Journal*, July 22, 1991, p. A1.

14

Structural Analysis of Japanese Economic Organization

A Conceptual Framework

MICHAEL L. GERLACH
JAMES R. LINCOLN

With the proliferation of various forms of strategic alliance in the global economy —from long-term supplier relations to international joint ventures to state-sponsored consortia—has come an increased theoretical interest in business networks as a topic of analysis. A brief sample of writings in this literature includes Aldrich (1979), Piore and Sable (1984), Miles and Snow (1987), Eccles and Crane (1987), Powell (1990), as well as edited volumes by Mizruchi and Schwartz (1987), Wellman and Berkowitz (1987), and Nohria and Eccles (1992). As the composition of this volume shows, Japanese industrial organization and business structures have taken a leading role in encouraging this shift in interest. [In addition to the chapters in this book, see Fruin (1992); Gerlach (1992a, b); Lincoln et al. (1992, 1996); and Imai and Itami (1984). Nor is this interest limited to Japan, because the network characteristics of Japanese industrial organization have also appeared in other East Asian economies, including in Korea (through its *zaibatsu*-like *chaebol*) and in Taiwan (through its own distinctive form of extended family groupings) (Hamilton and Biggart, 1988). Indeed, network forms are now recognized to be a pervasive form of economic organization in many countries, including those in the developing world (Leff, 1979) and those in continental Europe (Daems, 1979; Encaoua and Jacquemin, 1982; Cable and Dirrheimer, 1984).] In this chapter we have a dual agenda: We combine a general treatment of network organization in Japan with the presentation of a broad agenda for structural (network) analysis. The link between the two is our research program on Japanese economic organization, which is very much within the structuralist tradition but at the same time aims at pushing the frontiers of that tradition.

The questions that provide the motivation and organizing themes for the current chapter are as follows:

- What do we mean by network organizations?
- How do network theory and methodology generate insights into Japanese social, political, and (especially) economic organization, which are harder to come by—or even entirely overlooked—in alternative theories and research strategies?

- What are the current limits of structural analysis, and what concrete steps can be taken to overcome these limits?

Ultimately, it will be necessary to answer these questions in order for a network approach to comparative organization to reach its potential. Only then will it become useful to business leaders, policy-makers, and other practitioners who are actively involved in managing trade, diplomatic, and similar relations among the United States, Japan, and other countries.

The Nature of Network Organization: An Overview

The movement away from stark markets-or-hierarchies thinking about economic organization has both fostered and benefited from the simultaneous development of structural analysis, several distinguishing features of which are introduced here. First, network analysis is probably unique to the extent to which it emphasizes complex relations among a distinct set of actors, whether individuals, corporations, government agencies, or interest groupings as its central focus. As one early theorist described it, "The metaphorical use of the idea of the social network emphasizes that the social links of individuals in any given society ramify through that society. The analytical use of the idea of social network seeks to specify how this ramification influences the behavior of the people involved in the network" (Mitchell, 1974, p. 280). In its broad linking of micro- and macro-level phenomena, network reasoning offers a basic framework for comprehending the connections among diverse social actors and institutional spheres (from work groups within companies to overall economic systems) and for linking disparate theoretical perspectives (such as transactions costs economics and organizational ecology) in a unified explanatory framework.

This interrelatedness need not involve close, dense, or frequent interactions between *every* pair of actors (networks vary in these respects), but it does imply a high degree of overall *connectivity*. That is, actors are generally accessible to one another through some chain of intermediaries. A network characterized by high connectivity is well integrated; information and resources disperse easily to all its regions and are potentially available to all members of the population. Although any network will have localized dense patches of direct ties, bridged by fairly sparse or distant linkages, a well-connected network has few (perhaps no) complete breaks that isolate one set of actors from another (Lincoln, 1982).

In traditional formulations of network organization, the ties relating social actors to one another are for the most part informal, noncontractual, and governed by norms of reciprocity and obligation (Gouldner, 1960). In this view, face-to-face human interaction and long-term personal bonds are the fundamental building blocks on which large networks are erected. Network social organization is thus commonly cast as an informal, diffuse, and emergent configuration of ties. In Max Weber's classic writings, formal bureaucracy and market capitalism are both grounded in the same rationalist and universalist cultural ideals. These confer legitimacy on legalism, impersonality, and the competitive pursuit of self-interest within fixed rules of the game. In contrast, as Heimer (1992) wrote, particularistic and personalized commitments to identifiable others provide a much firmer foundation for strong social networks at the core of social and economic organization. We argue later in this chapter that an exclusive preoccupation with informal relationships is unnecessarily limiting and has hindered application of network methods to formal economic transactions. Nevertheless, this emphasis has the virtue of pointing to ways in which, in a network society, interpersonal and consequently interorganizational relations are less mediated or absorbed by formal, legal hierarchies, on the one hand, or atomized, arms-length markets on the other.

The structuralist paradigm is also distinctive in its insistence on the collection and analysis of rich behavioral data of real social and economic action and relations—including networks of friendship, information, influence, ownership, and trade—in contrast to the abstract conceptual exercises that dominate much of theoretical economics and a good deal of sociological and political theory as well. In the best structuralist inquiry, theory interacts with data in a series of iterative cycles. Network concepts (e.g., centrality, density, structural equivalence, diffusion) convert readily into operational procedures, and the information yielded from those operations lays the groundwork for the next round of theorizing.

This is not to say that measurement error does not loom large in network research. Its implications here, in fact, are far more serious than in modes of inquiry that assume away relations with postulates of independent observations. A single missing node or tie can wholly transform the revealed structure, leading to egregiously erroneous inferences. Structural inquiry has the advantage of a close correspondence between theory and measurement but also the heavy burden of ensuring that the data and measurement are of superior quality.

Finally, and of key importance, the structuralist perspective abhors the reductionism that seeks the determinants of social action—whether the actors are persons, organizations, or whole institutions—in the motives of autonomous individuals or fully socialized norms. Structuralist explanation takes as its core assumption the idea that causality itself resides with actors' positions in an extended network of social relations. As Leifer and White (1987, p. 85) described it,

> Structural analysis focuses upon the patterns of relationships among social actors. This emphasis rests on the often unspoken postulate that these patterns—independent of the content of ties—are themselves central to individual action. Moreover, structural analysis posits that the constraints associated with positions in a network of relationships are frequently more important in determining individual action than either the information or attitudes people hold.

Structuralist inquiry may thus seem out of step with the times in forcefully rejecting the now fashionable dogma that large-scale institutions emerge smoothly from a simple aggregation of rational choices based on individual utility functions. It furthermore stands in sharp contrast with the beliefs of an earlier generation of cultural determinists in anthropology and sociology, who sought explanation in internalized values and rules shared throughout society.

Japan as a Network Society

Although we believe structural analysis has the potential to extend the empirical and conceptual boundaries of all advanced economies, it is perhaps Japan—a country often described as a "network society" (Gerlach and Lincoln, 1992; Lincoln, 1990; Powell, 1990)—where its utility is greatest. (For evidence on the important role of networks elsewhere in East Asia, see the chapters 6 and 9 in this volume.) The network organization of Japanese society is a long-standing theme in sociological and anthropological work. Japan's social order is often discussed as one in which personal, obligatory, and diffuse relations permeate and dominate walks of life, where the "legal–rational" institutions of competitive markets, court-ordered contracts, and the like, are less conspicuous and consequential than in the West (Johnson, 1982; Kawashima, 1963; Packer and Ryser, 1992). To an extraordinary degree, the Japanese mold personal relationships to the conduct of political, economic, and community affairs and count on trust and obligation to ensure the credibility of commitments (see chapter 5 of this volume). In this section, we briefly consider these relationships as they are reflected in three areas: community and organizational studies, industrial structure, and politics.

Community and Organizational Studies

Ethnographic studies of family, gender roles, and community in Japan and their interplay with school, worklife, and politics highlights the vertically ordered interpersonal bonds, the in-group cohesion and out-group separation, and the evolution of these structures with economic growth and modernization (Dore, 1963; Vogel, 1963). Nakane's (1970) classic theoretical statement on Japanese social structure is the best known attempt to analyze formally the vertical ordering of Japanese social collectivities in explicitly structuralist terms. This tradition of fine-grained social structure research continues in the recent work on family, community, gender relations, and worklife by Bernstein (1983), Brinton (1993), and Kondo (1990).

The strong social networks typical of the Japanese workplace have been a source of special fascination for social scientists. Classic studies by Cole (1971), Dore (1973), and Rohlen (1974) have documented the informal vertical and horizontal bonds that Japanese companies strive to nurture and that figure so strongly in the motivation and commitment for which the Japanese workforce is renowned. Lincoln and Kalleberg's (1990) survey of more than 100 U.S. and Japanese manufacturing plants and 8,000 employees provided quantitative evidence of the same patterns: a markedly higher density and depth of affective co-worker ties within Japanese factories. As we argue, the Japanese firm is a less unitary entity than the U.S. firm from the standpoint of ownership, control, day-to-day management, and corporate strategy. But in terms of the cohesion of its internal social networks and the commitment, loyalty, and identification toward the company employees display, it is paradoxically much more of a unitary entity.

Industrial Structure

If strong networks are key to the internal organization of the Japanese firm and a source of its vitality and capacity for smooth, coordinated action, then economic relations *among* Japanese firms are also organized in network fashion to an extra-ordinary degree. Dore (1986), for example, referred to the singular importance in Japanese market organization of *goodwill*, or "the sentiments of friendship and the sense of diffuse personal obligation which accrue between individuals engaged in recurring contractual economic exchange" (p. 460). As a result, he continued in a well-known passage, it is tangible relationships rather than impersonal market processes that explain Japanese industrial organization:

> The Japanese, in spite of what their political leaders say at summit confer-ences about the glories of free enterprise in the Free World, and in spite of the fact that a British publisher with a new book about Adam Smith can expect to sell half the edition in Japan, have never really caught up with Adam Smith. They have never managed actually to bring themselves to believe in the invisible hand (p. 470).

Several authors in the present book clarify just how significant these relations are to understanding the management of production and technology in Japan. Dyer (chapter 11), and Fruin (chapter 12), each focus on the role of close supplier rela-tionships as alternatives to vertical integration for the Japanese firm. Although the automobile industry is the case that has received the most attention, similar (if more loosely organized) ties are common in other assembly industries in Japan. Fruin found in his detailed study of a Toshiba factory (chapter 11), for instance, that nearly four-fifths of the production value of a variety of high-technology elec-tronic products were sourced from outside suppliers—many of which are locked into long-term, informationally rich relationships with their core customers.

Others have focused on the role of cross-shareholding, dispatched directors, and bank capital as sources of cohesion within the Japanese corporate network (Gerlach, 1992; also see chapter 10 in the present volume). These writers empha-sized the special role played by large Japanese banks and industrial firms in defin-ing both the financial and the corporate governance systems of Japan. Companies use large-block shareholdings in each other as a means of consolidating their busi-ness relationships—and, not incidentally, protecting corporate managers from po-tential takeover threats. Whereas supplier relationships tend toward the vertical (i.e., marked by asymmetric power between parent and subcontractor), the rela-tionships among banks and large industrial firms are more likely to be viewed as among business equals.

Political Relationships

Similar to and overlapping with *keiretsu* networks in the Japanese economy is a complex matrix of political influence relations. The role of institutionalized cliques or factions in the ruling Liberal Democratic Party and elsewhere in Japa-nese political circles is well known. These nonideological clusterings comprise hi-erarchical relations of political loyalty and obligation. Much like decision-making within the Japanese firm, decision-making in the Japanese political arena is a behind-the-scenes process of informal coalition building and consensus formation. The legislative and executive machinery kicks in only at the point that consensus is reached and formal implementation begins.

The participation of government ministries such as the Ministry of International

Trade and Industry (MITI) and the Ministry of Finance (MOF) in setting goals and fostering cooperation among industrial firms and financial institutions is very much a key feature of the Japanese network political economy, as demonstrated in Broadbent and Ishio's systematic empirical work on political networks (chapter 4). Just as a formal market in corporate mergers and acquisitions is underdeveloped in Japan relative to the United States, formal court-enforced regulation is less the Japanese way than the development of strong, informal bonds of obligation and reciprocity between industry and government officials and the role of ministries in channeling information to firms (Johnson, 1982; Okimoto, 1989). An observation that has made the rounds for years is that MITI loves an oligopoly. The reason is that a dozen or so companies leads to the number of representatives who can be comfortably seated around a MITI conference table and with whom the Ministry bureaucrats can easily confer and build consensus (a process termed *nemawashi*).

Markets, Hierarchies, and Networks: Applying Structural Analysis to Economic Organization

The preceding discussion covers only a fraction of the significant institutional features of Japan that are amenable to network analysis. We believe that this book, as well as several others in recent years, represents an important shift in thinking about the structural underpinnings of Japanese society and political economy. Nevertheless, much conceptual and empirical work is necessary to flesh out the implications of this analytic shift in thinking. In this section, we compare structural perspectives to several other approaches, focusing on their application to comparative economic systems. Although we emphasize the advantages of structural analysis, particularly in comparison with textbook economic approaches that ignore the relational character of contemporary economies, we recognize that structural analysis also has a number of limitations. In the next section, we propose concrete steps that can be taken to overcome those limitations.

It is no small intellectual irony that the most complete paradigm in the social sciences—the neoclassical framework within economics—still dominates most economic textbooks at a time when its underlying premises have never seemed less realistic and tenable. In late twentieth-century capitalist societies, the vast majority of important economic decisions are made by social collectives of various forms (e.g., corporations, labor unions, government agencies) rather than by isolated individuals. Capital investment is largely mediated by banks and other major institutions, product markets are dominated by manufacturing enterprises, labor markets are internalized within formal hierarchies, and so on. Prices and quantities are adjusted by organizations often locked in long-term relationships, and these organizations directly factor in the identities and strategies of their partners in their decision-making. Therefore, markets and their constituent elements— competition, prices, and other terms of trade—are administered or managed to an extraordinary degree (Lincoln, et al., 1996a). Markets have come to resemble less and less the impersonal, abstract forces stressed in textbook theory. [By "textbook" we mean that version of orthodox price theory to which students are exposed in standard microeconomics courses. It should be noted that several authors have attempted to move beyond this approach in applying economic analysis to business organizations (e.g., Milgrom and Roberts, 1992). Although these authors introduced some real-world features into the discussion, their highly stylized portrayals of economic interaction, in our view, remains insufficiently attentive to relational features of firm and market organization.]

We further argue that, although these trends are universal, they characterize some national economies more than others. Consider first the case of labor. Internal labor markets, bounded by competitive ports of entry, have long existed in the United States, especially among larger corporations (Doeringer and Piore, 1971). These markets—particularly those for technical and professional personnel—tend to be organized around personal contacts and reciprocity, such that competitive market processes play a secondary role in recruitment, placement, and promotion (Granovetter, 1973; Kanter, 1977). Nevertheless, as recent corporate downsizing and other restructuring efforts suggest, commitments by U.S. companies to workers have declined over time (as, too, has corporate loyalty by those workers). As a result, industries in the United States are increasingly marked by fluid labor markets, wherein workers and managers freely compete for the remaining good jobs and firms compete for high-quality employees.

In contrast, and despite dire warnings about the end of permanent employment, the large-firm labor market in Japan continues to be dominated by very long employment tenure. Associated with this is a set of highly institutionalized arrangements that ritualistically operate to shift graduating cohorts of students into companies at fixed times of the year; lower-level employees into higher-status positions in step with seniority, age, and experience; and redundant and aging employees out of the firm and into subcontractors and affiliates. Also important are professor–firm relationships in linking graduates to jobs, plus school ties (*gakubatsu*) in keeping graduates in contact after they begin work (see Odagiri, chapter 7).

Workers' discretion to leave an employer for greener pastures is extremely constrained; not only will superiors (and perhaps relatives and neighbors, as well) berate and humiliate them for corporate disloyalty, but their odds of finding a better job are dim, for other companies also confine hiring to entry-level graduates and thereafter promote only from within. Even in the unlikely event that a firm takes on a mid-career entrant, that person's seniority clock is typically set back to zero. Experience and skill are sufficiently enterprise-specific in Japan that senior people (apart from a small corps of executive elite) find little external demand for their services.

National differences also exist in markets for capital and corporate control. *Relationship banking* and *relationship investing* are increasingly discussed in the United States (e.g., Eccles and Crane, 1988; Jensen, 1989). Yet the reality is that U.S. capital markets continue to be dominated by investors whose primary concern is direct financial returns and who are quite willing to sell off investments when it is in their short-term interest. Japanese companies are far more likely to tie themselves to a long-term relationship with a main bank that provides, in exchange for rights to monitor the company's affairs and to claim without competition its most lucrative fee-based business, steady financing, and substantial protection from downside risk (see Sheard, chapter 10). Even more striking are the contrasts in corporate control. A distressed U.S. company teetering on bankruptcy may find itself up for grabs in the takeover market—ousting the incumbent management and restructuring or disposing of the assets of the firm. A similarly distressed Japanese firm, in contrast, will be restructured at the hands of its main bank, long-term trading partners, and other *keiretsu* affiliates in a fashion more protective of its integrity as an ongoing concern.

In industrial markets, including intermediate products and technology trade, the differences between the two countries are generally less pronounced. Long-term, relational networks distinguish certain industries in the United States, such as the entertainment business (Hirsch, 1975). Moreover, high-technology firms in Silicon Valley and elsewhere have relied heavily on strategic alliances and informal information sharing to maintain their competitive edge (see Saxenian, chapter 13). Nevertheless, cross-national differences do exist in most industries. U.S. firms will outsource a component or material by putting out for bid a contract for which suppliers compete chiefly on price. Japanese manufacturers, in contrast, will informally adjust the terms of their ongoing procurement arrangement with long-term suppliers with whom they have an intimate and reciprocal set of obligations (Sako, 1992; see Fruin, chapter 12).

These characterizations of the Japanese and U.S. economy are highly stylized, to be sure. Long-term relationships are important in many areas of the U.S. economy and are increasing in certain fields (e.g., in the relations between automakers and their suppliers; see Helper, 1991). Conversely, arms-length markets do play a role in the Japanese economy and may be gaining ground as deregulation, recession, and foreign pressure (*gaiatsu*) force change. The essential point, however, is beyond dispute; the United States relies far more on competitive markets in the provision of goods, services, capital, and labor than does Japan (or Europe, for that matter), and the Japanese economy makes correspondingly greater use of thick, broad networks of mutual and stable relations. Moreover, policy-makers in the United States are more likely to assume that this competition creates socially desirable "efficiencies" than are Japanese policy-makers.

If markets in Japan are less well defined and abstracted from social structure, it follows that firms are so as well; the boundary between the two is less sharply drawn (Fruin, 1992). Clearly, the relatively small and specialized company that is Toyota Motor Corporation is just one piece (albeit a critical one) of the broad, malleable organization that is the Toyota network. Likewise, the denials of Japanese managers and bureaucrats notwithstanding, there is more to Mitsubishi or Sumitomo than merely a number of large firms that for historical reasons share a common name and logo and occasionally do a bit of business with one another. Yet it is just as misleading to characterize either group as diversified, centrally managed conglomerates in the style of TRW or Gulf & Western. Even in the case of vertical groups, there is little basis for the claim (alleged by T. Boone Pickens) that Toyota suppliers such as Koito are as subordinate to the authority and direction of Toyota as any General Motors wholly owned parts division is to that of GM. Firms and markets, then, are relative concepts, and are linked through an ongoing structure of economic and social relationships (Granovetter, 1985).

Consider by way of contrast the theoretical underpinnings of the neoclassical model. As Knight (1957), a sympathetic but reflective observer of economics pointed out, perfect competition assumes that there is "no exercise of constraint over any individual by another individual or 'society'; each controls his own activities with a view to results which accrue to him individually." There must also be "complete absence of physical obstacles to the making, execution, and changing of plans at will; that is, there must be 'perfect mobility'" (pp. 77, 79). Although Knight recognized that this was an idealized set of assumptions, he nevertheless believed it was sufficiently approximated in reality that its premises did not require substantial alteration.

This view is questioned by some within the discipline of economics who argue that neoclassical price auction models fail to capture important dimensions of how economic decisions are actually made and business transactions conducted (e.g., Nelson and Winter, 1982; Okun, 1981; Williamson, 1985). These observers have a strong interest in problems of organization, and several of the most active and exciting new areas of economic inquiry—such as agency theory, transaction cost economics, and evolutionary economics—include analysis of relations both within and between firms. Moreover, although contributors to these traditions are usually reluctant to use this language, their concerns lie clearly with the ties of control, communication, and even obligation and reciprocity, which are natural subjects of structuralist inquiry. How such flows and ties surround and regulate the exchange of goods and services among actors in a market, so as to economize on information and transaction costs, is the thrust of such theory. This set of concerns is not greatly different from that of sociological perspectives such as resource dependence, with its focus on organizational bridging mechanisms (such as interlocking directorates) to cope with dependence and uncertainty in exchange, or even that of "embeddedness" theory, with its attention to the myriad ways exchange relations are inextricably bound up with and facilitated by social resources, commitments, and ties (Coleman, 1986; Granovetter, 1985; Pfeffer and Salancik, 1978).

Nevertheless, although genuine efforts are being made to introduce real-world considerations into economic models, most such models continue to assume what we believe to be a structurally underdeveloped view of economic organization. Students of industrial organization, in which neoclassical assumptions about competition and anonymity have never really taken root, nevertheless typically conceive relations in terms of abstract categories such as concentration and market share (in the traditional Harvard approach) or, if social actors are considered at all, in terms of relatively simple two-person games (in the newer game theoretic approach). Closer to our relational view is the focus on transactions in the new institutional costs economics (Williamson, 1985) and interactional routines in evolutionary economics (Nelson and Winter, 1982). Even Hahn, one of the founding fathers of modern equilibrium theory, admitted later in his life to the need for a more concrete approach within economics: "There is something scandalous in the spectacle of so many people refining the analysis of economic states which they have no reason to believe will ever, or have ever, come about" (quoted in Loasby, 1976, p. 226). An analogy might be drawn here to the shift toward behavioral perspectives on managerial decision-making in organizational theory. Herbert Simon, James March, and others in the Carnegie School argued that how managers actually behave should be an important part of theory. If, for example, bounded rationality and opportunism are basic features of the psychological makeup of decision-makers, then these features need to be incorporated in models used to explain their decisions. Similarly, we argue that if economic actors view transactions not as isolated events but as socially interdependent, this view then becomes an important part of the framing of rationality in transactions, and the focus shifts to the social component of interaction.

The structural approach we favor differs from that of mainstream economics in two key respects. First, it is forthrightly relational. Economic action is analyzed in terms of concrete ties among economically powerful and socially significant actors (e.g., financial institutions, industrial corporations, state agencies), which are in turn located in complex economic, social, and political institutions. These relationships constitute the structural core of any advanced economy: formal and informal transactions; social and economic interests; patterns of competition and cooperation; and trade-offs among market, hierarchical, and alliance forms. The precise nature of their organization determines the constraints under which managers operate and the parametric features of the economic system as a whole.

This tilt toward viewing economic relations as part and parcel of the much broader and richer realm of social relations is unappealing to conventional economic inquiry, if for no other reason than the substantial sacrifice in parsimony that it entails. But the costs to explanatory power by ignoring these relations may be even higher, as the case of Japan makes clear. The "thick skein of relations" (Caves and Uekusa, 1976) through which Japanese economic activity is carried out is becoming fair game for economic models and, in so doing, making evident that certain efficiencies in the Japanese industrial system may be the product of its distinctive network institutions. The agency-theoretic role of banks as monitors in extracting information from and disciplining incumbent managements is nowhere better realized than in the Japanese "main bank" relationship chronicled in the case studies by Sheard (chapter 10) and other scholars. Moreover, the transaction cost ideas of "relational contracting" and "hybrid forms"—combining elements of market contracting with the bureaucratic mechanisms of authority and formal rules—have been quickly picked up by students of the Japanese economy, who see in the *keiretsu* networks of informal, long-term obligations among Japanese companies clear manifestations of these processes (Goto, 1982; Imai and Itami, 1984).

The structuralist paradigm is also distinctive in its explicit portrait of a unified, integrated national economy. Economic models typically disregard not only the social and organizational ties that bind players in lasting and constraining ways, but also the connections among economic outcomes and processes themselves. As Teece and Winter (1984, p. 199) pointed out, even the newer strategic models of industrial organization that are finding their way into economic analysis continue to "focus on the nature of competition with respect to a single variable (for example, irreversible capacity investment, lumpy investments, learning by doing, R&D) and ignore the interconnectedness of these processes.

A focus on interconnectedness defines the core of structural analysis. In our view, economic action is measured not at the level of isolated transactions, but in terms of networks of exchange that extend over time (in some cases, decades), across market boundaries (e.g., equity ties are used to reinforce business ties), and among larger groups of traders (e.g., in complex networks of reciprocal shareholding). The logic here is that economic transactions are themselves "embedded" in other ties, both instrumental and social (Granovetter, 1985; for a formal modeling approach to this issue, see White, Boorman, and Breiger, 1976). We believe structural inquiry is uniquely useful in its capacity to provide both direct measurement of localized transactions and to aggregate up to system-level outcomes.

Developing a Structural Paradigm: Steps
Toward Broadening the Network Approach

Unfortunately, the "potential" of structural analysis for the paradigmatic study of business organization and economic systems has been talked up for so many years that it has become something of a cliché. That fact is that, although the realization of that potential has been achieved in varying degrees in particular specialty areas, it is by no means accomplished on a broad scale. Structuralist inquiry is mired in an uneasy equilibrium among its constituent communities. In our view there are three such communities. The first is a hard core of self-conscious adherents whose chief commonality is their skill and interest in algorithm building and the formal modeling of network structures and processes. A second group is conversant in the methods and language of technical network analysis but sees itself as methods consumers, not innovators, and is chiefly interested in leveraging substantive insights from the network analysis of relational data (see, e.g., Wellman and Berkowitz, 1987). The third group has sprung up largely in the last 10 years and may have done more than the self-professed networkers to move network concepts and reasoning, if not methods and measurement, into the mainstream of social and economic inquiry. This tradition is almost wholly detached from the insular world of network scholarship but has independently hit upon network concepts and images as a way of portraying and analyzing what it sees to be distinctive and emergent forms of social and economic organization (for reviews, see Perrow, 1992; Powell, 1990).

In our view, true realization of the potential of structuralist inquiry demands significant development in several areas. We argue that much of the current network literature faces a dual set of limitations: first, by underestimating the power of the structural approach in tackling directly economic problems, and, second, by overestimating its ability to provide a universal explanation of social action. More specifically, by emphasizing empirical and conceptual analysis of social relations as the context or structure in which economic exchange is embedded, network studies may have underutilized the paradigm's potential to map transactions at the core of economic inquiry—the tangible flows of goods, services, capital, and technologies (exceptions include Burt, 1983, 1992; Pennings, 1980; and Pfeffer and Salancik, 1978).

Conversely, researchers have at times overestimated the power of structural analysis by ignoring or denying the institutional framing of networks. That is, network analysis in and of itself is insufficient to account for structural arrangements because their emergence and maintenance are shaped by historical and cultural forces that actors adopt as models in seeking to organize their worlds (Fligstein, 1990). A comprehensive structural theory of economic systems, therefore, must include both an extended analysis of overall patterns of economic relations and an explanation of the institutional ether that holds these relations together. In this, we part company with network analysts who take the strong-form structuralist position that the content of the relations, the motivations of the actors, and the cultural/historical/institutional context need not be introduced in structuralist models either as exogenous causes or endogenous outcomes. The formal properties of the network and the positions and roles revealed by a network analysis are sufficient (e.g., White et al., 1976). Note, however, that despite the extreme formalism urged on the structuralist agenda by these advocates, many of their applications are to highly historically and institutionally specific contexts, and their analysis combines a formal treatment of the network with thick description of the substantive features of the context. A comprehensive structural theory thus requires a detailed understanding not only of quantitative network methodology, but also a qualitative understanding of the nuances of the social and economic structure in question.

Data Requirements

There has been, in our view, an insufficient appreciation of the power of network analysis as applied to hard economic flows of the kind that empirical economists take as their livelihood. Early network theorists sought a framework for the analysis of community structures too complicated and subtle to be grasped as traditional concepts by social groups and as the roles or the structural–functional methodology then in vogue (Mitchell, 1974). This focus has persisted to the present, as the vast majority of researchers using network analysis stress diffuse, emergent ties, often among individuals. Yet, as various network scholars have stressed (Mintz and Schwartz, 1985; Mizruchi, 1982), director interlocks, friendship and kinship networks, and other "soft" or social measures of business relations must be coupled with investigations of the flows of goods and services that link large-scale business organizations. Although it is key to the structuralist perspective (and by and large ignored in orthodox economics) that these social and political bonds form an indispensable infrastructure for the conduct of economic exchange, the structuralist community has been overly absorbed in exercises of mapping and describing them (particularly true of interlocking directorate research), to the neglect of relations and data that economists (and businesspeople) consider critical—patterns of ownership and control, intermediate product transactions, strategic alliances, technological cooperation, and so forth.

Data on such processes are not, of course, easily obtained. Much useful information on corporate business activities is treated as proprietary and is thus excluded from public-domain sources. Interfirm network research would be facilitated immeasurably, for example, were companies mandated to report the names of their trading partners and the volumes of their transactions. But this information is obviously sensitive and is apt to remain inaccessible for the foreseeable future. However, smaller companies will sometimes report transactional data in 10-K reports and other securities filings because they have a significant bearing on these companies' financial health. In addition, large-scale transactions in corporate assets are reported even by large companies because these have major direct effects on financial performance. Similarly, joint ventures and major cooperative agreements are often available from the business press. These are promising sources of data for network analysts, although few attempts have yet been made to utilize these data. As a result, network scholars interested in addressing economic concerns attempt to proxy firm-level relationships with industry-level data on flows (Burt, 1983; Mintz and Schwartz, 1985). Direct survey methods offer an alternative means of obtaining information on flows and ties not recorded in archival sources, and some investigators have taken the challenge to measure through questionnaires and interviews supply relations and other concrete ties (Kelley and Brooks, 1991). But the obstacles to the wide use of survey methods to generate longitudinal data sets for representative samples of large corporations hardly need belaboring.

It is a matter of good fortune (and no accident) that Japan, the economy that has garnered the greatest interest and closest scrutiny for the density, complexity, and efficacy of its interorganizational networks, also makes widely available some of the richest relational data. A dizzying array of directories provides detailed, micro-level information on creditors, stockholders, trading partners, subsidiaries, and affiliates for Tokyo Stock Exchange-listed firms and for a large number of unlisted firms. Fine-grained information on boards of directors and management teams from sources such as *Kaisha Nenkan* and *Toyo Keizai* make possible inquiries into how corporate hierarchies interlock either contemporaneously through joint incumbency or sequentially via managerial career paths (Lincoln et al., 1992). Because the transfer or dispatch of management personnel from one large company to another is a pervasive practice in Japan and has profound implications for the network organization of the economy, such data are extraordinarily useful. Sources such as the *Jinji Koshin Roku* provide details for management personnel on educational history, family members, leisure interests, and early careers, thereby enabling assessments to be made of corporate linkages based on schooling (*gakubatsu*) or marriage (*kanbatsu*) ties. Finally, the quasiformal enterprise groupings —the big-six intermarket groups in particular—are researched and described in exhaustive detail in sources such as *Industrial Groupings in Japan* and *Keiretsu no kenkyu*. These identify the member companies of big-six President's Councils (*shacho-kai*) in addition to mapping the specific business and governance relations that account for group coherence.

One reason for this availability is the fact that the MOF requires all publicly traded corporations to provide in their annual securities reports detailed information on their borrowing positions with important banks, as well as lists of their major shareholders. This facilitates compilation of these lists in Japanese public sources. These more stringent reporting requirements may reflect the relatively high reliance by Japanese corporations historically on bank capital and cross-shareholdings in Japan, which makes these data of unusual importance to investors.

In some industries (e.g., steel and autos) it is also possible to get detailed information on specific trading relations among companies, whereas general lists of major trading partners are available across Japanese industry. This range of data enables the determination of "multiplex" network structures based on the diverse interests firms have in each other, and it points up the array of problems to which such data can be applied. (The data are readily available in print directories, but not in computer-readable form. Indeed, in attempting to obtain tapes on directors in Tokyo Stock Exchange-listed companies, we were informed by the publisher of the source that they were destroyed after the current year, because investors would have no interest in the information from prior years.)

The reason for the much greater availability of data on the network organization of the Japanese economy is clear. It is not so much that regulatory and information-gathering agencies are more enlightened as to the importance of relational properties and therefore more supportive of network research. As in the West, apart from the information provided by government sources (which tended to be particularly circumspect about disclosing actors' identities) the ministries, credit-rating agencies, and investor services that provide such information are responding to demand. The difference between Japan and the United States in this respect is that, in the Japanese economy, data on a company's network of creditors, suppliers, customers, stockholders, affiliates, government agencies, and the like are deemed essential for judging its credit worthiness and its soundness as an investment. Japanese companies in general are required to divulge far less information than are U.S. companies on their internal finances, but they are far more open about their external relationships and the backgrounds of their management teams.

Network Action and the Unit of Organization

We also believe it imperative that structural inquiry take on the challenge of analyzing inchoate, sparse, and sprawling networks. Real-world economies are much more populated by these than by the well-defined, dense, and bounded systems that tend to draw the attention of network research. Network analyses conducted within single organizations (Krackhardt, 1992; Lincoln and Miller, 1979) or in particular local communities (Galaskiewicz, 1985) or institutional sectors (Laumann and Knoke, 1987) have produced rich insights into the organization and functioning of such systems that alternative methods (e.g., sample surveys, ethnographies) fail to provide. Moreover, confining inquiries to such limited populations keeps the methodological problems tractable, that is, the number of potential relations is not so large as to exceed computing capacity or so sparse or segmented as to yield little variance to be explained.

The problems with the search for bounded network organization are highlighted in recent work on Japan's *keiretsu* groupings. Although the *keiretsu* appear a prototypical network organization, not all observers agree on the extent of coherence of these arrangements, especially that of the big-six horizontal groups (for skeptical views, see Miwa, 1990; for a critique of the view of Miwa and others, see Gerlach, 1992c). Internal analyses of single groupings are insufficient to establish group coherence because they fail to provide a set of references with which to anchor interpretations. Is an average of, say, 25 percent of total equity in a firm helped by other group companies a high figure? Is it possible that coalitions among the other 75 percent of shareholders are easily formed in ways that cancel intragroup effects? How do these cross-shareholdings vary with other types of ties, such as trade in intermediate products, where the evidence suggests that relationships are considerably less organized by group affiliations?

In short, it is impossible, without comparison points, to determine the extent to which nominal *keiretsu* groupings correspond to empirically meaningful clusters in a network of interorganizational relationships. This analysis requires both the systematic coding of network data among firms, regardless of nominal affiliation, and the use of methods of analysis that are capable of demonstrating the extent to which patterns of ties within groupings are distinct from ties across groupings. As it turns out, systematic group differences *do* emerge from fine-grained network data (Gerlach, 1992a,b; Lincoln et al., 1992). Equally important, however, is that other network patterns, such as hierarchies and regional clusters, also emerge, and these interact with formal group affiliations in ways not apparent in group-focused analyses.

In general, when networks take the place of vertically integrated and division-alized corporations, there is a problem of attributing coherence, identity, and goals to the system as a whole. In the case of the Japanese vertical supply and distribu-tion networks, one can at least ascribe leadership and control to the parent firm po-sition in the network. The big-six intermarket groups, on the other hand, continue to mystify and confound observers intent on finding a headquarters function re-sponsible for the coordination and coherence of the network as a system. The claim that none exists and, indeed, that such coherence is in any case illusory (e.g., Abegglen and Stalk, 1985) is hardly satisfying in light of accumulated evidence that substantial unity of action does periodically characterize groups and that the consequences for the member firms are far from trivial.

How networks "act"—where do their direction and coordination originate—is an important problem whose solution does not appear to be at hand. A logical first pass is that networks, which in some instances are but a shade closer to formal hi-erarchies than markets themselves, are likewise governed by an "invisible hand." Without a conscious attempt at intervention or control from any quarter, networks naturally "equilibrate"—move as a system toward the realization or maximization of participants' aggregate preferences. But whereas the "actions" of markets—to set prices and thereby allocate goods and services without central guidance—are intelligible in this sense, the more directed and focused actions of networks are not.

It is true of both the former *zaibatsu* groups (Mitsui, Mitsubishi, Sumitomo) and at least some vertical supply groups (e.g., Toyota) that at earlier points in their his-tories, these organizational forms better approximated formal hierarchies than they do today. Prior to the U.S. occupation, the *zaibatsu* were true conglomerates, cen-trally managed by a family-owned holding company and with greater unity and co-operation among the constituent divisions (Morikawa, 1992). During the occupa-tion, the holding companies were outlawed, the top management purged, and the largest business divisions split up, only to link up again in looser network al-liances. Less familiar is the history of vertical groups, which likewise evolved from a combination of forces both centripetal (drawing into an orbit of control and ex-change once independent firms) and centrifugal (a unitary parent firm spinning off divisions). In Toyota's case, business adversity and creditor pressure in the after-math of the war forced the divestiture of divisions Nippondenso and Toyota Motor Sales and their conversion into satellite, partially owned suppliers and distributors (Odaka et al., 1988).

The centrifugal strategy is now being emulated by U.S. corporations such as IBM, which have been hurriedly expelling divisions in a desperate search for the efficiencies and flexibility enjoyed by more nimble competitors (e.g., Sun and Compaq), who were quicker to see the need for and make the shift to network or-ganization.

The Economic Consequences of Networks

Another agenda item that, in our view, is essential for the structuralist paradigm to be taken seriously as an angle on the study of social and economic systems is that scholars must move beyond a fascination with structure *sui generis* and begin looking hard at *consequences*. Inherent perhaps in the nature of sociological inquiry is a preoccupation with social structure as an intellectual problem warranting explanation in its own right. Yet it is also true that for sociological theories and studies of structure to carry much weight with the outside world—policy-makers and business practitioners, not to mention economists—it must become transparent that structure makes a difference in outcomes about which these audiences care. How do networks affect costs, profits, flexibility and innovation, careers and compensation, competition and cooperation? If the structuralist paradigm was convincingly able to demonstrate that patterns of network organization make a unique and substantial contribution to the explanation of real-world variation in factors such as these, its credibility would be much enhanced.

Without question, a reason for the fast rise to prominence of the new network paradigms associated with the industrial district/small firm model is the strong and public claims made for the superiority of this form on a host of outcome dimensions: welfare, equity, innovation, efficiency, competitiveness, and the like (see Harrison, 1994, for an equally strong and public deflation of those claims). Because research within this tradition is in general not characterized by clear hypotheses and careful analyses of actual data, such claims are easily made and have been subject to little hard scrutiny. But equally unfortunate is the preoccupation of the hardcore network community with rigorous measurement and analysis to the neglect of social and economic consequences. It goes without saying that a marriage of the two would add substantial theoretical and practical value.

There are also some genuine methodological obstacles to an assessment of the economic consequences of network organization, although such obstacles are rapidly tumbling in the face of some interesting new methodological work (for a review, see Gerlach and Lincoln, 1992). The rational-choice paradigm utilizes a simple calculus for modeling economic outcomes: Easily identifiable unit actors— people, unions, firms—convert input resources (talent, effort materials, capital) into outcomes (goods and services, prestige and income, satisfaction and commitment) through an organizational apparatus (technology, division of labor, and authority relations) in accordance with a well-defined utility function. The deterministic models of structural–functional sociology likewise take some social or economic action (achievement, attitudes) to be a (typically) linear function of well-defined positions and roles in bounded social groups (family, organization, community) in combination with a set of rules and values that operate, not through external constraint (as network theory would have it), but through motives internalized via the socialization process. In both cases, the unit of analysis—individual, group, firm—is unambiguous and, as in a firm production function or a human capital earnings model, both input and outcome variables and the causal process linking them are defined at one level (Lincoln and Zeitz, 1980). The theory does not accommodate interdependencies across social units, and the assumptions of the statistical techniques used to estimate such models (independent sampling, random errors of measurement and prediction) cannot easily cope with such dependencies.

Proponents of the network paradigm, however, argue that outcomes are the joint product of complex interactions among numerous actors whose interdependent activities are not neatly packaged in simultaneous membership in the same well-defined, bounded organizations, industries, and markets. It states that boundaries are vague, permeable, and shifting and that actions and outcomes are weighted functions (where the weights are proportional to the strength of the ties), not simply of the inputs supplied by any given actor, but of the efforts, attributes, and resources of the network as a whole.

Although it is critical that structuralist researchers shift their attention from structure as outcome to structure as cause of economic outcomes, one of the strengths of this tradition is its skepticism of the kinds of optimizing arguments so prevalent in economic inquiry (Granovetter, 1985; Perrow, 1986). We thus view with some apprehension the claims that network organization necessarily reaps large gains in efficiency, flexibility, and innovativeness. Such claims are sometimes grounded in economic theories of relationships as governance modes that economize on information, control, and opportunism. Reasoning of this sort has been prevalent in economic explanations of the *keiretsu* (Goto, 1982; Imai and Itami, 1984), thereby displacing an older school of thought that cast such clusterings of firms as colluding oligopolists bent on the extraction of inefficient rents (Caves and Uekusa, 1976; Hadley, 1970). As we earlier observed, this view accounts for much of the appeal of the "flexible specialization" paradigm: That the appearance of network forms signals the demise of old-style, rigid, and inefficient mass production and with it, the dawn of a bright new era when networking strategies coupled with modern information technology preserve economies of scale and scope without the sacrifice in nimbleness and creativity that Fordist mass production entailed (Florida and Kenney, 1992; Perrow, 1992; Piore and Sabel, 1984; Womack et al., 1990).

Yet, in fact, the evidence from Japan for flat-out efficiency gains from network organization is mixed at best. The clear tendency for sales growth and profitability to be lower in firms affiliated with the big-six groups does not rest easily with claims that groupings of this sort economize on information and transaction costs. If networks lower costs, why do they not increase profits (Aoki, 1988; Nakatani, 1984)? Moreover, even the most ardent defenders of Japan's economic institutions do not claim that the distribution *keiretsu*—a dense thatch of stable and personalized small firm linkages if ever there was one—economize on much of anything. The case for efficiency is prima facie greatest with respect to the vertical supply networks, although even there, one finds room for doubt. Whether such networks generate genuine efficiencies or the clear gains to parent customer firms, such as Toyota, come at the expense of the profit margins, growth rates, and wages of their suppliers is still debated.

Even if the Toyota production network was the model of efficiency so often claimed, questions can be raised as to just how widely that form has diffused within the Japanese manufacturing economy. As Asanuma (1989) showed, the Japanese electronics industry conforms less well to the network model, wherein suppliers and customers are bound to one another through the sharing of assets such as know-how and technology and the joint pursuit of cost savings, product design, and innovation (also see Fruin, 1992; 1997). Even within the Japanese automobile industry, the Toyota model is a paragon of "networkness" and by no means the rule among Japanese auto producers (Fruin and Nishiguchi, 1992; Smitka, 1991). Some recent statistical work by Ahmadjian (1995) on our research team shows that, constant with Toyota's reliable standing as one of Japan's most profitable corporations, Toyota *kyoryokukai* (supplier association) members are likewise more profitable than the industry average. But the "Toyota effect" is unique; similar gains are not apparent for other carmakers' *kyoryokukai* members. Much of our impression of the efficiency of the Japanese network economy would appear to be inspired by the almost obsessive preoccupation of scholars and journalists with the Toyota case.

If the case for the efficiency of Japan's *keiretsu* groupings is uncertain, this by no means renders moot the broader question of economic consequences. A growing body of evidence paints a fairly clear portrait of the impact of Japanese business networks. Their economic effects are certainly nontrivial, but neither are they captured by the label "efficiency." What Japan's identifiable networks seem to do is manage terms of trade and lending with an eye toward the long-term fortunes of the membership as a whole and in accordance with what appear to be normative rules governing the distribution of risk, returns, and resources. In a word, groups *share* the burdens and benefits of economic activity through a system of ongoing, reciprocated obligations. The degree to which the network is committed to any company is proportionate to that company's linkage to it in terms of business (trade and lending) and governance (ownership and board representation) ties. The most dramatic and visible evidence for this intervention and redistribution process is the bailouts and turnarounds that groups launch to rescue financially distressed members from bankruptcy (Gerlach, 1992a; Hoshi et al., 1991; Sheard, 1994).

Yet there is also evidence of intervention at the high end of the performance distribution of member firms. As a function of the intensity of their network integration, strongly performing firms exhibit a subsequent tendency to drop back, reporting lower profitability a year or two hence (Lincoln et al., 1996a). It is not yet clear whether these processes of bolstering weaklings and reining in the high fliers are directly connected (e.g., through the strongest firms paying the premium on the implicit contract that insures all against the risk of failure) or whether they are distinct (e.g., groups prohibit profiteering or simply claim the right to redistribute "excess" returns). It does appear, however, that the same pattern of intervention and redistribution describes both the big-six group networks and the vertical supply networks in the Japanese electronics and automobile industries (Ahmadjian, 1995). This general phenomenon is quite consistent with a model of interfirm networks as *communities* that strive to limit inequality and opportunism in the membership while affording protection and support to the membership as a whole.

Space and Network Organization: Flexible
Specialization and Industrial Districts

One of the most influential of the "network forms" paradigms—the "flexible specialization" paradigm conceived by Piore and Sabel (1984)—has stimulated much investigation and discussion of industrial enclaves, such as Silicon Valley in Northern California (see chapter 13), where networks of small- and medium-sized firms achieve the scale and scope economies of large, diversified corporations at lower cost to quality of working life, employee participation and equity, and information and flexibility (for Japan, see Friedman, 1988; Fruin, 1992; Lincoln, 1990). The industrial districts perspective builds on the idea of economies of agglomeration in emphasizing the importance of space and distance in the evolution of interfirm networks. Indeed, although the "flex-spec" framework has popularized and dramatized the opportunities posed by regional concentration for the reciprocal sharing of resources, labor, and know-how—and thus the diminished need for any one organization to supply these inputs internally—a long tradition of serious network research by economic geographers and human ecologists were established well before the current fad (see, e.g., Hawley, 1986; Pred, 1977).

Because the constraints of geography vary markedly from one country to the next, there is good reason to suppose that the part it plays in determining national patterns of network organization is substantial. Few countries are as different in this respect as the United States, a vast expanse of territory with a moderate population thinly spread across it, and Japan, a small country whose mountain and island topography combine to crowd the population into dense, narrow regions. Space has no doubt set the stage for Japan's highly networked forms of social organization, but the spatial distribution of population and economic activity is in turn shaped by those network structures once in place. Of considerable concern to Japanese policy-makers is the continued shift of corporate headquarters and other strategic business activities to the Tokyo area, a decline that the expansive investment by the Kansai region in the new Osaka airport and other infrastructure is designed to stem. Yet the need to cultivate ties with Japan's ministry bureaucrats in Tokyo and the financial and media elites likewise centered there has made Tokyo the magnet for nationwide business migration.

Even Japan's highly networked manufacturing economy has evolved in accordance with the constraints and opportunities posed by the country's spatial organization. Sometimes overlooked in the numerous recent treatments of the efficiency and flexibility of the Toyota supply network is the close proximity in which the majority of Toyota suppliers stand in relation to the parent company's assembly operations in Nagoya. Japan's geographic concentration and dense population very likely played a historical role in fostering close and intricate relations between the customer and supplier firms—enabling, for example, the finely hewn articulation of production and delivery of the Just-In-Time system or the close collaboration on design and innovation of components and subassemblies. Proximity also doubtless plays a role in nurturing the personal ties (sustained through late night drinking and eating *tsukiai*) that link the managements of interacting firms. Indeed, one speculation on the demise of the supply *keiretsu* system in Japanese manufacturing is that Toyota and Nissan (largely owing to the labor shortages of the late 1980s' bubble economy) have in recent years begun dispersing their production facilities to the distant regions of Hokkaido and Kyushu.

However, the claim by "flex-spec" true believer David Friedman that regionalized networks of small firms *absent* the central coordinating role of a large parent firm explain the competitive dynamism of Japanese manufacturing just does not stand up to scrutiny, in our view (Friedman's interesting case study of the machine tool industry in one Nagano prefecture township notwithstanding). Although Japan's economy is riddled with networks, those networks at virtually all levels—the intermarket *keiretsu* clusters of the largest firms and financial institutions, the vertical supply and distribution *keiretsu*, and even the ties that define the internal structure of the Japanese firm—are fundamentally hierarchical (Nakane, 1970). Hierarchy is key to Japanese social organization (Clark, 1979). It is hard to contemplate organization at any level—certainly that of the interfirm network—that does not rest ultimately on status differences of some sort and the structuring of support, dependence, and control that these imply. Indeed, much of the reason that Japanese social organization gets by so well with so little formal, legal structure (e.g., the vague work roles and authority positions of Japanese managers and the absence either of hard contracts between suppliers and customers or full ownership and control within a corporate hierarchy) is because the natural status ordering and the attendant dependency relations are so clear, accepted, and determinative of action.

The Importance of Network Dynamics

Another agenda item that we believe is important, not only for structural inquiry but for the social sciences in general, is to move beyond static analyses to an appreciation of systems in flux. A typical network study reports a "snapshot" of a social structure at a single point in time, yet much social and economic action involves dynamic evolution. When a bank or manufacturer intervenes in the affairs of a client or supplier (by sending in a director or outside management team, for example), it does so as a result of *changing* performance conditions and firm strategies (Kaplan, 1991; Stearns and Mizruchi, 1986). Cross-sectional analyses cannot directly model this process.

The costs of collecting good data over time is one impediment to longitudinal analysis, but at least as significant is the huge increase in data complexity that the addition of a temporal dimension entails. Cross-sectional network data have a structure that is similar to that of panel data. In a panel, the data have the form of a matrix, the rows being times of observation and the columns being objects observed. Network data take the form of a matrix wherein rows and columns are the same units of observation (people, firms) and the cells are the measurements on the relations. A panel network data set is thus a three-dimensional matrix that presents the analyst with some huge computational obstacles. We, for example, are working with the relatively small population of the 250 largest financial and industrial institutions in the Japanese economy, observed approximately biannually from 1965 to 1988. With twelve waves of measurement, the three-dimensional data matrix has 747,000 distinct data points. When several different types of relationships are being measured, this figure multiplies. Furthermore, on certain key variables (e.g., director dispatch relations), the density of the matrix will be extremely low; the overwhelming majority of cells have values of zero.

Still, there is no denying that many of the most compelling contemporary issues pertaining to the network organization of the Japanese economy concern change, particularly during the "bubble economy" of the second half of the 1980s and the recession following it (Lincoln et al., 1996b). After more than 30 years of relative stability, some indicators point to the provocative conclusion that Japan is in the throes of shedding aspects of its "networkness." Large manufacturers are responding to pressure from international trading partners to increase their purchases from foreign parts suppliers. Those manufacturers, desperate to reduce costs in high-wage Japan, are finding it necessary to abandon traditional suppliers by shifting production offshore and entering into pacts with one another for the design and production of components.

In addition, press reports suggest that banks are writing off problem loans and thereby canceling their implicit insurance contracts with long-term clients in distress. These reports indicate that companies have come under enormous pressure to raise cash and dispose of underperforming assets by selling "stable" shares in *keiretsu* partners. The government's campaign of deregulation and political reform is undercutting powerful ministries, such as MITI and MOF, and forcing competitive practices on some of the most "managed" sectors of the Japanese economy, such as construction and government procurement. Even rising concerns over health, working hours, and family life (e.g., Japan's low fertility rate) may be indirectly eroding the foundation for the network economy as managers and officials spend less time in boozy, late night *tsukiai* building *jinmyaku* (personal network) ties that later will be the infrastructure for business decisions.

Whatever the validity of these trends, structural analysis is well suited to measure them empirically. Despite the methodological hurdles posed by dynamic network analyses, those systems in flux demand the kind of relational orientation that structural inquiry represents. As DiMaggio (1992, p. 122) pointed out, in emergent systems and those responding to rapid environmental or technological changes, many assumptions of traditional models, especially those based in static utility analysis, will be less applicable:

> [T]he population of engaged actors is not fixed (although the population of potential actors may be); actors improvise to create new relations or modify old ones; actors have more or less free access to one another; uncertainty is high; and actors may have numerous objectives, or, where they do possess something like a working utility function, be so uncertain about how to maximize utility as to find goals poor guides to action.

In these systems, durable and consistent attributes of actors (e.g., based on class identity industry affiliation, national origin) will be less important than ongoing changes in network position. But these changes can only be measured if systems are mapped over time.

Invoking Complementary Paradigms: Institutional Theory

Finally, whatever the virtues of the kind of network analysis proposed here, there are also limits to what even a fully developed structural approach can accomplish, and at these limits, other complementary paradigms must be invoked. Strong-form arguments for the power of network analysis suggest that knowledge of an actor's position in a social structure is sufficient to explain that actor's behavior (see, for example, White et al., 1976). We believe, in contrast, that network analysis must be supplemented by analysis of the institutional constraints under which networks operate, which serve to frame networks and give them form and substance. These constraints will reflect the combined effects of contextual factors in creating taken-for-granted modes of behavior that are neither codifiable in pure network form nor fully subject to reflexive, rational action. Indeed, these constraints factor especially in cross-national and comparative studies, wherein differences in history, politics, culture, social structure, and legal frameworks all figure prominently.

DiMaggio (1992) stated the case as follows. In his critique of overenthusiastic accounts of network analysis' potential, he argued that a complete description of social structure requires two features in addition to basic relational data: first, analysis of the "cultural typifications" of relationships—the substance of cognition (e.g., role definitions, action scripts) that define actor attributes within network ties and attitudes toward those ties—and, second, an overall theory of action, guiding assumptions about situated actors' orientations toward one another and the world. Together, these represent the working rules of exchange, defining the social order and assigning meaning to it. What this means in practical terms is that what we term "institutional framing" determines both the constitutive rules of social relations for the individual actors involved, at the micro level, and the overall models of how these relations are constructed across social settings, at the meta level.

One implication of the micro-level framing of relationships is that the *content* of ties is important. Whereas some network theorists have suggested that social structure exists outside the precise types of relationships involved (see Leifer & White's quotation, given earlier), we believe that tie content cannot be ignored. Networks may convey information to far-flung actors, but they also convey goods, services, people, capital, influence, and legitimacy. Each type of relation carries a set of historical and cultural associations that determine both how patterns are formed and how actors behave within those patterns. Ownership ties, for example, involve legal rights to influence others that operate quite differently from the informal information flows or gift exchanges that exist in personal networks; capital, however, has a universal fungibility that shapes its use as an exchange medium in ways quite different from the firm-specific assets of a particular investment in new technologies. Network effectiveness will also vary by tie content. In sharing knowledge of job opportunities, for instance, expansive "weak tie" networks may be most effective (Granovetter, 1973), but in the exchange of sensitive production data, narrow "strong tie" networks may be preferred (Gerlach, forthcoming).

At the meta level, networks are framed through a dual process involving internal isomorphism and external differentiation. By partially decoupling economic function from the organizational forms used to organize them and noting their reification as taken-for-granted models of the social world, institutional theorists are able to explain both movements toward similarities *within* social structure and differentiation *between* social structures. The first was the main focus of DiMaggio and Powell (1983), in their influential statement of the institutionalist position: "We ask . . . why there is such startling homogeneity of organizational forms and practices; and we seek to explain homogeneity, not variation" (p. 148). Less well understood is the converse of this argument: To the extent that actors within systems converge to common forms, they become increasingly differentiated from actors in other systems that have converged to alternative forms. Because the working rules of network construction vary significantly across setting, we may see the emergence of multiple solutions to the same economic problems in separate countries, industries, or historical periods.

It might help to make this discussion concrete by considering the institutional framing of networks in the context of the United States–Japan comparison. A leading student of U.S. corporate networks, Schwartz (1992), applied his knowledge to the study of Japan, arguing that the *keiretsu* are in fact less distinctive than is widely believed. He noted the following four institutions in the United States that he claims replicate functions performed by business groups: lending consortia, institutional stockholding, multidivisional corporations, and interlocking directorates. Lending consortia for example, are actively involved in the sharing of information and will come to the rescue of firms when their financial stakes are sufficiently challenged, as do Japanese main banks with their clients. Similarly, the multidivisional firm duplicates some joint decision-making processes found within groups, but it does so through full internalization of ownership and formal top-down control.

Yet despite these surface similarities, Schwartz (1992) also recognized that the underlying structure of the two economies vary in some important ways. Whereas Japanese enterprise groups foster regular and predictable information exchange among member companies, banks in the United States have looser relations with individual clients and are less consistent in the sharing of information. Localized banking ties in Japan, on the other hand, discourage the kind of economywide coordination of information interchange enjoyed by U.S. lending consortia, which tend to bring together most or all national banks for each major loan. In comparing U.S. multidivisional firms with Japanese business groups, Schwartz acknowledged that there is tighter coordination between major companies and their satellites in the United States than in Japan, because they exist within a common ownership structure. He concluded with the following assessment of the network structures in the two countries: "These mechanisms work together to create a set of parallel dynamics which are similar to, but nevertheless distinctive from, the Japanese pattern" (1992, p. 3).

Conclusions: The Role of Structural Analysis

We believe structural analysts must work toward developing a theoretical apparatus of sufficient sophistication to balance their formidable methodological arsenal. Old theories are not abandoned until compelling alternatives emerge, as Kuhn (1962) long ago observed in his famous study of the evolution of science. It is one thing to criticize orthodox economic analysis, but it is quite another to offer a systematic alternative that is capable of generating refutable predictions.

Although it is beyond the scope of this chapter to develop a fully realized paradigmatic approach to the study of economic systems, we close by suggesting here two key elements that we believe such a theory should feature. First, it should focus primarily on the economic terrain *intermediate* between the extremes of perfect competition and authority within simple hierarchies. In perfect competition, every player has unlimited choice among alternative relationships, whereas in administrative hierarchies, choice is concentrated in the hands of a dominant player (Burt, 1992). In both cases, the structural image is a fully determined and rigidly constructed system of relationships, and network analysis offers nothing new here. Perfect competition is itself handled quite nicely by general equilibrium theory, for which it was designed, whereas the structural underpinnings of pure hierarchy and formal authority relations have been systematically addressed elsewhere (Simon, 1962; Williamson, 1975, 1985). Network analysis, in contrast, adds substantial value to the study of indeterminate systems in which actors are capable of making choices and shaping their world but are constrained by the choices of others and the larger structures of which those choices are a part. As suggested previously, these systems encompass much of the activity of contemporary capitalist economies.

Second, a structural paradigm should lead to a refocusing of attention in understanding the terms of trade away from the role of *prices* toward those of *identities*. Orthodox economic analysts argue that trade is dominated by identity-neutral ties, as modeled in formal settings like stock and commodity exchanges. As such, they are concerned primarily with prices as determined by underlying conditions of supply and demand. Structural analysts, in contrast, put far greater emphasis on the identities and attributes of economic actors themselves, the extent to which specific characteristics of actors and their network positions condition the patterns of business relationships.

This view represents a fundamental shift in thinking, for it suggests that coordination and governance economies (i.e., control over successful completion of exchange) are as important or perhaps even more important than allocative economies. The identity of one's trading partners becomes important if it is a significant determinant of the terms of trade or the probability of its successful completion. This will be the case, first, when some traders are known in advance to be more reliable than others, and second, when one is able to enforce effectively whatever agreements are made. Because successful completion of a trade lowers transaction costs, the general rule is that it pays to deal with people one trusts and with people over whom one has some control. In a world dominated by corporate decision-makers and long-term customer markets, we believe that this is a realistic and powerful theoretical transformation.

Acknowledgment

This chapter is a revision of a paper presented to the Vancouver Network, Whistler, B.C., September 10–12, 1993. The comments of conference participants are gratefully acknowledged.

References

Abegglen, J. C., and G. Stalk, Jr. Kaisha: *The Japanese Corporation.* New York: Basic Books, 1985.

Ahmadjian, C. "Mutualism and Asymmetry in Japanese Supply Networks." Ph.D. diss., Walter A. Haas School of Business, University of California, Berkeley, 1995.

Aldrich, H. *Organization and Environments*. Englewood Cliffs, N.J.: Prentice Hall, 1979.

Acki, M. *Information, Incentives, and Bargaining in the Japanese Economy*. Cambridge: Cambridge University Press, 1988.

Asanuma, B. "Manufacturer–Supplier Relationships in Japan and the Concept of Relation-Specific Skill." *Journal of the Japanese and International Economies*, 3 (1989): 1–30.

Bernstein, G. L. *Haruko's World: A Japanese Farm Woman and Her Community*. Stanford, Calif.: Stanford University Press, 1983.

Brinton, M. C. *Women and the Economic Miracle: Gender and Work in Postwar Japan*. Berkeley: University of California Press, 1993.

Burt, R. S. *Corporate Profits and Cooptation: Networks of Market Constraints and Directorate Ties in the American Economy*. New York: Academic Press, 1983.

Burt, R. S. *Structural Holes*. Cambridge, Mass.: Harvard University Press, 1992.

Cable, J. and M. J. Dirrheimer: "Hierarchies and Markets: An Empirical Test of the Multidivisional Hypothesis in West Germany." *International Journal of Industrial Organization*, 1 (1983): 43–62.

Caves, R., and M. Uekusa. *Industrial Organization in Japan*. Washington, D.C.: The Brookings Institution, 1976.

Clark, R. *The Japanese Company*. New Haven, Conn.: Yale University Press, 1979.

Cole, R. E. *Japanese Blue Collar: The Changing Tradition*. Berkeley: University of California Press, 1971.

Coleman, J. S. "Social Theory, Social Research, and a Theory of Action." *American Journal of Sociology*, 16 (1986): 1309–35.

DiMaggio, P. "Structural Analysis of Organizational Fields: A Blockmodel Approach." Pp. 335–370 in B. M. Staw and L. L. Cummings (eds.) Research in Organizational Behavior, vol. 8. Greenwich, CT: JAI Press, 1990.

DiMaggio, P., and W. W. Powell. "The Iron Case Revisited: Institutional Isomorphism and Collective Rationality in Organizational Fields." *American Sociological Review*, 48 (1983): 147–160.

Doeringer, P. B. and M. J. Piore. Internal Labor Markets and Manpower Analysis. Lexington, MA: D. C. Heath, 1971.

Dore, R. P. *City Life in Japan*. Berkeley: University of California Press, 1963.

Dore, R. P. *British Factory, Japanese Factory: The Origins of Diversity in Industrial Relations*. Berkeley: University of California Press, 1973.

Dore, R. P. *Flexible Rigidities*. Stanford, Calif.: Stanford University Press, 1986.

Eccles, R. G., and D. B. Crane. *Doing Deals: Investment Banks at Work*. Cambridge, Mass.: Harvard Business School Press, 1988.

Encaoua, D., and A. Jacquemin. "Organizational Efficiency and Monopoly Power: The Case of French Industrial Groups." *European Economic Review*, 19 (1982): 25–51.

Fligstein, N. *The Transformation of Corporate Control*. Cambridge, Mass.: Harvard University Press, 1990.

Florida, R., and M. Kenney. *Beyond Mass Production*. New York: Oxford University Press, 1992.

Friedman, D. *The Misunderstood Miracle: Industrial Development and Political Change in Japan*. Ithaca, N.Y.: Cornell University Press, 1988.

Fruin, M. *The Japanese Enterprise System: Competitive Strategies and Cooperative Structures*. Oxford: Oxford University Press, 1992.

Fruin, W. M. and T. Nishiguchi. "Supplying the Toyota Production System: How to

Make a Molehill Out of a Mountain." Pp. 225–248 in B. Kogut, ed., *Country Competitiveness*. New York: Oxford University Press, 1993.

Galaskiewicz, J. *Social Organization of an Urban Grant Economy: A Study of Business Philanthropy and Nonprofit Organizations*. Orlando, Fla.: Academic Press, 1985.

Gerlach, M. L. *Alliance Capitalism: The Social Organization of Japanese Business*. Berkeley: University of California Press, 1992a.

Gerlach, M. L. "The Japanese Corporate Network: A Blockmodel Analysis." *Administrative Science Quarterly*, 37 (1992b): 105–39.

Gerlach, M. L. Twilight of the *keiretsu*? A Critical Assessment." *Journal of Japanese Studies*, 18 (1992c): 79–118.

Gerlach, M. L. "Economic Organization and Innovation in Japan." *Journal of Economic Behavior and Organization*, forthcoming.

Gerlach, M. L., and J. R. Lincoln. "The Organization of Business Networks in the U.S. and Japan." Pp. 491–520 in N. Nohria and R. Eccles, eds., *Networks and Organizations: Structure, Form, and Action*. Cambridge, Mass.: Harvard Business School Press, 1992.

Goto, A. "Business Groups in a Market Economy." *European Economic Review*, 19 (1982): 53–70.

Gouldner, A. W. "The Norm of Reciprocity: A Preliminary Statement." *American Sociological Review*, 25 (1960): 161–78.

Granovetter, M. "The Strength of Weak Ties." *American Journal of Sociology*, 78 (1973): 1360–81.

Granovetter, M. "Economic Action and Social Structure: The Problem of Embeddedness." *American Journal of Sociology*, 91 (1985): 481–510.

Hadley, E. Antitrust in Japan. Princeton, N.J.: Princeton University Press, 1970.

Hamilton, G., and N. Biggart. "Market, Culture, and Authority: A Comparative Analysis of Management and Organization in the Far East. *American Journal of Sociology*, 94 (Supplement) (1988): S52–S94.

Harrison, B. *Lean and Mean: The Changing Landscape of Corporate Power in the Age of Flexibility*. New York: Basic Books, 1994.

Hawley, A. *Human Ecology: A Theoretical Essay*. Chicago: University of Chicago Press, 1986.

Heimer, C. A. "Doing Your Job and Helping Your Friends: Universalistic Norms about Obligations to Particular Others in Networks." Pp. 143–164 in N. Nohria and R. G. Eccles, eds., *Networks and Organizations: Structure, Form, and Action*. Cambridge, Mass.: Harvard Business School Press, 1992.

Helper, Susan. "How Much Has Really Changed between U.S. Automakers and Their Suppliers?" Sloan Management Review 32 (Summer, 1991): 15–28.

Hirsch, P. M. "Organizational Effectiveness and the Institutional Environment." *Administrative Science Quarterly*, 20 (1975): 327–44.

Hoshi, T., A. Kashyap, and D. Scharfstein. "Corporate Structure, Liquidity, and Investment: Evidence from Japanese Industrial Groups." *Quarterly Journal of Economics*, 106 (February 1991): 33–60.

Imai, K., and H. Itami. "Interpenetration of Organization and Market." *International Journal of Industrial Organization*, 2 (1984): 285–310.

Johnson, C. A. MITI and the Japanese Miracle: The Growth of Industrial Policy, 1925–1975. Stanford University Press, 1982.

Kanter, R. M. *Men and Women of the Corporation*. New York: Basic Books, 1977.

Kaplan, S. N. "Internal Corporate Governance in Japan and the U.S.: Differences in Activity and Horizons." Mimeo. University of Chicago, 1991.

Kawashima, T. "Dispute Resolution in Contemporary Japan." In A. T. von Mehren, ed., *Law in Japan: The Legal Order in a Changing Society*. Cambridge, Mass.: Harvard University Press, 1963.

Kelley, M. R. and H. Brooks. "External Learning Opportunities and the Diffusion of Process Innovations to Small Firms: The Case of Programmable Automation." *Technological Forecasting and Economic Change*, 39 (1991): 103–25.

Knight, Frank H. *Risk, Uncertainty, and Profit*. New York: Kelley and Millman, 1957.

Kondo, D. K. *Crafting Selves: Power, Gender, and Discourses of Identity in a Japanese Workplace*. Chicago: University of Chicago Press, 1990.

Krackhardt, D. "The Strength of Strong Ties: The Importance of Philos in Organizations." In N. Nohria and R. G. Eccles, eds., *Networks and Organizations: Structure, Form, and Action*. Cambridge, Mass.: Harvard Business School Press, 1992, pp. 216–39.

Kuhn, T. S. *The Structure of Scientific Revolutions*. Chicago: University of Chicago Press, 1962.

Laumann, E. O. and David Knoke. *The Organizational State*. Madison: University of Wisconsin Press, 1987.

Leff, N. H. "Industrial Organization and Entrepreneurship in the Developing Countries." *Economic Development and Cultural Change*, 26 (1978): 661–75.

Leifer, E., and H. White. "A Structural Approach to Markets. Pp. 85–108 in M. S. Mizruchi and M. Schwartz, eds., *Intercorporate Relations: The Structural Analysis of Business*. Cambridge: Cambridge University Press, 1987.

Lincoln J. R. "Intra- (and inter-) Organizational Networks." IN S. B. Bacharach, ed., *Research in the Sociology of Organizations*. Greenwich, Conn.: JAI Press, 1982, pp. 1–38.

Lincoln, J. R. "Japanese Organization and Organization Theory." In B. M. Staw and L. L. Cummings, eds., *Research in Organizational Behavior*, vol. 12. Greenwich, Conn.: JAI Press, 1990, pp. 225–94.

Lincoln, J. R., M. L. Gerlach, and C. L. Ahmadjian. *Keiretsu* Networks and Corporate Performance in Japan. *American Sociological Review* 61 (1996): 67–88.

Lincoln, J. R., M. L. Gerlach, and P. Takahashi. *Keiretsu* Networks in the Japanese Economy: A Dyad Analysis of Intercorporate Ties. *American Sociological Review*, 57 (1992): 561–85.

Lincoln, J. R., and A. L. Kalleberg. *Culture, Control, and Commitment: A Study of Work Organization and Work Attitudes in the U.S. and Japan*. Cambridge: Cambridge University Press, 1990.

Lincoln, J. R., and J. Miller. "Work and Friendship Ties in Organizations: A Comparative Analysis of Relational Networks." *Administrative Science Quarterly*, 24 (1979): 181–99.

Lincoln, J. R. and G. Zeitz. "Organizational Properties from Aggregate Data: Separating Individual and Structural Effects." *American Sociological Review*, 45 (1980): 391–409.

Loasby, B. J. *Choice, Complexity and Ignorance*. Cambridge: Cambridge University Press, 1976.

Miles, R. E. and C. C. Snow. "Organizations: new concepts for new forms." *California Management Review*, 28 (1986): 62–73.

Milgrom, Paul, and John Roberts. *Economics, Organization, and Management.* Englewood Cliffs, N.J.: Prentice-Hall, 1992.

Mintz, B., and M. Schwartz. *The Power Structure of American Business.* Chicago: University of Chicago Press, 1985.

Mitchell, J. C. "Social Networks." *Annual Review of Sociology.* Palo Alto, Calif.: Annual Reviews, 1974.

Miwa, Y. *Nihon no kigyo to sangyo soshiki* [Japan's Enterprise and Industrial Organization]. Tokyo: Tokyo Daigaku Shuppan-kai, 1990.

Mizruchi, M. *The American Corporate Network: 1904–1974.* 1982.

Mizruchi, M., and M. Schwartz, eds., *Intercorporate Relations: The Structural Analysis of Business.* Cambridge: Cambridge University Press, 1987.

Morikawa, H. Zaibatsu: *The Rise and Fall of Family Enterprise Groups in Japan.* Tokyo: University of Tokyo Press, 1992.

Nakane, C. *Japanese Society.* Berkeley: University of California Press, 1970.

Nakatani, I. "The Economic Role of Financial Corporate Grouping." In M. Aoki, ed., *The Economic Analysis of the Japanese Firm.* Amsterdam: North-Holland, pp. 227–58).

Nelson, R. R., and S. Winter. *An Evolutionary Theory of Economic Change.* Cambridge, Mass.: Harvard University Press, 1982.

Nohria, N., and R. Eccles. *Networks and Organizations: Structure, Form, and Action.* Cambridge, Mass.: Harvard Business School Press, 1992.

Odaka, K., K. Ono, and F. Adachi. *The Automobile Industry in Japan: A Study of Ancillary Firm Development.* Tokyo: Kinokuniya, 1988.

Okimoto, D. I. *Between MITI and the Market: Japanese Industrial Policy for High Technology.* Stanford, Calif.: Stanford University Press, 1989.

Okun, A. M. *Prices and Quantities: A Macroeconomic Analysis.* Washington, DC: Brookings Institute, 1981.

Packer, F., and M. Ryser. "The Governance of Failure: An Anatomy of Corporate Bankruptcy in Japan." Working Paper No. 62, Center on Japanese Economy and Business, Columbia Graduate School of Business. New York: Columbia University, 1992.

Pennings, J. *Interlocking Directorates.* San Francisco: Jossey-Bass, 1980.

Perrow, C. *Complex Organizations: A Critical Essay*, 3rd ed. Glenview, Il.: Scott, Foresman, 1986.

Perrow, C. "Small Firm Networks." In N. Nohria and R. G. Eccles, eds., *Networks and Organizations: Structure, Form, and Action.* Cambridge, Mass.: Harvard Business School Press, 1992, pp. 445–70.

Pfeffer, J., and G. R. Salancik. *The External Control of Organizations.* New York: Harper & Row, 1978.

Piore, M. J., and C. F. Sabel. *The Second Industrial Divide: Possibilities for Prosperity.* New York: Basic Books, 1984.

Powell, W. W. "Neither Market nor Hierarchy: Network Forms of Organization." Pp. 295–336 in B. M. Staw and L. L. Cummings, eds., *Research in Organizational Behavior.* Greenwich, Conn.: JAI Press, 1990.

Pred, A. *City Systems in Advanced Economies.* London: Hutchison, 1977.

Rohlen, T. P. *For Harmony and Strength.* Berkeley: University of California Press, 1974.

Sako, M.. *Prices, Quality, and Trust: Inter-firm Relations in Britain and Japan.* Cambridge: Cambridge University Press, 1992.

Schwartz, M. "Japanese Enterprise Groups: Some American Parallels." Shoken Keizai 180 (1992): 1–10.

Sheard, P. "Interlocking Shareholdings and Corporate Governance." Pp. 310–349 in M. Aoki and R. Dore, eds., *The Japanese Firm: Sources of Competitive Strength*. Oxford: Clarendon Press, 1994.

Simon, H. "The Architecture of Complexity." Cambridge, Mass.: MIT Press, 1969. Proceedings of the American Philosophical Society 106 (1962): 67–82.

Smitka, M. J. *Competitive Ties: Subcontracting in the Japanese Automotive Industry*. New York: Columbia University Press, 1991.

Stearns, L. B., and M. S. Mizruchi. "Broken-tie Reconstitution and the Functions of Interorganizational Interlocks: A Reexamination." *Administrative Science Quarterly*, 31 (1986): 522–38.

Teece, D. J., and S. Winter. "The Limits of Neoclassical Theory in Management Education." *American Economic Review*, 74 (1984): 116–21.

Vogel, E. F. *Japan's New Middle Class*. Berkeley: University of California Press, 1963.

Wellman, B., and S. D. Berkowitz, eds. *Social Structures: Network Approach*. Cambridge: Cambridge University Press, 1987.

White, H. C., S. A. Boorman, and R. L. Breiger. "Social Structure from Multiple Networks: I. Blockmodels of Roles and Positions." *American Journal of Sociology*, 81 (1976): 730–80.

Williamson, O. E. *Markets and Hierarchies: Analysis and Antitrust Implications*. New York: Free Press, 1975.

Williamson, O. E. *The Economic Institutions of Capitalism*. New York: Free Press, 1985.

Womack, J. P., D. T. Jones, and D. Roos. The Machine that Changed the World. New York: Macmillan, 1990.

Index